BREAKING THE MIND

BREAKING THE MIND

NEW STUDIES IN THE SYRIAC "*BOOK OF STEPS*"

EDITED BY

Kristian S. Heal and Robert A. Kitchen

The Catholic University of America Press

Washington, D.C.

The paper used in this publication meets the minimum requirements of American National Standards for Information Science—Permanence of Paper for Printed Library Materials, ANSI Z39.48-1984.
∞

LIBRARY OF CONGRESS CATALOGING-IN-PUBLICATION DATA
New studies in the Syriac Book of steps / edited by Kristian S. Heal and Robert A. Kitchen.
pages cm. — (CUA studies in early Christianity)
Includes bibliographical references and index.
ISBN 978-0-8132-2166-3 (cloth : alk. paper)
1. Liber Graduum. 2. Christian life—Early works to 1800.
3. Monasticism and religious orders—History. 4. Spirituality—History.
5. Syriac literature. I. Heal, Kristian S., editor of compilation.
BX177.15.N49 2013
281'.5—dc23
2013024286

CONTENTS

Columba Stewart, OSB

BY WAY OF A PREFACE

The *Book of Steps* has always been overshadowed by more famous early Syriac literature, such as Aphrahat's *Demonstrations* and Ephrem's virtuosic memre, hymns, and commentary. The manuscript tradition is thin, with only one complete witness from the twelfth century (Paris, Syr. 201); accordingly, Western scholars have focused on other texts to the neglect of this substantial and fascinating collection of homilies on both the sublime and mundane aspects of the Christian life. Understanding the reasons for the relative paucity of manuscripts and the consequent small number of modern studies lies beyond the scope of this preface, but it is important to begin with this fact in order to appreciate the significance of the present collection of essays.

When I began my doctoral studies in the 1980s, the scholarly literature on the *Book of Steps* was truly negligible. It was largely concerned with links between the *Liber Graduum,* as it was always known then, and the Messalian controversy of the late fourth and fifth centuries. There was Kmoskó's fine edition in the *Patrologia Syriaca,* but no translation into any modern European language apart from Robert Murray's inclusion of memra 12 in *Symbols of Church and Kingdom.* The Latin column in Kmoskó's edition was the only crib. A couple of then-recent articles tried to set the distinctive pneumatology of the *Book of Steps* in a broader religious context, pointing readers beyond the Messalian pigeonhole to which the text was typically consigned. The situation has improved greatly since then, with several important studies, a complete

English translation by Robert Kitchen and Martien Parmentier, and now this most welcome *tour d' horizon.*

One spends time with a particular text for a reason, or for several. I came to the *Book of Steps* because of my interest in the origins of monasticism. As a Benedictine monk destined for teaching in our abbey's university apostolate, I knew that the primary interest of my students would be the monastic movement as known in the classical traditions of Egypt, Palestine, and Cappadocia and their heirs in the Latin West. To prepare myself for a career that would be largely focused on how it all turned out, I thought I should devote my doctoral studies to the prehistory of what is normally understood to be "monasticism." And as someone naturally inclined toward history, I always like to know something about the "before" of a subject. This led me to Syriac literature, which I first explored in translation under the tutelage of Gabriele Winkler, and then to the Syriac language, which I began to study at home in Collegeville, but then studied in earnest once I arrived at Oxford. Sebastian Brock kindly agreed to help me, and we chose the *Liber graduum* as our text, for reasons that are now obscure to me—perhaps it had to do with Messalianism, perhaps it was the neglected state of the text, perhaps my patient teacher thought it would be an easier work for a beginner. For an entire year he endured a weekly hour of my reading aloud and translating from the *Book of Steps.* In the dark depths of my first English winter, I thought I would never finish it. I leaned on Kmoskó's Latin version, while often marveling at his efforts to trap the looser syntax of the Syriac original in the much tighter constraints of Latin. As I gained a foothold in the language and the text, I began to see how I might link it to other ascetical writings of the same period that had clear, but unexplored affinities to it. My eventual doctoral thesis focused more on the Macarian *Homilies,* but it was the *Book of Steps* that gave me a lens through which to read them, searching for the Syriac substrate in their language of spiritual experience.

Like most Syriac literature, the *Book of Steps* relies heavily on biblical imagery, read with an emphasis on spiritual experience. The hermeneutic is distinctive, with an ascetic slant not unusual in Syriac writings. The pronounced sectarian tone of the *Book of Steps,* however, with its division of Christians into the ranks of "upright" and "perfect," probably explains its move to the margins of the Syriac literary tradition. Ephrem's ascetic vocabulary allowed for a more supple, mainstream interpretation by later readers. In genre the *Book of Steps* is close to the Macarian *Homilies,* but again, it is less susceptible to appreciation by a general audience. Many of Ephrem's writings moved into Greek translation (and inspired other compositions), and at least some of the Macarian *Homilies* were translated into Syriac; but the *Book of Steps* remained, as far as we know, only in Syriac. We owe the authors of these essays a great debt for pushing it a bit further out into the scholarly mainstream.

BREAKING THE MIND

Kristian S. Heal and Robert A. Kitchen

INTRODUCTION

We thought we knew a fair amount about the *Book of Steps,* even when it was called the *Liber Graduum.* We have spent decades exploring its nooks and crannies, but even what lies on the surface we know we have not yet fathomed.[1]

What do we know about the *Book of Steps?*[2] It is a late-fourth-century (several contributors to this volume dispute this and other matters!) Syriac collection of thirty *memre,* or discourses. The author is intentionally anonymous and tells us preciously little about the time and place in which he and his Christian community lived, though one reference implies a location in present northeast Iraq, part of the Persian Empire in the fourth and fifth centuries. The author, immersed in the language and thought-world of the Bible, is apparently the spiritual leader of a Christian community living in the midst of a town or village. This community contains two levels or groups of committed Christians—the Upright, who are married, work and earn income, and perform the active acts of charity in the community, and the Perfect, who are

1. References to the English translation of the *Book of Steps* appears as BoS followed by memra and section number, as found in Robert A. Kitchen and Martien F. G. Parmentier, trans., *The Book of Steps: The Syriac Liber Graduum,* Cistercian Studies 196 (Kalamazoo, Mich.: Cistercian Publications, 2004). References to the Syriac text appear as *LG* along with column and line numbers, as found in *Liber Graduum,* ed. Michael Kmosko, *Patrologia Syriaca* 3 (Paris: Firmin-Didot, 1926).

2. For a fuller introduction, cf. Kitchen and Parmentier, trans., *The Book of Steps.* For an updated bibliographical survey see, Grigory Kessel and Karl Pinggéra, *A Bibliography of Syriac Ascetical and Mystical Literature,* Eastern Christian Studies 11 (Leuven: Peeters, 2011), 53–60.

celibate, pointedly do not work, have no income or settled home, and spend their time in unceasing prayer, wandering in the region to teach and mediate conflicts. While the author treats a number of issues, theological and practical, many of which are discussed by the contributors to this volume, he initially appears to be reconstructing the standards for these two levels. However, by the end of the discourses, he noticeably expresses his disappointment in the decline of discipline among the Perfect, and ironically is delighted in the spiritual progress of the Upright. Unfortunately from a historical perspective, this is where the *Book of Steps* concludes, and one hears of no resolution. Anonymity exacts its price.

After a while it became apparent how very little the *Book of Steps* had been seriously studied. There was a fragmentary character to most of the studies, which can be attributed to the length and complexity of the thirty *memre.* In other words, it did not appear that many scholars had read the entire work and taken into account all the different themes and variations on a theme contained in this work, which teases the reader at first into believing it is a systematic exposition. A real flesh-and-blood community and author lurk behind the adventures of the Upright and Perfect, and so our task is to sort out and make sense of their story.

The translation of the *Book of Steps* and an introduction into its mysteries and apparent truths were intended to be only a beginning, a foundation, offering the opportunity for succeeding and brighter scholars to better apprehend the whole text and its world and then proceed to refine and correct what has not been well understood. We wanted to energize research on the *Book of Steps,* not only by senior scholars, but also by younger scholars and graduate students—who just might be able to look at the text with a different perspective and see something the rest of us had missed. And they have.

This volume of new essays on the *Book of Steps* has been gathered from several directions. A call for papers in a number of journals and academic societies mustered more than a few inquiries and offers of chapters. In order to draw attention to the *Book of Steps* on a wider stage, we arranged for sections at two major conferences in 2007. The fifth North American Syriac Symposium, hosted by the University of Toronto, heard four papers presented on the text—probably a record. It was a short-lived record, for less than two months later, at the fifteenth International Patristics Conference at the University of

Oxford, we conducted a three-day, nine-paper workshop on the *Book of Steps.* Attendance and participation was enthusiastic and adventurous. Following these sessions a few other chapters kept floating our way.

It is particularly gratifying to see how our aim of including graduate students was successful. Five chapters have been submitted by graduate students, and more than a few others eventually had to defer due to the pressures of their own dissertation work. We hope they do not forget the possibilities of the *Book of Steps* and will return for another look in their postdoctoral careers. The international character of this volume is evident by contributions from scholars from at least ten different countries, possibly a couple more depending upon which nationality they wish to claim.

One of the greatest problems of anonymity is not only in the authorship of the text, but also in our lack of knowledge of its political-social-geographic situation. Three chapters address the *Book of Steps'* situation in the wider world. The *Book of Steps* tells us only enough of its historical context to suggest a fourth-century date and a northern Mesopotamian provenance. With these facts as his guide, Geoffrey Greatrex presents a historical and political survey of these marchlands of the Roman and Persian empires in the period from A.D. 280 to 400. Through a comparison with contemporary Manichean material Timothy Pettipiece is able to expose some of the contours of the world of the *Book of Steps* and, in so doing, point to some striking similarities between the two communities and the texts they produced. Martien Parmentier tackles the reaction of the *Book of Steps* to the pervasive use of pagan magical practices as a cure for illness, pain, and suffering in the late antique world. The response in the *Book of Steps* is more than a simple rejection of magic, or, indeed, an affirmation that healing comes through the name of Christ by the gifts of the spirit. Rather, the community of the *Book of Steps* is reminded to accept that, though healing may come, when it doesn't, the pain and suffering caused should be accepted as steps toward eternal glorification.

Controversy surrounding the text of the *Book of Steps* has not disappeared, and several chapters examine some of these old and new issues, generating a little contemporary controversy, as well. Grigory Kessel reopens and extends the discussion of the textual history of the *Book of Steps,* with emphasis given to the reception of the work in the later tradition. He reviews the known sources and examines the context in which the homilies are found, the authors to whom selections and individual homilies are otherwise attributed, and the manner in which some of the homilies were recast. A newly identified fragment receives particular attention.

Kyle Smith provocatively posits that the preface to the *Book of Steps* was not a later addition, as it contends, but was actually written by the author of the *Book of Steps* in order to deliberately obscure its origins. Thus, instead of stemming from a fourth-century community, Smith contends that the *Book of Steps* is actually a fifth-century text written in reaction to the institutionalization of Syriac asceticism under Bishop Rabbula of Edessa.

There is nowhere to hide from the Bible in the *Book of Steps,* so several chapters examine different aspects of how the author utilized his roughly twelve hundred citations. René Roux posits that the central exegetical problem in the *Book of Steps* is the contradictions found in scripture. The author is aware that certain principles and rules need to be observed in order to tackle this problem. Roux systematically surveys these rules and the exegetical principles evident in the entire work, dividing them into three categories: direct exegesis, biblical theology, and dogmatic exegesis. He concludes that the target of many of these arguments was directed against a Marcionitic group that rejected the Old Testament as part of the Christian scriptures.

The *Book of Steps* has long been recognized as an important witness to the early text of Paul in the Syriac tradition. Matthias Westerhoff explores some of the broader questions surrounding the use of Paul in the text, such as the source of Pauline quotations, the reliance on earlier Syriac literary sources, the image of the apostle, and how Paul is rejected, extended, and reworked in the *Book of Steps.* The last portion of the chapter extends the discussion on the spiritual gifts begun by Parmentier.

The heavy engagement with the Bible by the author leads naturally to a plethora of theological themes in the thirty *memre.* Jeff Childers utilizes the insights of virtue epistemology in order to understand the epistemological assumptions at work in the *Book of Steps.* Childers reads the author presuming a vital connection between virtuous practices, the mind and its proper functioning, and the quest for truth. In particular he examines the nature of the key concept of "breaking one's mind" as a means of refining cognition through the practices of inner and outer humility.

The *Book of Steps* repeatedly insists that the hallmark of perfection is in unlimited love and forgiveness, following the admonitions of Jesus in the Sermon on the Mount. The Perfect are thus required to love and forgive all, without distinction: women, heretics, pagans, sinners, and even their own murderers. Pablo Argárate pursues this close association between perfection and love for enemies.

The *Book of Steps* is marked by strong group structures and hierarchies, the Upright and the Perfect being the most dominant and important. Kelli Bryant examines the recurrent use of dietary language—milk, vegetables, and solid food—as a nuanced way of distinguishing other hierarchies in the community of the *Book of Steps.* The terms primarily deal with the immaturity of the lower echelons of the church ("milk for the children," "vegetables for the sick") with little attention paid to the nature of solid food for the mature and perfect.

Underlying the varied discourse in the *Book of Steps* is the struggle of humanity with sin. Tera Harmon extracts the author's depiction of how the pledges of spirit and sin inhabit all people, including the Upright and Perfect. She identifies that for the author, sin is primarily a matter of broken relationships, which he details; he then prescribes various aspects of *imitatio Christi* and ascetic discipline as the corrective. Harmon pays particular attention to how the author works toward a reciprocal and reconciled relationship between the Upright and the Perfect.

The final section of this volume treats the best-known aspect of the *Book of Steps*—its particular practice of the ascetical life. Holiness in Syriac asceticism usually refers to sexual renunciation and celibacy, and that emphasis occurs frequently in the *Book of Steps,* particularly as an entrance requirement to perfection. Robert Kitchen examines theological holiness, utilizing definitions by Karl Barth and John B. Webster, noting that no saints are identified in the *Book of Steps* except Biblical characters. Perfection, while not identical to holiness, aims to return to the Edenic state before Adam had sinned by means of a *via negative*—no work, no anxiety, no sexual relationships or marriage. Barth's depiction of saints as "disturbed sinners" provides a lens through which to interpret the struggle for holiness among the author's community.

The *Book of Steps* is not monastic literature, but some of its concerns preview what will engage the monastic movement, the understanding and function of marriage and sexuality being two primary issues. Sergey Minov treats the sizeable amount of material on these topics dispersed throughout the *Book of Steps* and finds, not unexpectedly, a diverse range of perspectives, attitudes, and solutions. Minov points to the Encratite origins of the *Book of Steps,* but it is the angelomorphic concept of humanity that drives its attitudes toward sexuality. Grudgingly, the *Book of Steps* accepts the institution of marriage as God's alternative order for the Upright, but otherwise denigrates sexuality as originating in the activity of Satan.

Thomas Kollamparampil embarks on a pilgrimage through the *Book of Steps,* detailing how the concept of the holiness of the heart plays a central role. The author insists that the body and the heart must work together; that one does not have full legitimacy without the other. Kollamparampil shows the ways in which the work of the heart is a conscious and consistent method enabling the Upright and Perfect to progress spiritually.

Aryeh Kofsky and Serge Ruzer examine extensively the unique ascetical strategy of the *Book of Steps,* particularly in reference to the origins of humanity in the Garden of Eden, treated in most detail in *memra* 21. The authors identify the *Book of Steps* not as an exegetical treatise per se, but as an ascetical manifesto in which paradise is the center of perfect ascetical living. The author holds up Christ as the ultimate ascetical example of detachment from earthly existence, in which Christ demonstrates that the only way to *imitatio dei* is through humility and *kenosis.*

Jason Scully addresses the particular ascetical vocabulary of the *Book of Steps*—breaking one's mind, lowering and emptying oneself—and analyzes how these expressions help form the ascetical system of the text and how they are related to other contemporary ascetical systems and terminology. The *Book of Steps* is too large, too wide-ranging, too real in its depiction of a Christian community in a strange land not always welcoming for this collection to be the last word. We trust therefore that this will be the first of many collections of new essays on the *Book of Steps.*

PART I

THE WORLD AROUND THE *BOOK OF STEPS*

Geoffrey Greatrex

1. THE ROMANO-PERSIAN FRONTIER AND THE CONTEXT OF THE *BOOK OF STEPS*

As is well known, the *Book of Steps* is a notoriously hard work to pin down. The author quite deliberately provides few or no details, chronological or geographical, that would allow us to situate the work.[1] Nevertheless, a consensus seems to have been reached according to which the work belongs to the fourth century C.E., even if some prefer an earlier date within the century and others tend toward a later one.[2] Geographically the consensus favors the

1. Peter Nagel, "Die Märtyrer des Glaubens und die 'Märtyrer der Liebe' im syrischen Liber Graduum," in *Religion und Wahrheit: Religionsgeschichtliche Studien; Festschrift für Gernot Wiessner zum 65. Geburtstag,* edited by Gernot Wiessner and Bärbel Beinhauer-Köhler, 128 (Wiesbaden: Harrassowitz Verlag, 1998); Matthias Westerhoff, Das *Paulusverständnis im Liber Graduum* (Berlin and New York: Walter de Gruyter, 2008), 5–23; Robert A. Kitchen and Martien F. G. Parmentier, trans., *The Book of Steps: The Syriac Liber Graduum,* Cistercian Studies 196 (Kalamazoo, Mich.: Cistercian Publications, 2004), xlix–li. I am grateful to Matthias Westerhoff, Josef Wiesehöfer, and Scott McDonough for their help in preparing this chapter, as well as to Jing Feng, doctoral student at the University of Ottawa, for preparing the map.

2. Details in Westerhoff, "Das Bild vom Staat im *Liber Graduum,*" in *Christentum und Politik in der Alten Kirche,* edited by J. Van Oort and Otmar Hesse (Leuven: Peeters, 2009); cf. Irénée Hausherr, who places the work in the early fifth century; Hausherr, "Quanam Aetate Prodierit 'Liber Graduum?'" *Orientala Christiana Periodica* 1 (1935): 500–2; Klaus Fitschen, *Messalianismus und Antimessalianismus: Ein Beispiel ostkirchlicher Ketzergeschichte* (Göttingen: Vandenhoeck and Ruprecht, 1998), 110–18; Daniel Caner, *Wandering, Begging Monks: Spiritual Authority and the Promotion of Monasticism in Late Antiquity* (Berkeley and Los Angeles: University of California Press,) 2002, 106–7; Kitchen and Parmentier, *Book of Steps,* xlix–li, for an earlier (mid-fourth-century) date.

notion that the author was writing in Upper Mesopotamia, perhaps in Adiabene, a region undoubtedly more Christianized than many others. Several scholars suggest that the author originally may have lived on Roman soil, but chose to migrate during the Diocletianic persecution at the start of the fourth century.[3] Our aim here is not to pick through the slender evidence once again in a vain attempt to offer greater precision; rather, it is to place the work in its more general context, the marchlands of the Roman and Persian Empires in the fourth century. Because of the enduring uncertainty as to the provenance of the work, it will be necessary to examine the situation on both sides of the frontier—itself in any case subject to marked variation in the period—although we shall concentrate on the Persian side.

The chronological parameters within which we are working therefore are approximately C.E. 280 to 400. For most of this period the zone with which we are concerned, Upper Mesopotamia, was a battleground between the two most powerful states of the world at the time, the Roman empire and the Sasanian kingdom.[4] Simply put, the cause of this strife was the treaty concluded in 299 (some scholars prefer 298)[5], which assigned a large portion of Upper Mesopotamia, as far as the Tigris and in some cases even beyond it, to the Romans.

3. Fitschen, *Messalianismus,* 118; cf. Arthur Vööbus, *History of Ascetism in the Syrian Orient: A Contribution to the History of Culture in the Near East,* Corpus Scriptorum Christianorum Orientalium 500 (Louvain: Peeters, 1988), 3:17; Caner, *Wandering, Begging Monks,* 106–7.

4. Reasons of space dictate that we not go into detail about the nature of these two empires and their respective strengths. An excellent comparison of their structures and institutions is provided by J. D. Howard-Johnston, "The Great Powers in Late Antiquity: A Comparison," in *States, Resources and Armies: Papers of the Third Workshop on Late Antiquity and Early Islam,* edited by Averil Cameron, 3:157–226, Byzantine and Early Islamic Near East, Studies in Late Antiquity and Early Islam (Princeton: Darwin Press, 1995); cf. Z. Rubin, "The Reforms of Khusro Anūshirwān," in *States, Resources and Armies,* 3:227–97; see also Josef Wiesehöfer, *Ancient Persia: From 550 BC to 650 AD* (London: I. B. Tauris, 1996), 151–221, on the Sasanian state, with S. McDonough, "Power by Negotiation: Institutional Reform in the Fifth-century Sasanian Empire" (PhD diss., University of California, Los Angeles, 2005). On the Roman state in the fourth century see, e.g., Jean-Michel Carrié and Aline Rousselle, *L'Empire romain en mutation: Des Sévères à Constantin,* Nouvelle Histoire de l'Antiquité 10 (Paris: Seuil, 1999), 563–718, and in general Averil Cameron and Peter Garnsey, *Cambridge Ancient History,* vol. 13, *The Late Empire, A.D. 337–425* (Cambridge: Cambridge University Press, 1998).

5. We follow C. Zuckerman, "Les Campagnes des tétrarques, 296–98: Notes de chronologie," *Antiquité tardive* 2 (1994): 70, in placing the treaty in 299; cf. Timothy D. Barnes, *The New Empire of Diocletian and Constantine* (Cambridge, Mass.: Harvard University Press, 1982), 55, although many scholars continue to date it to 298—e.g., Engelbert Winter and Beate Dignas, *Rome and Persia in Late Antiquity: Neighbours and Rivals* (Cambridge: Cambridge University Press, 2007), 30–31; Karin Mosig-Walburg, *Römer und Perser: Vom 3. Jahrhundert bis zum Jahr 363 n. Chr.* (Gutenberg: Computus, 2009), 122–30.

Shapur II, whose reign extends from 309 to 379, was determined to regain this lost territory; he finally achieved this in the wake of Julian's abortive invasion of Persia in 363.[6] Thenceforth the eastern frontier, at least in Mesopotamia—some fighting continued in Armenia before its partition in 387—remained at peace almost without interruption until Kavadh laid siege to Amida in October 502.[7] On the Roman side of the border the period marks the transformation in the fortunes of the Christians of the empire. From an oppressed minority at the dawn of the fourth century they become the dominant force by the reign of Theodosius I (379–395), determined to eradicate the pagan cults that had hitherto survived in considerable numbers, even if this proved to be a slower process than has sometimes been imagined.[8] The conversion of Constantine has also usually been seen as a turning-point for the Christians of the Persian Empire: henceforth, their allegiance was suspect, and this is then held to be one of the primary grounds for the persecutions that broke out during the 340s. Given that much of the Roman Empire remained unchristianized at the time of the persecutions, however, the equation of Christian and Roman need not have been obvious to Shapur; thus, as Karin Mosig-Walburg has recently argued, we must not automatically infer a link between persecutions in Persia and the promotion of Christianity within the Roman Empire.[9]

6. This will be considered in greater detail later.

7. See Geoffrey Greatrex, *Rome and Persia at War: 502–532* (Leeds: Francis Cairns, 1998), 10–12; see also Greatrex, "The Background and Aftermath of the Partition of Armenia in A.D. 387," *Ancient History Bulletin* 14 (2000): 35–48, on the partition of Armenia; and Greatrex and Samuel N. C. Lieu, *The Roman Eastern Frontier and the Persian Wars (A.D. 363–630): A Narrative Sourcebook* (London: Routledge, 2002), 31–52, on the relatively peaceful years of the fifth century.

8. See, e.g., Peter R. Brown, in "Christianism and Religious Conflict," in *The Cambridge Ancient History,* vol. 13, *The Late Empire, A.D. 337–425,* edited by Cameron and Garnsey, 632–64 (Cambridge: Cambridge University Press, 1998). Brown, however, rightly stresses (640, 664) that Christian sources tend to exaggerate the rate of Christianization of the empire; cf. Brown, *Authority and the Sacred: Aspects of the Christianisation of the Roman World* (Cambridge: Cambridge University Press, 1995), 49–50, essentially the same text, as noted in Greatrex, review of *The Cambridge Ancient History,* vol.14, ed. A. Cameron, B. Ward-Perkins, and M. Whitby, *Phoenix* 57 (2003): 185; see also Cameron, *The Later Roman Empire, AD 284–430* (Cambridge, Mass.: Harvard University Press, 1993),75–78; A. Douglas Lee, *Pagans and Christians in Late Antiquity: A Sourcebook* (London: Routledge, 2000), 111–12.

9. Mosig-Walburg, "Christenverfolgung und Römerkrieg—Zu Ursachen, Ausmaß und Zielrichtung der Christenverfolgung unter Shapur II," *Iranistik* 7 (2005): 5–84, is the most thorough recent published treatment of the persecutions under Shapur II; cf. Mosig-Walburg, "Die Christenverfolgung Shâpûrs II: Vor dem Hintergrund des persisch-römischen Krieges," in *Inkulturation des Christentums im Sasanidenreich,* edited by Arafa Mustafa, Jürgen Tubach, and G. Sophia Vashalomidze, 171–86 (Wiesbaden: Reichert, 2007). The publication of McDonough, *"Power by Negotiation,"* is awaited.

We shall now consider the political and military context in which the *Book of Steps* was produced; we can then proceed to analyze the religious aspect of its genesis, and in particular the persecutions instigated by Shapur II.

The third century was a tumultuous one for the Roman East. As the author of the *Thirteenth Sibylline Oracle* put it, describing events of the 250s, "And then suddenly there will be famine, plague, dreadful lightning bolts, horrible wars, and destruction of cities. The Syrians will be terribly destroyed, for the great wrath of the lord on high will arise against them. There will be an uprising of the evil Persians, and Syrians joined with Persians will destroy the Romans."[10] Shapur I (239/240–270/272) inflicted numerous defeats on the Romans during his reign, and only with the reign of Aurelian (270–275) was Roman power definitively restored in the region, following the brief usurpation of power by Zenobia, ruler of Palmyra.[11] Even Aurelian, however, did not have time to take on the Persians himself, and it is quite possible that Mesopotamia remained under Persian control until the following decade. Not until the reign of Carus (282–283) did a Roman emperor cross the Euphrates and seek to avenge the defeat and capture of Valerian (253–260) in 260. His expedition was successful: he captured Ctesiphon in 283, but died on the re-

10. David S. Potter, *Prophecy and History in the Crisis of the Roman Empire: A Historical Commentary on the Thirteenth Sibylline Oracle* (Oxford: Oxford University Press, 1991), 173 (lines 106–11); see his commentary at 283–98 for an analysis; the allusion is to Shapur I's capture of Antioch (probably) in 252, although U. Hartmann, "Mareades—ein sasanidischer Quisling?" in *Ērān ud Anērān: Studien zu den Beziehungen zwischen dem Sasanidenreich und der Mittelmeerwelt,* edited by Josef Wiesehöfer and Philip Huyse, 106 and n5, Oriens et Occidens 13 (Stuttgart: Franz Steiner Verlag, 2006), argues for 253; cf. Michael H. Dodgeon and Samuel N. C. Lieu, *The Roman Eastern Frontier and the Persian Wars A.D. 226–363: A Documentary History* (London: Routledge, 1991), 49–67; and Peter M. Edwell, *Between Rome and Persia: The Middle Euphrates, Mesopotamia and Palmyra under Roman Control* (London: Routledge, 2008), 190–94.

11. For details, see Richard Stoneman, *Palmyra and Its Empire: Zenobia's Revolt against Rome* (Ann Arbor: University of Michigan Press, 1992); Dodgeon and Lieu, *Roman Eastern Frontier,* 68–110; Winter and Dignas, *Rome and Persia,* 22–26; Michael Sommer, *Roms orientalische Steppengrenze: Palmyra, Edessa, Dura-Europos, Hatra; Eine Kulturgeschichte von Pompeius bis Diocletian* (Stuttgart: Franz Steiner, 2005), 159–70; and Mosig-Walburg, *Römer und Perser: Vom 3. Jahrhundert bis zum Jahr 363 n. Chr.* (Gutenberg: Computus, 2009), 26–61. See also Andreas Luther, "Roms mesopotamische Provinzen nach der Gefangennahme Valerians (260)," in *Ērān ud Anērān: Studien zu den Beziehungen zwischen dem Sasanidenreich und der Mittelmeerwelt,* edited by Philip Huyse and Josef Wiesehöfer, 203–19 (Stuttgart: Franz Steiner Verlag, 2006), on the scanty evidence for events on the eastern frontier between 260 and 298, with Greatrex, Review of *Ērān ud Anērān,* by Wiesehöfer and Huyse, *Phoenix* 63 (2009): 208–11. Edwell, *Between Rome and Persia,* 149–200, deals with the earlier period, until the 250s.

turn journey, paving the way for the accession of Diocletian (284–305).[12] The frontier remained at peace for the following ten years, no doubt partly because of the multitude of problems facing the rulers of both empires, but under the Persian king Narses (293–302), hostilities broke out again. Although he was initially victorious against Diocletian's subordinate Caesar Galerius in 297, he suffered a crushing defeat in the following year and was forced to conclude a humiliating peace.[13] While most of the details of the peace terms need not detain us here, the extension of the Roman Empire further to the east than it had ever yet penetrated should be underlined (see map 1). We must be careful to note, however, that the "trans-Tigritane regions," much discussed by scholars, were almost certainly only under *indirect* Roman rule—that is, under rulers nominally subject to Roman control. An example of such a ruler is Jovinianus, satrap of Corduene, one of the trans-Tigritane regions. Although Jovinianus had received his education in Syria and was acquainted with Ammianus Marcellinus, Ammianus nevertheless states categorically that Corduene, at least in 359, "was subject to Persian power."[14] This need not mean that the Romans did not make some effort to implant themselves in these regions. Bezabde,

12. Dodgeon and Lieu, *Roman Eastern Frontier,* 111–21, with John Eadie, "The Transformation of the Eastern Frontier, 260–305," in *Shifting Frontiers in Late Antiquity,* edited by Ralph W. Mathisen and Hagith Sivan, 72–82 (Aldershot: Variorum, 1996). A gold medallion of Numerian from the Hermitage, published in 2006, depicts this triumph: the reverse displays two cavalrymen triumphing over six fallen adversaries; see Frank Althaus and Mark Sutcliffe, *The Road to Byzantium: Luxury Arts of Antiquity* (London: Fontanka, 2006), 146n58.

13. Details (from Peter the Patrician) in Dodgeon and Lieu, *Roman Eastern Frontier,* 121–22; Roger C. Blockley, *East Roman Foreign Policy: Formation and Conduct from Diocletian to Anastasius* (Leeds: Francis Cairns, 1992), 5–7; Winter and Dignas, *Rome and Persia,* 29–31; Mosig-Walburg, *Römer und Perser,* 100–19; and Bill Leadbetter, *Galerius and the Will of Diocletian* (London: Routledge, 2009), 89–95. For the chronology, see Zuckerman, who argues in "Campagnes des tétrarques," 65–66, that Galerius's campaign lasted from October 297 to spring 299.

14. Amm. Marc. 18.6.20. All citations of Ammianus are taken from John C. Rolfe, ed., *Ammianus Marcellinus: History,* 3 vols, Loeb Classical Library (Cambridge, Mass.: Harvard (University Press, 1935–39); see the discussion in John F. Matthews, *The Roman Empire of Ammianus* (London: Duckworth, 1989), 55–57. For discussion of the territorial provisions of the treaty of 298, see Blockley, "The Roman-Persian Peace Treaties of A.D. 299 and 363," *Florilegium* 6 (1984): 32–33; Winter, "On the Regulation of the Eastern Frontier of the Roman Empire in 298," in *The Eastern Frontier of the Roman Empire: Proceedings of a Colloquium Held at Ankara in September 1988,* edited by David H. French and Chris S. Lightfoot, 555–59, BAR International Series 553 (Oxford: British Institute of Archaeology at Ankara, 1989);Winter and Dignas, *Rome and Persia,* 122–30 (with map); Greatrex, "Roman Frontiers and Foreign Policy in the East," in *Aspects of the Roman East: Papers in Honour of Professor Fergus Millar FBA,* edited by Richard Alston, Samuel N. C. Lieu, and Fergus Millar, 117–18 (Turnhout: Brepols, 2007); and Mosig-Walburg, *Römer und Perser,* 134–47.

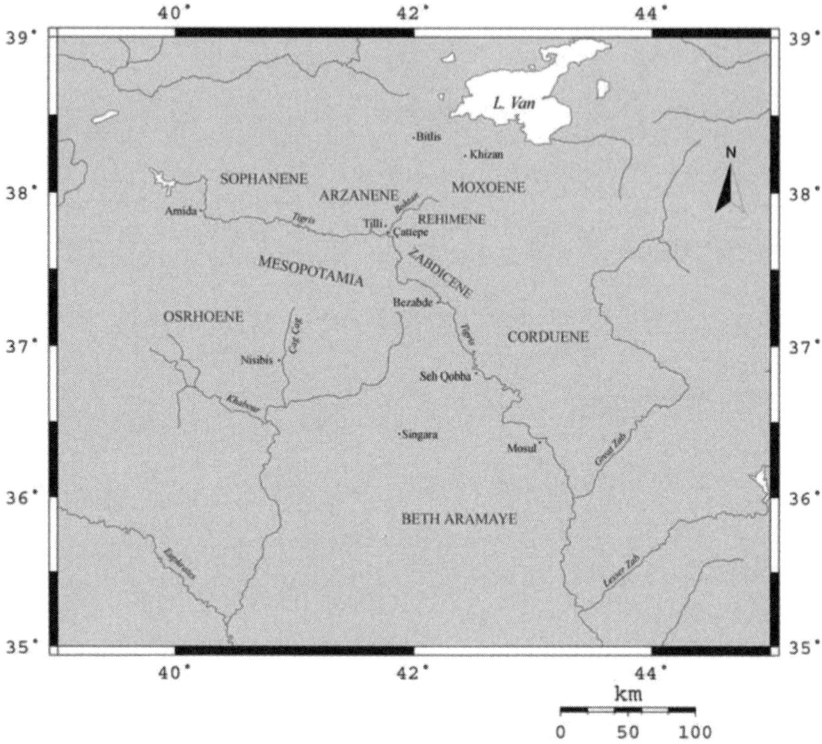

Map 1. Osrhoene and Northern Mesopotamia

for instance, lay on the west bank of the Tigris, across from Fenek,[15] and other more recently discovered sites, such as Tilli, just north of the Tigris and west of the Bohtan Su,[16] Çattepe at the confluence of the Tigris and Bohtan

15. See Lightfoot, "The Site of Roman Bezabde," in *Armies and Frontiers in Roman and Byzantine Anatolia: Proceedings of a Colloquium Held at University College, Swansea, in April 1981,* edited by Stephen Mitchell, 189–94, BAR International Series 156 (Oxford: British Institute of Archaeology at Ankara), 1989; Lightfoot, "The Year's Work," *Anatolian Studies* 40 (1990): 19–24.

16. Described in Lightfoot, "Tilli: A Late Roman *Equites* Fort on the Tigris," in *The Defence of the Roman and Byzantine East: Proceedings of a Colloquium Held at the University of Sheffield in April 1986,* edited by Philip Freeman and D. L. Kennedy, esp.518–21, BAR International Series 297 (Oxford: British Institute of Archaeology at Ankara, 1986). Anne E. Redgate, *The Armenians* (Oxford: Blackwell, 1998), 133, suggests that Constantius was responsible for its construction.

Su,[17] both on the border between Arzanene and Corduene, and Seh Qobba on the Tigris, close to Adiabene and only 100 kilometers from Mosul,[18] attest a Roman military presence beyond what has sometimes been supposed, even if it may have been only transitory.

This leads on naturally to a discussion of the frontier generally. In the wake of the treaty of 363, a quite perceptible frontier between the two powers came into being, marked by a network of fortified cities on the Roman side of the border.[19] But until then, the status of much of northern Mesopotamia was contested, and certain territories oscillated between Roman and Persian control. An inhabitant of a city such as Singara or Bezabde, for instance, may have been under Persian rule before Carus's invasion; in 360 both were retaken by Shapur and thenceforth remained again under Persian control, despite a Roman assault on Bezabde in late 360.[20] The experience of residents of the provinces beyond the Tigris would have been no less confusing: Arzanene, for instance, is named in the 299 treaty as one of the trans-Tigritane regions, thus within the Roman orbit. According to the Persian martyr acts, however, a persecution was unleashed here by Shapur in the eighteenth year of his reign (i.e., 326/327), which implies that it had already come into the Persian orbit

17. As described in Guillermo Algaze, Ray Breuninger, Chris S. Lightfoot, and Michael Rosenberg, "The Tigris-Euphrates Archaeological Reconnaissance Project: A Preliminary Report of the 1989–1990 Seasons," *Anatolica* 17 (1991): 191–92, the period of occupation is uncertain. An inscription in Greek attests the presence of a soldier in the second and third centuries. See also Winter, "Regulation," 560, on these two places; Winter argues that the Romans were seeking merely to occupy a few strategic places rather than exert full control over the trans-Tigritane regions.

18. See Warwick Ball, "Seh Qubba, a Roman Frontier Post in Northern Iraq," in *The Eastern Frontier of the Roman Empire: Proceedings of a Colloquium Held at Ankara in September 1988*, edited by David H. French and Chris S. Lightfoot, 1: 7–11, BAR International Series 553 (Oxford: British Institute of Archaeology at Ankara, 1989), which identifies the site with Ammianus's Castra Maurorum, ceded to Shapur in 363; cf. Ball, Stuart Campbell, and St. John Simpson, eds., *Ancient Settlement in the Zammar Region: Excavations by the British Archaeological Expedition to Iraq in the Saddam Dam Salvage Project, 1985–86*, BAR International Series 1096 (Oxford: Archaeopress, 2003), 18, 64–96, esp. 80–81. According to Carrié and Rousselle, *L'Empire romain*, 167, there was also a tetrarchic fort installed at Khizan, which they place in Zabdicene; in fact, it is rather in Rehimene or Moxoene, 120 kilometers due east of Matyropolis, 38 kilometers south of the western tip of Lake Van; see Robert H. Hewsen and Christopher C. Salvatico, *Armenia: A Historical Atlas* (Chicago: University of Chicago Press, 2001), map 93 D2; and Redgate, *Armenians*, 118, map 6.2 (Hizan); cf. B. Dixon, in "Journeys in Kurdistan," *Geographical Journal* 35 (1910): 368, who suggests it was the capital of Moxoene.

19. See Greatrex, *Rome and Persia*, 14; Greatrex, "Roman Frontiers," 119.

20. Amm. Marc. 20.62–67, with Mosig-Walburg, in "Zur Schlacht bei Singara," *Historia: Zeitschrift für Alte Geschichte* 48 (1999): 371, who suggests that Shapur may also have taken Singara earlier, perhaps in 348, but was forced to relinquish it again; cf. Dodgeon and Lieu, *Roman Eastern Frontier*, 190.

by this date, less than thirty years after Galerius's treaty.[21] The consequences of this point for the author of the *Book of Steps* are clear: it is possible that he experienced the Great Persecution in territory taken over by the Romans in 299, but which subsequently was recaptured by Shapur, which would explain why he is usually considered to have been writing under Persian rule. It is not necessary therefore to suppose that he actually moved from one region to another, although this, of course, remains possible.

We must resume our account of the dramatic events witnessed by the frontier region during our author's lifetime. The immediate aftermath of the treaty of 299 was peaceful, although it is possible that Hormizd II (302–309) made an unsuccessful attempt to exact vengeance for his father's defeat.[22] Epigraphi-

21. As noted by Marie-Louise Chaumont, *La christianisation de l'Empire iranien: Des origines aux grandes persécutions du IVe siècle,* Corpus Scriptorum Christianorum Orientalium 499 (Louvain: Peeters, 1988), 178, cf. 124, and Jérôme Labourt, *Le christianisme dans l'empire perse sous la dynastie sassanide (224–632),* 2nd ed., Bibliotheque de l'enseignement de l'histoire ecclesiastique (Paris: Librarie Victor Lecoffre, 1904), 50. Mosig-Walburg, "Christenverfolgung und Römerkrieg," esp. 6n2, is skeptical as to how much store can be put by these acts generally, and the early date of these persecutions is suspicious; nevertheless, given the evident looseness of Roman control beyond the Tigris, one should not reject the evidence out of hand. Jean-Maurice Fiey, *Nisibe: Métropole syriaque orientale et ses suffragants des origines à nos jours,* Corpus Scriptorum Christianorum Orientalum 388 (Louvain: Peeters, 1977), 25–26, correctly rejects some martyr accounts that place a Persian commander in Nisibis; cf. Joel Thomas Walker, *The Legend of Mar Qardagh: Narrative and Christian Heroism in Late Antique Iraq* (Berkeley and Los Angeles: University of California Press, 2006), 117–19, who notes that the account of the martyrdom of Qardagh dates from the late Sasanian period and thus likewise reflects the geography of this period (with Nisibis in Persian hands; Walker, *Legend of Mar Qardagh,* chap. 5, page 22; chap. 41, page 48). On the other hand, despite the arguments of Mosig-Walburg, "Christenverfolgung und Römerkrieg," 24n69, the ebb and flow of Persian and Roman control might explain the otherwise surprising statement of the Chronicle of Séert in Addai Scher, ed., *Chronique de Séert,* Patrologia Orientalis 4 (Turnhout: Brepols, 1908), 299, that a six-year persecution of Christians in the vicinity of Nisibis took place (apparently in the early 340s) at a time when the city itself was still under Roman control: in order to lay siege to the city (several times), Shapur must have controlled most of the adjacent region. See Georg Hoffmann, *Auszüge aus syrischen Akten persischer Märtyrer,* Abhandlungen für die Kunde des Morgenlandes, vol. 7, bk. 3 (Leipzig: Brockhaus, 1880), 22, the very start of the account of the martyrdom of Mar Sabā: the lands between Nisibis and the Tigris, the author claims, came sometimes under Roman control, sometimes under Persian; cf. Paul S. Russell, "Nisibis as the Background to the Life of Ephrem the Syrian," *Hugoye: Journal of Syriac Studies* 8 (2005): 70 (now 217).One might compare the uncertainty that surrounds the location of the martyrdom of Berikisho' (Paul Bedjan, comp, *Acta martyrum et sanctorum Syriace* [Paris and Leipzig: Harrassowitz Verlag, 1894], 4:166–70) and others, killed in 662 A.G. [Anno Graecorum], i.e., C.E. 351, somewhere on the Euphrates—but whether in Roman or Persian territory is unclear; see Labourt, *Christianisme,* 78n2; Sacha Stern, "Near Eastern Lunar Calendars in the Syriac Martyr Acts," *Le Muséon* 117 (2004): 468–69.

22. Winter and Dignas, *Rome and Persia,* 32; see also Chaumont, *Christianisation,* 122. Paul Kawerau, ed., *Die Chronik von Arbela* [*The Chronicle of Arbela*], Corpus Scriptorum Christianorum Orientalum 467:45 (text); 468:51 (translation) (Louvain: Peeters, 1985). Ilaria Ramelli, trans., *Il Chronicon di*

cal evidence has been used to argue for two Roman victories, one under Maximinus Daia in 310/311 and another in Cappadocia, under Licinius, in 313/314, but neither is particularly secure.[23] Otherwise the sources indicate a largely peaceful coexistence. Moreover, Constantine's taking control of the East from Licinius in 324 did not adversely affect relations between the two sides.[24] It appears that it was only in the mid-330s that tensions began to build once again following an unsuccessful Persian embassy to Constantine, by which Shapur demanded that negotiations about a (revised) frontier settlement begin. This took place probably in the winter of 336 to 337 and led to Shapur beginning hostilities in spring 337 while Constantine was still preparing for war in Constantinople. The emperor was not caught completely unawares, however, having simultaneously dispatched his nephew Hannibalian to Cappadocia in 336, appointing him king of Armenia, and putting his son Constantius in charge of the defense of the East.[25] These measures proved inadequate when

---

Arbela: Presentacione, traducione e note essenziali [Madrid: Universidad Complutense de Madrid, 2002], 51), a doubtful source, refers to a successful campaign of Hormizd. Mosig-Walburg, "Zur Westpolitik Shâpûrs II," in *Iran, questions et connaissances,* vol.1, *La période ancienne actes du IVe Congrès européen des études iraniennes, Paris, 6–10 septembre 1999,* edited by Philip Huyse, 329–47 (Paris: Association pour l'avancement des études iraniennes, 2002), surprisingly makes no mention of this episode, but see Mosig-Walburg, *Römer und Perser,* 176–82, suggesting that the reference is rather to a campaign launched against Arabs allied to the Romans.

23. Mosig-Walburg, "Westpolitik Shâpûrs II," 333–34 and nn.16–17; cf. Mosig-Walburg, *Römer und Perser,* 163–67, responding to Timothy D. Barnes, *Constantine and Eusebius* (Cambridge, Mass.: Harvard University Press, 1981), 39, 65. Mosig-Walburg, "Der Armenkrieg des Maximinus Daia," *Historia: Zeitschrift für Alte Geschichte* 55 (2006): 247–55, is rightly skeptical about an Armenian campaign attributed to Maximinus Daia.

24. The veiled threats contained in the letter of Constantine to Shapur cited by Eusebius, *Vita Constantini,* in *Über das Leben des Kaisers Konstantins,* edited by Friedhelm Winkelmann, iv, 8, rev. ed. (Berlin: Akademie-Verlag, 1991), are often considered to have augured ill for Romano-Persian relations, and indeed for the Christian community in Persia; see, e.g., Potter, *The Roman Empire at Bay: A.D. 180–395* (London: Routledge, 2004), 446–47. Mosig-Walburg, "Christenverfolgung und Römerkrieg," 8, 11–12, 8n5 (cf. Mosig-Walburg, *Römer und Perser,* 267–75), casts doubt, however, as to the extent to which Eusebius is here reproducing a genuine letter of Constantine; for a more positive assessment of Eusebius's evidence, see Averil Cameron and Stuart G. Hall, *Eusebius: Life of Constantine,* Clarendon Ancient History Series (Oxford: Oxford University Press, 1999), 313–14 (with references). Blockley, *East Roman Foreign Policy,* 10, believes that there were tensions in the East in the 320s, but see also Mosig-Walburg, "Westpolitik Shâpûrs II," 335.

25. I base myself here upon the research of Mosig-Walburg, "Westpolitik Shâpûrs II," 334–44, who examines all the sources in detail, rightly rejecting notices of earlier hostilities (to be found, e.g., in Richard W. Burgess and Witold Witakowski, *Studies in Eusebian and Post-Eusebian Chronography* (Stuttgart: F. Steiner, 1999), 199–200). On Hannibalian's appointment as king of Armenia as a way of strengthening Rome's hand in the East, see Mosig-Walburg, "Hanniballianus rex," *Millennium* 2 (2005): 229–54,

put to the test. While Constantine got no further than Nicomedia before falling ill and dying in May 337, Shapur overran much of Roman Mesopotamia and laid siege to Nisibis in June 337. The city bravely resisted the invader for two months, helped, so its inhabitants believed, by the prayers of its bishop, Jacob, who himself died in mid-July. In August Shapur withdrew to Persian territory.[26]

From this point to 363, with a brief lull for most of the 350s, the Roman East was under almost perpetual assault. Shapur II launched repeated invasions on Mesopotamia in an effort to back up his demands for a revision of the treaty of 299; Constantius II did what he could to ward off the Persians, but all too often proved unequal to the task. Although modern scholars are inclined to be more generous in their assessment of Constantius's performance than were some contemporaries, it is clear that he suffered a number of defeats in the course of the 340s, including at the much-discussed battle of Singara.[27] Yet for all his failures on the field of battle, Constantius nonetheless maintained his grip on Mesopotamia. Shapur laid siege to Nisibis two more times, once in 346 and again in 350, but its defenses held firm. Local sources, moreover, retain a favorable impression of the emperor: the *Life of Jacob the Recluse,* a sixth-century work, notes the care that he lavished on protecting

esp. 249–53, with Gerhard Wirth, "Hannibalian: Anmerkungen zur Geschichte eines überflüssigen Königs," *Bonner Jahrbücher* 190 (1990): 201–31, esp. 221.

26. The siege is sometimes dated to 338, but see Richard W. Burgess, "The Dates of the *First Siege of Nisibis* and the Death of James of Nisibis," *Byzantion* 69 (1999): 7–17, for justification of the 337 date. See page 16 for the chronological details of the siege; see also Burgess and Witakowski, *Studies,* 232–38, and now Muriel Debié, "Nisibe sauviée des eaux: les sources de Théodoret et la place des versions syriaques," In *Pèlerinages et lieux saints dans l'antiquité tardive et le moyen âge: mélanges offerts à Pierre Maraval,* edited by Beatrice Caseau, Jean-Claude Cheynet, and Vincent Déroche, 135–51 (Paris: Association des amis du Centre d'histoire et civilisation de Byzance, 2006),140–42; Mosig-Walburg, *Römer und Perser,* 216, 222.

27. As Mosig-Walburg, "Schlacht bei Singara," 343, concludes, following a thorough review of the evidence; cf. Mosig-Walburg, "Zu Spekulationen über den sasanidischen 'Thronfolger Narse' und seine Rolle in den sasanidisch-römischen Auseinandersetzungen im zweiten Viertel des 4. Jahrhunderts n. Chr," *Iranica Antiqua* 35 (2000): 111–57. B. H. Warmington, "Objectives and Strategy in the Persian War of Constantius II," in *Akten des XI. internationalen Limeskongresses,* edited by Jenó Fitz, 509–20 (Budapest: Akadémiai Kiadó, 1977), and Blockley, "Constantius II and Persia," in *Studies in Latin Literature and Roman History,* edited by Carl Deroux, 5:465–90 (Brussels: Latomus, 1989), offer useful overall assessments of Constantius's policy in the East; cf. Blockley, *East Roman Foreign Policy,* 13–23; Dodgeon and Lieu, *Roman Eastern Frontier,* 164–230; and Potter, *Roman Empire at Bay,* 467–68. Debié, "Nisibe," 142–50, considers the two sieges of Nisibis in detail; cf. Lightfoot, "Facts and Fiction: The Third Siege of Nisibis (A.D. 350)," *Historia* 37 (1988): 105–25.

and fortifying the frontier regions, describing how he bolstered the defenses of Amida, Cepha, and (perhaps) Rhabdion, which some have identified with Ammianus's Castra Maurorum.[28] The *Calendar of the Tur Abdin* commemorates Constantius alongside the numerous saints of the region, an honor by no means accorded to every emperor.[29] The inhabitants of Mesopotamia paid a heavy price for the emperor's grim determination to make no concessions to Shapur: Ammianus Marcellinus describes vividly the destruction wrought by both sides during the Persian incursions. While the population of the countryside sought refuge in the towns and cities, the crops would be destroyed, sometimes by Persian plunderers, sometimes by the Romans themselves in an effort to deny supplies to the invaders.[30] According to one Syriac source, in the course of one invasion, Karpos, bishop of Sawra, southeast of Amida, was killed by the Persians and his monastery burned to the ground; although there are grounds for skepticism about some aspects of this source, there is no reason to think that the Persians were not in control of this region for much of the time during Constantius's reign.[31] The extent of their control grew toward

28. See François Nau, "Résumé de monographies syriaques," *Revue de l'Orient Chrétien* 20 (1915): 7, for the translation; Matthews, *Empire of Ammianus,* 54–55, for a discussion. As Lightfoot, "Tilli," 519, notes, the work also attests to Roman interest in Arzanene, across the Tigris and Nymphius from Amida. On the date of the work and its provenance, see Gertrude Bell and Marlia M. Mango, *Churches and Monasteries of the Tur 'Abdin* (London: Pindar Press, 1982), 147. On the sieges of Nisibis, see the sources translated in Dodgeon and Lieu, *Roman Eastern Frontier,* 191–207.

29. Translation in Paul Peeters, "Le martyrologe de Rabban Saliba," *Analecta Bollandiana* 27 (1908): 168; his commemoration date was 16 Tešrin II (November). See Burgess and Witakowski, *Studies,* 277E–80, substantiating Constantius's work at Amida and dating it to 349; Mosig-Walburg, *Römer und Perser,* 221, prefers an earlier dating, however. Note also Ephrem, *Hymns against Julian,* 2.19 (translation in Lieu, ed., *The Emperor Julian: Panegyric and Polemic,* 2nd ed., Translated Texts for Historians [Liverpool: Liverpool University Press, 1989], 114), who refers to Constantius playing his part in defending Nisibis, despite his absence; cf. Lieu, *Emperor Julian,* 114n48.

30. Amm. Marc. 18.6.9 on Persians burning crops near the Tigris; 18.7.3–4 for the Romans setting light to their own crops in order to deny supplies to Shapur. *Exposition totius mundi et gentium,* a work compiled c.359, chap. 22, offers a more upbeat assessment of the region, noting its many thriving cities; cf. the translation in Dodgeon and Lieu, *Roman Eastern Frontier,* 221. A good general description of daily life in the region, and at Nisibis in particular, may be found in David Bundy, "Vision for the City: Nisibis in Ephrem's *Hymns on Nicomedia,*" in *Religions of Late Antiquity in Practice,* edited by Richard Valantasis, 189–206 (Princeton: Princeton University Press, 2000), drawing on Ephrem's *Hymns on Nicomedia;* see also Debié, "Nisibe," 137–38; Lightfoot, "Facts and Fiction," 106–11. Fiey, *Nisibe,* 32, based on Ephrem, *Carm. Nis.* vi.27 (24/26), asserts that only ten out of one hundred people survived these invasions, no doubt an exaggeration, but one that reflects their huge impact; cf. Ephrem, *Carm. Nis.* vii.2 (25/28), on the twenty years of suffering endured by the city.

31. See Andrew Palmer, *Monk and Mason on the Tigris Frontier: The Early History of Tur 'Abdin*

the end of the 350s. Amida fell after a protracted siege in 359, and although it was not garrisoned by the Persians, they did occupy both Singara and Bezabde, which were seized in 360.[32] The destruction was not confined to Roman Mesopotamia: even if Constantius was obliged to fight a largely defensive war, a strategy that was not to the taste of many Romans, it is probable that on at least one occasion Roman armies conducted comparable invasions of bordering Persian territories.[33] The massive invasion of Persia launched by Julian in 363, which penetrated as far as Ctesiphon, caused further damage to both Upper and Lower Mesopotamia; as Julian drew near to the Persian heartlands, they resorted to flooding large tracts of agricultural land in order to protect the city.[34]

The *Book of Steps* was thus composed against a backdrop of constant large-scale warfare. We may find an echo of this in memra 9, in which the author argues that God is not responsible for the conflict: "no longer when the Assyrian [i.e., the Persian] wakes up is it our Lord who awakens him; nor when the Roman descends to battle, is it our Lord who makes him descend."[35] Once Shapur had regained most of the trans-Tigritane provinces, along with Nisibis and the eastern part of Roman Mesopotamia, by the treaty of 363, the situation changed drastically. The region saw no further armed conflict between the two powers until 421. Indeed, relations between Constantinople and Ctesiphon improved considerably, partly in the wake of a devastating Hunnic

(Cambridge: Cambridge University Press, 1990), 21–22, using the (later) *Life of Samuel.* Whether the Persians deliberately targeted Christians, on the other hand, is doubtful, as will be discussed later.

32. See n. 20. One source reports that 9,000 prisoners were deported and taken to Persia: see Mosig-Walburg, "Christenverfolgung und Römerkrieg," 29n87, 38–40, who also draws attention to the role of the bishop in negotiating with the Persians (reported by Amm. Marc. 20.7.7), which implies a confidence in the adversary that would be unlikely if a thoroughgoing persecution of Christians were taking place on Persian territory at the time; Oscar Braun, trans., *Ausgewälte Akten persischer Märtyres, mit einem Anhang: Ostsyrische Mönchsleben* (Kempten: Verlag der Jos Köselschen Buchandlungen, 1915), 110; for the figure, cf. Labourt, *Christianisme,* 78n2. The *Acts of the Martyrs of Bezabde* (Bedjan, *Acta martyrum*, 316–24) is translated in Dodgeon and Lieu, *Roman Eastern Frontier,* 215–19.

33. Mosig-Walburg, "Schlacht bei Singara," 375, assembles the slender evidence for a raid by Constantius; cf. Dodgeon and Lieu, *Roman Eastern Frontier,* 179–81. She is scathing in her assessment of this "success": "Der angeblich bedeuntende Sieg des Constantius war kaum der Rede wert"; Mosig-Walburg, "Christenverfolgung und Römerkrieg," 9n9.

34. Amm. Marc. 24.3.10, with Matthews, *Empire of Ammianus,* 152–53. For details on Julian's invasion and retreat, see Matthews, *Empire of Ammianus,* 145–79; Glen W. Bowersock, *Julian the Apostate* (Cambridge, Mass.: Harvard University Press, 1978), 106–19; Dodgeon and Lieu, *Roman Eastern Frontier,* 231–74; and Winter and Dignas, *Rome and Persia,* 90–94.

35. *BoS* 9.6, *LG* 216; cf. 217.

raid in 395 that ravaged Roman and Persian lands in equal measure, and partly through the initiative of figures such as Bishop Marutha and the Persian king Yazdgerd I (399–420) himself.[36]

The author speaks on several occasions of persecutions. We may distinguish two bouts of persecution, one of which had taken place sometime in the past, but within living memory, the other very recent. It is necessary, therefore, now to turn to the religious environment in which the author was writing. We must bear in mind, of course, that religious and political factors, while clearly distinct for us, were hardly perceived as such by contemporaries: one need only think of the harsh measures imposed by Diocletian on Manichaeans in 302, at least partly motivated by their association with the Persians.[37] As has long been noticed, the vocabulary employed by the author betrays a familiarity with Roman institutions; the nature of the persecutions, moreover, points strongly to a Roman context, for example in the obligation mentioned to worship idols (rather than fire, for instance, as might be expected in Persia).[38] In this context we should note that persecutions in (Roman) Mesopotamia were infrequent under Diocletian, Galerius, Licinius, and Maximinus Daia; this is

36. Greatrex and Lieu, *Roman Eastern Frontier,* 10–17, on the situation in Mesopotamia from 363, with Greatrex, "Background and Aftermath," 35–43. On the Hunnic raid of 395, see Geoffrey Greatrex and M. Greatrex, "The Hunnic Invasion of the East of 395 and the Fortress of Ziatha," *Byzantion* 69 (1999): 65–73, and Gastone Breccia, "'Salus Orientis': Il nuovo sistema militare romano-orientale alla prova, 379–400," *Rivista di studi bizantini e Neollenici* 41 (2005): 50–54. On Marutha and the good relations established under Yazdgerd I, see Greatrex and Lieu, *Roman Eastern Frontier,* 31–36; McDonough, "A Second Constantine? The Sasanian King Yazdgard in Christian History and Historiography," *Journal of Late Antiquity* 1, no. 1 (2008): 127–36.

37. *Mosaicarum et Romanorum legum collatio,* in *Compiling the "Collatio Legum Mosaicorum et Romanarum" in Late Antiquity,* edited by R. M. Frakes (Oxford: Oxford University Press, 2011), §15.3, 191–92 (text); 233–34 (translation); cf. the translation and commentary of Winter and Dignas, *Rome and Persia,* 216–17. This law was formerly usually dated to 297, but scholars now favor 302 as the date for the rescript; see Roger Rees, *Diocletian and the Tetrarchy* (Edinburgh: Edinburgh University Press, 2004), 58–59; Simon Corcoran, *The Empire of the Tetrarchs: Imperial Pronouncements and Government, AD 284–324,* rev. ed. (Oxford: Clarendon Press, 2000), 135–36. Mosig-Walburg, *Römer und Perser,* 168–76, plays down the Persian connection in the law.

38. See Fitschen, *Messalianismus,* 111, citing *BoS* 8.4, *LG* 196; see also Westerhoff, "Bild vom Staat," 26–29; Westerhoff, *Paulusverständnis,* 8nn40–41. The punishments described in the same section include death by burning, by the sword, and at the hands of wild beasts, which also fit the Roman context better, as Fitschen, *Messalianismus,* notes. Nevertheless, one must note that some Persian martyr acts report deaths by the sword and at the hands of wild beasts; for the latter, see C. D. G. Müller, "Stellung und Bedeutung des Katholikos-Patriarchen von Seleukia-Ktesiphon im Altertum," *Oriens Christianus* 53 (1969): 228; and Bedjan, *Acta martyrum* 2:523; cf. Theodor Nöldeke, *Geschichte der Perser und Araber zur Zeit der Sasaniden: Aus der Arabischen Chronik des Tabari* (Leiden: E. J. Brill, 1879), 307, on elephants trampling Christians.

in contrast to Palestine, for instance, where many suffered martyrdom, as Eusebius relates at length.[39] We hear of a few martyrs at Edessa, in particular of Shmona, Gurya, and Habbib, village dwellers who were brought to Edessa in 309 and 310 and executed at the governor's orders. The former two notably refused to sacrifice to the sun, despite the insistence of the governor Mysianus. According to the martyr acts, whose reliability is by no means universally accepted, even Jews and pagans were moved by the execution of Habbib and took part in shrouding and burying his body. This popular sympathy would help to explain the infrequency of persecutions east of the Euphrates, where Christianity was much better implanted than in some other regions; governors may also have been aware that extensive persecutions risked jeopardizing the stability of the region under their command, which could in turn pose a serious danger in the event of renewed hostilities with Persia.[40] Other references to persecutions are vague and often to be found in sources writing considerably later (e.g., the account of the martyrdom of Sergius and Bacchus).[41]

It is always possible that our author emigrated from elsewhere in the Roman empire to Persian territory during the Great Persecution (303–13); it is not our

39. Eusebius, *Ecclesiastical History,* VIII–IX, on the persecutions generally, *Martyrs of Palestine* specifically; see Barnes, *Constantine and Eusebius,* 150–55.

40. The martyr acts are edited by E. von Dobschütz, *Die Akten der edessenischen Bekenner Gurjas, Samonas und Abibos,* vol. 37, bk. 2 of *Text und Untersuchungen zur Geschichte der altchristlichen Literatur* (Leipzig: J. C. Hinrichs, 1911); translation by F. C. Burkitt, *Euphemia and the Goth: With the Acts of Martyrdom of the Confessors of Edessa* (1913; Amsterdam: APA–Philo Press, 1981). See chap. 42 for the order to sacrifice to the sun (page 102 of Burkitt's translation). On the role of Jews and pagans in burying Habbib, see chap. 38a, page 126 of Burkitt's translation. See J. B. Segal, *Edessa: The "Blessed City"* (Oxford: Clarendon Press, 1970), 83–86, on the context on the sympathy for the martyrs among the local populace. These martyr acts exerted an influence in turn on the Persian martyr acts, as did those of the Palestinian martyrs; see Sebastian P. Brock, "Review of G. Wiessner's 'Zur Märtyrerübelieferung,'" *Journal of Theological Studies* 19 (1968): 305, who notes that the *martyrion* of Simeon bar Sabba'e likewise contains a demand upon him to worship the sun; cf. Mosig-Walburg, "Christenverfolgung und Römerkrieg," 21. It can thus be difficult to distinguish Roman and Persian types of persecution. For the governor Mysianus, see Arnold H. Jones, John R. Martindale, and J. Morris, *Prosopography of the Later Roman Empire,* vol. 1 (Cambridge: Cambridge University Press, 1971), which views his existence as questionable; Burkitt, *Euphemia,* 10–15, argues convincingly in favor of the historicity of the Edessene martyr acts; see also Fiey, *Nisibe,* nos.181–82, pages 88–89; he oddly dates Habbib's martyrdom to 322 rather than 310.

41. The acts of Shmona, Gurya, and Habbib (Dobschütz, *Akten,* 8, §5) refer to martyrs at Edessa at the hands of the *dux* Heraclianus—Hermas and companions; nothing further is known of them. On Sergius and Bacchus, see their *Passio* with the remarks of Elizabeth Key Fowden, *The Barbarian Plain: Saint Sergius between Rome and Iran* (Berkeley and Los Angeles: University of California Press, 1999), 8–17. She dates their martyrdom to 312, during the reign of Maximinus Daia, although some have placed it later; the work itself dates from the fifth century; Fowden, *Barbarian Plain,* 7–8.

intention, however, to consider the impact of the persecution throughout the empire.[42] It is worth underlining that if our author was a Roman subject who fled the empire at this time to find refuge in Persian territory, he would not have been alone in making such a choice. Already during the persecutions in the mid-third century refugees had moved east; many other Christians found themselves deported to Persia around the same time, in the wake of the capture of Antioch.[43] In the fourth century, according to one source, Jews began to take refuge in Persia from the worsening situation for them in Roman territory.[44] The frontier itself, despite occasional efforts by the two powers, remained porous, and refugees can have had little difficulty in crossing over to Persian soil; it will have helped them that the period of the persecution coincided with a lull in hostilities between the two empires. But even at a time of war the example of the deserter Antoninus, recounted by Ammianus Marcellinus, attests to the relative ease with which even a well-to-do citizen might defect to the opposing side: Antoninus, an accountant working for the *dux* of Mesopotamia, under severe pressure from creditors and realizing that he had no chance of extricating himself from his predicament, bought an estate right on the Tigris River, and, having acquainted himself thoroughly with the Roman military dispositions in the East, crossed over into Persian territory to act as an adviser to Shapur. He merely had to cross the river by night, along with members of his household, and no one attempted to intercept him.[45]

42. For convenient recent treatments, see Rees, *Diocletian and the Tetrarchy,* 59–71; Corcoran, *Empire of the Tetrarchs,* 51–53.

43. See Christelle Jullien and Florence Jullien, *Apôtres des confins: Processus missionaires chrétiens dans l'Empire Iranien,* Res Orientales 15 (Bures-sur-Yvette: Groupe pour l'étude de la civilisation du Moyen-orient, 2002), 163–64, on voluntary exiles; cf. Wolfgang Hage, "Die oströmische Staatskirche und die Christenheit des Perserreiches," *Zeitschrift für Kirchengeschichte* 84 (1973): 176. See Jullien and Jullien, *Apôtres des confins,* 154–63, on the deportees from Antioch; cf. Chaumont, *Christianisation,* 59–60. See also Michael G. Morony, "Population Transfers between Sasanian Iran and the Byzantine Empire," in *Convegno internazionale La Persia e Bisanzio: Roma, 14–18 ottobre 2002,* 163–70 (Roma: Accademia nazionale dei Lincei, 2002), who warns against overstating the number of Christians seized in Shapur's invasions and the impact they may have had on Christianity in Persia; cf. more generally Matthew P. Canepa, *The Two Eyes of the Earth: Art and Ritual of Kingship between Rome and Sasanian Iran* (Berkeley: University of California Press, 2009), 22–31.

44. Noted by Georg G. Blum, "Zur religionpolitischen Situation der persischen Kirche im 3. und 4. Jahrhundert," *Zeitschrift für Kirchengeschichte* 91 (1980): 31; cf. Braun, *Ausgewälte Akten,* 13n2 (citing an apocryphal letter from Papa to the Empress Helena).

45. Amm. Marc. 18.5.1–3. For a discussion, see Matthews, *Empire of Ammianus,* 68, and H. Elton, "Defining Romans and Barbarians," in *Shifting Frontiers in Late Antiquity,* edited by Ralph W. Mathisen

While it is likely that the persecutions alluded to in memra 8 took place in the Roman Empire, those described in memra 30 are generally interpreted as having taken place in Persia. Moreover, the very few geographical references in the *Book of Steps* also point in the direction of an eastern provenance: both the Euphrates and, more importantly, the Lesser Zab are mentioned, also in memra 30.[46] It is therefore necessary to consider the position of Christians in Persia in the fourth century.

By the end of the third century it may safely be asserted that the Christians were a significant minority within the Persian Empire. The origins and growth of this Christian community need not detain us here—an excellent recent treatment is offered in the work of the Jullien sisters[47]—but it would be appropriate to outline the status of its members at the dawn of the fourth century. We may first note that Christians had had to deal with persecutions only rarely and intermittently, most recently under the reign of Bahram II (276–93); according to some Christian sources, the king launched his persecutions because of confusion between Manichaeans and Christians and desisted when the distinction was explained to him. However that may be, the persecutions were neither long-lasting nor widespread and did little to check the spread of the new religion.[48] In fact, the main problem faced by the Persian church at this

and Sivan Hagith, 130–31 (Aldershot: Variorum, 1996) (who also cites evidence for the frontier region being shut during times of war). See Lee, *Information and Frontiers: Roman Foreign Relations in Late Antiquity* (Cambridge: Cambridge University Press, 1993), 54–57, on the general porousness of the frontier.

46. *BoS* 30.14, *LG* 896, on which see Fitschen, *Messalianismus,* 110, noting that the manuscript reading of Zab is contested; see also Kitchen and Parmentier, *Book of Steps,* l. The reference at *BoS* 30.4, *LG* 869, 872, to the destruction of pagan altars is likewise ambiguous: in the late 410s, zealous Christians tore down fire altars in Persia, thus precipitating persecutions; see Josef Rist, "Die Verfolgung der Christen in spätantiken Sasanidenreich: Ursachen, Verlauf und Folgen," *Oriens Christianus* 80 (1996): 33. The *Acta Mar Kardaghi,* chap. 47–48 (trans. Walker, *Legend of Mar Qardagh,* 53–54) also refer to the destruction of fire altars, apparently in 358 to 359 (see Fitschen, *Messalianismus*, 118), but this source is late and unreliable. From within the Roman empire the *Acts of the Council of Elvira,* chap. 60, a work from the early fourth century, takes a line comparable to that of the *Book of Steps,* condemning such gratuitous attacks. Michael Gaddis, *There Is No Crime for Those Who Have Christ: Religious Violence in the Christian Roman Empire* (Berkeley and Los Angeles: University of California Press, 2005), 39–40, also finds evidence for Christians (in this case, in North Africa) denying aid to imprisoned coreligionists during persecutions; cf. *BoS* 30.14, the persecution of "martyrs of love" by "members of the household of faith." Thus Westerhoff, *Paulusverständnis,* 8 nn40–41, citing Kmosko, considers all the persecutions to have taken place on Roman soil; see further note 66 in this chapter.

47. Jullien and Jullien, *Apôtres des confins;* cf. also Chaumont, *Christianisation,* and McDonough, "*Power by Negotiation,*" 234–46. Labourt, *Christianisme,* remains a useful work. On Christianity in Upper Mesopotamia, see Russell, "Nisibis," 72–95; Debié, "Nisibe," 137–39.

48. See Chaumont, *Christianisation,* 104–11, esp. on the martyr Candida; see also Hage, "Oströ-

stage was its fissiparous nature, a condition reflected not least in the diversity of names applied to Christians within Persia—*mshihaye,* Nazirites, and Christians.[49] The last of these seems to have been applied originally just to deportees from Roman territory, but came to be used generally for all Christians. The fact that such distinctions were made and continued to be made to the point that we find one city with two bishops, one for the indigenous community, one for the deportees, confirms the gravity of the problem.[50] It was against such a background that an ambitious bishop of Seleucia-Ctesiphon, Papa bar Aggai, now sought to impose himself as the *catholicos* of the entire church under Persian rule. His attempt was fiercely contested, and an initial synod in 315 overruled his venture; among his opponents was his own deacon, Simeon bar Sabba'e. Papa persevered, however, and appealed to the bishops of the Roman East. They therefore intervened, perhaps even coming to Seleucia-Ctesiphon, and ruled in his favor; Simeon, for his part, changed his stance and was designated as Papa's successor.[51]

Papa's project was undoubtedly a sensible one, whatever his own personal shortcomings. The time was ripe for the Christians of Persia to organize themselves and to set about putting their relations with the king on a regular footing, just as the Jews had their exilarch, who was responsible for the Jewish community and in return enjoyed access to the king and court.[52] Moreover,

mische Staatskirche," 176; Blum, "Religionspolitischen Situation," 21–22; Brock and S. Ashbrook Harvey, *Holy Women of the Syriac Orient* (Berkeley and Los Angeles: University of California Press, 1987), 64; Brock, "A Martyr at the Sasanid Court under Vahram II: Candida," *Analecta Bollandiana* 96 (1978): 167–81; and Rist, "Verfolgung der Christen," 28–29. The *Chronicle of Séert* is our main source on Bahram's persecutions; see Scher, *Chronique de Séert,* 237–38; cf. Kawerau, *Chronik von Arbela,* chap. 10; on the worth of this much contested source, see Jullien and Jullien, "La chronique d'Arbèles: Propositions pour la fin d'une controverse," *Oriens Christianus* 85 (2001): 41–83.

49. See Brock, "Some Aspects of Greek Words in Syriac," in *Synkretismus im syrisch-persischen Kulturgebiet: Bericht über ein Symposion in Reinhausen bei Göttingen in der Zeit vom 4. Bis 8. Oktober 1971,* edited by A. Dietrich, 92–94 (Göttingen: Vandenhoeck and Ruprecht, 1975); reprinted in Brock, *Syriac Perspectives on Late Antiquity* (London: Variorum Reprints, 1984); Chaumont, *Christianisation,* 113–17, on these terms.

50. See Blum, "Religionspolitischen Situation," 19–20; Jullien and Jullien, *Apôtres des confins,* 173–82; the latter are cautious, however, as to whether the double episcopacy was split between the deportees and the indigenous Christians; cf. Jes P. Asmussen, "Christians in Iran," in *The Cambridge History of Iran,* edited by Ehsan Yarshater, 3: 929–30 (Cambridge: Cambridge University Press, 1983).

51. The literature on these complex quarrels is extensive, starting with Labourt, *Christianisme,* 20–24; see also Blum, "Religionspolitischen Situation," 22–25; Chaumont, *Christianisation,* 140–44; Jullien and Jullien, *Apôtres des confins,* 238–41; and Jullien and Jullien, *Aux origines de l'église de Perse: les Actes de Mar Mari,* Corpus Scriptorum Christianorum Orientalium 604 (Louvain: Peeters, 2003), 105.

52. See Jacob Neusner, "Jews in Iran," in *The Cambridge History of Iran,* 918–19; Marie-Joseph Pierre,

Papa's successor Simeon bar Sabba'e, according to our sources, whose trustworthiness is a matter of debate, was on good terms with Shapur II, which augured well for the prospects for the Christian community.[53] Yet despite these promising circumstances, by the end of the 340s Simeon and his successor were dead—martyred—and numerous other clergy had suffered the same fate. The key to understanding this sudden reversal of fortune may lie in developments alluded to in the *Book of Steps.*

The most popular explanation for the outbreak of persecution under Shapur II links it to the Christianization of the Roman Empire. According to this view the conversion of Constantine led almost instantly to a change in the status of his coreligionists in Persia: henceforth, they all became an object of suspicion on the grounds that they would readily side with the Romans in any conflict that broke out. This interpretation has recently been subjected to a thorough analysis by Karin Mosig-Walburg, who concludes that it is in large measure incorrect. To be sure, there were some Persian Christians who looked to the West for the overthrow of the Sasanian king: the fifth *Demonstration* of Aphrahat, a contemporary of our author, dating from 337, expresses a hope for the victory of the "good man" over the "evil man"—that is, of Constantine over Shapur, although it also envisages the possibility that the latter might emerge victorious.[54] Yet there are a number of reasons for supposing that the persecutions, which broke out probably only in 340 or 341,[55] were by no means inev-

---

trans., *Aphraate le sage persan: les exposés,* 2 vols., Sources Chrétiennes 349, 359 (Paris: Les Éditions du Cerf, 1988–1989), 1:88–89; Wiesehöfer, "'Geteilte Loyalitäten': Religiöse Minderheiten des 3. und 4. Jahrhunderts n. Chr. im Spannungsfeld zwischen Rom und dem sasanidischen Iran," *Klio* 75 (1993): 362–82. McDonough, "*Power by Negotiation,*" 223–28; and Isaiah M. Gafni, "The Political, Social and Economic History of Babylonian Jewry, 224–638 CE," In *The Cambridge History of Judaism: The Late Roman-Rabbinic Period,* edited by Steven T. Katz, 4: 802 (Cambridge: Cambridge University Press, 2006).

53. The date of Simeon's succession is uncertain. It probably took place in the 320s; see Chaumont, *Christianisation,* 146–47; Pierre, *Aphraate,* 263.

54. Aphrahat, *Demonstration,* 5, §25, in Pierre, *Aphraate,* 357, on the possible victory of the evil man. On Aphrahat, see also Pierre, *Aphraate,* 33–41; Barnes, "Constantine and the Christians of Persia," *The Journal of Roman Studies* 75 (1985): 133–34; Potter, *Roman Empire at Bay,* 469–70; and Mosig-Walburg, "Christenverfolgung und Römerkrieg," 7, n. 4, and 50–51, arguing that Aphrahat is by no means representative; cf. Mosig-Walburg, "Die Christenverfolgung Shâpûrs II," 177–78.

55. The date of the outbreak of the persecution and the martyrdom of Simeon in particular remains disputed. Burgess, "The Dates of the Martyrdom of Simeon bar Sabba'e and the 'Great Massacre,'" *Analecta Bollandiana* 117 (1999): 37–41, puts Shapur's tax demand in 337, the arrest of clergy in 340, and the execution of Simeon in 344, followed by the "great massacre" in 345; see likewise Burgess, *Studies,* 244–69; Stern, "Lunar Calendars," 456–57, 468, also favors 344, while rejecting Burgess's calendar calcu-

itable. First, it must be remembered that the conversion of Constantine did not lead suddenly to the Christianization of the whole empire: many inhabitants, if not most, remained pagan for much of the fourth century. Thus there was at this stage no simple opposition between a Christian Roman empire and a Zoroastrian Persian empire. Second, the persecutions themselves were neither consistent nor all-embracing. The principal victims were members of the church hierarchy; ordinary Christians were rarely affected. Moreover, it is hard to see how it could have been in Shapur's interest to undertake large-scale pogroms within his own kingdom at a time of open war with his Western neighbor, especially since some parts of it, such as Adiabene, contained many Christians. This is not to deny, of course, the occurrence of the persecutions. Their outbreak, however, is to be attributed, as several sources indicate, to economic grounds: Simeon, summoned by Shapur to the court, was asked to exact money from his coreligionists to fund Shapur's war against the Romans. Whether he was asked for a levy from the Christians, or whether there already was a levy and Shapur demanded that it be doubled, is not entirely clear. In any case, Simeon, probably to the king's surprise, refused to comply. It is quite possible that the *catholicos* overestimated his own strength—a point to which we shall return—and believed that he was in a position to deny the request. As he may have realized, Shapur's initiative probably had a twofold motivation: on the one hand, it would provide additional funds for his lengthy struggle with Rome, and on the other, it would inevitably reduce the popularity of the religion, thus stemming the tide of conversions within his kingdom. Only when Simeon had rejected the king's demand did the persecutions break out; and, as Mosig-Walburg points out, the principal victims were the clergy and church hierarchy (i.e., those who would have been expected to cooperate in raising the funds). The actual contributors of the levy, the Christian people themselves, were left largely untouched, no doubt because Shapur's intention was still to raise funds from them.[56]

---

lations. Mosig-Walburg, "Christenverfolgung und Römerkrieg," 14n6, cf. 17, argues that it is unlikely that the events were so spread out and places Simeon's death already in 340 or 341.

56. I summarize here the arguments of Mosig-Walburg, "Christenverfolgung und Römerkrieg" and "Die Christenverfolgung Shâpûrs II"; cf. McDonough, "*Power by Negotiation,*" 248–49. The standard view on the connection between Constantine's conversion, the outbreak of war, and the persecutions may be found, e.g., in F. Decret, "Les conséquences sur le christianisme en Perse de l'affrontement des empires romain et sassanide," *Recherches Augustiniennes* 14 (1979): 140, and Blockley, "Constantius II

It would be beyond the scope of this chapter to examine Shapur's persecutions in detail; as has been made clear, they have been the subject of much recent work in any case. For our purposes it is sufficient to note that the 340s in particular were a troubled time for the Christians of Persia. This is reflected not only in the many accounts of the martyrs of the period—many of which, however, were substantially reworked at a later stage and cannot be taken at face value[57]—but also in contemporary works, such as *Demonstration* 14 of Aphrahat, and perhaps the *Book of Steps* itself. As Decret points out, the fifty years or so of growing prosperity in the Persian church that preceded the persecutions had exacerbated the internal dissensions and rivalries that were always one of its hallmarks; such was also the opinion of our author, who in memra 7 criticizes the complacency of his own generation, which had grown lax now that it found itself free of persecution.[58] Aphrahat's *Demonstration* 14 dates from January 344 and takes the form of a synodal letter to the church of Seleucia-Ctesiphon, which is replete with criticisms of the leadership.[59] It

and Persia," 474; cf. Asmussen, "Christians in Iran," 933–34, who also highlights the role of the Magi in spurring the persecutions. The argument is taken even further by Paul McKechnie and John A. Crook, "Roman Law and the Laws of the Medes and Persians: Decius's and Valerian's Persecutions of Christianity," in *Thinking Like a Lawyer: Essays on Legal History and General History for John Crook on His Eightieth Birthday,* edited by Paul McKechnie, 253–69 (Leiden: E. J. Brill, 2002), who argues that the Roman persecution of Christians in the empire in the mid-third century was a response to the aggressive Zoroastrian proselytism undertaken by the Persians in conquered Roman territories. See also Wiesehöfer, "Geteilte Loyalitäten," a more nuanced treatment, and Wiesehöfer, *Ancient Persia,* 210–14, rightly arguing against the notion of a "state" (Zoroastrian) church in Persia in the period with which we are concerned; cf. P. Gignoux, "Church-state Relations in the Sasanian Period," *Bulletin of the Middle Eastern Culture Centre in Japan* 1 (1984): 76–77, and McDonough, "*Power by Negotiation,*" 200–1; a priestly hierarchy only started to emerge during the reign of Shapur II. Mosig-Walburg, "Christenverfolgung und Römerkrieg," 65–66, on the other hand, believes that the notion of a "state church" is appropriate, while accepting that the influence of the clergy was by no means decisive. Rist, "Verfolgung der Christen," 30, sees the persecutions as a result of Shapur's anger in the wake of his failures at the start of hostilities with Rome; cf. Burgess, *Studies,* 37. On the question of the tribute raised from the Christians, see Mosig-Walburg, "Christenverfolgung und Römerkrieg," 27n71, 58n72, 60, who concludes that Shapur did aim to double the total; cf.Wiessner, *Zur Märtyrerüberlieferung aus der Christenverfolgung Schapurs II* (Göttingen: Vandenhoeck and Ruprecht, 1967), 183n1. The evidence of the Jewish situation does not help, since it is far from clear that the exilarch was responsible for raising taxes from among his community; see David M. Goodblatt, "The Poll Tax in Sasanian Babylonia: The Talmudic Evidence," *Journal of the Economic and Social History of the Orient* 22 (1979): 270, 293; Gafni, "Political, Social and Economic History," 803.

57. See Mosig-Walburg, "Christenverfolgung und Römerkrieg," 22–23, 30–31, building on the work of Wiessner, *Märtyrerüberlieferung.*

58. Decret, "Conséquences," 134; *BoS* 7.16. *LG* 176–77; cf. *BoS* 7.19–20, *LG* 184–85.

59. For the date, see Burgess, "Dates of the Martyrdom," 41; for a detailed analysis of the *Demonstration,* see Pierre, *Aphraate.* Both identify Simeon as the target; against this view, see Mosig-Walburg, "Christenverfolgung und Römerkrieg," 15–16.

is possible that it is directed against Simeon bar Sabba'e, if he was still alive in 344, but whoever is the target, the work is clearly highly critical of the close association between the church and the government: Aphrahat feels that the leader in question has proved oppressive and arrogant to his people and calls for disobedience.[60] This is undoubtedly the sort of milieu that must have inspired some sections of the *Book of Steps*, especially memra 30. Here we hear of "disciples of love," perhaps an equivalent category to the Perfect, being martyred at the hands of the "disciples of faith," for example, by fellow Christians; the latter are also persecuted, our author explains, partly because they provoke their persecutors by tearing down altars. They are inferior to the "disciples of love," however, in that they do not forgive their persecutors.[61] A similar distrust of the church leadership emerges from memra 19, in which our author makes clear that "the Perfect do not come near the positions of leadership."[62] He is willing to accept that the church hierarchy has a role: "They may discipline with mercy and wherever it is right they may separate justly what is better for the congregations in each place, and what is helpful for the infants and also for the sick, the corrupt, and the rebels." They should not, however, interfere with the Perfect nor oppress them: "take notice of the ways of Perfection and do not complain about us, nor accuse us in matters that concern us."[63] We

60. See Pierre, "Un Synode contestaire à l'époque d'Aphraate le sage Persan," in *La controverse religieuse et ses formes*, edited by Alain Boulluec, 253–54, 264 (Paris: Les Éditions du Cerf, 1995), thus one can perhaps grasp Simeon's overconfidence; see also McDonough, "*Power by Negotiation*," 231. In *Demonstration* 14, note especially §3 (Pierre, *Aphraate*, 609–11), corrupt and unjust leaders; cf. §37, 664–67), §4, 612, on the humiliation of the church because of its pride; cf. §7, 615 and §44, 684; §26, 646–47, for the call to disobedience. In general, see Pierre, *Aphraate*, 50–51, 86–91. Mosig-Walburg, "Christenverfolgung und Römerkrieg," 32–33, based on *Demonstration* 14, §4, 611, suggests plausibly that church leaders had tried to raise funds from the flock; cf. "Christenverfolgung und Römerkrieg," 60, on Simeon's overconfidence.

61. *BoS* 30.4, *LG* 871–73; see Nagel, "Märtyrer des Glaubens," esp. 130–31, who argues that the memra must refer to the persecutions of the 330s at the earliest, cf. Westerhoff, *Paulusverständnis*, 19. On the categories mentioned, see Kitchen and Parmentier, *Book of Steps*, xliv–xlvii. One wonders whether the *Book of Steps'* insistence, at memra 13.9 (*LG* 320–21), on the Upright not calling people by disreputable names also reflects an atmosphere of animosity.

62. *BoS* 19.4, *LG* 493. See, however, Westerhoff, *Paulusverständnis*, 21n119, who argues that the *Book of Steps*, unlike Aphrahat, offers no criticism of the church hierarchy: "Von einer Kritik des LG an machthungrigen Kirchenmännern kann keine Rede sein." The passages noted in note 63 of this chapter seem to the present author to represent at least some sort of implicit criticism of church leaders, even if they are mild in comparison to Aphrahat's invective.

63. *BoS* 19.31; *LG* 505, 508. Memra 12.3 (*LG* 292–93), on the other hand, does try to defend the visible church; cf. *BoS* 13.2, *LG* 308, enjoining the Upright to honor priests, and memra 27.5 (*LG* 777, 780).

are thus in a world of tension, if not outright conflict, between centralizing forces in the church, represented by Papa and Simeon, and more independently minded communities, who preferred to maintain their own traditions and distinctions. When persecutions broke out, different sections of the community reacted in different ways; inevitably, some Christians turned against their coreligionists, leading to the sort of events alluded to by our author. In the end the Persian church was able to stabilize the situation and to clear itself of the suspicion of being aligned with an increasingly Christian Roman empire: a synod held in Seleucia-Ctesiphon in 410 established an independent church, which fourteen years later, at another synod, broke off any remaining ties with its Western coreligionists.[64]

In conclusion, it is a difficult task to describe the world of the *Book of Steps;* such is the timeless nature of the work and the lack of chronological or geographical indicators. Its author quite deliberately minimizes specific references, a trait shared with Aphrahat and an indicator of the fraught times in which it was composed.[65] We should note, moreover, that both harbored the conviction that they were living through the last years of the world, a point that helps to explain the strong emphasis in the *Book of Steps* on the rejection of the world and its distractions.[66] We have nevertheless sought to describe the eventful circumstances that surround its genesis on both sides of the fluctuating frontier between the two powers. As we have underlined, even if we suppose that the author, having lived once on Roman territory, came later to inhabit the Persian Empire, it does not necessarily follow that he actually moved his residence: certain parts of Upper Mesopotamia changed hands frequently. It is hard to be certain whether, when he criticizes the laxity of "our generation," he is referring to the situation in Roman or Persian territory: references to a lack of fasting and a failure to observe the Sabbath could apply in either case.[67] The persecutions described in memra 30, on the other hand,

64. See Hage, "Oströmische Staatskirche," 181–83; Greatrex and Lieu, *Roman Eastern Frontier,* 34 and 43 (with references).

65. On the vagueness of Aphrahat's allusions and his deliberate omission of all names, see Pierre, *Aphraate,* 86.

66. On Aphrahat's belief in the imminent end of the world, see Barnes, "Christians of Persia," 134, citing *Demonstration* 5, §1 (Pierre, *Aphraate,* 322); *Demonstration* 2, §14, 254–55). For the *Book of Steps,* see especially memra 7.19 (*LG* 184): "the time for the punishment of our judgment is near."

67. *BoS* 7.20, *LG* 184–85; cf. *BoS* 4.5, *LG* 108, in which the author implies that now, unlike in

correspond closely to our picture of the events that took place at Shapur's instigation in the 340s. Since most of the *Book of Steps* gives the impression of a time of general laxity and ease as a result of toleration, it is tempting to infer that this last memra represents a subsequent addition, born out of the harsh experiences of the author's community at the hands of persecutors, both pagan and Christian.[68] Whether he survived to witness the treaty of 363 and the abatement of the persecutions is unknown.

---

apostolic times, there are not many pagans. Westerhoff, "Bild vom Staat," 27–28, argues that our author is more critical of civil than ecclesiastical authorities; he therefore prefers to place him in the generation after Aphrahat and to situate him in the Roman empire, where the venality of officials is well attested (e.g., in Ammianus Marcellinus). Such a possibility cannot be excluded, but the resemblances between Aphrahat and the *Book of Steps* are striking. While the *Book of Steps* may offer a defense of the visible church in memra 12, this does not prevent its author from issuing criticisms of church leaders, as noted above; see Kitchen and Parmentier, *Book of Steps,* lv–lvi.

The difference in attitude between generations is a feature also of Ephrem in Edmund Beck, ed., *Carmina Nisibena,* CSCO 218, 219 (Louvain: Peeters, 1961–1963), 15 (42 and 49–50) (the first number refers to the Syriac text, the second to the translation), especially in the final verses: the mildness of Bishop Vologaeses leads to splits among the generations and criticisms.

68. Fitschen, *Messalianismus,* 118, cf. Kmosko, *Liber Graduum,* clix; against this view, Hausherr, "Quanam Aetate," 496–97.

Timothy Pettipiece

2. PARALLEL PATHS

Tracing Manichaean Footprints along the Syriac Book of Steps

The Syriac *Book of Steps* is indeed a mysterious and remarkable piece of early Christian literature. While it has languished in the relative obscurity of the *Patrologia Syriaca* for nearly a century, accessible primarily to those with a specialized passion for its equally neglected language, Robert Kitchen and Martien Parmentier have recently done a great service to early Christian studies generally and to those interested in early Syriac literature in particular by publishing a complete and accessible translation of this important work.[1] Hopefully the publication of this text will facilitate further challenges to the longstanding paradigm of Latin West and Greek East that continues to influence so many reconstructions of early Christian history and open yet another window upon the fascinating vistas of Syriac Christianity. Yet in spite of our hopes that this publication will shed some much needed light on one of the more shadowy and poorly documented corners of the early Christian world, the reader is left with a certain degree of disappointment when faced with the fact that the *Book of Steps,* in its enigmatic and self-effacing way, provides precious little direct evidence of its own sociohistorical trajectory and milieu. Yet as adamant as the text is in refusing to disclose much about its environment

1. Robert A. Kitchen and Martien F. G. Parmentier, *The Book of Steps: The Syriac Liber Graduum* (Kalamazoo, Mich.: Cistercian Publications, 2004).

directly, perhaps we might trace some of its contours by juxtaposing some analogous textual material from a related tradition.

If, as we are told, the composition of the *Book of Steps* ought to be dated to sometime in the late fourth or early fifth century,[2] somewhere along the Romano-Persian borderland,[3] then it seems sensible to me to look in the same neighborhood for points of comparison. This is at least partly why the Manichaeans seem to be obvious candidates. After all, even though Mani had been executed by Vahram I in either 276 or 277 C.E., evidence of and allusions to his legacy can be found dispersed throughout some of the earliest examples of Syriac literature. For instance, while a veiled critique of Manichaeism has been detected in the *Odes of Solomon*,[4] a more direct Manichaean imprint may be visible in the famous "Hymn of the Pearl" from the *Acts of Thomas*.[5] More explicitly, Aphrahat, in the mid-fourth century, characterized the Manichaeans as "children of darkness,"[6] while somewhat later Ephrem polemicized against them in both his poetry[7] and prose[8] as heretics and purveyors of error. Even the "official" version of the introduction of Christianity into Syria found in the *Teaching of Addai* appears to be colored by anti-Manichaean polemic.[9]

2. Kitchen and Parmentier, *Book of Steps*, l.

3. See the fresh assessment of the situation by Geoffrey Greatrex in this volume.

4. Han Drijvers, "Odes of Solomon and Psalms of Mani: Christians and Manichaeans in Third-Century Syria," in *Gnosticism and Hellenistic Religions Presented to Giles Quispel on the Occasion of his 65th Birthday*, edited by Roelof van den Broek and Maarten J. Vermaseren, 117–30 (Leiden: E. J. Brill, 1981).

5. Albertus F. J. Klijn, trans., *The Acts of Thomas: Introduction, Text, and Commentary*, 2nd ed., Supplements to Novum Testamentum (Leiden: E. J. Brill, 2003); see also Paul-Hubert Poirier, *L'hymne de la perle des Actes de Thomas: Introduction, texte-traduction, commentaire* (Louvain-la-Neuve: Centre d'histoire des religions, 1981).

6. Alfred Adam, *Texte zum Manichäismus* (Berlin: Verlag Walter De Gruyter, 1969), 57, citing Aphrahat, *Demonstration* 3, §9.

7. See Edmund Beck, ed., "Hymni 56 contra haereses," in *Des heiligen Ephraem des Syrers Hymnen contra haereses*, Corpus Scriptorum Christianorum Orientalium 169, 170 (Louvain: L. Durbecq, 1957).

8. Charles W. Mitchell, ed., *Ephraim's Prose Refutations of Mani, Marcion, and Bardaisan*, 2 vols. (London: Williams and Norgate, 1912–21); John C. Reeves, "Manichaean Citations from the *Prose Refutations* of Ephrem," in *Emerging from Darkness: Studies in the Recovery of Manichaean Sources*, edited by Jason BeDuhn and Paul A. Mirecki, 217–88, Nag Hammadi and Manichaean Studies 43 (Leiden: E. J. Brill, 1997).

9. See Drijvers, "Facts and Problems in Early Syriac-Speaking Christianity," in *East of Antioch: Studies in Early Syriac Christianity*, 160–61 (London: Variorum Reprints, 1984); Drijvers, "Addai und Mani: Christentum und Manichäismus in dritten Jahrhundert in Syrien," in *Les contacts du monde syriaque avec les autres cultures: IIIe Symposium Syriacum 1980 (Goslar 7–11 Septembre 1980)*, edited by René Lavenant, 171–85, Orientalia Christiana Analecta 221 (Rome: Pont. Institutum studiorum orientalium, 1983).

Somewhat further west, around the mid-fourth century, Titus of Bostra composed his *Contra manichaeos,*[10] which, if not composed in Syriac, was almost immediately translated. This constellation of allusions and refutations reveals the degree to which Manichaeans were active, or at least vividly remembered, in and around the same milieu in which these early Syriac texts were composed. Thus it would not be inconceivable to find at least traces of similar Manichaean footprints along the *Book of Steps,* another key piece of the surviving literature of this formative period. As such this chapter will consider a number of possible parallels and points of contact between this enigmatic piece of Syriac literature and the equally enigmatic Manichaeans.

Ecclesiological Parallels: Bipartite Communities

Perhaps the most striking parallel between the *Book of Steps* and Manichaeism in general is at the level of community structure, something that has puzzled scholars for some time. Whereas the *Book of Steps* makes a rather clear distinction between the Upright (ܟܐܢ̈ܐ), those called to community ministry by feeding the hungry, clothing the naked, and visiting the sick,[11] and the Perfect (ܓܡܝܪ̈ܐ), who "do not take wives, nor work in the field, nor acquire possessions, nor have a place to lay their head like their teacher,"[12] this arrangement finds a structural parallel in the Manichaean division between the Elect, the strict ascetics who act as ritual vessels of light purification, and the Hearers (also known as "Catechumens") who provide for the material needs of the Elect under a less stringent regiment.[13] In this way both communities made a general distinction between two classes of believers: the first order called to a strict ascetic regime and the second order acting in support of the first.[14] The main question, as Peter Nagel has recently put it, is whether or not this similarity is the result of

10. Paul de Lagarde, ed., *Titi Bostreni contra Manichaeos libri quattuor syriace* (Berlin: C. Schulze, 1859). A new edition of this treatise is being prepared by a team at Université Laval led by Paul-Hubert Poirier.

11. *BoS* 3.2.

12. *BoS* 15.13; Kitchen and Parmentier, *Book of Steps,* xxxviii–xlix.

13. Peter Nagel, "Manichäisches im syrischen Liber Graduum?" in *Religionsbegegnung und Kulturaustausch in Asien: Studien zum Gedenken an Hans-Joachim Klimkeit,* edited by Wolfgang Gantke, Karl Hoheisel, and Wassilios Klein, 181, Studies in Oriental Religions 49 (Wiesbaden: Harrassowitz Verlag, 2002).

14. Nagel, "Manichäisches im syrischen Liber Graduum," 182.

analogy or influence.[15] For Nagel it seems unlikely that so-called "heretical" communities such as these would tend toward a bipartite structure as a rule. Rather, one might be able to postulate direct influence if it could be shown that the author of the *Book of Steps* knew something about Manichaeism.[16] While some have found little evidence of Manichaeans in the *Book of Steps,*[17] Nagel believes that traces do indeed exist—provided we look hard enough. For instance, memra 23's reading of the Exodus story[18] appears to parallel a Manichaean interpretation of the same passage found in book 3 of Titus of Bostra's *Contra Manichaeos,*[19] although one could also imagine that the anonymous author has Manichaeans in mind here when he attributes the evil acts committed by Pharaoh and the Israelites to free will rather than an independent, evil entity. Somewhat more compelling is Nagel's suggestion that rare designations for Christ from the *Book of Steps* such as "Tree of Life"[20] and "Judge of Truth"[21] echo language found in the Manichaean "Psalms of the Wanderers" and "Bema-Psalms," respectively.[22] Neither of these expressions, however, seems to me to be *distinctly* Manichaean. After all, as Robert Murray recognized, the Manichaean *Psalm-book* is itself firmly rooted in early Syriac tradition,[23] so much so that imagery of this sort could simply be drawn from a common spiritual font. Nevertheless, if we follow Nagel's lead, then such evidence could at least allow for the possibility that the anonymous teacher of the *Book of Steps* knew *something* about Manichaeans and, therefore, that the bipartite structure of his community could have been modeled on a Manichaean precedent, although based upon a different rationale.[24] While this hardly constitutes the "missing link" between Manichaeism and the *Book of Steps,* I would like to propose some other indicators that might help strengthen the connection.

15. Nagel, "Manichäisches im syrischen Liber Graduum," 182.

16. Nagel, "Manichäisches im syrischen Liber Graduum," 182–83.

17. Kitchen, "The Development of the Status of Perfection in Early Syriac Ascetism with Special Reference to the Liber Graduum and Philoxenus of Mabbug" (PhD diss., University of Oxford, 1997), 11.

18. *BoS* 23.3.

19. Nagel, "Manichäisches im syrischen Liber Graduum," 183, citing Lagarde, *Titi Bostreni,* 85.

20. *BoS* 20.7; see also *BoS* 21.2.

21. *BoS* 21.8.

22. Nagel, "Manichäisches im syrischen Liber Graduum," 183, citing *Psalm-Book* 154.22–29; 185.10–17, and *Psalm-Book* 21.18, 47.18, respectively.

23. Robert Murray, *Symbols of Church and Kingdom: A Study in Early Syriac Tradition,* rev. ed. (London: T. and T. Clark; Piscataway, N.J.: Gorgias Press, 2004), 27–28.

24. Nagel, "Manichäisches im syrischen Liber Graduum," 183.

Literary Parallels: The *Book of Steps* and the Manichaean *Kephalaia*

In my opinion the Syriac *Book of Steps,* in its general structure, bears a marked resemblance to one particular piece of Manichaean literature—namely, the *Kephalaia* or "Chapter-book."[25] Discovered near the town of Medinet Madi, Egypt, in 1929, the story of the recovery of this text, along with the *Psalm-book* and five other Coptic Manichaean codices, has been amply told.[26] While it is generally accepted that this Manichaean library dates from late-fourth- or early-fifth-century Roman Egypt, these Coptic versions are thought to be translations of either Greek and/or Syriac originals going back to the early days of the Manichaean mission along the Romano-Persian frontier during the late-third and early-fourth century.[27] More recently discovered evidence from Kellis (in western Egypt's Dakhleh Oasis), such as Syriac-Coptic translation exercises and bilingual glossaries, suggests that the transmission of this literature could have been relatively rapid and direct.[28] This means that the material eventually assembled and redacted into the *Kephalaia* should reasonably be situated in more or less the same sociolinguistic milieu that produced the *Book of Steps.*[29] Indeed, internal evidence confirms this hypothesis, since the *Kephalaia*'s "worldview" is decidedly Mesopotamian.

That Manichaeans formed part of the environment in which the *Book of Steps* was written should come as no surprise. After all, the suggestion that perceived references to persecution in the *Book of Steps* allude to the reign of Shapur II (340–372)[30] accords well with evidence from the martyr acts of

25. Hans Jakob Polotsky and A. Böhlig, *Kephalaia I: Hälfte (Lieferung 1–10)* (Stuttgart: Kohlhammer, 1940); Wolf-Peter Funk, ed., *Kephalaia I: Zweite Hälfte (Lieferung 13–14)* (Stuttgart: Kohlhammer, 1999); Funk, *Kephalaia I: Zweite Hälfte (Lieferung 15–16)* (Stuttgart: Kohlhammer, 2000).

26. For the initial assessment, see Polotsky and Carl Schmidt, *Ein Mani-Fund in Ägypten: Originalschriften des Mani und seiner Schüler* (Berlin: Akademie der Wissenschaften, in Kommission bei W. de Gruyter, 1933), 4–90, supplemented and updated by James Robinson, "The Fate of the Manichaean Codices of Medinet Madi: 1929–1989," in *Studia Manichaica: II. Internationaler Kongress zum Manichäismus, 6.–10. August 1989, St. Augustin/Bonn,* edited by Hans-Joachim Klimkeit and Gernot Wiessner, 19–62 (Wiesbaden: Harrassowitz Verlag, 1989).

27. See Iain M. F. Gardner and Samuel N. C. Lieu, "From Narmouthis (Medinet Madi) to Kellis (Ismant El-Kharab): Manichaean Documents from Roman Egypt," *Journal of Roman Studies* 86 (1996): 149.

28. Gardner, ed., *Kellis Literary Texts,* vol. 1 (Oxford: Oxbow Books, 1996).

29. Kitchen and Parmentier, *Book of Steps,* l.

30. Kitchen and Parmentier, *Book of Steps,* xlix.

Karka de Bet Selok, which suggests that Manichaeans were implicated in the murder of a group of "Daughters of the Covenant" during the same period.[31] Adda, Mani's great missionary to the West, had brought his teaching there sometime around 260,[32] where it seems to have taken root around Adiabene and the Lesser River Zab. This tributary of the Tigris constitutes practically the only concrete geographical reference in the entire *Book of Steps.*[33] In fact, Mani himself passed through the region as part of Shapur I's entourage.[34] Therefore, it seems reasonable to assume that after Mani's death Manichaeans maintained a prominent presence in the area close to Seleucia-Ctesiphon, seat of the Manichaean *archegos,* head of the Manichaean church.

Of course, while we might like to speculate as to whether or not memra and *kephalaion* could represent analogous literary forms, the general structure of the two texts is worthy of comment. Rather than being systematic treatises in the style of Origen's *On First Principles,* both works constitute a collection of more or less miscellaneous discourses on a variety of topics, although the *Kephalaia* is considerably larger and somewhat more embellished. In both cases the authors or editors are attempting to solve problems of interpretation and practice faced by their respective religious communities, a project not unlike that taking place in the nearby rabbinic academies of Babylonia. In the case of the *Kephalaia,* the compilers of the text are at least partly concerned with smoothing out ambiguities in canonical Manichaean tradition (that is, Mani's own writings, originally in Syriac) and in easing tensions between Elect and Catechumen,[35] whereas the anonymous author of the *Book of Steps* addresses a range of pastoral issues among the Upright and Perfect while rooting the community in the exegesis of his own canonical tradition of the Bible. This sort of quasi-scholastic, literary problem solving is perhaps a typical response among communities facing internal pressures of apostasy and conflict[36] as well as the external pressure of persecution and large-scale warfare.[37] In spite

31. Lieu, *Manichaeism in the Later Roman Empire and Medieval China,* 2nd ed. (Tübingen: J. C. B. Mohr, 1992), 111.

32. Lieu, *Manichaeism,* 90.

33. *BoS* 30.14.

34. *Kephalaia,* chap.16.1; Lieu, *Manichaeism,* 78.

35. See *Kephalaia,* chap. 88 and 91.

36. *Kephalaia,* chap. 97.23–99; *BoS* 4.1.

37. As discussed by Geoffrey Greatrex in this volume.

of their often bitter rivalries, Manichaeans and other Christians were sometimes caught in the same Sasanian net, as is evident in the late-third-century inscription of Kirdir, the Magian high priest, who claims to have persecuted not only "Jews, Buddhists, and Brahmans," but "Nazareans, Christians, Baptists, and Manichaeans" in his efforts to consolidate an Iranian state religion.[38] Thus we should also not be surprised that two communities struggling for survival in the same tormented milieu should make use of similar modes of literary expression in support of their competing claims of legitimacy.

Evidence for this struggle for legitimacy is borne out by the fact that, in addition to their apparent structural and functional similarities, both the *Book of Steps* and the *Kephalaia* are prefaced by hagiographic portraits of the teachers from which the texts seek to draw their spiritual authority. The Syriac editor of the *Book of Steps,* for his part, emphasizes in his "Preface" the "greatness and power" of the "blessed" teacher, whom he styles as a "prophet" inspired by the "Paraclete." We are presented with a portrait of a simple, holy man—one of the first to write in Syriac—who, in spite of his unadorned style, was capable of unlocking the depth of spiritual "mysteries" and whose authority is ultimately derived from an unbroken chain of "apostles and prophets." Such language, it seems to me, resonates strongly with some common features of Manichaean theological discourse. According to the *Kephalaia,* and Manichaean tradition more generally, the "Father of Greatness," ruler of the luminous realm, sent the "living Paraclete" to Mani, making him the last in a series of specially commissioned prophets and apostles.[39] From the Paraclete Mani received the capacity to interpret the "hidden mysteries" unknown to the world or misinterpreted by prior religious communities.[40] It seems, then, at least possible that the editor of the *Book of Steps* is attempting to support the prophetic claims of his own master against those of Mani by using what was likely a shared, albeit theologically charged, vocabulary. This enables him to contrast his master's humble character with Mani's often self-aggrandizing proclamations. In my opinion, notions of prophethood, Paraclete, mystery, and greatness resonate far more strongly with typically Manichaean values and

38. See Manfred Hutter, "Manichaeism in Iran in the Fourth Century," in *Studia Manichaica: IV Internationaler Kongreß zum Manichäismus, Berlin, 14.–18. Juli 1997,* edited by Ronald Emmerick, Werner Sundermann, and Peter Zieme, 308 (Berlin: Akademie Verlag, 1997).

39. *Kephalaia,* chap. 14.32.

40. *Kephalaia,* chap. 15.1.

themes than the more obscure appellations for Christ proposed by Nagel. After all, questions involving the provenance of prophetic and spiritual authority were at the heart of debates raging throughout the Christian communities of late antiquity, from Asia Minor to North Africa.

Moving now from prophecy to poetics, an additional similarity is apparent in the degree to which the *Book of Steps* and the Manichaean *Kephalaia* are marked by what Kitchen calls the "profoundly symbolic vision" inherent in early Syriac spirituality.[41] Not surprisingly, both texts make effective use of simile and metaphor, often employing imagery drawn from the Sasanian royal court—which, as we've seen, formed part of their common political milieu. For instance, in memra 6 the author compares the Perfect to "builders and workers (who) want to build a house or manufacture a chest for the king's possessions,"[42] whereas *Kephalaia,* chapter 16, relates how the advent of the Third Messenger, the Manichaean demiurge, is "like a great king who comes and inspects his artisans . . . builders and craftsmen."[43] In this way both the *Book of Steps* and the Manichaean *Kephalaia* not only employ analogous literary structures and hagiographic themes, but can also be seen to make use of a common stock of imagery drawn from their shared milieu.

A final feature of both texts that I submit may speak to their shared environment is their polemical tendencies, particularly those against imperial powers, magicians, and idol-worshippers. For instance, whereas memra 9 laments the "two antagonists" (i.e., Rome and Persia) who "raise their hands against one another . . . because they did not build upon the peace that our Lord Jesus made on earth,"[44] *Kephalaia,* chapter 6, condemns "those who rule over all of creation, humbling people in their tyranny according to their will."[45] Clearly both communities were not at ease with or impressed by their Romano-Persian overlords. On a somewhat more local level, however, we read in memra 7, "One should not consult oracles nor use magic arts, nor mutter incantations, which are whispered in the name of idols."[46] *Kephalaia,* chapter 6, in a similar vein, admonishes its readers to "keep yourselves away from magic and the sorcery of Darkness"[47] and to avoid "the idol-worshippers (and) the spirits of Error in every temple,"[48] since such things serve as clear signs of

41. Kitchen and Parmentier, *Book of Steps,* xviii.
42. *BoS* 6.1.
43. *Kephalaia,* chap. 52.22–25.
44. *BoS* 9.6.
45. *Kephalaia,* chap. 33.7–8.
46. *BoS* 7.3.
47. *Kephalaia,* chap. 31.25–26.
48. *Kephalaia,* chap. 33.21–22.

the dark lord's power in the world. As we can see, the authors of both texts were faced with similar problems of political oppression and religious rivalry. In this case, however, they are both on the same page in their opposition to their mutual adversaries.

Some Cautious Concluding Steps

As in the case of community structure, the evidence I have offered from the *Kephalaia* does not quite constitute the "missing link" or "smoking gun" that could definitively establish a connection between the *Book of Steps* and the Manichaeans. Both sets of evidence suggest *traces* of Manichaean influence on not only the organization of the community that the *Book of Steps* presents, but perhaps also the text's literary structure, its claim to prophetic authority, and its treatment of its adversaries. If nothing else, both texts reinforce the fact that the religious environment of fourth-century Mesopotamia was far from homogeneous. Any treatment of this context can no longer afford to ignore the contributions made to it not only by "Messalians," but, as the Magian high-priest Kirdir so severely evoked, by Nazareans, Baptists, and, of course, Manichaeans.

Martien Parmentier

3. THE *BOOK OF STEPS* ON MAGIC

Syriac Christianity is full of stories that describe the clashes between Christianity and pagan religions. Given this fact, it is not surprising that we find references to magic in the *Book of Steps*—it is only surprising that we find so relatively few of them. Was it because magic was associated with the lowest forms of spiritual life, much below the state of uprightness and perfection? Was it because the author of the *Book of Steps* expected his readership to be an unlikely prey of the passions for something as earthly as magic? In fact, most magic is concerned with some very important necessities of life: first, divination to guess what the future has in store; second, healing to live to see as much of that future as possible; and third, the power to manipulate the boundaries thereof.

Syriac is a magical language, and I will present three Greek texts to prove this point. Text number one, by John of Thessaloniki, is from the *Miracles of St. Demetrius,* which has a parallel in the *Book of Steps:*

An eparch named Marianos (. . .) excited the envy of the devil. Having failed to attack his virtue, the devil assailed the eparch's body, rendering him completely paralyzed. Hoping to cure Marianos, one of the eparch's close associates approached the sick man with the following words, which he whispered into his ear: "There is a certain man, who said to me that he could make you, Master, healthy, if you wished to tie around your neck and wear the inscribed parchment that he is giving to you." The eparch was immediately suspicious. He asked: "And what is it that he says is written on the parchment?" His servant replied: "When I enquired about this matter a little more carefully, (. . .) he said that he had written certain letters there and half circles, and certain other formulae with Hebrew letters and names of angels unknown to the many, written outside and inside." "But," added his servant, "what need is there to know the force and the forms of what is written there? For there is but one concern for all of us, your servants, that you should regain your health." But the pious eparch was not to be deceived; he responded indignantly as follows: "First, (. . .) from what is it manifest that I will escape the disease, having worn the parchment; but rather, since its writer did not wish to make clear the force of what was written, is it not plain that nothing good has been inscribed upon it? 'For whatsoever doth make manifest,' according to the apostle, 'is light.'"[1] The eparch concluded by saying that he did not wish to save his body while losing his soul.[2]

The same concern is expressed in a more general exhortation to the readers of the *Book of Steps.* The pivot of the argument is that there is only one name in which all Christian healing should happen:

Let us petition the Lord concerning all our trials as it is written, "Every sickness the Lord heals.[3] "He reviled and condemned the utterance of the lips of the unrighteous"[4]—that is, of magicians and soothsayers and of charmers and writers of amulets, snake charmers and diviners.

But if you wish to be healed without sins, wait for the Lord and pray to him, and he will heal you from numerous human and satanic temptations. If it is right that you should be healed in this world, our Lord will heal you in this world. If he does not heal you in this world, then it is to your advantage, for in that other world he shall give you rest, extol you, and make you cheerful, because you have waited for his redemption until your departure from this world. Do not be frightened by the stress of your illnesses so that for the sake of physical health you go killing your soul, whether your body is healed or not. It is better for you to endure a little temporal affliction rather than go to that affliction of which there is no measure.

If it happens that your body is healed by being with these false people, you will not know that your soul has become ill, with a sickness that will last until the day of judgment. Your condemnation will then be because you have fled from illnesses and afflictions of a short duration: you will go to the affliction from which it is not

1. Eph 5:14.

2. Text: Paul Lemerle, *Les plus anciennes recueils des miracles de saint Démétrius et la penetration des Slaves dans les Balkans* (Paris: Éditions du Centre national de la recherche scientifique, 1979), 61; summary in English: Henry Maguire, ed., *Byzantine Magic* (Washington, D.C.: Dumbarton; Cambridge, Mass: Harvard University Press, 1995), 62.

3. Psalms 103:3.2.

4. Psalms 59:12.

possible for you to escape because you have transgressed against the commandment of God. But if you have a disease and there is a doctor at hand, ask him as follows: "Are you a magician or a charmer, or someone who deals with the deceitful doctrine of error? May the Lord to whose judgement we shall go, testify against you. If you bring something to calm me, do it simply in the name of Jesus, and if not, do not bring it to me." Let him confirm to you that it is in the name of Jesus that he will make you healthy, and then let him come near you.[5]

The magic of the Syriac language can actually outwit the superior Greek. Normally, the Greeks win the rhetorical game. Yet, although Syrians are unskilled at rhetoric, one had better try to understand what formulas they utter, or else the spiritual power that they contain will render the elegant words of the Greeks powerless. What is at stake is not only the cultural tension between Greek and Syriac, but also the conflict between Christianity and paganism.

An anecdote from Leontius of Neapolis's *Life of Symeon the Holy Fool* (seventh century) is our second text; our third text is from Gregory of Nyssa's address to the fathers of the Council of Constantinople (381). These texts may mutually clarify each other.

During this time there was a woman clairvoyant and maker of amulets who performed incantations. The righteous one contrived to have her as a girlfriend and gave her things he had collected from those who gave him presents, whether coins or bread or even clothing. Then one day he said to her: "Do you want me to make you an amulet so that you will never be touched by the evil eye?" And she said to him, "Yes, Fool," reasoning that although he was a fool, perhaps he would succeed. So he went off and wrote in Syriac on a tablet: "May God render you impotent and stop you from turning his people away from him and toward yourself." Then he gave it to her and she wore it. And she was no longer able to make anyone either oracles or amulets.[6]

In passing, we note that the *Book of Steps* also knows a form of madness of which the author approves, as of holy foolishness.[7]

The power of Syriac culture is attested to also by Gregory of Nyssa in the context of an address he gave at the Council of Constantinople (381). Gregory seems to resist a defeatist dispensationalism that was adopted by some of his

5. *BoS* 7.14, *LG* 169–73.

6. Derek Krueger, *Symeon the Holy Fool: Leontius's Life and the Late Antique City* (Berkeley and Los Angeles: University of California Press, 1996), 165.

7. *BoS* 16.7; *LG* 404–5.

colleagues who believe that miracles no longer happen as in apostolic times. Miracles still happen, says Gregory. Look at those ascetic Syrians who have the power to exorcise demons. And we know that the early Christians demonized all pagan religion. This brings us back to the question of magic. Modern studies suggest that the best definition of magic is "not-my-religion." But first, let us hear Gregory of Nyssa:

Perhaps someone will say that at that time the wonders wrought by the apostles came to their aid and that the word [they proclaimed] received its plausibility through the charisms. I also hold that powerful works have a great persuasive force. So what are we to think of the present events?—Well, don't you see the same wonders of faith then? For I feel at home with the achievements of our fellow servants, who, on line in the same Spirit, witness to the truth of the Word by the power of healing. They are men who have come from abroad, countrymen of our father Abraham who have equally moved away from Mesopotamia, they have emigrated from their land and left their relations, indeed the whole world, they look up to heaven, are in a certain sense exiles from human life, stand above the vicissitudes of nature, touch upon this life only inasmuch as it is strictly necessary; for the most part they walk on high with incorporeal powers, they look like old men with solemn countenance, shining with grey hair; their mouths are secured because they have not learnt to dispute. But they have such a great authority against the spirits that they realize what they have in mind by a simple command and the demons withdraw, not by the art of drawing logical conclusions but by the authority of faith, not by irrefutable arguments, but because they are cast into outer darkness. This is the way in which the Christian is able to argue, these are the achievements of our faith. Why then are we not convinced if there is an exceeding grace of healing, if the teaching of the Word abounds?

"All these are affected by one and the same Spirit who apportions to each one individually as he wills."[8] Why do not those who are saved multiply? No one should think that I consider the present grace as insignificant.[9]

How, then, does the *Book of Steps* define magic, and how precisely does it regard the Christian alternative? Magic is associated with certain practices that are found in pagan religions: necromancy, eating the flesh of sacrifices, consulting oracles, practicing magical arts, muttering incantations and

8. 1 Corinthians 12:11.

9. Gregory of Nyssa, *De deitate adversus Evagrium* (= In suam ordinationem), in *Sermones,* edited by G. Heil, J. P. Cavarnos, and O. Lendle, Pars. 1, Gregorii Nysseni Opera 9 (Leiden: E. J. Brill, 1992), 337,11–38, 14.

charms, wearing amulets, using medicine laid under a spell.[10] However, most of these things remained in popular Christian use, and the eventual debate between Rome and Reformation on sacramentality is connected with this.[11] A central question here is, what spiritual power lies behind the concrete material object? The *Book of Steps* has no doubt about this: behind the Christian use of matter lies God's power, and behind magic and its objects stand the devil and his demons. God, more specifically, "our Lord," and the Holy Spirit, often called "the Paraclete,"[12] are the Giver of gifts of grace such as healing. The Upright receive the pledge of the Holy Spirit and his gifts;[13] the Perfect receive him more fully so that it is actually possible to say that they are "in the Spirit."[14] The nourishing and healing matter associated with the growth of the Upright and the Perfect (the milk of the children and the vegetables of the sick) gradually become superfluous as the spiritual child gets used to solid food and the spiritually sick person gets healed.

Perhaps it is true to say that the ascetic, anti-materialist tendency in Syriac Christianity led to a certain degree of progressive spiritualization of their universe, leading to a worldview not unlike that of Evagrius in his Letter to Melania—which was indeed only preserved in Syriac.[15]

But the charisms are not dogmatically neutral. They stand over against magic as Christianity does over against paganism—indeed, as the sphere of God and his angels stand opposite the devil and his demons. In the early days of Christianity this meant that the group that was able to manifest the gifts of the Spirit thereby proved itself to be Spirit-filled and vice versa; a group that had no charismatic life to show was regarded as less than perfect. When and where a church began to lack charismata (either through relaxation of the spiritual life by the *Parusieverzögerung,* the ending of the martyrdoms, or other causes), the fathers of the church often mourned the passing of the golden age of the apostles and chose a dispensationalist explanation (although presumably more in their sermons than in their anti-pagan works) in order to

10. *BoS* 7.3; *LG* 152–56; Robert A. Kitchen and Martien F. G. Parmentier, trans., *The Book of Steps: The Syriac Liber Graduum* (Kalamazoo, Mich.: Cistercian Publications, 2004), 67–69.

11. Cf. Richard Kieckhefer, *Magic in the Middle Ages* (Cambridge: Cambridge University Press, 2000), 15.

12. Cf. *BoS* 20.7, *LG* 544; and *BoS* 28.3, *LG* 789.

13. Cf. BoS 15.19.

14. *BoS* 14.3.

15. Martin F. G. Parmentier, "Evagrius of Pontus 'Letter to Melania'" Bijdragen 46 (1985): 2–38.

still be able to confute those who seemed to work more miracles than they themselves. Yet it was also a question of looking—who will tell which gifts are greater or lesser? The *Book of Steps* carefully discusses the different levels of the life with and in the Spirit, and it is clear that the author of this work does not believe that the gifts have died out.[16] But just how large a proportion of the community of the *Book of Steps* can be reckoned to have been "perfect," filled with the Spirit, rather than merely "upright"? In brief, to what extent the situation that was described by Irenaeus was still normal, we do not know. The description of the charismatic church by Irenaeus, quoted regretfully as no longer current by Eusebius of Caesarea,[17] reflects a spiritual state of affairs much like the author of the *Book of Steps* had in mind—but the fathers always made their ecclesiological statements prescriptive, rather than descriptive. Let us therefore now listen to Irenaeus:

Moreover, those also will be thus confuted who belong to Simon and Carpocrates, and if there be any others who are said to perform miracles who do not perform what they do either through the power of God, or in connection with the truth, nor for the well-being of men, but for the sake of destroying and misleading mankind, by means of magical deceptions, and with universal deceit, thus entailing greater harm than good on those who believe them, with respect to the point on which they lead them astray. For they can neither confer sight on the blind, nor hearing on the deaf, nor chase away all sorts of demons [none, indeed,] except those that are sent into others by themselves, if they can even do so much as this. Nor can they cure the weak, or the lame, or the paralytic, or those who are distressed in any other part of the body, as has often been done in regard to bodily infirmity. Nor can they furnish effective remedies for those external accidents that may occur. And so far are they from being able to raise the dead, as the Lord raised them, and the apostles did by means of prayer, and as has been frequently done in the brotherhood on account of some necessity—the entire church in that particular locality entreating [the boon] with much fasting and prayer, the spirit of the dead man has returned, and he has been bestowed in answer to the prayers of the saints—that they do not even believe this can possibly be done, [and hold] that the resurrection from the dead is simply an acquaintance with that truth that they proclaim.[18]

16. Cf. *BoS* 9.14; *LG* 233–35.

17. Irenaeus, Adversus Haereses II.31.2, 4–5; Eusebius, *Historia Ecclesiastica V.7.3–5*, in *Eusebius: Ecclesiatical History and Martyrs of Palestine,* translated and edited by H. J. Lawlor and J. E. L. Oulton (London: S.P.C.K, 1927–28), 1:152.

18. Adversus Haereses II.31.2, in *Ante-Nicene Fathers, vol. 1, The Apostolic Fathers: Justin Martyr, Ire-*

In the last part of this section, Eusebius begins to quote Irenaeus (what came before is only known in the Latin translation):

And what more shall I say? It is not possible to name the number of the gifts which the Church [scattered] throughout the whole world, received from God in the name of Jesus Christ, who was crucified under Pontius Pilate, exercises every day for the benefit of the heathen, neither deceiving any nor using the gifts for gain. For as she has received from God freely, so also freely she ministers.[19]

The quotation by Eusebius ends here, but the Latin translation of Irenaeus continues:

Nor does she perform anything by means of angelic invocations, or by incantations, or by any other wicked curious art; but, directing her prayers to the Lord who made all things in a pure, sincere and straightforward spirit accustomed to work miracles for the advantage of mankind, and not to lead them into error. If, therefore, the name of our Lord Jesus Christ even now confers benefits, and cures thoroughly and effectively all who anywhere believe on Him, but not that of Simon, or Menander, or Carpocrates, or of any other man whatever, it is manifest that, when He was made man, He held fellowship with His own creation, and did all things truly through the power of God, according to the will of the Father of all, as the prophets had foretold.[20]

For the *Book of Steps* the pouring out of the Holy Spirit is a self-evident fact of life. But the Spirit comes in greater and lesser measures, and our author specifically speaks of "contemporary gifts" as if wanting to distinguish within a variety of gifts for varying needs at varying times: "The apostle showed that God placed the Perfect in the Church, after them the prophets and after them the strong, the teachers, the builders, and the administrators and after them those who have the gifts of healing. He showed that one level is better than another level. The apostle spoke concerning these contemporary gifts that God has placed in the Church."[21] But who may claim which portion of the Spirit? How does the exercise of charisms, especially that of healing, relate to faith and knowledge (*gnosis*)? Memra 17 says,

---

naeus, edited by A. Cleveland Coxe (New York: Christian Literature Publishing, 1885), 407; cited as ANF 1.

19. Adversus Haereses II.32.4 (ANF 1, 409).

20. Adversus Haereses II.32.5 (ANF 1, 409).

21. *BoS* 9.14; *LG* 233.

Therefore, when you read that our Lord purified the lepers and opened the eyes of the blind, made the crooked straight, strengthened the paralyzed, calmed the people with dropsy, healed the sick, caused the lame to leap as harts, and straightened the tongues of the dumb, these are signs that our Lord did for whoever does not believe so that they may believe. But signs are not necessary for whoever does believe, yet suffering is necessary for him so that he may be perfected and suffer and mature and be glorified

Therefore, if you believe that Jesus is God, signs are not necessary for you. Do not inquire "how" and "why," but bring yourself to sufferings, and love, and watch the "how" and "why" these things happen are revealed to you. If a person thinks that he knows something, he does not yet know anything in the way he ought to know it. Whoever loves God will know this. Notice that with love, a person will know everything.[22]

Different charisms are given in different quantities at different times to different people. Among them the gift of healing and especially healers are most sought after. Yet when the healer prescribes something in another name than the name of Jesus, the help-seeking patient risks landing with a different God and ending up in the fiery abode of what is in fact a demon, like all would-be pagan gods. In view of the horizon of eternal punishment for the consultation of pagan healers—there is always the danger that they are better doctors—it is safer and more in line with the ascetic life to accept the suffering that the illness brings.

The occurrence of the charisms as outward signs, often used as a proof that God's Spirit is with us, is in fact an optional extra to the spiritual life. Outward signs serve to convince unbelievers, as Paul says, and the gnosis that certain people claim to have is in fact no knowledge at all. What is there to know? I would suggest this: True believers know that the life in the Spirit does not depend on outward and visible signs, and instead of risking their eternal salvation by passive misuse of the charisms or active overestimation of their own charismatic abilities, they go for a complete acceptance of physical suffering that might strike them here and now, leading them to eternal glorification.

Therefore, neither the active nor passive participation in the signs nor a would-be gnosis is the goal of the life in the Spirit, but another state, which the *Book of Steps* appreciates together with some apocryphal writings. This

22. *BoS* 17.1; *LG* 417.

is a characteristic denotation of the heavenly Jerusalem as the "City of the great rest" (or "peace").[23] And the central concept here is *neyacha—anapausis*—"rest," "resting place." The Perfect may come here to the rest of Christ.[24]

The concept of rest appears sixteen times in the Gospel of Truth[25] and in an invocation of the motherly Holy Spirit in the Acts of Thomas: "Come, holy name of the Messiah; come, power of grace, which art from on high; come, perfect mercy; come, exalted gift; come, sharer of the blessing; come, revealer of the hidden mysteries, come, mother of the seven houses, whose rest was in the eighth house."[26]

Differing denotations of the ascetic's eschatological goal are thus to be found scattered in the *Book of Steps.* As we have seen, the top step, which normally only the Perfect can reach, may be called "the city of the great rest" (or "the city of the great peace"), or simply "the place of rest," like in the *Gospel of Truth.* Other names are "the city of our king/the great king" (Jesus), "the hidden city," "that great city," "paradise," "the spiritual paradise," "the paradise of the kingdom," "the higher Jerusalem," "the heavenly Jerusalem," "the supernal Jerusalem." The ascetic can reach this place through suffering and future glorification if he does not prefer earthly healing and pagan magic. Could (one of) the purpose(s) of the *Book of Steps* have been to control the influence of the Valentinian Gnostics and their *Gospel of Truth*? It's not only the parallel use of the metaphor of "rest" that might point in this direction; in fact, the most common metaphor in the *Book of Steps* is "knowledge" (gnosis) and, like Irenaeus, it criticizes the "falsely thus-called knowledge" of certain Gnostic groups. This becomes especially evident when we look at the *Book of Steps'* attitude concerning suffering. Whosoever tries to evade the vicissitudes of life by seeking help from pagan magicians may attain to temporary solace that the church might not be able to give just now, but will find himself in the power of demons who serve the wrong god or are themselves pagan gods. They prevent the ascetic from becoming upright, let alone perfect. And the *Gospel of*

23. *BoS* 19.4, 19.6; *LG* 456, 461.

24. *BoS* 16.9; *LG* 408; and *BoS* 20.14; *LG* 505.

25. Cf. Jan Helderman, *Die Anapausis im Evangelium Veritatis* (Leiden: E. J. Brill, 1984), 16.

26. Albertus F. J. Klijn, trans., *The Acts of Thomas: Introduction, Text, and Commentary,* 2nd ed., Supplements to Novum Testamentum (Leiden: E. J. Brill, 2003), 77; Robert Murray, *Symbols of Church and Kingdom: A Study in Early Syriac Tradition,* rev. ed. (London: T. and T. Clark; Piscataway, N.J.: Gorgias Press, 2004), 317.

Truth belongs to this objectionable circuit. Helderman's thesis is that the concept of "rest" in the *Gospel of Truth* everywhere has an eschatological nature. Recently however, Judith Hoch Wray argued that the context of the *Gospel of Truth* shows that it takes the "rest" to refer to the present state of certain Gnostics. This could mean that we find a polemic here between this-worldly Gnostics and otherworldly Catholics.[27]

Therefore, it could be that the *Book of Steps* and the *Gospel of Truth* are two opposing voices within the larger context of the Catholic-Gnostic debate. The ecclesiastical environment of the *Book of Steps* becomes visible in memra 27, which says, "From the Catholic Church all truth shall be known. Let us love even idolaters and infidels, for the Catholic Church is great in our eyes." But that implies that there are conflicting claims as to the question through which Gospel the Christian can come to know the truth, the whole truth, and nothing but the Truth.[28]

27. Judith Hoch Wray, *Rest as a Theological Metaphor in the Epistle to the Hebrews and the Gospel of Truth* (New York: Scholars Press, 1998), 127n112.

28. BoS 27.5; *LG* 780.

PART 2

THE TEXT OF THE *BOOK OF STEPS*

Grigory Kessel

4. A PREVIOUSLY UNKNOWN REATTRIBUTED FRAGMENT FROM MEMRA 16 OF THE *BOOK OF STEPS*

The meticulous edition of the *Book of Steps* or *Liber Graduum* of the Hungarian scholar Micháły Kmoskó (1876–1931)[1] was published as the first part of the third volume of "Patrologia Syriaca" in 1926.[2] Ever since, it has been used extensively by students of Syriac Christianity in general and of the *Book of Steps* in particular, and there have been almost no objections to the accuracy of the edited text.[3] However, almost a century after the edition of Kmoskó, it is regrettable that no research done on the manuscript tradition of the *Book of Steps* has brought to light any new direct textual witnesses. The task is certainly worth undertaking, and it should especially focus on an investigation of the group of reattributed and recast memre, as will be demonstrated. In this chapter I will proceed first by making some observations on the transmission of the *Book of Steps,* and then, after a discussion of the results achieved by modern scholars, I will present a new find.

1. On Kmoskó's activity, see István Zimonyi, "Kmoskó Mihály és a magyar ostörténet," in *Ostörténet és nemzettudat 1919–1931,* edited by É. Kincses Nagy, 89–93 (Szeged: Magyar Őstörténeti Kutatócsoport, 1991).

2. The series was replaced by *Patrologia Orientalis.*

3. But see Lionel Wickham, "The *Liber Graduum* Revisited," in *VI Symposium Syriacum, 1992: University of Cambridge, Faculty of Divinity, 30 August–2 September 1992,* edited by René Lavenant, 177–87 (Rome: Pontificio Instituto Orientale, 1992). On the history of the *Book of Steps* scholarship, see Robert

Textual Evidence of the *Book of Steps*

The manuscript that served as *texte de base* for Kmoskó's edition was Bibliothèque nationale de France (BnF) syr. 201, dated by the editor back to the twelfth century.[4] Apart from the corpus of the *Book of Steps,* the manuscript also contains the complete text of the "Ascetical discourses" of Philoxenos of Mabbug,[5] one letter of Ammonios,[6] a letter of Basil to his brother Gregory,[7] some sayings of Xystus,[8] a letter of Antonius,[9] and some minor fragments. BnF syr. 201 is one of the most recent on the list of Kmoskó, but only one out of two manuscripts represents the complete corpus. The other manuscript containing the full text of the *Book of Steps* was the manuscript from the library of the Syrian Orthodox monastery of St. Mark in Jerusalem, which was copied, according to Kmoskó, around the seventh to eighth century.[10] Besides

A. Kitchen and Martien F. G. Parmentier, trans., *The Book of Steps: The Syriac Liber Graduum* (Kalamazoo, Mich.: Cistercian Publications, 2004), xxi–xxvi.

4. However, in the catalog of Zotenberg the manuscript dates to the thirteenth century; Zotenberg, *Catalogue,* 152.

5. The text was edited and translated by Ernest A. W. Budge, *The Discourses of Philoxenus: Bishop of Mabbôgh, A.D. 485–519,* 2 vols. (London: Asher, 1893–1894), who was not aware of BnF syr. 201 and made use only of the manuscripts preserved in the British Museum, although the catalog of Zotenberg was published twenty years earlier; for a description of used manuscripts, see Budge, *Discourses of Philoxenus,* lxvi–lxxiii, xciv–xcv (table), and André de Halleux, *Philoxène de Mabbog: Sa vie, ses écrits, sa theologie* (Louvain: Imprimerie Orientaliste, 1963), 280–83.

6. Following indication of the manuscript, Zotenberg states that it is a "sixth letter"; however, since the Syriac version of the collection of Ammonius' "Letters" is not a unified one, in the edition of Kmoskó this text appears under the number 11; Kmoskó, *Ammonii Eremitae Epistolae,* Patrologia Orientalis 10.6 (Paris: Firmin-Didot, 1915), 46–51. BnF syr. 201 was not known to the editor; for the description of the manuscripts, see Kmoskó, *Ammonii Eremitae Epistolae,* 3–8.

7. This remains unpublished; cf. Sebastian P. Brock, "Traduzioni siriache degli scritti di Basilio," in *Basilio tra Oriente e Occidente: Convegno Internazionale "Basilio il Grande e il Monachesimo Orientale," Cappadocia, 5–7 ottobre 1999,* edited by E. Baudry, (Monastero di Bose, Magnano, Italy: Edizioni Qiqajon, 2001), 175; and Paul J. Fedwick, *Basilius Caesariensis: The Letters,* Bibliotheca Basiliana Universalis 1 (Turnhout: Brepols, 1993), 451–52; BnF syr. 201 is mentioned in neither of those two studies. Jacques Grand'Henry, "La réponse de S. Basile a S. Grégoire: Édition critique de la lettre 2 en version arabe," *Le Muséon* 102 (1989): 321–59, contains a comparison of the Arabic and Syriac versions.

8. The text was published by Paul de Lagarde, who did not use the Paris manuscript, in his *Analecta Syriaca* (Lipsiae: B. G. Teubnerus, 1858), 2–31. For identification, see Hermann Zotenberg, *Catalogue des manuscrits syriaques et sabéens (mandaïtes) de la Bibliothèque Nationale* (Paris: Imprimerie nationale, 1874), 150.

9. Edited with French translation by François Nau, "La Version syriaque de la première lettre de Saint Antoine," *Revue de l'Orient Chrétien* 14 (1909): 282–97; Nau used the BnF syr. 201, but did not date it.

10. Kmoskó, *Liber Graduum,* viii–ix, ccxciv–ccxcvi. In a catalog of Dolabani the manuscript is num-

BnF syr. 201 and the Jerusalem manuscript, Kmoskó made use of thirteen manuscripts ranging from the sixth to the thirteenth century, each of which reproduces one or more memre.[11]

From the first view we can see that all the manuscripts used by Kmoskó for the edition have ascetic content[12] and consist of works (or fragments) originally written in Syriac or translated from Greek; furthermore, all of those thirteen manuscripts that contain only one or more memre are so-called monastic anthologies.[13] Already in the oldest textual witnesses of the *Book of Steps* (British Library Add. 14578 and Add. 14612), which both date back to the sixth or seventh century, the memre of the *Book of Steps* are located among the works of Evagrius, John the Solitary, and John Chrysostom. And if such ascetic context may seem to be quite predictable, what is puzzling is that all the manuscripts but one are of Syriac Orthodox provenance. The only exception is the priceless Syriac Chalcedonian (*Codex syriacus primus*) monastic anthology of the ninth century,[14] which is our sole witness of the presence of the text of the *Book of Steps* in the Syriac Chalcedonian (Melkite) tradition.

bered "180"; Filoksinos Y. Dolabani, *Catalogue of Syriac Manuscripts in St. Mark's Monastery*, Syriac Patrimony 8 (Aleppo: Syria Mardin, 1994), 377–80. Apart from the *Book of Steps,* the manuscript contains *Logoi* I–V of Abba Isaiah's "Asketicon," as published by René Draguet, *Les Cinq recensions recensions de l'Ascéticon syriaque d'Abba Isaïe,* Corpus Scriptorum Christianorum Orientalium 289, Scriptores Syri 120 (Louvain: Secrétariat du Sorpus SCO, 1968), 1–29, who did not use nor mention the Jerusalem manuscript; for the list of the manuscripts, see Draguet, *Cinq recensions,* 10*–36*, 28*–29* (table). Fortunately, this important manuscript was recently digitized by the Hill Museum and Manuscript Library, along with other manuscripts preserved in the library of St. Mark Monastery.

11. For a description of the manuscripts, see Kmoskó, *Liber Graduum,* i–viii, ix. The table contains two important misprints: Add. 18812 should be corrected for Add. 18814, and Add. 17728 for Add. 14728.

12. The only exception from that observation could be British Library Add. 12160, which in its present form contains the lives of the saints, but may well have originally had a more varied content.

13. On monastic anthologies, see Herman Teule, "Les Compilations monastiques syriaques," in *Symposium Syriacum VII: Uppsala University, Department of Asian and African Languages, 11–14 August 1996,* edited by René Lavenant, 249–62, Orientalia Christiana Analecta 256 (Roma: Pontificio Istituto Orientale, 1998).

14. Anton Baumstark dated it to the early ninth century; Baumstark, *Karl W. Hiersemann's Katalog 500. Orientalische Manuskripte: Arabische, syrische, griechische, armenische, persische Handschriften des 7.–18. Jahrhunderts* (Leipzig: Karl W. Hiersemann, 1922), 3–6. The manuscript was destroyed in May 1940, when it was being held in the library of the University of Leuven with the shelf number G. 197. On the history of the manuscript, see Werner Strothmann, "Die orientalischen Handschriften der Sammlung Mettler (Katalog Hiersemann 500)," in *XIX. Deutscher Orientalistentag vom 28. September bis 4. Oktober 1975 in Freiburg im Breisgau. Vorträge, Sektion IV,* edited by Wolfgang Voigt, 292 nn30, 33, Zeitschrift der Deutschen Morgenländischen Gesellschaft, Supplement, vol. 3, part 1 (Wiesbaden: Steiner, 1977); and Bernard Outtier, "Le Sort des manuscrits du Katalog Hiersemann 500," *Analecta Bollandiana* 93 (1975): 377. On its probable relation to the East Syriac milieu, see below in this chapter.

The evidence of the previously mentioned British Library Add. 14578 is also important in another respect. In this oldest witness of the text of the *Book of Steps,* memra 14 appears under the name of Evagrius Ponticus. This fact is not an accidental one, for, as one can learn from the introduction of Kmoskó, some memre can be found with attribution to both Evagrius (memra 14) and John the Solitary (memre 16 and 19), whose original writings were foundational in the development of Syriac ascetic and mystical tradition.

Moreover, in addition to a few reattributed memre, Kmoskó adds a witness of another kind. According to Wright's description of the manuscript BL Add. 17193, folios 3r–3v contain "an extract from the *Κλῖμαξ,* the 'Ladder,' or 'Book of Steps,' here ascribed to Eusebius the monk, on 1 Corinthians 5:5."[15] Kmoskó studied the piece[16] and demonstrated that it contains a brief commentary on 1 Corinthians 5:5 in which a fragment from memra 29 was incorporated without reference to the original source.[17]

Thus the evidence provided by Kmoskó enables one to discern different branches of the textual transmission of the text of the *Book of Steps* during the period of the sixth through the thirteenth century. First of all, the corpus continued to be copied as a whole in (at least) two different forms.[18] Some selected memre were introduced in the corpora of the writings of Evagrius Ponticus and John the Solitary. Some memre were also used for compiling monastic anthologies (in which reattributed memre can be found, as well). And last, a relevant fragment was excerpted for exegetical commentary.

Although no systematic quest for new witnesses of the text of the *Book of Steps* has been undertaken,[19] scholars working on the heritage of a particular

15. William Wright, *Catalogue of Syriac Manuscripts in the British Museum, Acquired Since the Year 1838* (London: British Museum, 1871), 2:989.

16. Kmoskó, *Liber Graduum,* xii (Syriac text and Latin translation).

17. *BoS* 19.4. Thus we see that the text of the *Book of Steps* experienced a certain amount of reinterpretation, because it was considered an exegetical work (or as a source of exegetical materials), which led to the incorporation of the *Book of Steps* fragment into exegetical compilations (similar to the *Demonstration* of Aphrahāṭ, for which see Grigory Kessel, "A Note on One Borrowing from Aphrahat: St. Petersburg, Institute of Oriental Studies, Diettrich 2," *Parole de l'Orient* 31 (2006): 295–307.

18. The text of the Jerusalem manuscript differs considerably from that of the BnF syr. 201.

19. However, it should not be neglected. It is worth noting in passing that the situation with textual witnesses for Aphrahāṭ's *Demonstration* is even worse: as one can learn from the introduction of Parisot, there is one manuscript of the fifth century and two of the sixth century; one *Demonstration* is preserved in the West Syriac manuscript dated 1364 C.E. However, the recent discovery of Sebastian Brock in Sinai Syr. 16 of two fragments from *Demonstration* 23, written in the estrangelo hand of the sixth century

Syriac author (or a Greek one, but whose works were translated into Syriac) have discovered additional texts and manuscripts. While investigating the minor works of Evagrius Ponticus, Jules Muyldermans discovered one more manuscript with memra 14 attributed to Evagrius,[20] while Werner Strothmann, in his study on the œuvre of John the Solitary, discovered fragments from memra 29 incorporated into the treatise that was circulating with an attribution to either John the Solitary or Macarius.[21] And finally, Charbel Chahine managed to identify a fragment from the *Book of Steps* in a piece attributed to an East Syriac author of the sixth-to-seventh century, Abraham of Nathpar.[22]

In order to get a better idea to whom memre from the *Book of Steps* have been attributed, I have placed all the data in the following table (new findings are underlined):

To start the analysis of the new evidence procured by these scholars, we should say that the eleven new manuscripts are of ascetic content and with dates ranging from the ninth century to 1576 C.E. Only one manuscript contains a complete memra (memra 14 under the name Evagrius), while the majority of the manuscripts (viz., nine) reproduce selected extracts from memra 29 joined together with those of *Historia monachorum in Aegypto* (1.19–24)[23] that were circulating within a treatise attributed to either John the Solitary or Macarius. Nine manuscripts belong to the group of ascetic anthologies, while one (Vat. sir. 121) contains the *corpora* of Macarius and Mark the Solitary and

(Brock, "The Genealogy of the Virgin Mary in Sinai Syr. 16," *Scrinium* 2 [2006]: 71, as well as my findings [Kessel, "Note," 295–307]) prove that there is still room for discovery of new witnesses of the text.

20. Jules Muyldermans, *Evagriana syriaca: Textes inédits du British Museum et de la Vaticane,* Bibliothèque du Muséon 31 (Louvain: Publications universitaires, 1952), 81–82 (general discussion), 105–9 (edition), 143–46 (French trans.). Muyldermans did not manage to identify the text, and considered it part of the work of Evagrius; the first scholar who identified the provenance of the piece was Arthur Vööbus, "Liber Graduum: Some Aspects of Its Significance for the History of Early Syrian Asceticism," in *Charisteria Iohanni Kopp octogenerio oblata,* 113, Papers of the Estonian Theological Society in Exile 7 (Stockholm: Estonian Theological Society in Exile, 1954). This manuscript was taken into account in Kitchen and Parmentier, *Book of Steps,* xxviii.

21. Strothmann, Werner, *Johannes von Apamea,* Patristische Texte und Studien 11 (Berlin: De Gruyter, 1972), 37–38, no. 3.6; Strothmann, *Die Syrische Überlieferung der Schriften des Makarios,* Göttinger Orientforschungen I Reihe, Syriaca, Bd. 21 (Wiesbaden: Harrassowitz, 1981), 1:213–20; 2:143–44 (translation of final paragraph only).

22. I follow the conventional spelling of Abraham's name, although Chahine argued that "Nethpar" reflects original vocalization, while "Nathpar" is an Arabism; C. Chahine, *Abraham de Bēt-Netprā: Discours (Mēmrē) : Introduction, texte critique et traduction* (PhD diss., Augustinianum: Roma, 2004), 32.

23. The excerpts from the *Book of Steps* constitute approximately a fourth of the treatise.

Table 4-1. Attribution of Memre in the *Book of Steps*

Memra	Evagrius Ponticus	John the Solitary	Macarius	Abraham of Nathpar
Memra 14	BL Add. 14578 (6th/7th c.), Add. 14621 (802 C.E.), *Add. 17217* (9th/10th 10th c.), Add. 7190 (12th c.)			
Memra 16		BL Add. 18814 (7th/8th c.)		
Memra 19		BL Add. 18814 (7th/8th c.)		
Memra 29 (selected extracts only)		§ 9, 16, 17–18, 19: *Sachau 352* (13th c.), *Sharfeh, Raḥmani 38 212* (1466 C.E.)	§ 9, 16, 17–18, 19: *Vat. sir. 122* (769 C.E.), *BL Add. 14582* (816 C.E.), *Add. 18814* (9h c.),[a] *Add. 14637* (10th c.), *Vat. sir. 126* (1223 C.E.), *Mingana Syr. 330* (13th c.), *Vat. sir. 121* (1576 C.E.)	§§ 1, 2: *BL Or. 6714* (9th–10th c.)

a. Thus this manuscript contains two memre from the *Book of Steps:* one is attributed to John the Solitary, the other to Macarius.

the other (BL Or. 6714, ninth to tenth century)[24] comprises different works by Syriac (Shūbḥālmāran, Abraham of Nathpar, Barḥadbshābbā, Gregory the Monk) and Greek (Theodore of Mopsuestia and Gregory Nazianzen) au-

24. Lane dates the manuscript between the ninth and eleventh centuries (David J. Lane, *Shubhalmaran: The Book of Gifts,* Corpus Scriptorum Christianorum Orientalium 612, Scriptores Syri 236 [Louvain: Peeters, 2004], 5), while it is the appraisal of Nau, who considered the manuscript to be written in the ninth or tenth century (Nau, "L'Histoire ecclésiastique," de Bar Ḥadbešabba ʿArbaia et une controverse de Théodore de Mopsueste avec les macédoniens," *Revue de l'Orient Chrétien* 6 [1911]: 237), that was upheld by recent scholarship e.g. Chahine, *Abraham de Bēt-Netprā,* 138; Paul Géhin, "Manuscrits sinaïtiques dispersés I: les fragments syriaques et arabes de Paris," *Oriens Christianus* 90 (2006): 27.

thors.[25] What strikes one most of all in respect to the last mentioned manuscript is that among the majority of Syriac Orthodox witnesses, it is the only one that has an East Syriac provenance.[26] And as is the case with the treatise that can be found with attribution either to John the Solitary or Macarius, manuscript British Library Or. 6714 also contains a fragment from memra 29 incorporated into the longer version of Abraham of Nathpar's "Commandments and admonitions." The work was previously identified in Mingana syr. 601 by Sebastian Brock as consisting of Aphrahāṭ, *Demonstration* 6.8–9.19.[27] Charbel Chahine found in British Library Or. 6714 the same text that is supplemented with four additional fragments: two from the same *Demonstration of* Aphrahāṭ (6.19, 7), one from the *Book of Steps* (*BoS* 29.1, 2), and one that remains unidentified.[28] Thus British Library Or. 6714 is to be considered a precious piece of evidence that provides us with a unique hint that the text of the *Book of Steps* was known in the East Syriac milieu[29] at least by the time

25. For description of the manuscript, see Lane, *Shubhalmaran,* 5–8.

26. Nevertheless, it seems to be quite remarkable that, judging from the extant evidence, the *Book of Steps* was almost completely forgotten by later East Syriac tradition. That might be due to the fact that this text, written in a Syriac proto-monastic community, was considered as alien in view of traditional reformed East Syriac monasticism; but perhaps some reasons of theological nature may lurk behind the exclusion.

27. Brock, "John the Solitary: On Prayer," *Journal of Theological Studies* 30 (1979): 85.

28. Chahine, *Abraham de Bēt-Netprā,* 46.

29. Although the manuscript contains exclusively the works of East Syriac origin, a sound supposition of Brock linked it with the Chalcedonian monastery of St. Catherine on Sinai; Brock, "Mingana Syr. 628: A Folio from a Revision of the Peshitta Song of Songs," *Journal of Semitic Studies* 40 (1995): 51–52. This claim was recently supported by Géhin, "Manuscrits sinaïtiques," 27: "il ne fait guère de doute que l'ensemble du manuscrit a appartenu, malgré son origine nestorienne, au monastère de Sainte-Catherine." The connection of British Library Or. 6714 with a Chalcedonian milieu is also confirmed by the manuscript tradition of the memre of Abraham of Nathpar present in that manuscript: according to the stemma, established by Charbel Chahine, the textual evidence of BL Or. 6714 is related to both a Syriac Chalcedonian manuscript *olim* Hiersemann 500/3 (known as *Codex syriacus secundus* [it is worth noting in passing that this unique manuscript was auctioned off at Christie's on June 27–28, 2006 for $96,000, together with other items from the Cornelius J. Hauck collection that had been housed at the Cincinnati Historical Society, and its new owner is currently unknown]); and a fragment from a Syriac Chalcedonian manuscript, A 296 inf./Chabot 34 from the Bibliotheca Ambrosiana, while in turn all of those three witnesses represent the original East Syriac *Vorlage* of the text (Chahine, *Abraham de Bet-Nētprā,* 213–18, 234 [stemma]). Although one knows nothing about the provenance of the Syriac Chalcedonian manuscript (*Codex syriacus primus*) used by Kmoskó, it is quite plausible that, not unlike *Codex syriacus secundus* it comes from the the Palestine/Sinai region and has evident kinship with the East Syriac tradition (e.g., this manuscript contains the text of "Commandments and admonition" of Abraham of Nathpar, which normally features only in the East Syriac manuscripts); for the presence of East Syrians in the Holy Land in general and in Jerusalem in particular during the seventh to ninth century, see

of its incorporation into the text that is attributed to Abraham of Nathpar (*terminus ante quem* is set by the date when the manuscript was produced).[30]

Available data demonstrates that as early as the sixth or seventh century, the text of memre 14 and 16 was already transmitted with attribution to Evagrius and John the Solitary. A few centuries later, selected fragments from memra 29 supplemented with those of *Historia monachorum in Aegypto* are attested with attribution to Macarius and afterward to John the Solitary, while roughly at the same time two excerpts from the same memra appear in the text attributed to Abraham of Nathpar.

The exact reasons for such partitions of memra 29 are still to be revealed, but one may suppose that it could have happened due to the practical necessity when the scribes, delineating the composition of the codex, sought to include the most appropriate material.[31] From Kmoskó's list of the manuscripts, we know that memre 14, 19, and 20 are attested by far better than the others.[32] New evidence of reattributed and recast memre in general supports the case (with an exception of memra 20, for which no new witnesses have yet been found).

Fragment from Memra 16

Not intending to search for new textual witnesses of the *Book of Steps,* I accidentally, while studying Syriac monastic anthologies, came across a fragment from one of its memre that is attributed to a virtually unknown monk Thomas.

Otto Meinardus, "The Nestorians in Egypt," *Oriens Christianus* 51 (1967): 124; Brock, "Syriac into Greek at Mar Saba," in *The Sabaite Heritage in the Orthodox Church from the Fifth Century to the Present,* edited by Joseph Patrich, 203, Orientalia Lovaniencia Analecta 98 (Leuven: Peeters, 2001).

30. Charbel Chahine lists some other manuscripts (predominantly of East Syriac provenance) that contain "Commandments and admonitions." Although I am aware of two more manuscripts with the text of Abraham's "Commandments and admonitions"—Greek Orthodox Patriarchate 34, fol. 168r–69v (1593 C.E.), Metropolitan Library of the Church of the East in Baghdad 145–47 (1742 C.E.)—both of them represent the shorter version of the text. It should be noted that there is one more branch of the textual tradition of that piece. The same shorter version supplemented by one more fragment from Aphrahāṭ, *Demonstration* 6.19, features under the name of John the Solitary in the manuscripts British Library Add. 17170, fol. 49v–51r (774–775 C.E.), Sachau 352, fol. 105v–106r (thirteenth century), Sharfeh, Raḥmani 38 (1466 C.E.), fol. 94v–95r. Strothmann considered the attribution of the piece to John the Solitary to be dubious; Strothmann, *Johannes von Apamea,* 33.

31. The principles that governed the formation of the monastic anthologies are not yet clear; for preliminary discussion, see Teule, "Compilations monastiques syriaques," 249–62.

32. "Together these three memre could readily have served as a digest of the themes of the *Book of Steps*—as was probably the intention of some of the scribes—for in the majority of cases these were

The text of the fragment is preserved in eight manuscripts:

1. Berlin, Staatsbibliothek Preussischer Kulturbesitz, Sachau 352 (thirteenth c.).[33]

2. Paris, Bibliothèque Nationale, syr. 195 (1469/1470 C.E.).[34]

3. Mardin, Church of Forty Martyrs 420 (*olim* Deir al-Zaʿfarān/Dolabani 110, 1472 C.E.).[35]

4. Mardin, Church of Forty Martyrs 422 (*olim* Deir az-Zaʿfarān/Dolabani 109, 1473/1474 C.E.).[36]

5. Mardin, Church of Forty Martyrs 417 (*olim* Deir az-Zaʿfarān/Dolabani 108,[37] 1474 C.E.).[38]

6. Mardin, Church of Forty Martyrs 157 (*olim* Deir az-Zaʿfarān/Dolabani 75; sixteenth to seventeenth c.).[39]

7. Sharfeh, Patriarchal Library (Raḥmani 302; 1698/1699 C.E.).[40]

8. Cambridge, Mass.: Harvard Houghton Library, Syr. 48 (1796/1797 C.E.).[41]

All of the manuscripts that contain the fragment belong to the genre of monastic anthologies (i.e., collections of complete and excerpted treatises of

included as sole representatives of the *Book of Steps* in larger manuscripts"; Kitchen and Parmentier, *Book of Steps,* xxviii–xxix.

33. Eduard Sachau, *Verzeichniss der Syrischen Handschriften der Königlichen Bibliothek zu Berlin* (Berlin: A. Asher, 1899), 2 :638–46.

34. Zotenberg, *Catalogue,* 138–40.

35. Dolabani, *Catalogue,* 67–76. There is no list of correspondence between Dolabani's catalog of the Deir az-Zaʿfarān collection and the present shelf numbers of the library of the Syrian Orthodox Archbishopric in Mardin, where the former was transferred to. The identification between Dolabani's catalog and the present shelf numbers (used, for instance, by Arthur Vööbus in his studies) is mine and based on the description of Dolobani and the details provided by Vööbus, as well as on the direct consultation of the manuscripts.

36. Dolabani, *Catalogue,* 62–67.

37. In Dolabani's *Catalogue* the manuscript is numbered as 109. However, the number is a result of an erroneous numeration and, following the order of the list, the manuscript should be numbered 108.

38. Dolabani, *Catalogue,* 52–62.

39. Dolabani, *Catalogue,* 292–95.

40. Polycarp Sherwood, "Le Fonds patriarcal de la bibliothèque manuscrite de Charfet," *L'Orient Syrien* 2 (1957): 102"; Behnām Sōnī, *Fihris al-maḫṭūṭāt al-baṭriarkīyya fī Dair aš-Šarfa: Lubnān/Le catalogue des manuscrits du Patriarcat au Couvent de Charfet—Liban* (Beirut: 1993), 78–80.

41. Moshe H. Goshen-Gottstein, *Syriac Manuscripts in the Harvard College Library: A Catalogue,* Harvard Semitic Studies 23 (Missoula. Mt.: Scholars Press, 1979), 57; a more detailed description by J. F. Coakley can be found at the online catalog of the Harvard University Library.

ascetic and mystical content). They have Syriac Orthodox provenance and were copied in the region of Ṭur ʿAbdin. The oldest manuscript dates back to the thirteenth century, while the most recent one was copied in 1796/1797 C.E.

The fragment is introduced either with attribution to Thomas (BnF syr. 195) or using the standard expression ܕܝܠܗ ܒ ܕܝܠܗ ("of the same," as in Sharfeh Raḥmani 302 or Houghton Library Syr. 48). Fortunately, the explanation of the attribution is ready at hand, for in all the manuscripts, the fragment stands next to two other fragments (most often between them) that bear an attribution to monk Thomas, who is called more often "the blessed Thomas." Even a cursory reading of those two fragments creates an impression that they are not two independent pieces, but the parts of one text. Such an assumption was confirmed by further investigation, for I had the good luck to find some seven more manuscripts, each of them containing a complete text attributed to Thomas.

A study of the manuscript tradition enabled me to distinguish three recensions of Thomas' text that I tentatively call a "Letter."[42] Two of them represent a complete or nearly complete text, while the third one is much different. The latter recension presents Thomas' "Letter" divided into two parts arranged in reverse order and supplemented with an inauthentic fragment that can be easily identified as a fragment from memra 16 of the *Book of Steps.*[43]

One may proceed further and wonder if there is any available data concerning the author of the "Letter" and the time of its composition. Unfortunately, no direct hints can be found in the extant text of the "Letter," which has a common ascetic character. Much more suggestive is the manuscript tradition of the "Letter," which points at the period close to the twelfth to thirteenth century and at a Syriac Orthodox milieu situated in the region of Northern Mesopotamia (perhaps in the region of Ṭur ʿAbdin) as the most plausible period and place of its composition.

One may also inquire if there is any possibility of finding who the author

42. Detailed treatment of the issue can be found in Grigory Kessel, "The 'Letter' of Thomas the Monk: An Edition and Study of the Syriac Text and Its Author," *Journal of Eastern Christian Studies* 61 (2009): 43–100. It is worth noting that only recently have I managed to get access to three Mardin manuscripts (Orth. 417, Orth. 420, and Orth. 422) that were not available to me at the time I was writing the article. The new witnesses allow one to reconstruct the textual history of the "Letter" with more precision, and I am planning to investigate their evidence at a future occasion. Though the present study was generally conducted without access to the aforementioned manuscripts, it has still been possible during the editing process to introduce some additions and corrections to the initial text.

43. *BoS* 16.11 (*LG* 408, line 25–409, line 23).

of the "Letter" was. Syrian Orthodox Patriarch Aphram Barṣoum conjectured that the author of the text is to be identified with the monk Thomas, whose life was described by Michael the Great (1126–1199 C.E.) in his "Chronicle."[44] Regrettably, the learned patriarch does not give arguments in favor of his supposition, but merely refers to three manuscripts containing Thomas' text and to Michael's "Chronicle." I have undertaken an investigation of the available data and have come to the following conclusion.[45]

Fifteen manuscripts of Syriac Orthdox provenance that were written in the period from the thirteenth to the beginning of the twentieth century contain a brief text attributed to an otherwise unknown monk, Thomas. The considerable number of copies indicates that the text enjoyed a steady popularity among Syriac Orthodox monks and scribes. A quest for information concerning the author does not reveal more than one can read in a vivid account of Michael the Great concerning the life of a certain monk Thomas, with whom the author of the "Letter" was identified by Patriarch Barṣoum. Michael reports how a young man, due to a famine, decided to go to the monastery of Zabar (near Melitene), where he was destined to live as a solitary until his death by the hands of the Turks in 1146 C.E.; he gained great esteem in the eyes of his contemporaries and predicted a dramatic fall of Edessa. Michael is silent concerning the literary activity of Thomas, but considering his authoritative position, it is indeed likely that he could have written such an exhortation as the given "Letter." No direct data concerning the period and place of its composition can be found in the extant text of the "Letter"; however, the external evidence of the manuscript tradition makes it plausible to bring together the Thomas who is the author of the text with the Thomas portrayed by Michael the Great, and thus to confirm the probability of Patriarch Barṣoum's conjecture.

If one tries to ascertain when and how the fragment from the *Book of Steps* came to be attributed to Thomas and started to be transmitted among two parts of that author's text, it seems that a clue to the answer can be found in Sachau 352, for it is the only extant manuscript in which the *Book of Steps* fragment is not attributed to Thomas, and—what is much more important—

44. Ignatius A. Barsoum, *The Scattered Pearls: A History of Syriac Literature and Sciences,* trans. M. Moosa, 2nd ed. (Piscataway, N.J.: Gorgias Press, 2003), 138 and 171.

45. Kessel, "Letter," 74–75.

stands directly next to Thomas's "Letter." Being the oldest witness of the *Book of Steps* fragment (Eduard Sachau dates it back to the thirteenth century), Sachau 352 seems to belong to the period when the fragment had not yet been attributed to Thomas and just followed (or preceded) Thomas's original text with its personal and independent title. Since its title included no mention of its author, later on, in the course of its transmission, the *Book of Steps* fragment received the attribution to monk Thomas and eventually was placed in between two parts of the "Letter."

Actually, the fragment is attributed explicitly to Thomas only in four late-fifteenth-century manuscripts (BnF syr. 195, Mardin Orth. 417, Orth. 420, and Orth. 422). The evidence of those four manuscripts represents the next stage of the textual history of the *Book of Steps* fragment as compared to Sachau 352—namely, we see that the fragment was already attributed to Thomas, but was still transmitted independently from the "Letter" (by that time already circulating in a form of two divided parts placed in a reverse order).

Not too long afterward one may observe a final change that occurred to the *Book of Steps* fragment. In manuscript Mardin Orth. 157 (sixteenth-seventeenth c.) the fragment from the *Book of Steps* can be found between two parts of Thomas' "Letter." This arrangement of text is witnessed by few other manuscripts and can be characterized as a final stage of the textual history of the fragment.

Thus, irrespective of the date of composition of the "Letter," the extant manuscript evidence allows us to reconstruct the history of the *Book of Steps* fragment as follows. By the thirteenth century the fragment from memra 16 appears in a Syrian Orthodox monastic anthology next to the text of the "Letter" of Monk Thomas. By that time the "Letter" was already transformed into a sequence of two parts, and in due course (but certainly before the second half of the fifteenth century) the *Book of Steps* fragment received an attribution to the same monk Thomas on the grounds of some points of similarity between the texts. Given a very changeable character of content of Syriac monastic anthologies, it is no surprise that eventually the *Book of Steps* fragment could be placed between two parts of Thomas' "Letter." An appearance of a fragment that was extracted from a complete text of the memra corresponds rather well to what we know about the manuscript tradition of the *Book of*

Steps. A period of the transmission of a complete corpus of memre was followed by a circulation of single (or groups of selected) memre. Moreover, there are four manuscripts that date back to around the twelfth and thirteenth centuries that contain the text of only one memra.[46]

Title of the Fragment

The majority of the manuscripts provide the following title (with some slight variations)[47]: ܕܠܗ ܠܬܗܪܐ ܕܪܒܘܬܗ ܕܐܠܗܐ: ܘܕܠܐ ܣܦܩܝܢ ܠܗ ܪ̈ܘܡܐ ܘܥܘܡ̈ܩܐ ܕܢܫܒܚܘܢܗ ("Of the same on the amazement upon the magnificence of God and that neither the heights nor the depths are capable of praising him.")[48] The title was most likely introduced by a scribe who extracted it from the text of the memra; it seems to be a successful summary of the fragment's content.

Variant Readings

The comparison of the fragment against the edition of Kmoskó and its *apparatus* reveals a number of significant divergences that should be considered not as merely alternative readings, but as a result of deliberate correction introduced by scribes. Some of them can be viewed as attempts to simplify the original text by way of omission of pleonastic constructions:

BoS 16.11 (LG 408, lines 25–409, line 3): "*If all people who have existed and who will exist—the children of Adam,* from the beginning until the end—were alive."

Fragment: "*If all the children of Adam—who have existed and who will exist,* from the beginning until the end—were alive."

BoS 16.11 (LG 409, line 7–line 9): "They would be too few *to confess* and to praise the kindness of God toward people."

Fragment: "They would be too few to praise the kindness of God toward people."

46. It is notable that there is no extant witness of the *Book of Steps* later than the thirteenth century.

47. The manuscripts are, however, at variance in the form and position of Thomas's name.

48. The title of Sachau 352 is only slightly different. The only divergent wording is provided by BnF syr. 195, which contains the rather succinct title ܬܘܒ ܡܡܠܠܐ ܡܘܬܪܢܐ ܕܡܪܝ ܬܐܘܡܐ ("A profitable discourse of Mar Thomas").

Yet there is one variant reading that deals not with the form of the narration, but with its content.

BoS 16.11 (LG 409, line 14–line 16): "And [even] *if they progress* more than the apostles and [more] than the example of lowliness that our Lord had shown them."

Fragment: "And [even] *if they consider* [*to have achieved*] (variant readings in other manuscripts: if they live/if they suffer) more than the apostles and [more] than the example of lowliness that our Lord had shown them."

The alteration can be seen as an effort to play down the assumption that a person is able to surpass the sufferings of Christ;[49] an idea that could have appeared to an ordinary monk to be audacious, and maybe even inadmissible. One more variant reading can be found in the quotation from Romans 8:18:

BoS 16.11 (LG 409, line 17–line 20): "*I consider that the sufferings of this time are not comparable, and the life that the Perfect are pursuing, to the glory and the beauty that we will come to receive.*"

Fragment: "*I consider—says Paul,—that the sufferings of this time are not comparable to the glory and the beauty that will be revealed in us.*"

The quotation in question was considered by Josef Kerschensteiner, who studied ancient Syriac versions of Paul's "Epistles" (which preceded the redaction of Peshitta) as a witness to that text.[50] On the contrary, the reading of the fragment is different and corresponds to the Peshitta. The scribe might have been stricken by the unusual wording and decided to replace it with the corresponding verse from the Peshitta, following a widespread practice of the time.

The other quotation from Paul's "Epistles" (1 Corinthians 2:9) reveals an emendation of the same kind. One may again observe how seemingly unusual wording was replaced with the common rendering of the Peshitta.

BoS 16.11 (LG 409, line 20–line 23): "The thing that eye has not seen

49. For justice's sake it is necessary to say that the author of the *Book of Steps* seems to be willing to express the idea that a person can fulfill and thus surpass not the Christ's personal sufferings, but the commandments given by Christ (which is the issue of the memra 16—"On how a person may surpass the major commandments"—from which the fragment was extracted).

50. Josef Kerschensteiner, *Der altsyrische Paulustext,* Corpus Scriptorum Christianorum Orientalium 315, Subsidia 37 (Louvain: Secrétariat du Corpus Scritporum Christianorum Orientalium, 1970), 25 n39. In a more recent study of Andreas Juckel and Barbara Aland, the words "and the life that the Perfect are pursuing" are considered to be an author's deliberate addition to the original text (Barbara Aland and Andreas Juckel, eds., *Das Neue Testament in Syrischer Überlieferung, Die paulinischen Briefe,* Arbeiten zur Neutestamentlichen Textforschung 14 (Berlin and New York: de Gruyter, 1991), 182).

and ear has not heard, and the thing that God has prepared for them has not ascended to the heart of a person in the higher levels, for those who loved him."[51]

Fragment: "The thing that eye has not seen and ear has not heard, and the thing that God has prepared for those who love him and do his will has not ascended to the heart of a person."

The expression "and do his will" is attested solely by BnF syr. 195 and does not feature in any other extant witness to that Bible verse.[52] This addition may reflect extensive liturgical usage of the phrase.[53]

Conclusions

Although the reattributed fragment presented here does not provide us with any new hint concerning authorship, origin, and date of the *Book of Steps* (which would, of course, be very welcome), it nevertheless reflects certain aspects of its reception history.[54] As was demonstrated in the first part of this chapter, the vast majority of the textual witnesses of the *Book of Steps* are of Syriac Orthodox provenance, while two unique witnesses provide us with valuable indication that the text of the *Book of Steps* was circulating and read also in the East Syriac and Syriac Chalcedonian communities approximately at the turn of the millennium. With only one exception, all the manuscript witnesses have ascetic content. There are only two witnesses that contain the complete text, whereas a vast majority of all other manuscripts belong to the genre of the monastic anthologies that contain selected memre. The manuscripts in question were copied during a period ranging from the sixth and seventh centuries up to 1576 C.E. As early as the sixth or seventh century, memre from the *Book of Steps* started to be transmitted under the names of

51. I follow Kerschensteiner's opinion regarding the end of the quotation (Kerschensteiner, *Altsyrische Paulustext,* 35–36), while in Kitchen's translation the reference sign stands after the word "levels" (Kitchen and Parmentier, *Book of Steps,* 167). The reason of such ambiguity is that in the original text of the *Book of Steps* it is far from clear where the quotation terminates.

52. At least among those that were used by Barbara Aland and Andreas Juckel, *Neue Testament,* 218.

53. Cf. Psalm 103:21, 145:20.

54. It is well known that the absence of any quotations from the *Book of Steps* in later Syriac literature caused many scholars to consider that text as an idiosyncratic one that did not leave its mark in history (leaving aside, of course, the issue of Philoxenus of Mabbug, for which see Kitchen and Parmentier, *Book of Steps,* lxxxii–lxxxiii).

such renowned authors as Evagrius Ponticus and John the Solitary. By the eighth century there appeared a treatise that made use of some fragments from memra 29 and that was extensively copied over eight centuries, attributed to either Macarius or John the Solitary, while some other excerpts from the same memra were appended to the piece attributed to Abraham of Nathpar. A fragment from the *Book of Steps* can be found in the Syriac Orthodox exegetical compendium in a text clarifying 1 Corinthians 5:5.

Despite the variety of the ways in which the text of the *Book of Steps* was transmitted, it is possible to detect a number of selected memre (namely, 14, 16, 19, 20, and 29) that were copied especially often in a Syriac Orthodox monastic milieu for the compilation of monastic anthologies.[55]

The present finding of a fragment from memra 16 fits this ecclesiastical, literary, and chronological frame of the general line of the textual history of the *Book of Steps,* while extending it up to 1796/1797 C.E. The fragment was excerpted from memra 16, which undoubtedly enjoyed popularity in the manuscript tradition and is preserved in the monastic anthologies of Syriac Orthodox provenance. The special significance of the new fragment lies in the fact that it reveals one more branch of the textual transmission of the *Book of Steps.* To the witnesses of complete memre (sometimes attributed to another author) and of the fragments embedded into another texts (also with different attributions) we can now add a new type of witnesses—namely, a fragment from a memra that was extracted from a memra to be included in the monastic anthology. Most probably it was the consequence of a scribe's decision to keep the valuable fragment separate from the text of the memra. Such excerption might eventually result in attribution of the excerpt to another author (in the present case, monk Thomas).

One more observation can be made. All distinctive branches of the textual transmission of the *Book of Steps* tend to flourish during particular periods. Thus the copying of the complete corpus evidently represents the primitive layer, which is represented by St. Mark Monastery Library/Dolabani 180 (seventh or eighth century). The use of selected memre in monastic anthologies (generally with pseudo-attributions) is generally attested during the period from the eighth to thirteenth century, while excerpted fragments (sometimes

55. One may cherish hopes that a detailed investigation of the monastic anthologies will result in finding of the new witnesses for the text of the *Book of Steps.*

being introduced into another text) constitute a later period that extends up to the eighteenth century.[56]

To sum up, all available evidence demonstrates that at least some memre of the *Book of Steps*—being written at the dawn of the history of Syriac monasticism for a particular community—were appreciated mainly by Syriac Orthodox, but also by East Syriac and Syriac Chalcedonian, monks who, while reading them more than a thousand years after their composition, still found in them valuable impetuses contributing to the accomplishment of their monastic commitment. Ranging from copies of the complete corpus of memre to excerpts incorporated into other texts, all the manifold branches of the textual transmission of the *Book of Steps* are an unambiguous indication of the wide circulation of its text (at least in a partial form) during the Medieval period and reaching even the modern times.

Edition of a Fragment

BnF syr. 195 was used as the main manuscript for edition of the fragment. One of the main arguments in favor of such a decision was the consideration of its close kinship to the original text of the *Book of Steps.* As the apparatus and the foregoing presentation of the variant readings demonstrate, all other witnesses differ from the Paris codex and apparently reflect a somewhat recast and adapted text.

Index siglorum:

F: Berlin, Staatsbibliothek Preussischer Kulturbesitz, Sachau 352 (thirteenth c.), fol. 200v

G: Sharfeh, Patriarchal Library (Raḥmani 302) (1698/9 C.E.),[57] fol. 65r

H: Cambridge, Massachusetts, Harvard Houghton Library, Syr. 48 (1796/1797 C.E.), fol. 29v

56. This general line of textual history of the *Book of Steps* reflects the pattern of the development in the transmission of Syriac literature discerned by Sebastian Brock, according to whom complete texts and corpora tend to stop to be copied *in toto* after approximately 1000 C.E.; afterward they are transmitted predominantly partially; Brock, "Without Mushē of Nisibis, Where Would We Be? Some Reflections on the Transmission of Syriac Literature," *Journal of Eastern Christian Studies* 56 (2004): 15–24.

57. I am grateful to Monsignor Gabriel Dib, abbot of the monastery of Sharfeh, who graciously provided me with a copy of the necessary manuscript.

K: Mardin, Church of Forty Martyrs 157 (sixteenth–seventeenth c.),[58] fol. 145r

L: Mardin, Church of Forty Martyrs 417 (1474 C.E.), 561

M: Mardin, Church of Forty Martyrs 420 (1472 C.E.), 469–70

N: Mardin, Church of Forty Martyrs 422 (1473/1474 C.E.), 331–32

Paris, Bibliothèque Nationale, syr. 195 (1469/70 C.E.), fol. 241v–242r:

ܬܘܒ ܡܡܠܠܐ ܡܥܕܪܢܐ ܕܡܪܝ ܬܐܘܡܐ[59] ܣܗܕ ܗܘ ܠܝ ܓܝܪ ܐܠܗܐ. ܕܐܠܘ ܦܢܫܝܢ ܗܘܘ ܟܠܗܘܢ ܒܢܝ̈ܘܗܝ ܕܐܕܡ. ܕܗܘܘ ܘܕܗܘܝܢ. ܡܢ ܫܘܪܝܐ ܘܥܕܡܐ ܠܚܪܬܐ. ܘܗܘܐ ܠܟܠ ܚܕ ܡܢܗܘܢ ܪܒܘ ܦܘ̈ܡܝܢ. ܘܠܟܠ ܚܕ ܚܕ ܦܘܡܐ ܪܒܘ ܠܫ̈ܢܝܢ. ܘܠܟܠ ܚܕ ܠܫܢܐ ܪܒܘ ܡ̈ܠܝܢ. ܘܠܟܠ ܚܕܐ ܚܕܐ ܡܠܬܐ ܪܒܘ ܡܫ̈ܒܚܢ. ܘܠܟܠ ܚܕ ܚܕ ܡܫܒܚܐ ܪܒܘ ܡܫ̈ܠܡܢܝܢ. ܠܡܫܡܥ ܐܝܟ ܕܢܫܬܡܥܘܢ ܠܡܫܒܚܘܬܗ ܕܐܠܗܐ[60] ܕܗܘܐ ܠܒܢܝ̈ܢܫܐ. ܠܐ ܡܣܬܦܩܝܢ ܘܠܐ [242r] ܡܫܬܟܚܝܢ. ܘܠܐ ܡܣܬܦܩܝܢ. ܘܡܫܬܡܥܝܢ[61] ܐܝܟ ܚܢܢܐ ܠܐܠܗܘܬܐ ܕܢܫܒܚܘܢ[62] ܘܢܬܪܘܡܡܘܢ ܠܗ[63] ܠܥܠܡ ܐܝܟ ܪܒܘܬܗ. ܘܐܝܟ ܡܫܒܚܘܬܗ. ܘܐܝܟ ܕܐܦܠܐ ܢܥܡܬܗ[64] ܘܐܬܡܪܘܗܝ[65]. ܠܐ ܡܫܟܚܝܢ[66] ܬܘܒ ܡܠܠ ܡܢ ܡܠܝܐ. ˥ܘܡܢ ܡܕܡ ܕܣܓܝ ܠܗܘܢ ܡܢܗ ܬܘܩܦܐ ܕܡܫܒܚܘܬܐ[67]. ܗܟܢ ܐܡܪܝܢ[68]. ܡܢ ܡܕܡ ܕܡܛܠ ܠܗܘܢ ܡܢܗ. ܡܫܬܒܚܐ ܐܢܐ ܐܡܪ ܦܘܡܗܘܢ. ܘܠܐ ܩܝܡܝܢ ܢܬܩܢܘܢ ܕܡܫܬܡܠܝܐ ܗܘ ܠܡܫܬܥܝܘ ܐܝܟ ܕܐܝܬܘܗܝ ܘܕܐܠܗܐ ܗܘ. ܘܐܦܠܐ ܚ̈ܝܠܘܬܐ ܫܡܝ̈ܢܐ. ܘܐܪ̈ܥܢܝܐ ܕܒܥܠܡܐ. ܠܡܫܒܚܘ ܒܫܘܠܡܐ ܗܘ ܕܠܐ ܡܬܡܠܠ ܘܡܫܬܘܕܥ. ܡܕܡ ܕܚܝܠܐ ܠܐ ܣܦܩ ܘܐܦܠܐ ܡܫܬܟܚ. ܘܡܛܠ ܗܢܐ ܕܥܠܝܐ ܠܐ ܡܫܬܒܩ. ܡܕܡ ܕܡܛܠ ܐܠܗܐ ܠܐܠܡܝܢ ܕܬܫܒܘܚܬܐ ܠܗ. ˥ܐܡܝܢ ܘܐܡܝܢ[69]

Translation

Next, a profitable discourse of Mar Thomas.[70] God witnesses to me: If all the children of Adam—who have existed and who will exist, from the begin-

58. Copies of the four Mardin manuscripts were made available to me thanks to Columba Stewart, OSB (Hill Museum and Manuscript Library).

59. Titulus: GHK ܕܝܠܗ ܕܝ ܕܝܠܗ ܕܥܠ ܬܗܪܐ ܕܪܒܘܬܗ ܕܐܠܗܐ ܘܕܠܐ ܣܦܩܝܢ ܠܗ ܪ̈ܘܡܐ ܘܥܘܡ̈ܩܐ ܕܢܫܒܚܘܢܗ
F ܕܥܠ ܬܗܪܢܝܬܐ ܪܒܘܬܗ ܕܐܠܗܐ ܘܕܠܐ ܣܦܩ ܠܗ ܪ̈ܘܡܐ ܘܥܘܡ̈ܩܐ ܕܢܫܒܚܘܢ
L ܬܘܒ ܕܝܠܗ ܕܬܐܘܡܐ ܚܣܝܐ: ܥܠ ܬܗܪܐ ܕܪܒܘܬܗ ܕܐܠܗܐ ܘܕܠܐ ܣܦܩܝܢ ܠܗ ܪ̈ܘܡܐ ܘܥܘܡ̈ܩܐ ܕܢܫܒܚܘܢܗ
M ܥܠ ܬܗܪܐ ܕܪܒܘܬܗ ܕܐܠܗܐ ܘܕܠܐ ܣܦܩܝܢ ܠܗ ܪ̈ܘܡܐ ܘܥܘܡ̈ܩܐ ܕܢܫܒܚܘܢܗ. ܡܡܠܠܗ ܕܡܪܝ ܬܐܘܡܐ
N ܕܬܐܘܡܐ ܥܠ ܬܗܪܐ ܕܪܒܘܬܗ ܕܐܠܗܐ ܘܕܠܐ ܣܦܩܝܢ ܠܗ ܪ̈ܘܡܐ ܘܥܘܡ̈ܩܐ ܕܢܫܒܚܘܢܗ

60. ܕܐܠܗܘܢ GHKLM.

61. sg. FGHKMN.

62. om. FGHKLMN.

63. om. FGHKLMN.

64. pr. ܘ GHK.

65. lege ܘܐܬܡܪܘܗܝ FGHKLM.

66. GKLM, ܫܟܝܢ HN, ܫܟܚܝܢ F.

67. ˥ ܘܐܝܟ ܬܘܩܦܐ ܕܣܓܝ ܠܗܘܢ ܡܢܗ ܡܫܒܚܘܬܐ FLMN, ܘܐܝܟ ܬܘܩܦܐ ܕܣܓܝ ܠܗܘܢ ܡܢܗ ܡܫܒܚܐ GHK.

68. sg. GHKMN.

69. ˥ om. FGHKLMN.

70. Title: "Of the same on the amazement upon the magnificence of God and that neither the heights nor the depths are capable of praising him" GHK, "On the marvelous magnificence of God and that neither the heights nor the depths are capable of praising him" F, "Of Thomas on the amazement upon the magnificence of God and that neither the heights nor the depths are capable of praising him" L, "On the amazement upon the magnificence of God and that neither the heights nor the depths are

ning until the end—were alive—each having ten thousand mouths, and each mouth having ten thousand tongues, and each tongue having ten thousand words, and each word having ten thousand praises, and each praise having ten thousand blessings—they would be too few to praise the kindness of God toward people, whether at first, in the middle or at the end. [The number of] people would be too few in comparison to the places of rest[71] that are prepared for everyone, in accordance with his works and his level, and with how he has afflicted and exhausted[72] himself; and [even] if they consider [to have achieved][73] more than the apostles and [more] than the example of lowliness that our Lord had shown them,[74] they would be too few for what our Lord has prepared for them. "I consider—says Paul,—that the sufferings of this time are not comparable to the glory that will be revealed in us"[75] and neither are the arduous labors nor the afflictions of the Perfect [comparable] to the glory and delight that we will come to receive. "The thing that eye has not seen and ear has not heard, and the thing that God has prepared for those who love him and do his will[76] has not ascended to the heart of a person."[77]

capable of praising him, a discourse of Mar Thomas" M, "Of Thomas on the amazement upon the magnificence of God and that neither the heights nor the depths are capable of praising him" N.

71. of rest] om. FGHKLM.

72. emended based on the reading of FGHKLMN; the Paris ms provides a corrupted reading.

73. if they consider] if they suffer F] if they live GHKLMN.

74. and [more] than the example of lowliness that our Lord had shown them] according to the example of lowliness that our Lord had shown them FGHKLMN.

75. Rom 8:18.

76. and do his will] om. FGHKMN.

77. 1Cor 2:9.

Kyle Smith

5. A LAST DISCIPLE OF THE APOSTLES

The "Editor's" Preface, Rabbula's Rules, *and the Date of the* Book of Steps

This chapter suggests that the *Book of Steps* is less anomalous than scholars have previously imagined. The prevailing theory is that the text is a fourth-century witness to a marginal, proto-monastic (possibly Messalian), Syriac Christian community. Alternative interpretations about the origins of the text have hardly been considered. In an attempt to spur other revisionist studies of the text, this chapter challenges traditional notions about the authorship of the *Book of Steps.* The theory preliminarily advanced here is that the *Book of Steps* was written in reaction to the fifth-century institutionalization of Syriac asceticism under Bishop Rabbula of Edessa. In order to create plausible conditions for the serious consideration of this theory, the traditional interpretation of the text is deconstructed. Then, in order to provide a revised contextual framework for a renewed interpretation of the text, the *Book of Steps* is juxtaposed with Rabbula's *Rules.* As textual evidence for a date of authorship well into the fifth century, this chapter considers the "editor's" preface—a brief, hagiographical introduction to the author of the *Book of Steps* that was supposedly added by a later scribe. Considering the possibility that the editor's preface was not a later addition, but was rather an integral part of the original fifth-century composition, it is further argued that the *Book of Steps* could be a pseudepigraphon of sorts. To be sure, the *Book of Steps* is an anonymous work, even though parts of it have been attributed to various monastic authors. In the new interpretation advanced in this chapter, the reasons for the text's anonymity are called into question. Instead of trusting the editor that the text was written anonymously on account of the humility of its author, this chapter suggests that the preface was in fact written by the author of the thirty memre himself and was a rhetorical move designed to obscure the true origins of the *Book of Steps.* Under this interpretation the *Book of Steps* can thereby be read as a pious fraud—a supposedly first-century biblical commentary justifying the way of life of the Perfect and the Upright that was penned by none other than "a last disciple of the apostles."[1]

Confronting Messalian Proto-Monasticism

As students of the *Book of Steps* know well, the earliest studies of the text were largely concerned with debating its orthodoxy given an assumed connection to the Messalian controversy. As Robert Kitchen remarks in the introduction to his English translation of the text, "To mention the *Liber Graduum* to an earlier generation of scholars is to conjure up its alleged role in one of the on-going controversies of the late-fourth to early-fifth centuries—the Messalian controversy."[2] The presumption of this heretical association was based primarily on Michael Kmoskó's theory in his 1926 edition of the Syriac text. Kmoskó compiled, in a lengthy preface, a list of anti-Messalian references from numerous late ancient commentators.[3] On the basis of this reading of the text and Kmoskó's suggestion of a mid-fourth-century date of authorship concurrent with the rise of the Messalian controversy, the heretical proclivities of the community described in the *Book of Steps* were thoroughly indicted. Irenée Hausherr, while accepting with little reservation Kmoskó's characterization of the *Book of Steps* as a Messalian text, argued that it did not represent

1. The "editor" writes in his preface, "Since this blessed one desired to remain anonymous, and no other author tells us anything about him, and since we do not know precisely when he lived, we can only accept the tradition that he was one of the *last disciples of the Apostles*" (*BoS* Preface, *LG* 1:3–8).

2. Robert A. Kitchen and Martien F. G. Parmentier, *The Book of Steps: The Syriac Liber Graduum* (Kalamazoo, Mich.: Cistercian Publications, 2004), xviii–xxiv.

3. Michael Kmoskó, ed., *Liber Graduum,* Patrologia Syriaca 1.3 (Paris: Firmin-Didot, 1926), cxv–cxlix.

an *early* witness to Messalian thinking, but instead revealed well-developed communal and ascetic structures that must have matured from an early Messalian substrate. As such, Hausherr was inclined to date the text later than Kmoskó—not to the mid-fourth century, but likely to the early fifth century, or at least somewhere between 370 and 435 C.E.[4] For both Kmoskó and Hausherr interpretation of the *Book of Steps* and its probable date of authorship are premised upon the theory that the text is inextricably connected with some form of Messalianism. As a result, all of the earliest interpretations of the text began with an assessment of Messalian theology.[5]

Such theologically strident lines of inquiry were for the most part abandoned as philological, historical, and literary critical studies replaced inquisitions of orthodoxy. Nevertheless, the specter of Messalianism has been difficult to escape. In many ways it continues to haunt interpretations of the *Book of Steps.* One can hardly find a study that does not at some point at least address a footnote to the question of Messalianism. Even recently one finds defenders of Kmoskó's preferred mid-fourth-century date for the *Book of Steps* among scholars of the Messalian controversy.[6] Usually it is on account of the misgivings about manual labor that are so prominent in the *Book of Steps* that a Messalian connection is dredged up: the Perfect are not to labor in the fields, exchange money or goods in the marketplace, or even assuage the corporal decrepitude of the poor.[7] Rather, they fast, pray, teach, and perform a spiritual ministry.[8]

4. Irénée Hausherr, "Quanam Aetate Prodierit 'Liber Graduum?'" *Orientalia Christiana Periodica* 1 (1935): 495–502, and Hausherr, "L'erreur fondamentale et la logique du messalianisme," *Orientalia Christiana Periodica* 1 (1935): 328–60.

5. For an overview of the earliest scholarship on the *Book of Steps* linking it to the Messalian controversy, see Robert A. Ratcliff, "Steps Along the Way of Perfection: The *Liber Graduum* and Early Syrian Monasticism" (PhD diss., Emory University, 1988), 61–69.

6. See, for example, Klaus Fitschen, *Messalianismus und Antimessalianismus: Ein Beispiel ostkirchlicher Ketzergeschichte* (Göttingen: Vandenhoeck and Ruprecht, 1998), 108–19.

7. The author of the *Book of Steps* distinguishes the ministry of the Perfect both by explicitly stating what it *is* and by detailing what it is *not*—namely, the lesser ministry of the Upright. Consider the following passages: "The Perfect do not take wives, nor do they work in the field, nor acquire possessions, nor have a place to lay their heads on earth like their teacher" (*BoS* 15.13, *LG* 365:26–68:2). "Those who bind and loose in the world and buy and sell, owning possessions justly and treating the needy well while not treating anyone badly, are the Upright who are inferior to the Perfect" (*BoS* 15.9, *LG* 357:6–10). "It was to these Upright ones that our Lord said, 'If you are not pursuing Perfection, then satisfy the hungry, clothe the naked, visit the sick, give relief to the oppressed, visit those in prison and supply their needs, welcome strangers, and whatever you do to those,' thus our Lord says to these, 'you do to me'" (*BoS* 3.2, *LG* 48:21–49:1).

8. "Why do we not fast twice a week as it is written for the Upright? The Perfect fast every day. Why

In his assessment of wandering, non-laboring monks, Daniel Caner argues convincingly that "modern studies have tended to identify objections to manual labor with marginal or heretical ascetic groups such as 'Manicheans,' 'Messalians,' or 'circumcellions.' Moreover, they have treated such groups as separate historical phenomena, or rather, as distinct and isolated historical 'movements.'"[9] This, Caner says, merely perpetuates the labels that "orthodox" groups assigned to the practices of "heretical" communities. An example that Caner summons is the community described in the *Book of Steps,* which is in many ways disregarded as an anomaly in the wider scheme of ascetic movements within the Syriac milieu. But, as Caner shows, "an apostolic ascetic lifestyle characterized by wandering and material dependency was widely advocated and practiced in the fourth and fifth centuries all around the Roman Empire."[10] As Caner suggests, neither the bipartite community structure described in the *Book of Steps* nor the efforts by opposing parties to condemn non-laboring ascetics such as the Perfect was particularly anomalous in late antiquity. Caner's work demonstrates that there is no reason the *Book of Steps* must necessarily be linked with Messalianism or, for that matter, be considered the written testament of but a marginal Syriac Christian community.

Perhaps on the basis of Caner's conclusions one can suggest that the lingering bond in the scholarly imagination between the Messalian controversy and the *Book of Steps* is based in part on the plausible consensus opinion that the text was written in a contentious age of transition. To broadly generalize, that is to say that it was written between, on the one hand, the era of the unregulated, apostolic vagrancy of early Syrian asceticism—an era described in vivid prose not only by Peter Brown,[11] but more recently by Caner—and, on

do we not pray three times a day—as well as in the morning and in the evening—as it is written for the Upright? The Perfect praise [God] the whole day. Why do we not keep the Law of God and do alms, nor do we pray with them, as it is written for the Upright? . . . the Perfect perform the rites all their days and pray unceasingly before our Lord" (*BoS* 7.20, *LG* 184:24–85:8).

9. Daniel Caner, *Wandering, Begging Monks: Spiritual Authority and the Promotion of Monasticism in Late Antiquity* (Berkeley and Los Angeles: University of California Press, 2002), 13.

10. Caner, *Wandering, Begging Monks,* 14.

11. Of course, the obvious reference here is to Brown's characterization of the Syrian "holy man" in his famous article on the subject; see Peter R. Brown, "The Rise and Function of the Holy Man in Late Antiquity," *Journal of Roman Studies* 61 (1971): 80–101. Additionally, Brown discusses the Perfect of the *Book of Steps* in his overview of asceticism in Christianity; see Brown, *The Body and Society: Men, Women, and Sexual Renunciation in Early Christianity* (New York: Columbia University Press, 1988), 334–38.

the other hand, the rise of coenobitism, monastic rules, and ecclesiastical oversight. Because this age of transition in ascetic and monastic circles was contemporaneous with the Messalian controversy, and because a parallel (deserved or not) has historically been drawn between Messalian thinking and the community presented in the *Book of Steps,* we are left with two mutually reinforcing propositions that end up being ascribed the weight of an argument. In other words, the implicit presumption that one can glean lurking beneath the surface of scholarly studies is that the *Book of Steps* is a fourth-century text for two reasons: (1) because it presents a community before the age of developed monasticism—the term "proto-monasticism" is often applied; and (2) because even though a direct Messalian connection is nowadays regarded as an overstatement, the text at least reeks of enough of a Messalian influence to lead some to conclude that it can only be a fourth-century text.[12]

There is little justification, however, to present as evidence of a fourth-century date of authorship either the text's supposed "Messalianism" or its "proto-monasticism." As Hausherr's work indicates, even if one is insistent on connecting the Messalian controversy with the *Book of Steps,* there is no reason that the *Book of Steps* could not have been written well into the fifth century.[13] And, in Syriac Christianity, the transition to the prevalence of a more coenobitic form of monastic asceticism did not truly begin in earnest until the fifth century—and as late as the sixth century in the geographic area, later home to the Church of the East, where the *Book of Steps* seems to have originated.[14] To say that the ascetic community presented by the *Book of Steps* is "proto-monastic" thus says little about the date it was probably written. Moreover, calling the *Book of Steps* "proto-monastic" can be as ideological-

12. The conclusion about Messalianism was challenged over fifty years ago, but still seems to be the starting point for any discussion about the *Book of Steps;* see Arthur Vööbus, "Liber Graduum: Some Aspects of Its Significance for the History of Early Syrian Asceticism," in *Charisteria Iohanni Kopp octogenerio oblata,* 108–28, Papers of the Estonian Theological Society in Exile 7 (Stockholm: Estonian Theological Society in Exile, 1954). To my knowledge the issue of "proto-monasticism" has not been addressed at length.

13. As the very title of Columba Stewart's book on the Messalian controversy indicates, the controversy raged at least until the Council of Ephesus; see Stewart, "*Working the Earth of the Heart*"*: The Messalian Controversy in History, Texts, and Language to A.D. 431* (Oxford: Clarendon Press, 1991), 42–51.

14. Abraham of Kashkar, the sixth-century founder of the monastery on Mount Izla near Nisibis, is the preeminent example of the later monastic reforms and coenobitic restructuring in the eastern regions of Syriac Christianity; see Sabrino Chialà, *Abramo di Kashkar e la sua comunità: La rinascita del monachesimo siro-orientale* (Comunità di Bose: Edizioni Qiqajon, 2005).

ly loaded as calling it "Messalian." In the context of Syriac Christianity, "proto-monasticism" implies the ecclesiological and doctrinal development from a more primitive (or even heretical) form of Christian practice to an apotheosis once the antecedent practice has fully morphed into an officially sanctioned orthodox one. In his published works on the *Book of Steps,* Kitchen uses the term "proto-monastic" in scare quotes, citing Sebastian Brock and Sidney Griffith, who tend to use the term likewise.[15] For instance, Kitchen suggests "the real significance of the *Liber Graduum* is not ultimately in its Biblical and extra-Biblical witnesses, nor in its Messalian connections, but in the historical role it played during the late fourth century transition from the 'pre/proto-monastic' period of early Syriac asceticism to the subsequent era when the Greek image of Egyptian monasticism colored the lens through which we are allowed to perceive Syrian asceticism."[16] While the *denotation* of "proto-monastic" is relatively innocuous, indicating—as Kitchen, Brock, Griffith, and others use the term—simply a community or a form of asceticism that existed prior to the formal establishment of Greek-influenced coenobitic monasticism, the *connotation* of the term seems to me to be more slippery in that it carries negative theological valuations of ascetic practices prior to what would

15. Brock puts the *Book of Steps* in the "first stage" of Syriac ascetic development: "*Première étape:* la tradition primitive du troisième et surtout du quatrième siècle, que j'appellerai 'le proto-monachisme.' Nos meilleurs témoins sont les écrits d'Aphraate, d'Ephrem et de l'auteur anonyme du *Liber Graduum,* c'est-à-dire du *Livre des Degrés*"; see Sebastian P. Brock, "Le monachisme syriaque: histoire et spiritualité," in *Le Monachisme Syriaque: Aux premiers siècles de l'Église. IIe–Début VIIe siècle,* 21–31, Patrimoine Syriaque: Actes du colloque V. (Antélias, Lebanon: Éditions du Cerf, 1998).

Griffith notes, "modern scholars prefer to speak of the period of St. Ephraem's own Nisibene ministry, and of earlier times, as the period of premonasticism or protomonasticism"; see Sidney H. Griffith, "Asceticism in the Church of Syria: The Hermeneutics of Early Syrian Monasticism," in *Asceticism,* edited by Richard Valantasis and Vincent L. Wimbush, 237 (New York: Oxford University Press, 1995).

16. Kitchen, "Conflict on the Stairway to Heaven: The Anonymity of Perfection in the Syriac *Liber Graduum,*" in *Symposium Syriacum VII: Uppsala University, Department of Asian and African Languages, 11–14 August 1996,* edited by René Lavenant, 211–20 (Rome: Pontificio Instituto Orientale, 1998).

Adam Becker discusses this sort of "Egyptianization," too, by which more is meant than just the trend in Syriac late antiquity to look to and draw upon for spiritual sustenance the monastic literature of and about the Egyptian desert. The influx of Egyptian monastic texts into Syria, according to Becker, "effected a rewriting of monastic history, thus obscuring the origins of Syriac Christianity and early Syriac monasticism." It is a process that Becker says belongs to "a broader erasure of the Syriac past" that "led to a transformation of Syriac monastic historiography"—a transformation, that is, of the indigenous, Syriac tradition; see Becker, *Fear of God and the Beginning of Wisdom: The School of Nisibis and Christian Scholastic Culture in Late Antique Mesopotamia* (Philadelphia: University of Pennsylvania Press, 2006), 173–74.

later come to be known and accepted as monasticism proper.[17] Indeed, "proto-monastic" may well be read to indicate less a period of *time* prior to the influence of Greco-Egyptian forms of monasticism than an ecclesiological *situation* wherein a particular community (the one from which the *Book of Steps* derived, for instance) resists these forms of asceticism in favor of retaining its indigenous communal and ecclesiological structures. As such, "proto-monasticism" says something more than just the period to which the community in question can be dated, and I do not believe that it is pedantic to therefore insist on caution in applying the term.[18] If the *Book of Steps,* as suggested in this chapter, is in part a response to Rabbula's fifth-century regulation of Syrian asceticism, then its importance as a textual witness demonstrating how an autochthonous, and perhaps liminal, Syriac Christian community stood in struggle against an encroaching and hybrid Edessene style of asceticism cannot be overestimated.

In addition to claims about Messalianism and proto-monasticism, those who date the *Book of Steps* to the fourth century typically advance two other arguments. First, the sense of crisis and trial that pervades much of the text is linked to the mid-fourth-century persecution of the Persian king Shapur II. The *Book of Steps,* it is suggested, was likely written during, or in the wake of, these persecutions. This is, however, a very unconvincing argument for two reasons: there is little internal or external evidence that would lead one to conclude that the *Book of Steps* was written following this persecution in particular; and the Syriac martyrological literature can hardly be relied upon as historical evidence documenting the time, scope, and geographic extent of Shapur's persecution.[19] Moreover, if the *Book of Steps* was supposedly written following a per-

17. The use of the term "proto-monasticism" as indicating something less than favorable can be seen, for example, in Tim Vivian and Apostolos N. Athanassakis, "Montanism, Heresy, or Proto-Monasticism? The Martyrdom of St. Theodotos of Ancyra and of the Seven Virgins with Him," *Studia Monastica* 44 (2002): 239–92.

18. Columba Stewart refines Reinhart Staats's assessment of Messalianism to say, "The imagery and terminology associated with Messalianism is no more and no less than a dramatic manifestation of Syrian Christianity in Greek guise, and can be considered utterly heterodox only from the viewpoint of the orthodoxy of a Greek-speaking imperial church." One might employ similar logic when reassessing the use of the term "proto-monastic" vis-à-vis the community presented in the *Book of Steps;* see Stewart, "*Working the Earth,*" 10.

19. Kitchen acknowledges this, too, conceding, "there is too little evidence to be able to pinpoint the identity of any perpetrator [of violence against the community of the *Book of Steps*]"; see Kitchen and Parmentier, *Book of Steps,* liv. For a reassessment of the traditional explanation of Shapur's persecution, see Kyle Smith, "The Persian Persecution: Martyrdom, Politics, and Religious Identity in Late Ancient Syriac Christianity" (PhD diss., Duke University, 2011).

secution—or at least in an era when Persian Christian communities may have perceived that they were being persecuted—then there are other possibilities to choose from—namely, the "persecution" that began about 420 C.E. under Yazdgard I.[20] But it is far from clear that the text does in fact describe a "persecution" in the sense of a sustained campaign of violence or intimidation against Christians, such as was the case, for example, earlier in the West under Diocletian.[21] The passage in memra 30 cited as evidence of "persecution" speaks in such broad terms that it is unclear whether the author is waxing generally about Christians (or even speaking biblically, given the allusion to Acts 14), or whether he is speaking about specific, contemporary events.[22] And *where* exactly was the persecution we are looking for? Localizing the text's probable place of origin would be helpful in this regard, but the only useful geographic reference provided in the *Book of Steps* is to the Lesser Zab River, an eastern tributary of the central Tigris that separates Adiabene and Bet Garmai.[23] Even if, on the basis of this reference, we can reasonably approximate the geographical area in which the *Book of Steps* was written, this alone is not enough evidence to then conclude that it must have been Shapur's persecution that resulted in the crisis seemingly described in the text.

20. Lucas Van Rompay, "Impetuous Martyrs? The Situation of the Persian Christians in the Last Years of Yazdgard I (419–420)," in *Martyrium in Multidisciplinary Perspective: Memorial Louis Reekmans*, edited by Mathijs Lamberigts, Louis Reekmans, and Peter van Deun, 363–76 (Leuven: Peeters, 1995).

21. For an overview of the *Acts of the Persian Martyrs* and the early periods of "persecution" in Persia, see J. Rist, "Die Verfolgung der Christen in spätantiken Sasanidenreich: Ursachen, Verlauf und Folgen," *Oriens Christianus* 80 (1996): 17–42. For an excellently argued rejection of the view that Christians were outsiders to Persian society, and for a reinterpretation of Christian martyr texts as a means of negotiating Christian belonging in Persia, see Richard E. Payne, "Christianity and Iranian Society in Late Antiquity, ca. 500–700" (PhD diss., Princeton University, 2010).

22. "The disciples of faith also endure the heretics, are persecuted by the idolaters—because they are their opponents—and, being killed, become martyrs. They are known as martyrs of faith and as [martyrs] of love. The martyrs of faith are persecuted and killed by idolaters and pagans because they resolutely confront them for their evil doctrine, tearing down their altars and enduring wherever they are persecuted in order not to become vain idolaters in the land of the Lord our God, but [in order to] 'Serve only the Lord God who made heaven and earth and all which is in them'" (*BoS* 30.4, *LG* 869:14–72:5). On the "tearing down" of pagan altars, see the discussion of the martyrs under Yazdgard I, some of whom were supposedly killed for demolishing Zoroastrian fire altars and refusing to rebuild them, in Van Rompay, "Impetuous Martyrs," 364–68.

23. "The teacher has the right to say to one of his disciples, 'Go among the tax-collectors and sinners and adulterers and among the wicked and heathens,' because he knows he is a good swimmer and is able to cross over the Euphrates while it is stormy and the sea while it is troubled. He commands his other disciple, who knows that he is not able to cross over the Lesser Zaba, 'You should not talk with such and such a person, and you [should not] go to such and such a place'" (*BoS* 30.14, *LG* 893:23–96:5).

Given this lack of evidence, it seems that hypothesizing Shapur's mid-fourth-century persecution as the culprit is merely a subtle way of localizing chronologically and geographically the two premises that have already been assumed—namely, the proto-monasticism and Messalianism supposedly inherent in the text. Add these former premises together with the conclusions drawn about the persecution in the text, and it appears that the only possible conclusion is that the Messalian-leaning, proto-monastic community described in the *Book of Steps* suffered under Shapur's tyranny sometime in the fourth century and probably somewhere in Adiabene.[24] But again, this way of reading the text is based almost entirely on assumptions taken over in the wake of Kmoskó's theories about the text's Messalianism and what "monasticism" might have looked like among Syriac communities in the Christian east. This is a plausible theory based on the available evidence, but other ways of reading the text are warranted.

The "Editor's" Preface

There is one final reason that the *Book of Steps* is often attributed to the fourth century: the witness of the so-called editor's preface. This brief, rather hagiographical introduction to the *Book of Steps* has typically been given short shrift in studies of the text.[25] Kmoskó discusses the editor's preface briefly in the preface to his own edition, but the potential importance of the editor's preface has, I think, been overlooked. Typically, following Kmoskó, the preface is read as an early, but nevertheless secondary, addition to the thirty memre of the *Book of Steps*—a preface penned by a later, anonymous editor who vigorously champions not so much the biblical interpretation, the theological instruction, or the bipartite community of Perfect and Upright presented in the text, but rather the holiness and apostolic credentials of the anonymous *author* of the *Book of Steps* himself.

24. On the martyrs of Adiabene during Shapur's "Great Persecution," see Gernot Wiessner, *Zur Märtyrerüberlieferung aus der Christenverfolgung Schapurs II* (Göttingen: Vandenhoeck and Ruprecht, 1967).

25. In her extensive study of prefaces in Syriac literature, Eva Riad does not consider (or even acknowledge) the preface to the *Book of Steps.* This is especially disappointing, since the preface to the *Book of Steps* is very different from the rhetorical tropes common to Syriac prefaces that Riad outlines; see Riad, *Studies in the Syriac Preface,* Studia Semitica Upsaliensia 11 (Uppsala, Sweden: Uppsala University, 1988).

The preface does not show up very often in the manuscripts that preserve portions of the *Book of Steps.* Of the fifteen manuscripts to which Kmoskó had access, only two retain the preface.[26] This is, however, not terribly surprising, since the great majority of the extant manuscripts in which parts of the *Book of Steps* are preserved contain only a fraction of the full text. For example, just three manuscripts (mss. α, β, and R) contain more than five of the thirty original memre, and most of the other manuscripts preserve only a single memra.[27] If the *Book of Steps,* as the manuscript evidence suggests, was circulating in such a fragmentary form, then it is no wonder that the (dispensable) preface is found solely in those manuscripts that preserve the majority of the text. Indeed, even assuming that a scribe had access to all of the *Book of Steps,* there would be little reason for him to include the preface if he was interested in transcribing only a couple of memre.[28]

Kmoskó's base manuscript, which he calls ms. α (Paris *Syr.* 201), is a twelfth- or thirteenth-century manuscript, and it is the only complete text of the *Book of Steps* that we have. In addition to ms. α, the editor's preface is found in Kmoskó's second most important witness, what he calls ms. β (BL *Add. 14,613*), a tenth-century manuscript that preserves eighteen of the thirty memre. Finally, the third manuscript in which a substantial number of memre can be found is ms. R (St. Mark's *Syr.* 103), a seventh- or eighth-century manuscript from the Syrian Orthodox monastery of St. Mark's in Jerusalem. Ms. R closely parallels ms. β, but it is not likely from the same manuscript tradition. The preface is not preserved in what *remains* of ms. R, but there is evidence that the preface might originally have been included in the manuscript. Because ms. R was not available to Kmoskó until his edition was nearly complete, he addresses it only

26. Kmoskó provides a helpful conspectus chart of which manuscripts contain which sections of the *Book of Steps;* see Kmoskó, *Liber Graduum,* ix. While Kmoskó's preface is unquestionably the starting point for any study of the *Book of Steps,* renewed study of the manuscripts that contain memre from the *Book of Steps* is necessary. Of particular importance are the *names* under which the memre were transmitted—Philoxenus, Evagrius, John the Solitary, et al.

27. In addition to the manuscripts referred to by Kmoskó, one more manuscript has recently come to light in the library of the Coptic Deir al-Surian in Egypt. It probably dates from the tenth century, and it retains both the preface and long extracts from twenty-eight memre. Unfortunately, this manuscript is not yet readily available for further research; Van Rompay, oral communication.

28. Interestingly, there is a common theme in the manuscripts in which just one or two memre are found. Later scribes were interested in memre addressing issues common to ascetic communities in particular—prayer, fasting, and bodily discipline. Memre that deal more explicitly with the Upright, however, are found only in manuscripts that preserve large sections of the *Book of Steps.*

in an appendix, but this fact should not devalue its importance as a textual witness. Kmoskó explains that although the first twenty-one folios of ms. R are indeed missing, one can surmise from what remains (as I will explain) that it was once a *complete* text of thirty memre, including the preface.[29]

Kmoskó's conclusion that the preface was a secondary insertion by a later editor (and not part of the original text of the *Book of Steps*) seems to rest on the assumption that the preface is unique to the manuscript tradition represented by mss. α and β. Ms. α is the only complete extant manuscript, and it is quite late, dating from the twelfth or thirteenth century. But it is ms. C (BL *Add. 18,812*), a much earlier manuscript probably from the seventh or eighth century, that, according to Kmoskó, preserves the earliest known version of the *Book of Steps* because it retains the most ancient biblical quotations. Assuming Kmoskó is correct that ms. C does preserve the most "original" reading of the *Book of Steps* and more ancient biblical quotations, what does this tell us about the preface? Very little, it seems to me. Like so many other manuscripts that transmit parts of the *Book of Steps,* ms. C preserves only two memre (memre 16 and 19). It does not mean much that the preface is not also preserved along with these memre. The biblical quotations may be more ancient in ms. C than they are in mss. α and β, but this indicates only that mss. α and β are from a different textual tradition, or are possibly "updated" versions of the text, and not (as Kmoskó would have it) that the broader conclusion that the preface was always absent from the manuscript line from which ms. C was copied.

Admittedly, we have a very odd situation in that there is only one complete text of the *Book of Steps,* which is found in quite a late manuscript, while there are excerpts that antedate the complete text by several centuries. Kmoskó, surely recognizing this situation, contends that nothing is certain about the author of the recension from which mss. α and β are derived; "However," he continues, "if it is weighed carefully that texts α and β are quite similar, then it seems probable that the author of this more recent recension of the *Liber Graduum*

29. Kmoskó, *Liber Graduum,* ccxciii–cccvi. The scribe who copied ms. R inserted the name "Philo" in the margin of the final memra. As Kitchen notes, "the scribe apparently could not stand the thought of anonymity [of the author of the *Book of Steps*] and while Kmoskó made a tentative suggestion about Philo's identity, he did not seem all that convinced himself"; see Kitchen and Parmentier, *Book of Steps,* xxvii.

was the same person who added that preface to the entire book shared by both codices [i.e., mss. α and β]."[30] This conclusion is unfounded. If ms. C or one of the other pre-tenth-century manuscripts (mss. A, B, D, E, R, and Z) included a large number of memre without also including the preface, then one could hypothesize that the preface was a later addition—possibly one originating with the manuscript tradition from which α and β are descended. But of the manuscripts dated prior to the tenth century, ms. R is in the only one that preserves more than four memre, and, as noted, it may well have been a complete manuscript had it not been partially destroyed. Lacking evidence in the earliest manuscripts, it is pure speculation to draw conclusions not only about the preface, but also about the vast majority of memre (twenty-three out of thirty!) that are absent from the textual tradition (except in ms. R) until the tenth century. More importantly, perhaps, even though the preface is not extant in any manuscript older than the tenth century, there is reason to believe that the editor of ms. R was well aware of the preface. Ms. R is acephalous: the preface (if there was one), the first six memre, and most of the seventh are lost. Nevertheless, the colophon at the end of memra thirty in ms. R rehashes what we already know from the preface: it indicates that a blessed one, who did not want his name known, wrote all the memre.[31] This seems to me to be good evidence that the preface existed in the seventh or eighth century when ms. R was written. Certainly the colophon of ms. R does not prove that the preface was an original part of the composition of the *Book of Steps,* but it *does* suggest that the preface is in no way unique to the manuscript tradition of mss. α and β.

Interestingly, the idea that the preface was a secondary addition works to reinforce the conclusion that the rest of the *Book of Steps* is a fourth-century text. The basis for this conclusion is the passage in the preface that indicates that the author of the memre was a "peer in the things of God" to three Greek fathers who flourished in the final decades of the fourth century: "Gregory the Great [i.e., Gregory of Nazianzus], blessed Basil the Great, and blessed Evagrius."[32] This comparison to Gregory, Basil, and Evagrius is important, for

30. Kmoskó, *Liber Graduum,* x. "De auctore huius recensionis eiusque aetate nil certi constat; si autem perpendatur textum α et β quam maxime affines esse, probabile videtur auctorem recensionis recentioris Libri Graduum eundem virum fuisse, qui et illam praefationem utrique Codici communem toti Libro praemisit."

31. Kmoskó, *Liber Graduum,* ccxciv–ccxcv.

32. *BoS,* Preface, *LG* 5:14–18.

it is the only time in the text that someone who lived later than the first century is mentioned by name. In fact, other than the glancing reference to Thecla and Thecla's "evil and cruel" parents,[33] every other person identified by name in the text is a *biblical* character. And then we have this remark about three Greeks from Asia Minor.

These four names—Thecla, Gregory, Basil, and Evagrius—merit consideration. Finding the name Thecla in memra 27 militates against a fourth-century date of composition for the *Book of Steps.* In addition to being an early Syriac reference to the Thecla narrative, a point that has escaped notice in studies of the spread of Thecla's cult, the mention of Thecla appears to presuppose both the existence of a Syriac version of the Thecla story and, probably, considerable familiarity with it as well.[34] For unless readers of the *Book of Steps* were quite familiar with the story of Thecla, such a glancing reference to her would not make much sense. Valentina Calzolari's research on the cult of St. Thecla in the Armenian sources indicates (confirming Conybeare's earlier hypothesis) that there was probably not a Syriac version of the *Acts of Paul and Thecla* until the early fifth century.[35] If the Conybeare-Calzolari hypothesis is correct, then one would have to question a fourth-century date of authorship for memra 27.

The reference to Gregory, Basil, and Evagrius is just as vexing. Robert Kitchen comments on the rather out-of-place comparison to the two Cappadocians and the monk from Pontus by saying, "Since all three gained renown in the late fourth century, the editor could not have done his work before that period."[36] This is certainly true. Logistically, however, it is unlikely that the preface was written even at the very end of the fourth century. Evagrius, the

33. *BoS* 27.3, *LG* 772:4–9.

34. For a major study on the cult of Thecla and its spread throughout the late ancient Christian world, see Stephen J. Davis, *The Cult of St. Thecla: A Tradition of Women's Piety in Late Antiquity* (Oxford: Oxford University Press, 2001). In response to Davis's book, Catherine Burris and Lucas Van Rompay wrote two articles about Thecla in Syriac Christianity. The reference to Thecla found here in memra 27 should be added to the data that Burris and Van Rompay compiled; see Burris and Van Rompay, "Thecla in Syriac Christianity: Preliminary Observations," *Hugoye: Journal of Syriac Studies* 5 (2002): 225–36, and "Some Further Notes on Thecla in Syriac Christianity," *Hugoye: Journal of Syriac Studies* 6 (2003): 337–42.

35. F. C. Conybeare, *The Armenian Apology and Acts of Apollonius and Other Monuments of Early Christianity,* 2nd ed. (New York: Macmillan, 1896), 59, and Valentina Calzolari, "Notes sur la traduction arménienne du texte syriaque des Actes de Thècle," in *Proceedings of the Fifth International Conference on Armenian Linguistics: McGill University, Montreal, Quebec, Canada, May 1–5, 1995,* edited by Dora Sakayan, 233–43 (New York: Delmar, 1996).

36. Kitchen and Parmentier, *Book of Steps,* l.

last of the three Greeks named herein to die, was not dead until 399 C.E. It is not impossible, but it is rather improbable to suppose that the author of the editor's preface—on stylistic grounds undoubtedly written by a native Syriac speaker—would have had reason to consider Evagrius enough of an enduring blessed one by 399 C.E. to want to compare him with the author of the *Book of Steps.* Additionally, there is the textual evidence: Antoine Guillaumont and others who have examined the Syriac (and Armenian) Evagriana propose that Evagrius did not exist in Syriac until well into the fifth century.[37] Unless Evagrius's reputation was firmly cemented in Syriac ascetic circles, it would make no sense for the author of the preface to compare the author of the *Book of Steps*—a "prophet" and "a last disciple of the apostles"—to Evagrius. Thus it is highly unlikely that the editor's preface to the *Book of Steps* was written before the end of the fourth century.

Demonstrating that the *terminus post quem* of the preface to the *Book of Steps* is probably somewhere around 430 C.E. does little to help ascertain when the thirty memre of the *Book of Steps* were written—if, of course, the two were in fact written separately and by different authors. Additionally, it is important to remember that establishing the *terminus post quem* of the preface does not entail that the rest of the *Book of Steps* had to have been written prior to the turn of the fifth century; unless the preface and the memre were written at the same time, the *terminus post quem* of the preface cannot be used to definitively date the memre one way or the other. And although it is certainly possible that the preface was written subsequent to the memre, there are reasons for supposing that the preface was *not* a later editor's addition, but was rather an integral part of the anonymous author's original scheme. As such, more than just being read alongside the rest of the *Book of Steps,* the preface could be considered a hermeneutical key to the text.

The preface is quite short. At not even four full columns of Syriac text, it accounts for less than one percent of the *Book of Steps.* Nevertheless, it says a lot. At the outset the author of the preface claims several things about the author of the *Book of Steps,* calling him "that blessed one who published this simple doctrine of his."[38] We are told that because the blessed one desired ano-

37. Antoine Guillaumont, *"Les Képhalaia gnostica" d'Évagre le Pontique et l'histoire de l'origénisme chez les Grecs et chez les Syriens,* Patristica Sorbonensia 5 (Paris: Éditions du Seuil, 1962).

38. *BoS,* Preface, *LG* 2.1–2.

nymity, and because no one else says anything about him, "we can only accept the tradition that he was one of the last disciples of the Apostles."[39] Moreover, we are told that he was one of the first teachers to write in Syriac, and that his style is that of an ancient one in the Syriac language.[40] He "was a great and perfect man who ranks with the apostles and prophets, like Agabus and his companions who are mentioned in Acts."[41] He did not learn what he teaches in schools or from wise men, and "the simplicity of his speech shows that he was not a scholarly writer."[42] Instead of "an account of his great achievements of the kind that we find in the biographies of fathers like Gregory the Great, blessed Basil the Great, and blessed Evagrius,"[43] we are given a long quotation from the "last section of the last memra of his work . . . in order that the greatness and power of this person of God's spiritual understanding might be clear and manifest to the reader."[44] This supposed final section is an admonition to the cynics, to those who might "reject the testimonies of the Scriptures—of the prophets, of our Lord and of the Apostles—by saying, 'Who knows whether this is true?'"[45] Effectively, the quotation from the "last section of the last memra" is a justification of the prophecy of the blessed one who wrote the work and a plea that his words should be heeded even if he wrought no signs or miracles in conjunction with his prophecy.[46]

Robert Murray, who acknowledged that the *Book of Steps* "could be a conservative work of the fifth century," famously insisted, "there *is* something 'sectarian,' something isolated and defensive, about the *Liber Graduum*."[47] Perhaps the most insistently defensive aspect of the text can be found right here in the preface. The author of the preface seems overly keen to ensure that the author of the *Book of Steps* gets a fair hearing. Not only does he argue that

39. *BoS,* Preface, *LG* 2.3–9.
40. *BoS,* Preface, *LG* 2.9–10.
41. *BoS,* Preface, *LG* 4.7–10.
42. *BoS,* Preface, *LG* 4.10–14.
43. *BoS,* Preface, *LG* 5.14–18.
44. *BoS,* Preface, *LG* 2.13–18.
45. *BoS,* Preface, *LG* 5.21–23.

46. The quotation supposedly preserved from the last memra is not from what is now known as memra 30. In ms. α there is in fact a brief, partly illegible, thirty-*first* memra that is effectively just a recitation of the quotation found in the preface. Unfortunately, one can only speculate about this memra. Whether memra 31 ever existed independently (it is not attested by any other manuscript), or whether it was added after memra 30 by the copyist who transcribed ms. α so that the preface would make more sense, is a puzzling question.

47. Robert Murray, *Symbols of Church and Kingdom: A Study in Early Syriac Tradition,* rev. ed. (London: T. and T. Clark; Piscataway, N.J.: Gorgias Press, 2004), 36.

the author of the *Book of Steps* is a "last disciple of the Apostles," but he is also punctilious in insisting that those who reject the teachings of these memre do so at their own peril and can be compared to those naysayers who also reject "the testimonies of the Scriptures . . . [and] our Lord."[48] The writer of the preface preemptively counters those who might dismiss the *Book of Steps* as uninspired and bereft of miracles by claiming that "if the prophets of our time do not perform any signs, it is because our Lord does not want to perform signs through them, seeing that in our time everybody believes in him, and whoever does not believe in the ancient signs will not believe in recent ones either."[49]

Are these the words of a later proponent of the *Book of Steps?* Possibly. But how does our reading of the text change if we ask: what if these words in the preface that justify the text and its author were penned by the same person? Read this way, the *Book of Steps* goes from being merely an anonymous, hard-to-place text to a sort of pseudepigraphon—a text by a late ancient author who purports to speak with the authority of an ancient one, indeed one who was a disciple of the Apostles.[50] Our author leaves the dirty work of establishing his identity to his alter ego, the admonishing editor who stops cold those who are foolish enough to doubt the veracity of a text with apostolic links. Indeed, the preface is an example of measured caution. The editor, affecting the guise of the discoverer of the text, is silent about where he found it and how he came to know of its existence. Since our author claims no name for himself, and since we do not know when he lived, and since no one else speaks

48. *BoS,* Preface, *LG* 5.21–23.

49. *BoS,* Preface, *LG* 8.22–9.3.

50. This would not be a unique situation in Syrian literature. The author of the *Book of the Holy Hierotheos* wrote under the guise of a disciple of Dionysius the Areopagite. In the brief preface to this text, the one who postures as an anonymous translator claims he has been asked to translate "from Greek into Syriac that mystic and holy book of illustrious words"; see Fred Shipley Marsh, *The Book Which Is Called the Book of the Holy Hierotheos: With Extracts from the Prolegomena and Commentary of Theodosios of Antioch, and from the "Book of Excerpts" and Other Works of Gregory Bar-Hebraeus* (London: Text and Translation Society, 1927). More recently Karl Pingérra has argued that there are two different layers to the *Book of the Holy Hierotheos,* carving out early and late (Evagrian and Dionysian) sections; see Pingérra, *All-Erlösung und All-Einheit: Studien zum "Buch des heiligen Hierotheos" und seiner Rezeption in der syrisch-orthodoxen Theologie* (Wiesbaden: Reichert, 2002).

Quite famously, Ps.-Dionysius himself claims apostolic roots. The author of the preface to *Book of Steps,* if we can consider it an analogous situation, is more circumspect than Ps.-Dionysius and claims that the author of the memre only "ranks" among those mentioned in Acts and, by deduction, was probably one of them, but *which* one is wisely left unspecified.

of him, "we can only accept the *tradition* that he was one of the last disciples of the Apostles." Whence this tradition derives is unsaid, and, on the basis of the sharp warnings elsewhere in the preface, it does not need to be explained. Invoking the "tradition" that the author was a disciple is sufficient in itself, and this claim is only bolstered by the assessment that the author wrote in an ancient Syriac style[51] that bespeaks a simplicity unencumbered by training in rhetoric—this, of course, in contradistinction to Gregory, Basil, and Evagrius. The comparison of our anonymous author to these three Greeks is ingenious in its subtlety. The quotation in the preface that is said to be the last section of the last memra displays the author's holiness and the legitimacy of his inspired teachings, and this quotation, we are told, is purposefully given in lieu of a hagiographical account. Thus the editor, in comparing our author to Gregory, Basil, and Evagrius, quietly trumps them, for they—*educated Greeks*—require biographical accounts of their great deeds; for our author, on the other hand, it is his connection to "Agabus and his companions who are mentioned in *Acts*"[52] that serves as sufficient evidence of the truth of his words.

Biblical Interpretation in the Book of Steps

The link with the disciples mentioned in Acts seems especially important to the author of the *Book of Steps.* On five different occasions the Protomartyr Stephen is cited as an icon of fortitude in the face of suffering and violence. When discussing the martyrs of faith and the martyrs of love in memra 30, Stephen is invoked as the example to follow.[53] It is striking that no later "Christian" martyr is ever mentioned by name, though the author has ample opportunity to adduce the example of many. That no heralded martyrs are mentioned would be a strong indication to late ancient readers that the author, as the preface suggests, is an heir to the apostles—and it bolsters the "editor's" case that the author's teaching is an ancient one. Indeed, the author's silence on the topic of the trials of earlier Christians is remarkable. Stephen, moreover, is an excellent example of how the author of the *Book of Steps* reads the New Testament to advance a type of biblical exegesis that supports a division between Perfect and Upright. Stephen, the author is sure to make clear

51. *BoS,* Preface, *LG* 4.15.

52. *BoS,* Preface, *LG* 4.7–10.

53. *BoS* 30.4, *LG* 873:4–6.

when he first mentions him in memra 3, "was killed while teaching the word and not while giving material alms,"[54] the task for which he was initially chosen by the apostles. That is, he was martyred while acting the part of a Perfect one who engages in spiritual ministry and not while giving alms and engaging in the material ministry indicative of an Upright one.

Stephen is not the only example of how the author of the *Book of Steps* interprets the New Testament in such a way as to support his distinction between the Perfect and the Upright. The entirety of the text, as others have more or less pointed out, albeit with certain qualifications, is an extended exercise in biblical exegesis.[55] The first sentence of the first memra is an exhortation to "inquire into the words of our Lord one by one."[56] The subsequent memre support this agenda as the author defends a division of people into the Perfect and the Upright, often freely expanding upon the words of Jesus to support this interpretation. Needless to say, the author's *bona fides* as a disciple of the apostles—he is no mere scholar of the Bible—is a substantive aid in advancing the ancientness and purity of his exegesis over and against those who do not share a fondness for his ecclesiastical arrangements. The author's text, then, is in large part a biblical commentary (in a supposedly ancient style of the Syriac language, no less) that purports to be a pure reading of the Bible from an apostolic perspective. It is a reading unencumbered by theological disputes, competing hermeneutical agendas, or the ornate prose and rhetorical education that is shrewdly criticized in the preface.

Explaining the paradoxical nature of commentary, Michel Foucault explains that "commentary must say for the first time what ha[s] . . . already been said, and must tirelessly repeat what ha[s] . . . never been said." Foucault goes on to make a subtle, yet important distinction between "the text itself" and the commentary *on* the text: commentary, he explains, "allows us to say something other than the text itself, but on condition that it is this text itself which is said, and in a sense completed."[57] Foucault's paradox (wherein the

54. *BoS* 30.4, *LG* 77:25–26.

55. See the article by René Roux in this volume. For studies specific to the use of particular biblical passages in parts of the *Book of Steps,* see, for example, Fiona J. Parsons, "The Nature of the Gospel Quotations in the Syriac *Liber Graduum*" (PhD diss., University of Birmingham, UK, 1969).

56. *BoS* 1.1, *LG* 12:6–10.

57. Michel Foucault, "The Order of Discourse," in *The Archaeology of Knowledge,* translated by A. M. Sheridan Smith, 215–37 (New York: Pantheon Books, 1972).

commentary is other than the text and yet the text itself) underscores the intricate relationship between the biblical text "itself" and the commentary on the biblical text found here in the *Book of Steps.* Karlfried Froehlich summarizes the tripartite matrix of text-tradition-interpretation—the hermeneutical circle of the text—as a process in which "biblical language [determines] theology and . . . theological presuppositions [shape] the reading of the Bible." In other words, "text and interpretation are like twin brothers; one can scarcely tell the one from the other."[58] Commentary, then, is not merely a hermeneutical *tool* for the sort of exegesis found here in the *Book of Steps;* rather, commentary is integral to the text itself.

What I am suggesting is that the *Book of Steps* can be read as a *purposefully anonymous* (and in that sense, pseudepigraphic), fifth-century biblical commentary wherein the author masquerades as a first-century writer (and also as a later editor) in order to ensure that the ecclesiastical arrangements he supports will be taken seriously, given the apostolic roots and biblical warrants he claims for them. As others have suggested, I would further propose that the *Book of Steps* shows strong signs of having been written during a tense transitional period between a less regulated form of what Caner terms "wandering" asceticism and a more hierarchically controlled form of coenobitic monasticism. This would explain the author's motivation to write a work of biblical commentary designed to describe and highlight the biblical bases for a distinction between the Perfect and the Upright and their separate, but interdependent, ways of life. Indeed, the *Book of Steps* might be read as a reaction to a combination of social and ecclesiastical conditions—on the one hand as a response to the disgruntled Upright, some of whom seemed tired of supporting

58. Karlfried Froehlich, *Biblical Interpretation in the Early Church* (Philadelphia: Fortress Press, 1984), 1. I am surely not the first to suggest that the *Book of Steps* is a work of biblical commentary. Readers of the *Catena Severi,* a collection of commentaries, scholia, and notes on the entire Bible compiled in the mid-ninth century, also recognized that the *Book of Steps* is, at least in part, a biblical commentary. In the marginalia that became incorporated into later manuscripts of the commentary (ms. *Vat. Syr.* 103, f. 116r, mg.), a ninth- or tenth-century monk added to the commentary on 1 Kings a reference he cites as being from the *Book of Steps*—a paraphrase of David's pursuit of perfection as discussed in memra 9 (*BoS* 9.7, *LG* 217:21–24). This indicates, if only in a small way, that the *Book of Steps* was used by and familiar to at least one later monk searching for a reference to add to a biblical commentary. The *Book of Steps* was read not as an exclusively "ascetic" treatise, though the manuscript evidence shows that this is certainly part of the story, and the text was surely not a "lost" piece of foreign literature irrelevant to later times and places. The number and diversity of manuscripts of the *Book of Steps* alone testify to that.

the Perfect, and on the other hand to ecclesiastical regulations such as those of Bishop Rabbula of Edessa in the late 420s and early 430s. To broaden the hypothesis: there may well be something of a dialectical relationship between the admonitions to the Perfect in the *Book of Steps* and Rabbula's *Rules* for the monks, the clergy, and the *bnay qyâmâ* ("sons of the covenant").[59] That is, Rabbula's *Rules* can be read as a response to communities such as those represented by the *Book of Steps,* and the *Book of Steps* can be read as a defense of the kind of communal structures and standing of ascetics such as the Perfect that Rabbula's injunctions sought to reign in. The *Book of Steps* and Rabbula's *Rules* thus constitute a back-and-forth between sometimes contradictory and sometimes complementary rules on work, buying and selling, providing for the holy poor, wandering, and teaching.[60]

Rabbula's *Rules* and the *Book of Steps*

"Rabbula," in Susan Ashbrook Harvey's words, "legislated his church into order, writing strict canons for clergy of all levels [including monks and the *bnay qyâmâ*] . . . providing some of the earliest institutionalized controls on the flourishing but unregulated Syrian ascetic movement."[61] This "long list of injunctions" for the as-yet-unregulated ascetic movement is an appropriate description of the *Book of Steps,* too. In many ways a manual of proper ascetic practice—bolstered by biblical commentary that explains and justifies the rules while giving them an apostolic warrant—the *Book of Steps* describes in detail why the Perfect are to be celibate and are not to work. The main argument of the text is easily summarized: sex and work mimic the conditions

59. On the *bnay qyâmâ,* see especially George Nedungatt, "The Covenanters of the Early Syriac-Speaking Church," *Orientalia Christiana Periodica* 39 (1973): 191–215, 419–44; and Griffith, "Asceticism in the Church of Syria," 220–46.

60. David Brakke argues convincingly that Athanasius of Alexandria effectively reined in the monks of Egypt under his ecclesiastical oversight by regulating proper ascetic practice. Thus those who were not in accord with the bishop's notions of ascetic orthopraxy, in Athanasius's view, separated themselves from both the church and orthodoxy. Perhaps a similar situation developed under Rabbula in fifth-century Edessa; see David Brakke, *Athanasius and the Politics of Asceticism* (Oxford: Clarendon Press, 1995); reprinted as *Athanasius and Asceticism* (Baltimore: Johns Hopkins University Press, 1998).

61. Susan Ashbrook Harvey, "The Holy and the Poor: Models from Early Syriac Christianity," in *Through the Eye of a Needle: Judeo-Christian Roots of Social Welfare,* edited by Emily Albu Hanawalt and Carter Lindberg, 47 (Kirksville, Mo.: Thomas Jefferson University Press, 1994).

of the Fall, whereas celibacy and the forgoing of manual labor reenact the prelapsarian condition—the life of the angels in paradise. On account of Adam's transgression, we are told, "[God] discouraged them with labor."[62] But, by not laboring, the ascetic is able to recapture the Edenic state: for the "Perfect road is this, 'Do not be anxious about what you shall eat and what you shall wear.' The path that leads you away from this is, 'Work and eat the bread [you have earned] and do not be a burden on anyone.'"[63] This is, no doubt, quite difficult advice to follow, and there are a number of snares along the way, since, in the view of the author of the *Book of Steps,* there can be no acquiescing to the concerns of the world for the Perfect one:

> [The evil one] deluding the Perfect one, says the following, "It is virtuous that you should *acquire a little* [wealth] through Uprightness, sufficient for your own comfort and for whomever comes to you. *Build for yourself* a dwelling that is just adequate for strangers to come and rest in it. *Plant a little crop* and *make for yourself a vegetable garden* that will be for the healthy and the sick." Under the pretext of the comfort of the afflicted [the evil one] schemes to make [a Perfect] one fall from that major commandment that [Jesus] directs to the Perfect, "Do not be anxious even about yourself," and by that [other] commandment, "Think about what is above and not of what is on the earth."[64]

Ultimately, according to the author of the *Book of Steps,* the Perfect one strives to be able to say, "'If I die, I will die; and if I live, I will live,' as long as I do not abandon the journey of the great road on account of nourishment and clothing."[65]

Rabbula, in his rules for monks, also recognizes the problem of labor and the acquisition of nourishment and clothing that binds one to the earth. But Rabbula's monks are far from the ascetic ideal—far from the example of the Perfect—that is outlined by the author of the *Book of Steps.* In economic matters, at least, monks in Rabbula's day more closely parallel the Upright. As Harvey indicates, "Rabbula's legislation strictly curtailed any possibility of economic growth for monastic communities and severely limited their standard of living, a move that would seem to indicate concern about monastic wealth."[66] Rabbula controlled the monks by controlling their economic activity and by

62. *BoS* 21.7, *LG* 601:8–11.

63. *BoS* 19.13, *LG* 473:16–20.

64. *BoS* 25.5, *LG* 741:22–44:9.

65. *BoS* 20.2, *LG* 529:11–15.

66. Harvey, "Holy and the Poor, 52.

regulating their movement. But whereas the Perfect are not to own anything at all, or even tend a little garden for the sick, Rabbula's monks, on the other hand, are given more leeway and are allowed enough to tend a little garden: "The monks shall not possess the goods of sheep and of goats or of horses and mules or of other animals, except one donkey (for those) who need it, or one yoke of oxen, (for those) who seed (the field)."[67] Rabbula's monks fall between the Perfect, who spurn the affairs of the marketplace, and the Upright, who possess wealth righteously and buy and sell as is appropriate. The monks are told that there is never to be "business-affairs of buying and selling in the monasteries, except only for that (thing) which is sufficient for their needs, without greediness."[68] What is earned from the sale of crops to benefit the monastery shall be sold at a fair price and no more;[69] moreover, the monks are not to own anything privately: everything belongs collectively to the community, "and is under the authority of the *rêsh dayrâ*."[70] So, in contradistinction to the Perfect of the *Book of Steps,* the begging ones who do not labor, Rabbula's ideal monks must undertake some sort of agrarian labor to earn their bread and to help sustain the community—but only enough to survive without the largesse of others. While the Perfect, in emulation of their teacher, do not have a place to lay their heads—a characteristic that has been interpreted to mean that the Perfect were some sort of itinerant teachers, wandering about from town to town—Rabbula's monks are prohibited from going out to meet even with their relatives,[71] or from leaving the monastery under any condition to "roam in the towns."[72] They must not work when they are supposed to be praying.[73] They should live in community rather than dwell in isolation.[74] Unlike the Perfect, who teach and perform a spiritual ministry, the monks are commanded not to give answers from scripture to anyone,[75] and they are forbidden from receiving into the community "a brother that moves from monastery to monastery without a word (assignment) of the *rêsh dayrâ* with whom he stayed."[76]

67. Rules for Monks 9. The quotations from the Rules for Monks and Rules for the Clergy and *bnay qyâmâ* are from Vööbus, *Syriac and Arabic Documents Regarding Legislation Relative to Syrian Asceticism,* Papers of the Estonian Theological Society in Exile 11 (Stockholm: Estonian Theological Society in Exile, 1960), 27–33; 36–50.

68. Rules for Monks 11.

69. Rules for Monks 25.

70. Rules for Monks 12.

71. Rules for Monks 13.

72. Rules for Monks 14.

73. Rules for Monks 16.

74. Rules for Monks 18.

75. Rules for Monks 19.

76. Rules for Monks 26.

Quite interestingly, there seems to be more of a parallel between the Perfect and the *bnay qyâmâ* than between the Perfect and the monks. Indeed, on at least one occasion in the *Book of Steps,* the Perfect are specifically called *bnay qyâmâ.*[77] The Perfect are told they must not worry about food or clothing, for the Upright will provide for their material needs. Providing for the Perfect is, one senses from the *Book of Steps,* part of the very reason that the Upright are upright. As Daniel Caner points out, the *Book of Steps* is premised upon the notion "that ascetics who devoted themselves to the spiritual work of prayer and edification merited support from other members of the Christian community. This premise," he continues, "was closely bound to the Syro-Mesopotamian tradition of providing maintenance for the ascetic 'Sons and Daughters of the Covenant'"—the *bnay* and *bnât qyâmâ.*

This notion of a reciprocal relationship is found, for example, in Aphrahat's *Demonstration* XX, as well. Adam Becker, in an article on Aphrahat and care for the poor, indicates that, for Aphrahat, gift giving is itself a gift from God and that the almsgiver (the *mzaddqânâ,* or the "one who justifies") is justified by the act of justly caring for the poor.[78] Like the Perfect of the *Book of Steps,* whose material needs are provided for through the justice of the Upright, the *qyâmâ* of Rabbula's *Rules* are similarly cared for by the community in exchange for the spiritual ministry they perform. In the spirit of encouraging the just and cheerful giver, Rabbula specifies that the clergy are not to "impose tributes" on the people on behalf of the *bnay qyâmâ;* rather, the *bnay qyâmâ* are to be cared for "by (the help) of what (everyone) gives by his will."[79] This is the clearest indication in the *Rules* that the *bnay qyâmâ*—a sort of holy poor—were supported by the alms of the community. In response to the gifts of food and clothing they are given, "all the sons of the church" (and here the text seems to mean the *bnay qyâmâ*) are required to "persevere in fasting and be diligent in prayer."[80] The most interesting point comes in the next rule, where it is specified that the priests are required to "take care of the poor that come to them, and relieve them, especially those who are the *bnay qyâmâ.*"[81] This rule demonstrates a clear distinction between the clergy and the "holy

77. *BoS* 10.9, *LG* 265:19.

78. Adam H. Becker, "Anti-Judaism and Care for the Poor in Aphrahat's *Demonstration* 20," *Journal of Early Christian Studies* 10 (2002): 305–27.

79. Rules for *bnay qyâmâ* 6.

80. Rules for *bnay qyâmâ* 11.

81. Rules for *bnay qyâmâ* 12.

poor" (such as the *bnay qyâmâ*), and it provides further evidence that the *bnay qyâmâ* were to be cared for by the people of the church *and* by the clergy. Effectively, this is an institutional decree to care for the praying ones. The Perfect of the *Book of Steps* are clearly not the only ones who are to be provided for by others. Rabbula's *Rules* state definitively, "If there is anyone of the *bnay qyâmâ* or of the *bnât qyâmâ* who are in want, the priests or the deacons of their villages shall take care of them." The rule continues: "But if this is not in his power he shall inform us that we may be solicitous about them, so that because of their need they may not be compelled to do something that is not suitable."[82] One wonders what sort of "unsuitable" things that the *bnay* or *bnât qyâmâ* may have felt compelled to do should their material needs not have been adequately met. Certainly they are not to be traveling around, or buying and selling in the marketplace, but they are never specifically commanded *not* to do some sort of labor. On the other hand, they are enjoined to "be continually in the worship-service of the church and shall not neglect the times of prayer and psalmody night and day."[83]

Conclusions

It is evident that a more in-depth study of the possible relationship between the *Book of Steps* and the *Rules* of Rabbula is necessary. Rabbula's injunctions are only one possible way of situating and understanding the motives of the author of the *Book of Steps.* Still, whether or not a connection with Rabbula is plausible, there is good reason for distancing the text from the methods and conclusions of its earliest scholarly interpreters. Indeed, the primary aim of this chapter was not to definitively resituate the *Book of Steps* in conjunction with Rabbula, but only to deconstruct earlier ways of reading the text and to thereby advance a preliminary new reading, suggesting possible connections and intriguing parallels. A fifth-century date of authorship and a reading of the text as a "pious fraud" (constructed in such a way so as to cloak its true provenance with a covering of apostolic roots) are two hypotheses that stand or fall irrespective of the proposed link with Rabbula. At this point what does seem to be clear is that the fifth century was an important period of

82. Rules for *bnay qyâmâ* 19.
83. Rules for *bnay qyâmâ* 27.

transition in Syriac Christianity and that the *Book of Steps* can be read in ways that make it fit naturally into this period. Of course, the text was used later in completely different circumstances, which is what makes the manifold questions about later excerpts taken from the *Book of Steps* so interesting, but the new historical context for the composition of the *Book of Steps* proposed in this chapter shows that the text need not be read as a historical oddity from an isolated community in the Persian hinterlands. Rather, the very distance that the *Book of Steps* takes from the increasing institutionalization of the church exemplifies its role in the struggle over ecclesiastical control—a struggle highlighted by the contentious reign of Bishop Rabbula in an urban, fifth-century Syriac Christian milieu.

PART 3

BIBLICAL EXEGISIS IN THE *BOOK OF STEPS*

René Roux

6. BIBLICAL EXEGESIS IN THE SYRIAC *BOOK OF STEPS*

A Preliminary Survey

In his introduction, the ancient Syriac editor of the *Book of Steps* compares its anonymous author to Basil the Great, Gregory the Theologian, and Evagrius Ponticus for his great theological achievements.[1] History has certainly taken a different view on this point. Up to the first critical edition in 1926,[2] the *Book of Steps* was hardly known outside the Syriac world. But, in spite of the weariness caused by its repetitive style, the *Book of Steps* strikes the modern reader with the originality of its theological insight. Its author has provided us with a very original and highly coherent vision of the essence of Christianity.[3] This originality also appears in his approach to exegetical problems, where he follows a method that distinguishes itself from the main exegetical traditions of Christian antiquity. The entire *Book of Steps* seems to be an answer to the problem of the contradictions that are found in scripture. Whereas the Greek exegetical tradition had produced careful analysis of the contradictions

1. See Michael Kmoskó, ed., *Liber Graduum,* Patrologia Syriaca 1.3 (Paris: Firmin-Didot, 1926); *English translation,* Robert A. Kitchen and Martien F. G. Parmentier, *The Book of Steps: The Syriac Liber Graduum* (Kalamazoo, Mich.: Cistercian Publications, 2004) (BoS), Preface.

2. Kmoskó, ed., *Liber Graduum,* Patrologia Syriaca 1.3.

3. Cf. René Roux, "The Doctrine of the Imitation of Christ in the *Liber Graduum:* Between Exegetical Theory and Soteriology," in *Studia Patristica: Biblica Et Apocrypha, Ascetica, Liturgica,* vol. 30, edited by Elizabeth A. Livingstone and E. Peters, 259–64 (Leuven: Peeters, 1997).

among the four gospels—especially the genealogy of Christ and the narratives of the resurrection[4]—the *Book of Steps,* which was reading a gospel harmony, the Syriac Diatessaron, is only interested in the contradictions among the divine commandments.

The centrality of exegetical themes in the *Book of Steps* has recently been rediscovered,[5] and various studies have been done concerning the problem of the biblical text actually used by the *Book of Steps,*[6] his canon of inspired texts, the relation to Jewish and early Christian traditions,[7] the reception of Paul,[8] and other texts. But there is still a need for a systematic attempt at describing the kind of exegetical material to be found in the *Book of Steps* and the method followed by our author in dealing with the scriptures. In the present chapter I shall first attempt to sketch the general setting of the exegetical problem in the *Book of Steps* and the doctrinal premises that determine the author's hermeneutical method. Second, I suggest a possible classification of the exegetical material into three main categories: "direct exegesis," which I call "Christian halakha," since it is almost exclusively concerned with moral themes; "biblical theology"; and "dogmatic exegesis." As a conclusion, I would like to draw attention to the new light that a better understanding of the *mens exegetica* of our author seems to cast on the recent obscure problem of his theological milieu.

4. Cf. Helmut Merkel, *Die Widersprüche zwischen den Evangelien: Ihre polemische und apologetische Behandlung in der alten Kirche bis zu Augustin* (Tübingen: Mohr Siebeck, 1971); Helmut Merkel, *Die Pluralität der Evangelien als theologisches und exegetisches Problem in der alten Kirche* (Bern: Lang 1978).

5. Cf. Paolo Bettiolo, "Confessare Dio in perfetta spogliazione: La via del discernimento dei comandamenti nel *Liber graduum,*" *Cristianesimo nella storia* 19 (1998): 631–51.

6. Cf. Dom Aelred Baker, "The Significance of the New Testament Text of the Syriac *Liber Graduum,*" in *Studia Evangelica 5: Papers Presented to the Third International Congress on New Testament Studies, Held at Christ Church, Oxford, 1965; Part 2: The New Testament Message,* edited by Frank L. Cross, 171–75 (Berlin: Akademie-Verlag, 1968).

7. Cf. Aleksander Kowalski, *Perfezione e giustizia di Adamo nel Liber Graduum,* Orientalia Christiana Analecta 232 (Rome: Pontificium Institutum Orientale, 1989), 183–92; Alexander Golitzin, "Recovering the 'Glory of Adam': 'Divine Light' Traditions in the Dead Sea Scrolls and the Christian Ascetical Literature of Fourth-Century Syro-Mesopotamia," in *The Dead Sea Scrolls as Background to Postbiblical Judaism and Early Christianity: Papers from an International Conference at St. Andrews in 2001,* edited by James R. Davila, 275–308 (Leiden: E. J. Brill, 2003).

8. Cf. Matthias Westerhoff, "Zur Paulus-Rezeption im Liber Graduum: der Apostel als Vorbild," in *Syriaca: zu Geschichte, Theologie, Liturgie und Gegenwartslage der syrischen Kirchen,* edited by Martin Tamcke, 253–59 (Münster: LIT Verlag, 2002).

Interpreting the Scripture: The Need for a *Regula Fidei*

The *Book of Steps* begins with an invitation to inquire into the words of our Lord.[9] This invitation is composed of seven biblical citations[10] that stress the importance of studying the Word of God, the necessity of humility as a particular attitude of the mind, the fundamental role of the Holy Spirit, and the fruit of his presence, which are peace and love. In fact, the main intention of the *Book of Steps* is to solve the hermeneutical problem caused by contradictory statements in the scriptures. Two entire homilies, the first and the eleventh, deal with setting the general rules for interpreting the scriptures. The commandments seem to entail contradictory requests. Moreover, some of the examples set by the prophets and by Christ himself seem to break the commandments instead of illustrating them. The only solution lies in realizing that those commandments were not addressed to the same people, and therefore one needs to inquire to whom the commandments were given. "Notice how the words of Jesus become the opposite of one another. So that you shall recognize that they were spoken to two types of people, our Lord said, 'Do not judge';[11] and he also said, 'Shame a person before the whole church.'[12] If both of them are intended for you, which one will you choose? If you judge, you have isolated yourself from that major commandment, 'Do not judge.' And, if you do not judge, you will be blameworthy because of that other commandment, 'before the whole church shames him.'"[13]

To justify this hermeneutical procedure, the author of the *Book of Steps* quotes those commandments that were obviously meant for just one person in rather exceptional circumstances. Two such cases are mentioned:[14] the commandment given to Abraham, "Sacrifice to me your son whom you love so much,"[15] and the one to the prophet Hosea, "Go, take yourself a harlot as your wife."[16] Nobody would think that these two commandments were meant for general implementation. They had their function at a particular historical

9. Cf. *BoS*, 1.1, *LG* 12.9–10.

10. (1) Apocryphal; (2) Heb 3:13; (3) Rom 12:2;(4) Phil 4:8; (5) 1 Cor 14:27–28; (6) Gal 5:22; and (7) John 8:32.

11. Matt 7:1.

12. Matt 18:17.

13. *BoS* 11.2.

14. *BoS* 1.6.

15. Gen 22:2.

16. Hos 1:2.

moment. By the first one, God wanted to teach that we have to love God's commandments more than our children. The second one was an admonition to those Israelites who lived in fornication themselves. However, from these two examples the author of the *Book of Steps* deduces the general rule that in order to understand the meaning of a commandment, the interpreter has to first establish its addressees.[17] This method allows the interpreter to overcome the previously mentioned contradictions and points to the different levels of spiritual development.

The idea that the Bible is not a monolithic collection of universally valid laws, but rather a store case of all that people might need for their spiritual growth, to be wisely dispensed according to actual needs, is confirmed by the teaching of the Apostle Paul, who uses the metaphor of the milk for the children and the solid food for the grown-up in order to justify his progressive approach in instructing the believers.[18] In this way it is possible to harmonize apparent contradictory commandments: they fit into the same general divine purpose, and their differences are an adaptation to the different human conditions. Even those biblical passages that show a rather violent God can be thus justified. Their purpose is just to prevent misunderstandings. If God never showed his authority, people might not realize that he is the real almighty God.

The biblical exegesis of the *Book of Steps* is in fact based upon a specific way of looking at the problem of God. Ancient biblical exegesis was always theological. The author of the scriptures was thought to be God or the Holy Spirit. While interpreting a group of texts so numerous and varied as those making up the Christian Bible, ancient Christians felt the need of elaborating summaries of the main truths, more or less similar to baptismal creeds. They were needed not only for catechetical purposes, but also for reading the Bible. These summaries or "*regulae*" were not meant to explain particular points, but to set the framework for the exegetical activity.[19] They provided the inter-

17. The possibility of an "individual" commandment is confirmed by another individual judgment: the pardon given to the good robber, even though he had no works to his credit; cf. *BoS* 1.7.

18. 1 Cor 3:1–3 and Heb 5:12–14.

19. Cf. Prosper Grech, "The Regula Fidei as a Hermeneutical Principle in Patristic Exegesis," in *The Interpretation of the Bible: The International Symposium in Slovenia,* edited by Joze Krasovec, 589–601 (Sheffield: Sheffield Academic Press, 1998).

preter of the Bible with some sort of general guidance and with "boundaries," which delimited the field of possible orthodox exegesis from unacceptable ones. One rather difficult point was the relationship between Father and Son and the related problem of the divinity of Christ. Another one was, for instance, the problem of humanity and divinity in Christ. Biblical texts, as history has shown, were open to contradictory interpretations. Even though it was based on a particular understanding of revelation, the rule of faith became normative for subsequent exegetical activity.

The author of the *Book of Steps* faced a similar problem when he wanted to explain the contradiction among divine commandments. The pedagogical character of the commandments allowed him to organize them in a progressive or hierarchical order. But the direction of this order implies a specific understanding of the nature of God. For our author it is clear that, with the incarnation, Christ has shown not only the way to go back to the lost paradise, but also something of the characteristics of God. God commands humility because he is good, patient, and in a way "humble." He does not destroy Satan when Satan tries to become like him. He does not punish Adam for his disobedience, but gives him a possibility of penance. In the same way, he does not expose and denounce Judas Iscariot when he is about to betray him.[20] In the entire history of salvation, God has shown that the humility of Moses,[21] Noah, and Jacob was more important to him than the arrogant achievements of other people.[22] The Virgin Mary was chosen as mother of our Lord because she was the humblest of all women, and Christ himself is the humblest of all men and loves humility.[23] Humility is thus a characteristic of the divinity: "God lives without law and has authority over his creation. The creation is fit to be under God and subservient to him. 'If I, who am without law, am your Lord and Master, have humbled myself in this way, how much more ought you who are beneath God to bring yourselves to be humbled more than me, the Lord and Master.'[24] But not even when we imitate the lowliness of our Lord is our lowliness comparable to his. When we offer our cheek to blows

20. In the *Book of Steps* "God" and "Christ" are almost interchangeable.

21. The humility of Moses was an important theme in Jewish tradition as well; cf. Num 12:3.

22. Cf. *BoS* 21.12–14.

23. *BoS* 21.16, *LG* 624.22–25.4.

24. Cf. John 13:14.

according to our tangible nature, this lowliness is smaller than that lowliness, because the nature, which was neither tangible nor wounded, became limited and was wounded."[25] In the same logic, the Holy Spirit will be given only to those who humble themselves and consider themselves lower than any other people. This general understanding about the nature of God and of Christ enjoys the status of a *regula fidei* and becomes a general rule for exegesis. All the statements that do not agree with it, because they show an arrogant or violent God, have to be harmonized or somehow explained away.[26]

Who is the interpreter that can understand the scriptures correctly? He is the one who has humbled himself and received the gift of the Holy Spirit. In order to know all the truth, one needs to receive the Holy Spirit in its highest form, the Paraclete, and so he is able to distinguish the truth from falsehood and to teach others.[27] It is important to notice that the author of the *Book of Steps* is aware of interpreting the Bible from a particular perspective, and we might say that he is aware of the originality of his own approach. "Our Lord did not dictate [the commandments] one by one [i.e., distinguishing them] and it is not because we are more perfect than him and his apostles that we write them down one by one but because today there are hardly any people who expound them, so that even simple people may attain insight, and everyone may struggle to enter by the narrow gate[28] of Perfection, or inherit the place of Uprightness below it."[29] He does not justify this approach, but he insists on explaining that if "the letter will kill you," as Paul says,[30] it is because "you do not know how to distinguish his commandments."[31] Anyone who is humble and has received the Paraclete is able to understand the scriptures. Otherwise, it is necessary to interrogate an experienced man of God. Even though some passages of the *Book of Steps* hint at a spiritual master acting for a particular community,[32] it seems clear that this teaching is directed to the entire church.

25. *BoS* 22.13, *LG* 664.7–20.

26. We shall return to the philosophical and historical implications of this at the end of this chapter.

27. Cf. *BoS* 5.19, 28.2–3.

28. Cf. Matt 7:13.

29. *BoS* 1.1.

30. 2 Cor 3:6.

31. *BoS* 16.9. In the Alexandrian tradition, this Pauline text was used to justify all sorts of allegorical interpretations.

32. *BoS* 30.10–14.

Hermeneutical Typologies in the *Book of Steps*

In order to find the logic underlying the hermeneutical procedure in these ancient homiletical texts, it is necessary to distinguish between direct exegesis, on the one hand, where the interpreter tries to establish the meaning of the biblical text—a word, a sentence, or a longer section—and, on the other hand, the use of the Bible in a broader sense, where the preacher makes use of a biblical citation or even just a reminiscence of it in order to develop a doctrinal or historical theme. This second case implies a certain understanding of the text, but obeys different rules.[33] If we apply this distinction to the exegetical material of the *Book of Steps,* it appears that the author practiced direct exegesis almost exclusively to points linked with moral teachings, which results in a rather remarkable and original Christian halakha.[34] Some theological problems, like the nature of sin, Satan, or free will, have led him to develop a sort of "biblical theology." Even if he occasionally suggests interesting explanations of some biblical passages, his intention is not to explain the text of scripture, but to explain something else making use of scriptural evidence. Finally, attention shall be devoted to the only example of a dogmatic exegesis in the *Book of Steps.*

A Christian Halakha

"Our Lord appeared physically so that he might win the whole world and so that the world might know the will of God from God himself and from his footsteps [. . .]. Our Lord was born for the education of everyone so that all might learn the truth of his lowliness and love in a visible way, because not everyone is capable of hearing the will of the Lord through the Holy Spirit."[35] The scope of the divine revelation is to bring lost humanity back to paradise. Through *praecepta* and *exempla* humanity is shown the way; the analysis of commandments and moral examples scattered throughout Bible is the center of the exegetical activity of the *Book of Steps* and arranges a coherent program for Christian life and spiritual growth.

33. On this complex epistemological problem, see Basil Studer, *Schola Christiana: Die Theologie zwischen Nizäa (325) und Chalzedon (451)* (Paderborn: Ferdinand Schöningh, 1998), 131–35.

34. God has walked among us (root: hlk) as a man so that we may imitate him; see *BoS* 20.10.

35. *BoS* 9.1.

The Exegesis of the Praecepta

In this section we shall make a quick survey on what the precepts are called, how they are classified in at least six main categories, and how the relation between the Old and the New Testament is to be understood.

Most likely the author of the *Book of Steps* considered the discernment of the *praecepta* as his most important contribution to the life of the Christian community. *Praecepta* fall into different categories because they are meant for different people. *Praecepta* can be major or minor, *praecepta* of justice or of perfection, of faith, or of love. There is also a group of *judicia* that do not bring salvation, but eventually a less severe eternal punishment. This terminology underlines the importance of the two main categories of *praecepta,* but it has the drawback that it looks very static and might give the impression of a radical distinction between the two. That may explain why, when referring to the categories of commandments, the author of the *Book of Steps* often makes use of two metaphors, one taken from food, the other one from the way. According to the first one, which is of Pauline origin,[36] there are commandments that are like the milk given to small children; other commandments are like solid food for adults, still others like medical herbs meant for the sick. This image underlines the differences among the precepts, the idea of spiritual life as a sort of natural growth from one stage to the next (obviously against any notion of Gnostic determinism), and the importance of giving the right nourishment to the right people.

The other metaphor, the one of the way, is a development of the two ways of teaching of the *Didache,*[37] a text the *Book of Steps* considered canonical, and of the image of the holy mountain with the city of God at its top.[38] The great commandments are the ways that lead directly to the top. They are a very steep climb. That's why many people need the lower commandments that are like gentler paths. The main point is that one should not go down, but always up. This image underlines the variety, I dare say almost at an individual level, in the spiritual path toward God.

The author of the *Book of Steps* goes on trying to systematize and classify all the commandments found in the Bible. Commandments are explained in

36. Cf. 1 Cor 3:1–3 and Heb 5:12–14.

37. Cf. *Didache* I.1–2.

38. Cf. *BoS* 19.1.

their literal or historical meaning and are organized in long lists of *testimonia,* a typical feature of Judeo-Christian exegesis,[39] conceived as a further help in order to grasp the intention of the divine legislator. A first group of commandments is the already mentioned individual commandments to Abraham and Hosea. They are justified in their symbolical meaning: God wanted to tell something to his people and does it through his servants. The symbolic meaning of the actions is not "allegorical" in the sense that it is the only meaning of it, and as such is already to be found in the biblical text.[40]

A second group of commandments is made up of those judgments that do not save those who follow them,[41] as it is written in Ezekiel 20:25: "I have given them judgments by which no one may be saved."[42] Four commandments are mentioned: the *lex talionis,* "an eye for an eye, a tooth for a tooth, a blow for a blow, an insult for an insult, a wound for a wound, a soul for a soul,[43] in other words, everything evil for evil";[44] second, Matthew 5:43, "Love him who loves you and hate your enemy";[45] third, Mark 7:11, "If you strike your father bring an offering into the temple"; and finally, Matthew 5:31, "Let whoever wishes to leave his wife give her a writ of divorce while she has not committed adultery." Even if these commandments have been abolished by Jesus Christ, it remains to know why they have been given in the first instance. The *Book of Steps* is obviously struggling against the idea that the legislation of the Old Testament was given by an inferior or wicked God. In fact, God was almost forced to give these commandments because this is what the people wanted. "They loved murder and enmity and hidden hatred,"[46] and "they loved the curse and did not desire the blessings."[47] In fact, these commandments, even though they cannot lead to salvation, have played a positive role in educating humanity by condemning excessive revenge[48] and treating mildly exceedingly barbaric customs. Those who follow these commandments will go to hell, but their punishment will be less severe.

39. Cf. Jean Daniélou, *Etudes d'exégèse judéo-chrétienne: Les testimonia* (Paris: Beauchesne 1966).

40. Cf. *BoS* 1.5–6. On the problem of symbolic and allegorical meaning, cf. Manlio Simonetti, *Lettera e/o allegoria* (Rome: Institutum Patristicum "Augustinianum", 1985), 14n13.

41. Cf. *BoS* 22.

42. *BoS* 22.7.

43. Exod 21:24; cf. Matt 6:38.

44. *BoS* 22.1.

45. Cf. Lev 19:18.

46. Ezek 20:25, in *BoS* 22.7.

47. Ps 109:17, in *BoS* 22.8.

48. Cf. *BoS* 22.16–20.

A third group of commandments is represented by the so-called commandments of uprightness, or corporeal service, or milk of the children, or path of uprightness. They are best explained when compared with a fourth group, the commandments of perfection or major commandments, or solid food. In fact, most of the *Book of Steps* is written to describe and explain these commandments and to clarify their relationship. Memra 19, the longest of the *Book of Steps,* contains a group of twenty-five pairs of commandments; each commandment of perfection is called a "way" according to the metaphor of climbing up the mountain of God.[49] Each "way of Perfection" is associated with a "path of Uprightness" or "inferior commandment."[50] The commandments of perfection are also listed on their own in the second homily.[51] The commandments of uprightness are dealt with in homilies 5 to 8.[52] To the group of the major commandments belong, for instance, Matthew 22:30, "Whoever does not leave his wife and his children and his family and everything he has in the land, is not worthy of me";[53] Matthew 6:25, "Do not be anxious about what you shall eat and what you shall wear";[54] and Matthew 5:14, "Bless him who curses you and love him who hates you, and pray for whomever harms you and persecutes you."[55] Their counterpart on the level of uprightness are Matthew 19:6, "Whatever God has joined together do not separate";[56] 2 Thessalonians 3:12, "Work and eat your bread and do not be a burden on anyone";[57] and Matthew 18:17, "Consider whomever does not listen as a Gentile and a tax-collector."[58] It is possible to say that the commandments of righteousness are meant for those people living in the world, getting married, and earning their bread with their own work. The major commandments imply the readiness to abandon everything, live in humility, and experience dispossession according to the example of our Lord. Those following the minor commandments have received the pledge of the Holy Spirit, as Paul said.[59] The Perfect

49. A "commandment" may be obtained through a combination of biblical texts; cf. *BoS* 19.14 (Matt 22:30 and Matt 10:37), or *BoS* 19.17 (Matt 9:39 and Luke 6:37).

50. The same ideas are restated in memra 3, "On the physical and spiritual services," and memra 14, "On the conduct of the Upright and the Perfect," not like an exegesis of biblical passages, but more like a description of saintly behavior.

51. Memra 6 being then a description of the way of living of the Perfect.

52. And again in memra 13, but as a description of the behavior of the Upright.

53. Cf. *BoS* 19.14.

54. Cf. *BoS* 19.13.

55. Cf. *BoS* 19.12.

56. Cf. *BoS* 19.14.

57. Cf. *BoS* 19.13

58. Cf. *BoS* 19.12.

59. 2 Cor 1:22, 5:5; Eph 1:14.

have received the fullness of the Spirit, which is the Paraclete promised by our Lord.[60]

There are two further groups of commandments that show a different nuance and might even point to an evolution in the attitude of the author. In memra 16 he explains how a person may spiritually grow even above the level of perfection: "If you wish, listen to me and I will show you how you may grow and be elevated above these major commandments."[61] He then lists six commandments of perfection, showing in each case how they can be surpassed. Matthew 5:39 says, "Whoever strikes you upon your cheek, offer him the other." To go above it, you should offer your entire body. To go above Matthew 18:21, "Forgive a wrongdoer seventy times seven," you should not require anything at all for a wrong. According to this logic, the author explains all the remaining commandments.[62] Reading this section, one has the impression that perfection is something that can actually be reached relatively easily, as in a sort of juvenile enthusiasm. Such an enthusiasm seems to make room for more realism in memra 30, where a final distinction is introduced, if not developed. The last homily of the collection is the second longest and contains a summary of the main ideas of the *Book of Steps* with some new nuances, and, as far as exegesis is concerned, with two innovations: the only example of dogmatic exegesis,[63] and a new distinction between the commandments of faith and the commandments of love.[64] "Commandments of faith" is a synonym for "minor commandments," but the "commandments of love" are somewhere between the minor ones and those of perfection. "Perfection teaches the disciples of love something better and greater, and raises them up to be perfect in Christ."[65] The *Book of Steps* says that there is peace between the disciples of love and those ministering in perfection, thus implying that they are not the same group of people, and that anyway the perfect has reached a higher level.[66] In particular, the "commandment" of Paul in 1 Corinthians 2:15, "A man in the Spirit judges everything but he is not judged by anyone," which implies a clear teaching responsibility toward the community,[67] applies to the perfect,

60. John 14:26.

61. *BoS* 16.1.

62. That is Matt 5:41; Luke 6:37; Matt 2:22; and Matt 6:9-12; cf. *BoS* 16.1–3.

63. On Col 1:15; see discussion later.

64. Cf. *BoS* 30.1.

65. *BoS* 30.3.

66. *BoS* 30.7.

67. *BoS* 30.3.

but not to the disciples of love. Given that the classification of the commandments is strictly linked to specific categories of people, we might speculate on the reason for such a development. It might be that within the group of ascetics who have followed the teachings of the *Book of Steps,* the attempt at seeking perfection has proved more difficult than it was thought to be at the beginning, so that it was deemed reasonable to introduce an intermediary level. At any rate, the method of classifying the commandments according to the levels in spiritual growth allows the author of the *Book of Steps* to overcome the contradictions of the biblical text while adhering to its strict literal meaning.

A specific problem is caused by the entire civil and ritual legislation of the Old Testament. It no longer had validity for the Christian community, but a need was felt to explain its presence and its function in the scriptures. The Alexandrian tradition had found a way to make relevant those regulations via allegorical interpretation, while the Antiochene tradition stressed so much the newness of the incarnate economy that the old legislation had just a historical interest.[68] The author of the *Book of Steps* explains the relation between the old law and the law of Christ through a particular interpretation of Matthew 5:18. "When he said, 'He made both of them one Testament,'[69] and he annulled the law of the commandments by his commandments, so that he might make everything new with one testament. 'From now on not a single letter "iota" will pass away from the Law and the Prophets.'"[70] As for the rest, "the whole Law and Prophets up to John were established in order to serve and then pass away."[71] "For the thing that has become old is worn out and close to destruction,"[72] and from then on we ought not to speak about these.[73] From then on, that one letter iota will remain—which is the Ten Commandments, which are called iota, for there are Ten Commandments in the number of the signs. These ten commandments [. . .] are the iota that do not pass away from the Law or the Prophets."[74] The apparent contradiction between Matthew 5:18 and the texts claiming the abolition of the ancient law is thus solved by in-

68. Striking in this sense is the attitude of Theodore of Mopsuestia; cf. Manlio Simonetti, *Lettera e/o allegoria: Un contributo alla storia dell'esegesi patristica* (Rome: Institutum Patristicum Augustinianum, 1985), 167–74.

69. Eph 2:14.

70. Matt 5:18.

71. Matt 11:13.

72. Heb 8:13.

73. Heb 9:15.

74. *BoS* 22.21.

terpreting the letter yud with its numerical value—ten, which is immediately related to the Decalogue.[75]

The Exegesis of the Exempla

The second main field for exegetical inquiry in the *Book of Steps* is represented by the exempla given by the prophets and by Jesus Christ himself. Memra 9 deals entirely with the study of the conduct of the prophets of the Old Testament. In spite of being filled with the Holy Spirit, their behavior was at times quite far away from the ideal of humble love praised throughout the *Book of Steps*. In order to justify their seeming misconduct, the *Book of Steps* has to elaborate a rather complex theology of history. Had the prophets been allowed to follow their own will, they would have lived according to the law of perfection. However, God prevented them from reaching it and occasionally forced them to behave at a level that was even lower than righteousness because of the harsh era they lived in, when there was a wall of enmity between God and humanity caused by original sin. The occasionally violent acts that they had to perform in obedience to God's will were necessary in order to teach humanity who was punishing them: "If the Lord had killed the rebellious without the prophets, they would have said, 'our idols killed us, not the Lord,' and they would have continued to have sacrificed their sons to their idols in order to appease them and they would not have known the Lord."[76] Since they were acting under divine orders, they were not held responsible for those killings (God does not punish somebody for obeying his orders). When Jesus Christ destroyed the wall of enmity between God and humanity, the prophets were finally allowed to become perfect and enter the city of God together with the apostles. Moses is the best example for what has been said. "When our Lord sought to kill the Israelites, Moses said in his prayer concerning these who were embittering his spirit every day and abusing him, 'If you blot them out, blot me out from your book of life.'[77] Look, what did Moses do to the evildoers? As he wished that the righteous might do to him if he

75. For a similar interpretation, cf. Aphrahat, *Demonstrations*. Transl. from Syriac and introd. by Kuriakose Valavanolickal. (Kottayam: St. Ephrem Ecumenical Research Inst., 2005), 2.7.

76. *BoS* 9.2.

77. Ex 32:32.

had done wrong, that they might pray for him. See how the Upright pursued Perfection!"[78] "In another place in scripture, the Lord brought Moses down to a stage lower than Uprightness when he said to him, 'Command the Levites to slay their brothers and fathers because they worshipped the calf,'[79] exchanging God for a dead calf. When Moses saw that evil had targeted him, and it was no use if he prayed for them, he did to them that thing he hated for someone to do to him if he sins; that is, he acted by the word from the Lord's mouth, and not by the will of Moses."[80] The *Book of Steps* goes on applying this hermeneutical criteria to scriptural evidence related to Jeremiah,[81] David,[82] Abraham,[83] Elijah,[84] Elisha,[85] Abel,[86] Adam,[87] Isaac,[88] Jacob,[89] and Joseph.[90] In each case the author carefully distinguishes those acts that are supposed to be imitated from those that were necessary because of the harshness of the ancient times and that no longer apply.

The life of Jesus is even more important for the theological system of the *Book of Steps*. In Jesus Christ God himself has shown the way of perfection. Unfortunately, Christ's acts do not always reflect that ideal. The problem is clearly stated by one of the contradictory pairs in memra 19: "The Perfect road is this, 'do not allow a spiteful word to come out of your mouth.'[91] But, the path that will make you turn back without coming near to the road is this, when you seek to imitate our Lord and call the people, 'brood of vipers, how can you do what is virtuous, being evil ones and sons of the evil ones?'"[92] When reading the New Testament it is therefore necessary to distinguish between the passions of Christ, which are for us to imitate, and the signs, whose purpose were to reveal the divine identity of Jesus.[93] Five passions or sufferings are carefully listed and analyzed in memra 17: when Jesus gives his cheek to whoever strikes him, speaks peacefully with him and prays for him;[94] when he submitted himself and washed the feet of Judas Iscariot;[95] when he was heal-

78. *BoS* 9.5.
79. Ex 32:27.
80. *BoS* 9.5.
81. *BoS* 9.2–4.
82. *BoS* 9.7.
83. *BoS* 9.8, 19.
84. *BoS* 9.9.
85. *BoS* 9.10.
86. *BoS* 9.11.
87. *BoS* 9.11.
88. *BoS* 9.19.
89. *BoS* 9.20.
90. *BoS* 9.21.
91. Eph 4:29.
92. *BoS* 19.22, *LG* 488:10–18, citing Matt 12:34.
93. Cf. *BoS* 17.1 and *BoS* 19.22, *LG* 488:18–21.
94. Cf. *BoS* 1.2.
95. Cf. *BoS* 17.3.

ing the ear of the one who took the sword and came to kill him;[96] when he prayed God to forgive those who had crucified him;[97] and when he says to his disciples to go and teach those who had tried to kill him.[98] Another example of suffering is naturally when Jesus prayed with tears in Gethsemane in order to set an example.[99] On the other hand, the acts that are not intended for imitation are called "signs." They are designed to show the divine identity of Jesus Christ. Interestingly enough, the *Book of Steps* puts in this category not only the miracles, which manifest Christ's supernatural power,[100] but also his harsh acts, which are perfectly human, but necessary to prevent misunderstanding, lest someone should think that, at Doomsday, God will not distinguish between good and evil.[101]

This method of classifying the acts of Christ into passions and signs is so far-reaching that we find in the *Book of Steps* an original interpretation of Philippians 2:6: "Jesus Christ, being in the form of God, thought it not robbery to be equal with God." In the Greek-speaking church of the fourth century, this text had often been used by orthodox theologians as a proof of the divinity of Christ. Only later did Arian theologians suggest that this passage implies an inferiority of Christ.[102] In both cases the term "robbery" is understood as a predicative of "be equal to God": it refers to the *res rapienda.* The *Book of Steps,* on the contrary, refers it to the verb, to the *actio rapiendi.* While Satan and Adam had tried to get hold of the divinity by robbery and had failed, Christ, who is God, shows the right way to become equal to God, not by robbery, but by humility.[103] The text is not read as referring to the relation between Father and Son, but as an example for us.

In conclusion, the exegesis of *praecepta* and *exempla* in the Bible reveals

96. Cf. *BoS* 17.4. In this case, the BoS is not impressed by the miraculous healing, but by the bounty of Christ, who decided to help his enemy.

97. Cf. *BoS* 17.5.

98. Cf. *BoS* 17.6.

99. Cf. *BoS* 18.

100. For example, cf. the list of miracles in *BoS* 17.1, performed so that people might believe in Christ.

101. That's the case of *BoS* 19.22 and *BoS* 23.10.

102. Cf. Manlio Simonetti, *La crisi ariana nel IV secolo* (Rome: Institutum patristicum Augustinianum, 1975), 475–76.

103. Cf. André Louf, "Une ancienne exégèse de Phil 2,6 dans le Ketaba DeMasqata (Livre des Degrés)," in *Studiorum paulinorum congressus internationalis Catholicus 1961,* 2:523–33, Analecta Biblica 17–18 (Rome: Pontificio Instituto Biblico, 1963). Impressed by the exegesis of Phil 2:6 in the *Book of Steps,* the author argues for a possible Aramaic origin of the hymn.

a systematic approach to hermeneutical problems inspired by practical concerns, based upon a coherent understanding of salvation and revelation, and far away from allegorical developments.

A Biblical Theology

The entire economy of this Christian halakha implies that we are endowed with free will and calls for an explanation of the origin of evil. The author of the *Book of Steps* tries to find in scripture the answers to these problems, but, in doing so, he is not so much interested in explaining a given biblical text; rather, on the basis of a number of biblical passages related to the subject, he tries to elaborate a Christian doctrine. The wording of *dicta* or *facta* related by the Bible are no longer examined per se, as was the case in the halakhic section, but they become the starting points in order to solve broader theological problems. Occasionally the *Book of Steps* mentions specific interpretations that cast more light into his theological system and might suggest possible theological affiliation. For instance, we can consider the sin of Adam, which is narrated in the first chapters of Genesis. To explain it, the *Book of Steps* expands on the role of Satan, drawing from Jewish and Christian extra-biblical traditions according to which Satan was an angel who wanted to take the place of God, rebelled, and fell.[104] So that we might better understand what happened at the beginning, Jesus Christ called Judas Iscariot among his disciples. He knew that Judas was going to betray him out of his own free will, but he wanted to show, by the example of Judas, what had happened with Satan.[105]

In this theological context the two trees in the Garden of Eden get an allegorical interpretation: they are Jesus and Satan.[106] The tree of life is Jesus;[107] if we eat from him (i.e., if we follow his teachings) we shall reach perfection. Eating from the tree of "knowledge" equates to listening and learning from

104. Cf. Aleksander Kowalski, *Perfezione e giustizia,* 195–98; and Tryggve Kronholm, "The Trees of Paradise in the Hymns of Ephraem Syrus," *Annual of the Swedish Theological Institute Leiden* 1 (1978): 48–56.

105. Cf. *BoS* 23.5.

106. Cf. *BoS* 21.2.

107. The same image was used by the Manicheans; cf. Peter Nagel, "Manichäisches im syrischen Liber Graduum?" in *Religionsbegegnung und Kulturaustausch in Asien: Studien zum Gedenken an Hans-Joachim Klimkeit,* edited by Wolfgang Gantke, Karl Hoheisel, and Wassilios Klein, 179–84 (in particular 183), Studies in Oriental Religions 49 (Wiesbaden: Harrassowitz Verlag, 2002).

Satan. While explaining why God permits free will in evil people, the *Book of Steps* has to explain that God does not force anyone to be evil. If he did—he occasionally prevented the prophets from acting according to the law of perfection—he would not punish him. The expressions in Romans 11:22, "He compelled the Israelites not to obey," has to be understood as Exodus 11:10, "The Lord hardened the heart of Pharaoh—so that he would not obey." By a careful reading of the exodus narrative, the *Book of Steps* concludes that the Pharaoh was ready to let the Israelites go when Egypt was suffering under the plagues. But when the Lord was showing mercy stopping the plagues, Pharaoh changed his mind by his own will. The Lord does not harden the heart of Pharaoh in the sense that he compels him to behave badly, but because when he shows his goodness, Pharaoh despises him.[108] The same argument is applied to Romans 11:22: the Jews have rejected Jesus Christ because of his humility.[109] It is, in a way, a tragedy that as soon as God reveals his meek and humble nature, human beings start to despise him.

An Example of Dogmatic Exegesis: The Case of Colossians 1:15

The only example of a "dogmatic" interest in exegesis is to be found in memra 30. The question is how to understand the expression "first-born of creation," which is said of Christ, without endangering his divinity. "Our Lord has been called, 'the first-born of creation.' It was not about these first creatures the apostle spoke, but about these creatures who were created anew through the Son of God."[110] Colossians 1:15 had traditionally been interpreted as related to the role of the Logos in the creation of the world.[111] From the beginning of the Arian crisis this verse has been used by heretics to show that Christ had in fact been created as a part of creation.[112] The *Book of Steps* reacts against this second interpretation by referring the "first-born" to the new creation, to the economy of salvation. It seems as if an early echo of the Arian crisis had finally reached the author of the *Book of Steps.*

108. Cf. *BoS* 23.9.

109. Cf. *BoS* 23.10, with extra citation of Isa 53:2–3: the suffering servant.

110. *BoS* 30.23.

111. Cf. Manlio Simonetti, *Crisi ariana,* 3.14; and Alfred Hockel, *Christus der Erstgeborene: Zur Geschichte der Exegese von Kol 1.15* (Düsseldorf: Patmos Verlag, 1965), 48–88. In Afrahat, *Demonstration* 17, the title "first-born" indicates Christ's divinity.

112. Cf. Manlio Simonetti, *Crisi ariana,* 52–53.

Final Observations

In conclusion, the biblical exegesis in the *Book of Steps* shows some very archaic features, like the use of *testimonia,* and is essentially concentrated on halakhic matters. There is almost no trace of allegory, and none in the halakhic section, all the explanations being looked for at a historical level. The separation between Old and New Testament is clearly defined, but only as far as precepts are concerned. There is a need to "purify" the biblical language by dividing the *praecepta* and the *exempla* in exact categories, which seems to anticipate the antiochene exegesis of the gospels, where it was felt important to distinguish between what applies to divinity and what applies to humanity.[113]

It would be helpful to know if the author had any theological adversaries, but this can only be deduced from his arguments. Faithful to his own teachings, our author does not betray the names of the "sinners." Still, if we look at how he defines the nature of God and how he organizes his exposition of the *praecepta,* it would not seem to be impossible to formulate a hypothesis. The exegesis of the *Book of Steps,* where Old and New Testament clarify each other, is based on the identity of God the Creator with God the Savior, a common feature of all orthodox exegesis of the time. But there is a difference between the theological debate in Greek Christianity and what we read in the *Book of Steps.* Most of the Greek theologians were concerned by the relation between Father and Son in the divinity. A possible contemporary of the *Book of Steps,* Eunomius, was trying to define the nature of divinity on the basis of the concept of *agennesia,* thus excluding the Son and the Holy Spirit from the fullness of divinity. The biblical texts at the center of exegetical discussions were those dealing with the relation among the divine persons, in terms of priority in time and being. We could say that during the Arian controversy the problem of God was looked at from the metaphysical perspective of being and of how to conceive a plurality within the first being to accommodate the Son and later the Holy Spirit. The author of the *Book of Steps* looks at the problem of God from the transcendental perspective of "*bonum.*" The nature of God as

113. For an ancient critic to such a method, cf. Severus of Antioch, *Homiliae Cathedrales,* Hom. 22, Les homiliae cathedrales de Sévère d'Antioche, Homélies XVIII à XXV. Trad. syriaque de Jacques d'Édesse. Éd. et trad. en français par Maurice Brière et Francois Graffin (Paris: Firmin-Didot, 1975) 88–112.

revealed by Christ is goodness and meekness (not to be misunderstood with weakness). Accordingly, the elements that are likely to create problems in the scriptures are not those related to the relations between Father and Son, but those that seem to show two different faces of God, a good one and a violent one. The entire efforts of the *Book of Steps* are, as we have seen, to harmonize the seeming contradictions at this level. In the light of the above, it does not look improbable to suggest that the author of the *Book of Steps* was thinking of Marcionitic groups.[114] We know from Theodoret,[115] from Eznik of Kolb,[116] and even from archaeological remains[117] that Marcionitic communities were well established in the Middle East at the time the *Book of Steps* was written. According to the testimony of Tertullian, Marcion, impressed by the contradictions between the two Testaments, produced a theory of two opposite Gods: "Dispares deos constituere, alterum iudicem, ferum, bellipotentem, alterum mitem, placidum et tantummodo bonum atque optimum."[118] The God revealed by Christ is good and meek; the God of the Old Testament is violent and belligerent. There is a striking similarity between the definition of God in the *Book of Steps* and what we know of Marcion's doctrine. The author of the *Book of Steps,* though, does not admit two principles, but elaborates a theological system to explain why some violent features are occasionally applied to the one good God. Moreover, given the undeniable presence of Jewish elements in the New Testament, Marcion came to the conclusion that the New Testament in its traditional form had been contaminated by the evil God and set off to devise a new canon according to his own principles. We know from Tertullian[119] that Marcion accompanied his new recension of the Bible with a sort of apologetic work called *Antithesis,* in which he had collected a list of contradictory statements from the two testaments in order to show that they could

114. For the *status quaestionis* on Marcionitic studies, cf. Gerhard May, Katharina Greschat, and Martin Meiser, eds., *Marcion und seine kirchengeschichtliche Wirkung: Vorträge der Internationalen Fachkonferenz zu Marcion gehalten vom 15.–18. August 2001 in Mainz* (Berlin: Walter de Gruyter, 2002); and Gerhard May, *Markion: Gesammelte Aufsätze,* edited by Katharina Greschat and Martin Meiser (Mainz: Von Zabern, 2005).

115. Cf. Theodoret of Cyrus, *Ecclesiasticae Historiae* V.31.

116. Cf. Eznik de Kolb, *De Deo* 358–432 (a long refutation of Marcionism).

117. Cf. Simon Légasse, "Les autres voies de la mission," in *Histoire du Christianisme 1: Le Nouveau Peuple (des origines à 250),* edited by Jean-Marie Mayeur, et al, 185–86 (Paris: Desclée, 2000).

118. Tertullian, *Adversus Marcionem* I.6.1.

119. Tertullian, *Adversus Marcionem* IV.3–6.

not have the same origin, "Hae sunt Antitheses Marcionis, id est contrariae oppositiones, quae conantur discordiam evangelii cum lege committere, ut ex diversitate sententiarum utriusque instrumenti diversitatem quoque argumententur deorum."[120] This would describe the method followed by our author in memra 19, but obviously in an opposite understanding of the uniqueness of God.[121] In conclusion, the *Book of Steps'* exegetical effort can partly be described as an orthodox answer to a marcionitic theological milieu.

A second aspect is the fight against anthropological dualism. In spite of the importance of the distinction between upright and perfect, our author makes it clear that these are just two levels within a path of spiritual growth. Everyone is called to attain the highest possible level and is warned against the temptation of going back or falling down. By emphasizing free will, the *Book of Steps* takes a general stand against Gnostic and Manichean anthropologies, where the differences between spiritual and material people were considered part of their nature and therefore not modifiable at will.

Finally, the core message of the *Book of Steps,* focused as it is on the goodness of God, which should be irradiated in religious behavior against an understanding of faith propositions that lead to religiously motivated violence, goes well above the needs of an ascetic movement and becomes an invitation to every believer in any religion to critically reconsider the relation between discourse on God and human attitude toward persons of different faiths or opinions.

120. Tertullian, *Adversus Marcionem* I.19.4.

121. In his long introductory study, Kmoskó had noticed some analogies between the *Book of Steps* and Marcion, but, obsessed as he was to show the Messalian heresy in the *Book of Steps,* he was unable to see the "orthodox" intention of our author; cf. Michael Kmoskó, *Liber Graduum,* CX–CXI. The relationship between the *Book of Steps* and Marcionism does require further investigation.

Matthias Westerhoff

7. DID THE AUTHOR OF THE *BOOK OF STEPS* UNDERSTAND PAUL?

Whereas the Syriac editor's opinion that the anonymous author of the *Book of Steps* was one of the last pupils of the apostles must be dismissed as apocryphal,[1] the editor's appreciation still makes sense insofar as the author has been learning from "the Apostle." The author places Paul second in authority after our Lord himself: "Our Lord and the Apostle" is a frequently used formula of reference to his main scriptural authorities.[2] In one instance, when it seems that the apostle's word outweighs that of Jesus, the author clarifies the relationship between the two: "It is not in dissolving he dissolves, rather in building up he builds on them (i.e., the words of Our Lord)."[3] Thus the relation between the apostle and our Lord resembles that of the prophets and the Torah in Judaism: the apostle functions as the true interpreter of the teaching of our Lord.

This chapter may be seen as a summary sketch of my more comprehensive study: Matthias Westerhoff, *Das Paulusverständnis im Liber Graduum,* Patristische Texte und Studien 64 (Berlin and New York: Walter de Gruyter, 2008).

1. *BoS* Preface, *LG* 1:7f.

2. E.g., *BoS* 5.5, *LG* 108:15.

3. *BoS* 8.2, *LG* 192:24f.

Listening

The whole message of the *Book of Steps* is based on scriptural exegesis. Since the author keeps silent about the exact historical circumstances in which he drew up this "sum of Christian life under the sign not only of asceticism but of the consequent rejection of the world as such,"[4] as Peter Nagel characterizes the *Book of Steps,* we should accept this reticence and listen to the word that the author felt compelled to compose as a legacy for generations to come.

Since Michael Kmoskó's remarks in chapter 6 of his introduction on some specific features of the Pauline epistles in the *Book of Steps* that do not conform to the Peshitta, but to Aphrahat,[5] and particularly since Joseph Kerschensteiner's study on the Old Syriac text of the Pauline epistles,[6] the *Book of Steps* has emerged as a witness to a postulated text of the apostle prior to that of the Peshitta. In the vast synopsis of the Pauline epistles in Syriac by Barbara Aland and Andreas Juckel, the *Book of Steps,* following Aphrahat and Ephrem, forms the third in order of age of the witnesses to the apostle in Syriac.

However, when inquiring into our author's understanding of the apostle, we first must have a look at his textual basis. It appears that the author did not have at hand a copy of the *corpus paulinum* when dictating his discourses. His quotations are drawn from memory and are often free. The creative manner in which the author quotes Paul—which distinguishes him from Aphrahat, who faithfully keeps to the wording of the biblical text[7]—testifies to the author's self-understanding as an heir of the living Word that was communicated by the prophets and apostles.

The fact that he quotes from memory is apparent from quotations in which two verses are merged. "For you have not received the spirit of fear"[8] merges Romans 8:15—"For you have not received the spirit of bondage again to fear"—with 2 Timothy 1:7: "For God did not give us the spirit of fear." The

4. Peter Nagel, "Das Gleichnis vom verlorenen Sohn (Lk 15:11–32) im syrischen Liber Graduum," *Hallesche Beiträge zur Orientwissenschaft* 29 (2000): 17.

5. Michael Kmoskó, ed., *Liber Graduum* 164, Patrologia Syriaca 1.3 (Paris: Firmin-Didot, 1926).

6. Josef Kerschensteiner, *Der Altsyrischer Paulustext,* Corpus Scriptorum Christianorum Orientalium 315, Subsidia 37 (Louvain: Secrétariat du Corpus Scritporum Christianorum Orientalium, 1970).

7. Cf. Paul Schwen, *Afrahat: Seine Person und sein Verständnis des Christentums, Ein Beitrag zur Geschichte der Kirche im Osten,* Neue Studien zur Geschichte der Theologie und der Kirche 2 (Aalen: Scientia-Verlag, 1973), 52.

8. *BoS* 5.19, *LG* 133:23–36:1.

straightforward "spirit of fear" replaces the more complex phrasing in Romans.

A telling example of a free quotation can be seen in the warning, "Watch out, lest the root of bitterness push the flower out and harm many."[9] Here the author condenses the elaborate sentence of Hebrews 12:15 into a more easily comprehensible sentence.

Some quotations betray a tradition of citation to which the author is indebted; so the combination of 1 Timothy 1:9 with Romans 2:14—"The law is not made for the righteous, for they are a law unto themselves"[10]—occurs already in Aphrahat: "And for their (i.e., the righteous of the Old Testament) righteousness the law was not made. And they were a law unto themselves."[11]

The atomizing way the author quotes Paul results in "sentences." Although he is acquainted with the whole of the *corpus paulinum* apart from Philemon and including Hebrews, he does not seem to have any idea of the specific features of the individual letters. This point may be illustrated by the fact that only once is the title of one of the letters mentioned—namely, "to the Galatians."[12] Did he get to know the apostle by an anthology of "sentences" that was intended to be taught at some school?

Certainly one source of the author's textual basis for the Pauline letters was Aphrahat. However, inspirations clearly came from other sources, as is apparent from a prominent feature in the picture the author draws of the apostle—namely, his love of his enemies. Moreover, when the author seems to allude to Romans 9:1–3, where Paul is prepared to become a curse on behalf of his kinsfolk, we see a reflection of a passage already prefigured in Origen[13] and repeated in John Chrysostom, a contemporary of our author.[14] So the author

9. *BoS* 20.4, *LG* 536:22f.

10. *BoS* 22.10, *LG* 657:7–9.

11. Aphrahat, *Demonstration* 2.2; Jean Parisot, ed., *Aphraatis Sapientis Persae Demonstrationes,* Patrologia Syriaca 1.1 (Paris: Firmin-Didot, 1894), 52.7.

12. In *BoS* 5.18, *LG* 133:13; the author is referring to the incident at Antioch when Paul rebukes Peter for avoiding the gentiles.

13. *Comm. in Rom.* 7:13, in *Commentarii in Epistulam ad Romanos: Liber Septimus, Liber Octavus,* translated and edited by Theresia Heither, 134:4–12, Fontes Christiani 2, 4 (Freiburg: Herder, 1994).

14. *De laud. s. Pauli* 1:13, translated in *The Heavenly Trumpet: John Chrysostom and the Art of Pauline Interpretation,* by Margaret M. Mitchell (Louisville: Westiminster John Knox Press, 2002); Paul was even more excellent than Moses in choosing "for others to be saved while he was deprived of the boundless glory."

is also familiar with standard topics of the apostle's aretalogy. It is quite certain that in this particular case he is indebted to an extant homiletic tradition rather than to his own study of Romans 9:1–3: Paul was also a very great person who loved wicked people more than himself. He said, "The Lord bears witness to me that I wished to die [in order that] the evil ones might glorify the Lord of Glory, if the Lord wishes to receive me and exchange my death for their salvation so that I may imitate our Lord who died for sinners."[15]

The contact with scripture for the author is primarily an acoustic experience of listening to lessons to be read, as is stated in memra 11: "When the apostle and the gospel are read."[16] It is characteristic for the author of the *Book of Steps* to give special prominence to the ear in comparison to other human body parts. The voices of God and Satan make themselves to be heard, and it is up to a human being to discern.[17] The act of listening must result in obedience (Syriac ܡܫܡܥܬ ܐܕܢܐ lit.: ear-listening): "The apostle said, 'These things I say: As you have prepared your members as a weapon for sin, so be prepared to the obedience of Uprightness' (Romans 6:19, with intrusion of 6:16)."[18]

The author knew scripture in general and the apostle in particular by listening, which for him is an existential act. Although he does not quote, or perhaps does not know, Romans 10:17, it is clear for him that "faith (comes) by what is heard."

Distinguishing

The hermeneutic key for how scripture must be read is found in Romans 12:2 and is pointed out to the reader right in the first paragraph of the first discourse: "Be distinguishing and see what is the acceptable and perfect will of God."[19]

The author understands ܦܪܫ in ܗܘܘ ܦܪܫܝܢ "be distinguishing" according to its basic meaning of "separating" rather than in its derived meaning of an act of attentive, critical perception or discretion. Thus the apostle emerges as the authority for the strictly applied technique of distinguishing scripture, which is carried through the whole of the *Book of Steps.* It is here that we find

15. *BoS* 21.15 (modified), *LG* 624:5–12.
16. *BoS* 11.1, *LG* 273:22f.
17. This is the theme of memra 25.
18. *BoS* 15.9 (modified), *LG* 356:15–19.
19. *BoS* 1.1 (modified), *LG* 12:14–16.

the scriptural evidence for the author's way of thinking in antitheses of the great and small commandments, the Old and New Testament, the visible and invisible, and even miracles and suffering. If this is a misrepresentation of the apostle, it certainly is a creative one. For with that hermeneutic key in mind, the author is enabled to be a true follower of the apostle, when Paul's own distinctions between law and gospel, old and new, are at stake.

The law, the author states in accordance with Paul, was given to the sinful human being to prevent him from further deterioration: "For the Apostle says: The law was added to on account of transgression, this [law] which was given through Moses" (Galatians 3:19).[20] Now, in the eschatological era that was brought about in Jesus, love is the label of that set of ethics that overcomes the law: "The law does not have power over a person who in the Spirit pursues love, for he is above the law."[21] A peculiar feature of the law, which may reflect some existential experience, is that it is marked off by borders, whereas love, which, according to 1 Timothy 1:5 with Romans 13:10 is the sum of the law,[22] is unlimited.[23] Whoever has transcended the law "is for himself a law of love."[24]

A progression in theology from Aphrahat to the author will be noted here. Whereas Aphrahat understands that the just of the Old Testament "are a law unto themselves" because they showed the requirements of the law by their deeds,[25] our author places the act of "being a law unto themselves" in the new order of love. This is to be distinguished from the law, even if the order of love can be called the "law of love."[26] Love belongs to the order of the gospel.[27]

When the author comes to interpret Paul's idea of the law as tutor in Galatians 3 and 4, he differs from the theological tradition initiated by Irenaeus, which is further developed by Clement and Origen. This tradition maintains the idea of the law as a nursery school that prepares one for Christ.[28] The author, however, envisages the law as a guardian, and he rejoices that he is no longer under its hand: "But today, [as] the heir of the household is revealed, we are no longer under guardians, but under the hand of the master of the

20. *BoS* 26:4 (modified), *LG* 764:1–3.
21. *BoS* 16:8, *LG* 405:10f.
22. *BoS* 16:9, *LG* 405:20f.
23. *BoS* 22:14, *LG* 668:1.
24. *BoS* 22:14, *LG* 668:17.
25. Aphrahat, *Demonstration* 2.2; Parisot, *Aphraatis Sapientis,* 52:6–9.
26. *LG* 22:10, *LG* 657:10.
27. Cf. *BoS* 26:4, *LG* 761:23–64:1.
28. Cf. *Adv. haer.* IV:14.3, 15.1; *Quis div. salv.* 9:2; Origen, *Comm in Mt.* 10:9.

household, who is the Son, the Christ in the New Testament, who is our Lord Jesus Christ."[29]

In his understanding of the incompatibility of law and gospel the author is clearer than the theological tradition to which he is indebted: "This is to say, he freed us from the yoke of servitude of sin and from the heavy burdens of the Old Testament. He yoked us with a sweet and light yoke and with the light burdens of the New Testament."[30]

At this point the author again shows deeper insight than his (possible) teacher Aphrahat. For Aphrahat the coming of Jesus resulted in the abolition of the ceremonial law (i.e., the temple service of sacrificing animals),[31] whereas our author, feeling its heavy load, looks at the meaning of the law in a more essential way.

The limitations of the author become apparent when he identifies the gospel of Jesus with ethical perfection and sexual abstinence (memra 26), thus understanding it as a kind of new law.[32] Nevertheless, whereas Origen defends the unity of law and gospel against Marcionism, our author does not shy away from stating the difference, thus showing more understanding of Paul than the Alexandrian mainstream.

The author is committed to the ideal of distinguishing, and so holds to the ultimate distance between God and humanity, not blurring it in mysticism as Macarius does. The voice of his master Paul is echoed when the author exclaims, "Can the servant find fault with his creator? No!" [33] The awareness of God's sovereignty corresponds to the insight that humanity is sinful. Here Paul functions as an example for the sinful person, whom God's mercy has acted upon. Thus the author is offering hope for any sinner when he writes, "Yet, who knows whether Our Lord will not deal with them as with Paul or the publican or the woman taken in sin?"[34]

Paul belongs to the category of people who repented and are saved, or who

29. *BoS* 19.7, *LG* 464:17–21.

30. *BoS* 19.7, *LG* 465, 8–11.

31. Aphrahat, *Demonstration* 2, 6; Parisot, *Aphraatis Sapientis,* 57:3.

32. The earliest evidence of the concept of Christ as legislator is found in Barn. 2:6. This line can be followed up to Origen, as Hasler has shown in his study on law and gospel in the early church; see Victor Ernst Hasler, *Gesetz und Evangelium in der Alten Kirche bis Origenes: Eine auslegungsgeschichtliche Untersuchung* (Zürich: Gotthelf Verlag, 1953).

33. *BoS* 19.22, *LG* 489:17f; cf. Rom 10:20: "O man, who art thou that repliest against God?"

34. *BoS* 5.2, *LG* 104:10–12.

are weeds and finally became good wheat: "There are people, like Paul, those publicans and those harlots, who were weeds in the beginning, but became good wheat in the end."[35] Whereas many aspects of the author's picture of Paul turn out to be rather conventional, he is original at least at this point.

Protesting

There are some instances when the author protests against the apostle, at least against one interpretation cherished by Christians who entertained a liberal approach to the world. When confronted with people attempting to justify their dealings with the affairs of this world by Paul's eschatological approach—"But this I say (. . .) let those who have wives live as though they had none (. . .), and those who buy as though they had no goods, and those who deal with the world as though they had no dealings with it, for the form of this world is passing away"[36]—the author repudiates this with bitter sarcasm and unmasks his opponents as spiritualizing Christians who shy away from a real renunciation of the world. Quoting his opponents, "We possess while not possessing, and we own but our mind is not bound by it,"[37] he labels them as liars: "Therefore, if a possession can be acquired while not being possessed, and a building can be built while we are not attached to it, then even a theft could be committed while [we are] not being robbed, and hateful deeds could be done while not being done."[38] Applying his hermeneutical key of distinguishing, the author looks at Paul's advice for dealing with the affairs of this world in an eschatological perspective as counsel that is applicable only to fallen humanity, not for someone striving toward perfection.[39]

Another area in which the author parts ways with Paul is the question of the right of political authorities. In memra 22 the author rebukes Christians who dare to behave like a judge by appealing to Romans 13: "If you say, 'I will imitate the judges for there is no authority that does not exist apart from God,' notice that they have authority over evil, and they administer judgments by which no person is saved."[40]

35. *BoS* 5.11, *LG* 120:5–7.

36. 1 Cor 7:29–31.

37. *BoS* 10.8, *LG* 264:6–8.

38. *BoS* 10.8, *LG* 264:17–21.

39. *BoS* 26.3, *LG* 761:4–10, with allusion to 1 Cor 7:30f.

40. *BoS* 22.4, *LG* 641:25–44:3; Rom 13:1.

Having drawn a rather sinister picture of the political authorities of his time who abuse their power by bribery, buying one's way into office, enrichment, and judicial murder, the author still must concede that they are somehow appointed by God. He does this by having recourse to the Old Testament prophetic criticism of kingship, thereby explaining the appointment of political rulers as a dispensation of God's wrath. If humanity would only keep to the ethical level of righteousness, judges and kings would be redundant.[41]

Conclusion: Leading On

Even if in the aforementioned arguments the author appears to tear down the bridge the apostle has built with the culture and the state of the Roman Empire, there is another even more essential point of Pauline teaching that the author develops further, thereby opening up his own charismatic heritage to the present and even times to come: it is Paul's rationality.

The author is able to transfer the charismatic heritage into his own times, in which there are no more miracles and in which one is left to rely on the Word. In fact, when rendering 1 Corinthians 14:27, the author replaces speaking in tongues by reading scripture. So the author renders, "And if someone speaks in tongues, two should speak, and three at the most. And one after the other they should speak and one should interpret"[42] as "when the scriptures are read, two or three or more, then let the interpreter (that is, whoever participates in the Spirit) interpret it."[43]

When the author sees liturgical reading as a replacement of *glossolalia,* this is to say that lessons and address must be perceived as living prophecy. The author firmly believes in the charismatic form of the church, although he shifts the emphasis to the gift of teaching. By the order in which the apostle lists the charismata in 1 Corinthians 12:28, he already stresses the kerygmatic gifts as against the miraculous: "For God has appointed in the church first apostles, after them prophets, after them teachers, after them miracle workers, after them gifts of healing and helpers and leaders, and diversities of tongues."[44]

In his rendering the author replaces the apostles by their true followers, the Perfect, and leaves out miracle workers and the tongues: "And the apos-

41. *BoS* 22.9, *LG* 653:22–56:5.

42. Rendering of the Peshitta.

43. *BoS* 1.1, *LG* 12:18–13:2.

44. Rendering of the Peshitta.

tle shows that God has appointed in the church the Perfect and after them prophets and after them strong ones and teachers and edifiers and helpers, and after them [those who have] the gifts of healing."[45]

So it is only the gift of healing that has remained of the miraculous. The author trusts solely on the Word that creates faith, thereby abrogating the miraculous as is stated in the so-called "last paragraph" rendered in the Syriac editor's preface: "If the prophets of our times do not perform any signs, it is because Our Lord does not want to perform signs through them, seeing that in our time everybody believes in him."[46]

What is more, suffering is preferred to miracles: "When you, therefore, believe that Jesus is God, the miracles are not necessary for you, and you should not inquire into the How and Why, but take resort to the sufferings and love, and behold: it will be revealed unto you how and why these things are."[47]

It was a debated issue at the time in which the author wrote whether the charismata were still present.[48] Resorting to the kerygmatic gifts is a commonplace strategy. However, when John Chrysostom states that the prophetic gift of preaching is prominent because it is the source of all other gifts,[49] the author is more radical in that he relies on the weakness of the Word alone. Developing a tendency that is already present in Pauline thought, the author results in presenting a form of faith that is compatible with his own age and certainly with our present age.

45. *BoS* 9.14, *LG* 233:18–21.

46. *BoS* Preface, *LG* 8:25–9:2.

47. *BoS* 17.1, *LG* 417:17–22.

48. For Theodore of Mopsuestia (d. 428), speaking of the charismata means speaking of something passed away; cf. Adolf Martin Ritter, *Charisma im Verständnis des Joannes Chrysostomos und seiner Zeit: Ein Beitrag zur Erforschung der griechisch-orientalischen Ekklesiologie in der Frühzeit der Reichskirche* (Göttingen: Vandenhoeck and Ruprecht, 1972), 128.

49. *In ep. I ad Cor. hom.* 32, in Patrologia Graeca 61, 265:55–60. "However, it is proper that the gifts of healing are second in rank in comparison to prophecy. Why that of teaching also? Because it is not the same thing to proclaim the word of preaching, to sow religion in the souls of those who listen, and to perform miracles, as these come into existence by that one"; cf. Ritter, *Charisma,* 70.

PART 4

THEOLOGICAL PERSPECTIVES IN THE *BOOK OF STEPS*

J. W. Childers

8. A BROKEN MIND

The Path to Knowledge in the Book of Steps

"We must seek the truth, for, as our Lord said, the truth will set us free. That implies, however, that we must humble ourselves and break our minds."[1] The modern scholar will identify with the impulse to seek truth that the author of the *Book of Steps* expresses here, but even the most demanding teacher might wonder how useful "breaking the mind" would be toward that end. In this text "breaking the mind" relates in a particular way to the practice of humility and is necessary for excellent living and for the proper functioning of the cognitive processes. Those who do not break their minds "are ignorant of the truth," for "pride is an obstacle preventing knowledge."[2]

Ancient writers commonly correlate knowledge and virtue, linking sound cognitive processes to the exercise of praiseworthy dispositions. In contrast, modern epistemology has been largely obsessed with the problem of adjudicating truth claims, justifying true belief, and answering skepticism. Moral qualities have been judged as mostly irrelevant to the rigorous analysis of knowledge in the sterile laboratory of dispassionate critical reflection. Only in recent decades have contemporary epistemologists been discussing in earnest a subject that so captivated some of the ancient sages—the possibility of

1. *BoS* 1.2.

2. *BoS* 1.2. Unless indicated otherwise, translations of the *Book of Steps* are from Robert A. Kitchen and Martien F. G. Parmentier, trans., *The Book of Steps: The Syriac Liber Graduum* (Kalamazoo, Mich.: Cistercian Publications, 2004).

a vital link between virtue and knowledge. "Virtue epistemology" prescribes a change in the direction of analysis—from properties of beliefs to properties of persons, so that, for instance, epistemic justification might be explained in terms of a belief's relation to intellectual virtue.[3] Some epistemologists seek to work out proposals in which virtue plays a central role in resolving the thorny epistemological problems of the twentieth century—especially the analysis of truth claims and the justification of knowledge. But others legitimately question whether virtue can play such a role, since some beliefs at least may be reliably formed and held apart from the exercise of some virtue.[4]

Some "responsibilist" virtue epistemologists refocus the discussion to illuminate the place of virtue in enhancing the intellectual life and regulating the scholarly enterprise.[5] Rather than subjugating virtue to the project of jus-

3. This shift parallels somewhat earlier developments in the field of ethics. Influential "virtue reliabilists" include Ernest Sosa, "Raft and the Pyramid: Coherence versus Foundations in the Theory of Knowledge," in *Studies in Epistemology,* edited by Peter French, Howard K. Wettstein, Robert Feleppa, and Theodore E. Uehling, Jr., 5:3–25, Midwest Studies in Philosophy 5 (Minneapolis: University of Minnesota Press, 1980); John Greco, "Virtues in Epistemology," in *The Oxford Handbook of Epistemology,* edited by Paul K. Moser, 287–335 (Oxford: Oxford University Press, 2002). Influential "virtue responsibilists" include Lorraine Code, *Epistemic Responsibility* (Hanover, N.H.: University Press of New England for Brown University Press, 1987); James A. Montmarquet, "Epistemic Virtue," *Mind* 96 (1987): 482–97; Montmarquet, *Epistemic Virtue and Doxastic Responsibility* (Boston: Rowman and Littlefield, 1993); Linda Trinkaus Zagzebski, *Virtues of the Mind: An Inquiry into the Nature of Virtue and the Ethical Foundations of Knowledge* (Cambridge: Cambridge University Press, 1996); W. Jay Wood, *Epistemology: Becoming Intellectually Virtuous* (Downers Grove, Ill.: Intervarsity Press, 1998). Other helpful sources for understanding the development of modern virtue epistemology include Guy Axtell, "Recent Work in Virtue Epistemology," *American Philosophical Quarterly* 34 (1997): 1–27; Axtell, *Knowledge, Belief, and Character: Readings in Virtue Epistemology* (Lanham, Md.: Rowman and Littlefield, 2000), xi–xxix; and Abrol Fairweather and Linda Zagzebski, eds., *Virtue Epistemology: Essays on Epistemic Virtue and Responsibility* (New York: Oxford University Press, 2001), 3–14.

4. "An exercise of intellectual virtue simply is not a necessary ingredient of justification in any traditional sense"; Jason S. Baehr, "Character in Epistemology," *Philosophical Studies* 128 (2006): 500; cf. Zagzebski, *Virtues of the Mind,* 281.

5. E.g., Jonathan L. Kvanvig, *The Intellectual Virtues and the Life of the Mind* (Savage, Md.: Rowman and Littlefield, 1992); Baehr, "Character in Epistemology," 501–8, 479–514; Frederick D. Aquino, "The Healing of Cognition in Deification: Towards a Patristic Virtue Epistemology," in *Immersed in the Life of God: The Healing Resources of the Christian Faith,* edited by Paul Gavrilyuk, Douglas M. Koskela, and Jason E. Vickers, 123–42 (Grand Rapids, Mich.: Eerdmans, 2008); Baehr, "On the Reliability of Moral and Intellectual Virtues," *Metaphilosophy* 38 (2007): 456–70; William P. Alston, *Beyond "Justification": Dimensions of Epistemic Evaluation* (Ithaca: Cornell University Press, 2005); Robert C. Roberts and W. Jay Wood, *Intellectual Virtues: An Essay in Regulative Epistemology* (Oxford: Oxford University Press, 2007); Christopher Hookway, "How to Be a Virtue Epistemologist," in *Intellectual Virtue: Perspectives from Ethics and Epistemology,* edited by Michael R. DePaul and Linda T. Zagzebski, 193–97 (Oxford: Clarendon Press, 2003); Wayne D. Riggs, "Understanding 'Virtue' and the Virtue of Understanding,"

tifying true belief, the appeal to virtue can inform our understanding of how traits such as open-mindedness, desire for truth, attention to detail, diligence, and honesty can lead to understanding. For instance, Robert Roberts and Jay Wood have noticed that the virtue of humility generally leads a person to be unconcerned about status and appearance, to avoid exercising power over colleagues and students, and to avoid the complacent assertion of unwarranted claims on the basis of one's supposed superiority. The authors observe, "over the long run, just about everybody will be epistemically better off for having, and having associates who have, epistemic humility."[6]

It is here that ancient writers find a fresh voice in contemporary discussions. Although they typically offer no insights contributing to the modern project of justifying true belief, many are able to converse fluently about the benefits of virtue and wisdom in the quest for knowledge. Like virtue ethicists, virtue epistemologists appeal to ancient models, routinely alluding to the parallels that exist between their own assumptions and those of classical authors. Yet few attempts have been made to explore the texts of specific ancient authors and intellectual traditions with this in mind;[7] Aristotle stands as a recurring exception.[8]

One intellectual tradition in which notions of virtue play a prominent role in shaping epistemological assumptions is that of early Syriac-speaking Christianity.[9] The recent appearance of a complete English translation of the *Book of Steps* creates an opportunity to explore its contemporary relevance in this vein. This chapter conducts a preliminary overview of the epistemological assumptions at work in the text, showing that the *Book of Steps* stands as a worthy participant in the aforementioned conversations, since it presumes that a vital connection exists between virtuous practices, the mind and its proper functioning, and the quest for truth.

---

in *Intellectual Virtue,* edited by DePaul and Zagzebski, 223–26; see also Axtell, "Blind Man's Bluff: The Basic Belief Apologetic as Anti-Skeptical Stratagem," *Philosophical Studies* 130 (2006): 131–52.

6. Roberts and Wood, "Humility and Epistemic Goods," in *Intellectual Virtue*, edited by DePaul and Zagzebski, 271–72.

7. E.g., Aquino's treatment of Maximus Confessor, in "Healing of Cognition."

8. Especially Aristotle's *Nicomachean Ethics.*

9. E.g., see J. W. Childers, "'Humility Begets Wisdom and Discernment:' Character and True Knowledge in Aphrahat," in *Studia Patristica,* edited by Frances Young, et al, 41:13–22 (Leuven: Peeters, 2006); Childers, "'We Must Seek the Truth': Theological Scholarship in the Early Syriac Tradition," *Restoration Quarterly* 49 (2007): 193–216.

"There Is Life in Each of the Three Churches and Their Ministries": Sustaining Unity in Diversity

The thirty anonymous memre of the *Book of Steps* (ܟܬܒܐ ܕܡܣܩܬܐ)[10] probably composed in late-fourth-century Persia,[11] treat a range of topics, but it is the problem of sustaining practical unity within a diverse community that provides the most vivid backdrop against which to understand the entire corpus.[12] Echoing the proto-monasticism of the early Syrian tradition,[13] the *Book of Steps* primarily addresses Christians consecrated to the ascetic life of the solitaries (ܝܚܝܕܝܐ) or children of the covenant—covenanters (ܒܢܝ ܩܝܡܐ), yet these ascetics are situated within an ecclesial context that includes non-ascetics.[14] The practice of very different styles of Christian discipleship side by side has pro-

10. Heading cites *BoS* 12.4. The "three churches" are the visible church (largely associated with the Upright), the invisible church of the heart (largely associated with the Perfect), and the "higher church" of heaven "that perfects all the saints" (*BoS* 12.3); see Robert Murray, *Symbols of Church and Kingdom: A Study in Early Syriac Tradition,* rev. ed. (London: T. and T. Clark; Piscataway, N.J.: Gorgias Press, 2004), 262–64.

11. The standard edition is that of Michael Kmoskó, ed., *Liber Graduum,* Patrologia Syriaca 1.3 (Paris: Firmin-Didot, 1926). For introductory discussions of the *Book of Steps,* see Kmoskó, *Liber Graduum,* i–clxix; Anton Baumstark, *Geschichte der syrischen Literatur: Mit Ausschluss der christlich-palästinensischen Texte* (Bonn: A. Marcus and E. Webers, 1922); Kitchen and Parmentier, *Book of Steps,* xxi–lxxxiii; Arthur Vööbus, *History of Asceticism in the Syrian Orient: A Contribution to the History of Culture in the Near East,* Corpus Scriptorum Christianorum Orientalium 500 (Louvain: Peeters, 1988), 3:1–18; Guillaumont, "Liber Graduum," in *Dictionnaire de spiritualité ascétique et mystique: Doctrine et histoire* 9:749–54 (Paris: Beauchesne, 1976); Seely J. Beggiani, *Introduction to Eastern Christian Spirituality: The Syriac Tradition.* London: Associated University Presses, 1991), 29–34; and David J. Lane, "The Book of Grades, or Steps," *The Harp* 14 (2001): 81–88.

12. "It is the persistent witness of conflict that makes the greatest impression"; Kitchen and Parmentier, *Book of Steps,* lxi–lxii, li–liv; see also Kitchen, "Conflict on the Stairway to Heaven: The Anonymity of Perfection in the Syriac *Liber Graduum,*" in *Symposium Syriacum VII: Uppsala University, Department of Asian and African Languages, 11–14 August 1996,* edited by René Lavenant, 211–20 (Rome: Pontificio Instituto Orientale, 1998).

13. See Kitchen and Parmentier, *Book of Steps,* xiii–xxi; Sebastian P. Brock, "Early Syrian Asceticism," *Numen* 20 (1973): 10–19; Robert Murray, "The Features of the Earliest Christian Asceticism," in *Christian Spirituality: Essays in Honour of Gordon Rupp,* edited by Peter Brooks, 72–73 (London: SCM, 1975); Vööbus, *History of Asceticism,* 1:178–84, 190–94; 1–18; Shafiq Abouzayd, *Ihidayutha: A Study of the Life of Singleness in the Syrian Orient, From Ignatius of Antioch to Chalcedon 451 AD* (Oxford: ARAM Society for Syro-Mesopotamian Studies, 1993). Even after the primitive style of Syrian asceticism had begun to be supplanted by the Egyptian-Greek model, "the church of Syria long preserved adepts of the old ways, who continued to live in the general community and to use the traditional ascetical vocabulary, although much of it was also adopted by the new enthusiasts"; Sidney H. Griffith, "Asceticism in the Church of Syria: The Hermeneutics of Early Syrian Monasticism," in *Asceticism,* edited by Richard Valantasis and Vincent L. Wimbush, 223 (New York: Oxford University Press, 1995). Griffith joins others in situating the *Book of Steps* during a period of transition from the primitive form of asceticism (222).

14. Decades of reflection on Kmoskó's identification of the *Book of Steps* as "Messalian" have rightly

duced tensions, manifested in conflicts arising from the misunderstanding, elitism, and factionalism that often accompany such diversity. Even episodes of physical violence have become a feature of life within this community.[15]

The author strategically draws on the diversity of scripture's own commands and examples in order to promote a vision of appropriately stratified, but interdependent classes within the Christian community.[16] Principally, these consist of (1) the Upright, or Just (ܟܐܢܐ), who are fully involved in the affairs of the material world and find their ethical guidance in the Golden Rule; and (2) the Perfect, or Mature (ܓܡܝܪܐ), who embody a higher path of radical ascetic renunciation and the extreme ethic of treating others better than oneself and loving one's enemies.[17] Although the author regards the way of the Perfect as the more excellent one, he also underscores the legitimacy and value of the Upright,[18] picturing for them a noble place within the community and stressing the need for harmonious unity between the two classes.[19]

---

yielded the consensus that his accusation is basically unjustifiable as such; Vööbus, "*Liber Graduum:* Some Aspects of Its Significance for the History of Early Syrian Asceticism," in *Charisteria Iohanni Kopp octogenerio oblata,* 108–28, Papers of the Estonian Theological Society in Exile 7 (Stockholm: Estonian Theological Society in Exile, 1954); Peter Bäss, "Der Liber Graduum—ein messalianisches Buch?" In *XVII. Deutscher Orientalistentag, vom 21. bis 27. Juli 1968 in Würzburg,* edited by Wolfgang Voigt, 2:368–84 (Wiesbaden: Franz Steiner Verlag, 1969); Guillaumont, "Situation et significance du 'Liber Graduum' dans la spiritualité syriaque," in *Symposium Syriacum 1972: Célébré dans les jours 26–31 octobre 1972 à l'Institut pontifical oriental de Rome: Rapports et communications,* edited by Ignacio Ortiz de Urbina, 311–25, Orientalia Christiana Analecta 197 (Rome: Pontificium Institutum Orientalium, 1974); Robert A. Ratcliff, "Steps Along the Way of Perfection: The Liber Graduum and Early Syrian Monasticism" (PhD diss., Emory University, 1988), 33–93; Klaus Fitschen, *Messalianismus und Antimessalianismus: Ein Beispiel ostkirchlicher Ketzergeschichte* (Göttingen: Vandenhoeck and Ruprecht, 1998), 108–28; Lionel Wickham, "The Liber Graduum Revisited," in *VI Symposium Syriacum, 1992: University of Cambridge, Faculty of Divinity, 30 August–2 September 1992,* edited by René Lavenant, 177–87 (Rome: Pontificio Instituto Orientale, 1992). See the survey and discussion in Kitchen and Parmentier, *Book of Steps,* xxi–xxiv, lvi–lxi. Columba Stewart's study has challenged traditional assumptions about "Messalianism," showing that the controversy owed more to linguistic and cultural differences than doctrinal ones; Columba Stewart, *"Working the Earth of the Heart": The Messalian Controversy in History, Texts, and Language to A.D. 431* (Oxford: Clarendon Press, 1991); see also Murray, *Symbols,* 35–36; Ratcliff, "Steps," 33–61; Peter R. Brown, *The Body and Society: Men, Women, and Sexual Renunciation in Early Christianity* (New York: Columbia University Press, 1988), 333–38.

15. Abouzayd, "Violence and Killing in the *Liber Graduum,*" *ARAM* 12 (2000): 451–65; Kitchen, "Conflict," 219–20.

16. Kitchen and Parmentier identify six levels of discipleship in the *Book of Steps,* xxxviii.

17. Passages summarizing the characteristics of the Upright and the Perfect include *BoS* 2.1, 3.3, 7.2, 13, 14, 18.19, 19.20, 24.7, and 25.6–9. See the descriptions in Kitchen and Parmentier, *Book of Steps,* xxxviii–xliv; Vööbus, *History of Asceticism,* 3: 11–14.

18. *BoS* 3, 8, 13.

19. *BoS* 21.2, 28.2; Kitchen and Parmentier, *Book of Steps,* xxxvi–xxxviii; Kitchen reads the *Book of Steps* as a "sect-canon," a major function of which is to clarify relationships between people within the

For our author such unity requires, among other things, the cultivation of basic epistemic virtues that help regulate the enterprise of acquiring and using knowledge. Underlying his vision of communal life are certain assumptions regarding the mind and knowledge that are traceable within the coherent depiction of salvation history occurring in the text.

"Their Mind Stood Before God in Heaven:" A Narrative Framework for Understanding the Mind and Knowledge

A commonly recognized epistemic virtue is the ability to achieve coherence. Knowers seek to interrelate discrete items of knowledge by fitting them into a cogent framework that will clarify their significance.[20] Coherentists propose to evaluate knowledge based on coherence.[21] Although such analysis is not a concern in the *Book of Steps,* fitting knowledge and experience into a coherent framework is a strong interpretive principle for the author. The *Book of Steps* presupposes a framework based on the biblical narratives, especially the creation and gospel accounts.[22] Attending to this narrative structure enables the author to discover a richly nuanced role for the mind and to construct a set of norms for its ideal functioning.[23]

According to the *Book of Steps,* in the beginning the human mind (ܪܥܝܢܐ) was situated immediately in God's presence.[24] Adam and Eve initially had a

community; Kitchen, "The Gattung of the Liber Graduum: Implications for a Sociology of Asceticism," in *IV Symposium Syriacum 1984,* edited by H. J. W. Drijvers, et al, 174–82, Orientalia Christiana Analecta 229 (Rome: Pontificium Institutum Studiorum Orientalium, 1987).

20. Heading cites *BoS* 21.8.

21. See Richard Fumerton, "Theories of Justification," in *The Oxford Handbook of Epistemology,* edited by Paul K. Moser, 226–30 (Oxford: University Press, 2002).

22. "The most notable feature of the *Liber Graduum*'s description of creation, disruption, and recovery is a detailed analysis of humankind's movement away from and then once more toward the perfection intended for them by God. The approach is both historical and moral"; Stewart, *"Working the Earth,"* 87.

23. For a descriptive summary of the *Book of Steps'* account of the Fall, see Diana Juhl, *Die Askese im Liber Graduum und bei Afrahat: Eine vergleichende Studie zur frühsyrischen Frömmigkeit,* Orientalia Biblical et Christiana 9 (Wiesbaden: Harrassowitz Verlag, 1996), 38–68. For a detailed study, see Aleksander Kowalski, *Perfezione e giustizia di Adamo nel Liber Graduum,* Orientalia Christiana Analecta 232 (Rome: Pontificium Institutum Orientale, 1989), 35–175.

24. Cf. Aphrahat's similar, but distinctive teaching: humanity was first "conceived and dwelt in the mind of God" prior to its full birth, thereby enabling humanity reciprocally to conceive of God within its mind; Aphrahat, *Demonstration* 17.7; see also J. W. Childers, "'Humility Begets Wisdom and Discern-

sort of bifurcated experience: their minds "stood before God in heaven" while their bodies were on the earth,[25] apparently destined for eventual exaltation to an experience of fuller integration in heaven.[26] In their primal state the minds of Adam and Eve were completely oriented on heavenly realities, fully absorbed by the divine presence.[27] They were students only of good, focused on him who supplies all good teaching: "Because God had only taught what is good to Adam and Eve when he created them, they did not know evil."[28] This was the state of perfection (ܓܡܝܪܘܬܐ),[29] which the author frequently compares to the angelic life.[30] Feigning concern for their well-being,[31] Satan convinced Adam and Eve that fulfilling their aspirations to become like their Creator would require eating fruit from the tree of knowledge. By doing so, he offered, they could gain possession and control of material things and attain divine dignity: "Look, gold and silver are on the earth and all sorts of pleasures. Possess and enjoy yourself; rule, increase, and multiply," the evil one counseled. "Cast off from yourself asceticism and renunciation and holiness, also lowliness, and know evil as well as good things and grow and become like God who created you."[32] Exercising their free will,[33] "Adam and Eve accepted the evil idea and coveted the beauty of the earth. . . . They initially desired these things in the hope that they could become like their Creator . . . [they did so] in that hope that they could become great like God."[34] The inclination was profoundly arrogant.[35] Their motive for seeking knowledge was to usurp God's place

ment': Character and True Knowledge in Aphrahat," in *Studia Patristica,* edited by Frances Young, et al, 15 (Leuven: Peeters, 2006).

25. *BoS* 21.7–8; see also *BoS* 21.3.

26. See Kowalski, *Perfezione e giustizia,* 86–88.

27. Kitchen, "Syriac Additions to Anderson: The Garden of Eden in the Book of Steps and Philoxenus of Mabbug," *Hugoye: Journal of Syriac Studies* 6 (2003): 43–45.

28. *BoS* 21.1.

29. *BoS* 1.4.

30. "See, O man, what [kind of] thought Adam had about the one who created him from dust and mingled him with the heavenly angels"; *BoS* 21.10. The theme of the ascetic life as an anticipation of angelic existence was prominent in Syrian asceticism; see Brock, "Early Syrian Asceticism," 5–6; Abouzayd, *Ihidaya,* 269–77.

31. *BoS* 21.9.

32. *BoS* 21.9.

33. "However, in the end, Adam had a will, and if he had not so desired, the evil one would not have oppressed him"; *BoS* 21.10. In keeping with other Syriac authors (e.g., Ephrem, Aphrahat), the author of the *Book of Steps* firmly upholds a belief in human free will and personal responsibility.

34. *BoS* 15.2.

35. See Kitchen, "Syriac Additions," 29.

in an effort to possess and control other creatures, to become the guarantors of their own welfare, and to procreate independently.[36] Upon eating from the tree of the knowledge of good and evil, they became knowers of both and were thereby corrupted, "and from there the enmity of impiety bound Adam and his children."[37] The mind's attention shifted decisively from its heavenly communion with God in heaven to the captivating entanglements of mere earthly existence.[38]

Whereas in the views of Aphrahat and Ephrem the fruit of the tree of knowledge was meant for eventual human consumption and to play a proper role in the process of human divinization,[39] in the *Book of Steps* the fruit appears to be more sinister. It poisons humanity due to its mixed nature as a provider of evil knowledge alongside the good knowledge that they already had. In the introduction to memra 21, "On the Tree of Adam," the author claims that "the tree of the knowledge of good and evil" was in fact "the evil one, toil, anxiety, and the thought of transitory things by which Adam and Eve tasted death. For through it they came to know evil, which they had not known."[40] Yet it is unclear whether the author believed the fruit to be inevitably lethal in its original essence or only to be corrupting in its effects because of the way in which it was obtained and used. The latter view is closer to that of Aphrahat and Ephrem, but even in the former view there are significant parallels. For all three Syriac authors, knowledge and knowing relate to the divine nature and are tied to fundamentally moral dimensions of humanity. "Knowing truth" is as much a state of being and a way of acting as an experience of cognitive awareness or precision. For each author the Genesis narrative teaches that

36. See Michela Aveta's study of the *Book of Steps'* teachings about the connections between sex, celibacy, and the impulse to play God; Aveta, "Ad instar angelorum: Per un'analisi storico-religiosa dell'antropologia del *Liber Graduum*," *Christianesimo nella storia* 8 (1987): 481–500.

37. "Because God had only taught what is good to Adam and Eve when he created them, they did not know evil until they had obeyed Satan and he taught them evil. Because of this Satan is called the 'Tree,' through which Adam and Eve knew evil and good. . . . They became 'knowers of good and evil'"; *BoS* 21.1.

38. Kitchen, "Syriac Additions," 9–11.

39. Childers, "'Humility Begets Wisdom,'" 15–16; Juoko Martikainen, "Das Böse in den Schriften des Syrers Ephrem, im Stufenbuch und in Corpus Macarianum," in *Makarios-Symposium über das Böse: Vorträge der Finnisch-Deutschen Theologentagung in Goslar 1980,* edited by Werner Strothmann, 39–41, Göttinger Orientforschungen 1, Reihe: Syriaca 24 (Wiesbaden: Harrassowitz Verlag, 1983); see Kowalski, *Perfezione e giustizia,* 132–36.

40. *BoS* 21.1; see also *BoS* 20.6.

primal humanity stood at the brink of divinization, but forfeited its original potential by eating from the tree of knowledge in arrogant willfulness. At that point pride and the desire for autonomy got in the way, and true knowledge became more elusive as humanity slipped into an existence defined by the ill-advised ambitions on which it had acted.[41]

Having diverted their minds from heaven toward earth in a bid to gain mastery, Adam and Eve effectively left heaven and fell from perfection,[42] thereby enslaving themselves to the burdens of anxiety, labor, and marriage.[43] The inclinations took root and were passed on to their descendants, who continue to struggle with the same temptations.[44] Desiring also to be like God, they eat the same fruit and become entangled in the same snares as their original parents, who "abandoned heaven and heavenly wealth and loved the earth and all that is in it. . . . They erred because there is nothing that is able to become like the Creator of all the worlds."[45] Not only did the fall separate the human mind from God, but its surrender to materialism "resulted in an inability to live in that kind of loving and accepting relationship with other human beings which had been God's original intention for humanity."[46] The corrupting entanglements that came with their prideful venture to control earthly existence produced patterns of greed, jealousy, lust, manipulation, and violence.

In a tragic irony, the elevated status that Adam craved and the desire to do such things as procreate would have been granted him if he had been humble enough to receive these things spiritually from God according to the divine arrangements.[47] But by pridefully trying to obtain these things in an earthly fashion—in the wrong way and for the wrong reasons—Adam fell from perfection to uprightness (ܟܐܢܘܬܐ).[48] This latter state exists by God's merciful concession as an opportunity for humans to enjoy a somewhat limited salvation[49] by adher-

41. "God punished them by giving them what they wanted; their fascination with earthly things resulted in their bondage to them. . . . The difficulty of meeting one's own physical needs led to anxiety over them, which in turn erected barriers between individuals and produced enmity and hatred of others"; Ratcliff, "Steps," 138–39.

42. *BoS* 15.8.

43. *BoS* 20.6, 21.10, 15.2, 6; Ratcliff, "Steps," 82–84.

44. *BoS* 5.14.

45. *BoS* 21.10.

46. Ratcliff, "Steps," 72.

47. *BoS* 15.6; see also *BoS* 21.7.

48. See Kowalski, *Perfezione e giustizia,* 117–74.

49. See *BoS* 3.3 for notice of the common belief that some would receive more noble heavenly rewards, in keeping with the quality of their spiritual lives.

ing to the lower code of God's law in their earthly environment—especially the Golden Rule.[50] In this state humans can exploit their earthly entanglements for the sake of avoiding evil and doing good.[51] Those who do so have an inferior spiritual existence during their earthly life, but they anticipate a heavenly reward, since "God desires that all people should live."[52] Of course, it is possible to fall from that level to even lower levels of debauchery and abuse.[53]

Yet with the advent of Jesus Christ, a new eschatological possibility emerges—a chance to regain paradise and the state of perfection by participating in the mind of Jesus and imitating his radical ethic:[54] "No person has shown clearly how Adam was created, except Jesus through his way of life."[55] Jesus reveals original humanity,[56] inviting people to enter into a dynamic experience of new creation through him: "Because people fell short of the Perfection through which God created Adam and [fell short of] the purity of heart that belonged to Adam while he had not yet sinned, and [fell short of] the holiness in which he was created in the image of the angels, on account of this, the apostle witnesses, saying, "In Jesus everything is made new again."[57] Jesus is the perfecter of perfection.[58] He is the Tree of Life, the fruit of which is the definitive remedy for those who have partaken of the toxic fruit of the tree of knowledge of good and evil. Although those who love God may yet pursue uprightness, an eschatologically charged state of perfection is accessible to those who "do not take wives, nor do they work on the land, nor acquire possessions, nor have a place to lay their heads on earth like their teacher."[59] Those

50. See Martikainen, *Gerechtigkeit und güte Gottes: Studies zur Theologie von Ephrem und Philoxenos von Mabbug,* Göttinger Orientforschungen 1, Reihe: Syriaca 20 (Wiesbaden: Harrossowitz Verlag, 1981), 24–27.

51. *BoS* 21.20. Whereas the Upright engage in human commerce in order to minister to the material needs of the poor, the Perfect become poor in order to be free to love and forgive others fully; Ratcliff, "Steps," 89–92. Memre 13 and 14 have the most detailed descriptions of the ethics of physical purity and ministries of compassion by which the Upright are to live; memra 8 focuses on the Upright's duty to give of their means to support the poor; see Nancy Khalek, "Methods of Instructing Syriac-Speaking Christians to Care for the Poor: A Brief Comparison of the Eighth Memra of the Book of Steps and the Story of the Man of God of Edessa," *Hugoye: Journal of Syriac Studies* 8 (2005): 16–21.

52. *BoS* 7.21.

53. *BoS* 1.4.

54. See the summary in *BoS* 30.24; Kitchen, "Syriac Additions," 30–32; Juhl, *Askese im Liber Graduum,* 71–89.

55. *BoS* 25.2.

56. See Ratcliff, "Steps," 148–50.

57. *BoS* 30.24; see also *BoS* 23.1, 25.2.

58. *BoS* 20.8.

59. *BoS* 15.13.

who imitate Christ in these ways are reversing the Fall by humbly refusing to usurp God's place,[60] choosing instead to empty themselves through the renunciation of property, marriage, work, and violence, thereby reorienting their minds toward heavenly realities and effectively beginning a reentry into the angelic life of paradise.[61] Like Jesus, the Perfect will pursue extreme love within the framework of their heavenly orientation, refraining from judgment, violence, and retribution.[62] By their habits they "become attached to our Lord in heaven and become dead from the use of the world."[63]

The Holy Spirit plays a crucial role in the recovery of paradise, bringing the mind back into God's presence. The Spirit had originally dwelt within Adam, instructing him in doing right.[64] In the postlapsarian economy, the person who unites his or her interior self with the exterior actions of obedience to God receives "the gifts of the Holy Spirit who will be given to them in the form of a pledge, and a person will be established as a trinity and live."[65] This is the experience of the Upright. Applying the Pauline notion of a "pledge of the Spirit,"[66] the *Book of Steps* teaches that they receive the Spirit only as a partial indwelling of the Spirit that enables them to do good according to the measure of their disciplined submission to God's will (ܥܘܪܒܢܐ).[67] The more they seek God, the greater the effectiveness of the pledge within them. But when a person advances so far that she empties herself and pursues the way of perfec-

60. See André Louf, "Une ancienne exégèse de Phil 2,6 dans le Ketaba DeMasqata (Livre des Degrés)," in *Studiorum paulinorum congressus internationalis Catholicus 1961,* 2:523–33, Analecta Biblica 17–18 (Rome: Pontificio Instituto Biblico, 1963).

61. By living "free from care" as Jesus commanded, they could "recapture the angelic freedom that had characterized Adam before his Fall"—and that was characteristic of Jesus as well; Daniel Caner, *Wandering, Begging Monks: Spiritual Authority and the Promotion of Monasticism in Late Antiquity* (Berkeley and Los Angeles: University of California Press, 2002), 109.

62. Ratcliff, "Steps," 194–96.

63. *BoS* 13.5.

64. *BoS* 28.1–4.

65. *BoS* 28.5. The author shows no interest in ontological speculation about the nature of God and Trinity, but is chiefly concerned with God's manner of relating to humans and the potential for humans to emulate his character; see Wickham, "Teachings about God and Christ in the Liber Graduum," in *Logos: Festschrift für Luise Abramowski zum 8. Juli 1993,* edited by Hanns Christof Brennecke, Ernst Ludwig Grasmück, and Christoph Markschies, 490–96 (New York: Walter de Gruyter, 1993).

66. See 2 Cor 1:22, 5:5.

67. *BoS* 3.7. For a discussion of this obscure term, see Guillaumont, "Les Arrhes de l'Esprit' dans le Livre des degrés," in *Mémorial Mgr Gabriel Khouri-Sarkis (1898–1968): Fondateur et directeur de l'Orient syrien, 1956–1967,* edited by François Graffin, 107–13 (Louvain: Imprimerie Orientaliste, 1969); see also Kitchen and Parmentier, *Book of Steps,* xlvii–xlix; cf. Stewart, *"Working the Earth,"* 199–203.

tion, loving and being merciful to everyone, "even our murderers," she receives the plenitude of the Paraclete.[68] Such people "belong to our Lord continually, and our Lord is in them."[69] As Jesus promised, the Paraclete becomes a channel of truth within these people, enabling them to discern and to know with extraordinary skill.[70] The presence and activity of the Paraclete within the Perfect reinstates the mind to its place as a locus of direct experience of God, but this mental rehabilitation occurs only when a person practices habits of extreme lowliness and service.

Each group has its place: "Thus God desires that all humanity act, each one according to the stage on which he stands."[71] The Upright will engage in worldly affairs, avoid traditional vices, practice basic devotion, administer the church, and live according to the standards of the Golden Rule—including the practice of hospitality and charity toward the Perfect and others. For their part the Perfect contribute to the community's well-being from within a rigorous asceticism, discussed further later in this chapter. They represent God's love and forgiveness, refuse to judge, and minister among those who are not part of the Christian community.[72] For both classes the author pictures the Christian life as an experience of ongoing growth. "Incompleteness, not error, limits the spiritual advance of the Upright,"[73] who by the assistance of the Holy Spirit are able to advance to the state of perfection. Fervent application of the minor commands will, over time, enable a person to achieve the major ones—or perhaps surpass them.[74] Even the Perfect, once they receive the Paraclete, are just at the beginning of a lifelong course of maturation into their original, divinely focused states[75]—"he immediately knows all the truth and begins to grow and to eradicate all his defects."[76] A new creation is underway. One's growth potential is limited only by one's desire and discipline: "Everyone as he seeks you, so he will find you. As he compels his disposition to keep your law, so he will grow. As much as he humbles himself, so he will be glorified."[77] For both groups, growth in spiritual status occurs in proportion to

68. *BoS* 20.7.

69. *BoS* 3.11.

70. *BoS* 1.2; see also *BoS* 3.11.

71. *BoS* 7.21.

72. Ratcliff, "Steps," 135.

73. Kitchen and Parmentier, *Book of Steps,* xlii.

74. *BoS* 2.2–4, 15.16–17.

75. *BoS* 5.18–19, 16.3–4.

76. *BoS* 28.2.

77. *BoS* 14.4. In some contexts the *Book of Steps* seems to indicate that the growth potential of some is limited; see *BoS* 15.18; cf. the author's hopeful claim that growth in perfection "is an easy enterprise for

one's degree of self-lowering. Practical humility, originating within the mind, is fundamental. This is especially evident within the Perfect, who have the opportunity to experience mental functioning according to its original design and purpose.

"We Must Humble Ourselves and Break Our Minds:" Refining Cognition through the Practice of Inner and Outer Humility

As the principal venue of divine experience and a major actor in the events of the Fall, the human mind plays a crucial role in adopting and sustaining the way of perfection.[78] Its proper functioning is regulated by the exercise of external and internal virtues consistent with the original ideals for humanity, beginning with humility. In a thematic passage near the beginning of the first memra, the author touches on many of his most pervasive themes,[79] situating mental habits alongside humility in the center of his vision: "We must seek the truth, for as our Lord said, the truth will set us free. That implies, however, that we must humble ourselves and break our minds, for these are the sacrifices of God and this is his will; to such a one he reveals his truth."[80] The key phrase is "break the mind" (ܬܒܪ ܪܥܝܢܐ). Kitchen and Parmentier translate the phrase "subdue the mind." Their translation works here, since the phrase is basically parallel to "humbling oneself." But the more literal rendering of "break" (ܬܒܪ) reminds us that the term is a richly evocative one of shattering and pounding; it connotes the grinding pulverization that happens when the material of a thing has been abraded by relentless wearing action or sharp impact.[81] The passage echoes Psalm 51, for which the Peshitta reads, "the sacrifices of God are a humble spirit; a broken heart God does not despise" (ܕܒܚܘܗܝ ܕܐܠܗܐ ܪܘܚܐ ܗܝ ܡܟܝܟܬܐ ܠܒܐ ܬܒܝܪܐ ܐܠܗܐ ܠܐ ܡܣܠܐ).[82] For the psalmist, the heart that is humbly broken in

everybody; the only thing necessary is a deliberate effort of the will to empty oneself and to lower oneself, and then one can reach the highest level of Perfection"; *BoS* 3.16.

78. Heading cites *BoS* 1.2.

79. E.g. humility, the Holy Spirit, knowing truth and discerning the commands, and fulfilling ministries according to one's station.

80. *BoS* 1.2.

81. See Robert Payne Smith, *Thesaurus Syriacus* (Oxford: Clarendon, 1879–1901), 2:4122–25.

82. Psalm 51:19. Certain manuscripts amplify the expression: ܠܒܐ ܬܒܝܪܐ ܘܡܟܝܟܐ, "broken *and lowly*

penitence and acknowledged dependence before God creates an opportunity for redemption. The *Book of Steps* uses "mind" (ܪܥܝܢܐ) rather than the Peshitta's "heart" (ܠܒܐ), focusing on the intellect as the primary location for redemptive humility to begin taking root in one's life.

In the *Book of Steps,* humility is the virtue that impacts knowledge most deeply.[83] Whereas "pride is an obstacle preventing knowledge of the truth," breaking one's mind in the practice of being "the gentlest and humblest of all people" removes the obstacle and renders a person capable of attaining knowledge. Specifically, it creates space for the Spirit to enter and transform cognitive processes by attuning him or her to the truth: "None can know the will of God from ink, but only when he partakes of him in the Spirit, that is to say, unless he is the gentlest and humblest of all people. . . . Therefore only the person who partakes of God in the Spirit can understand scripture and discern the commandments."[84]

Simply addressing oneself to a propositional object such as the biblical text will not do. In order to gain access to the truth, one must be attuned to the life and mind of him who is its source—by imitating his humble nature, a move that is both a condition of the Spirit's presence and a sign of it. "A Spirit-filled person is recognized by the following characteristics: he is obviously instructed by that Spirit, he loves all people, even his enemies."[85] The *Book of Steps'* theory of knowledge is highly pneumatic.[86] The Spirit empowers the cognitive faculties to work most effectively. Whereas for Aphrahat the rationality of a discourse is accessible to any who genuinely attend to it,[87] knowledge in the *Book of Steps* is more exclusive. In fact, within the *Book of Steps* the deepest knowledge is available only to the Perfect, whose humble inner and outer practices invite and sustain the full measure of the Paraclete.[88] People who will not fully

heart"; viz. 12t2.5.7 in Donald M. Walter, ed., *The Old Testament in Syriac according to the Peshitta Version,* part 2, fasc. 3, *The Book of Psalms* (Leiden: E. J. Brill, 1980), 57. *BoS* 30.16 adapts the passage in the following way: ܕܒܚܘܗܝ ܕܐܠܗܐ ܪܘܚܐ ܗܝ ܡܟܝܟܬܐ܃ ܘܠܒܐ ܬܒܝܪܐ ܪܚܡ ("the sacrifices of God are a humble spirit, and a broken heart he loves").

83. See Stewart, *"Working the Earth,"* 221.

84. *BoS* 1.2; see Ratcliff, "Steps," 163.

85. *BoS* 3.12; see also *BoS* 24.7.

86. Guillaumont sees the *Book of Steps'* "mystique pneumatique" as characteristic of Syriac spirituality, though the *Book of Steps'* particular emphasis is distinctive; Guillaumont, "Situation et significance," 315–18; see also Vööbus, *History of Asceticism,* 3:14–17.

87. Childers, "Humility Begets Wisdom," 18–21.

88. See *BoS* 30.4. Comprehending "the height and the depth and the length and the width" requires the full measure of the Paraclete and the radical love that attends it; *BoS* 8.5, 19.34.

break their minds in combination with concretely lowering themselves before everyone on the earth remain "ignorant of the truth."

This association of extreme inner humility, concrete expressions of lowliness, and "breaking the mind" shows up elsewhere in the *Book of Steps.* For instance, in memra 6 the Paraclete is promised to the "person who has lowered himself from all things that are on the earth, has *broken his mind* night and day, who counts everyone else better than himself, has emptied himself of all he possessed, and kisses the feet of his enemies."[89] Memra 14 promises that a person will be exalted to the same extent that she "*breaks her mind*" and "humbles herself."[90] Some contexts do not mention ܪܥܝܢܐ, but nevertheless refer to the function of disciplines and rigorous experiences in "breaking" a person. Memra 29 indicates that the ascetic "death of the body" happens when a person is "*broken* by prayer and by lowliness and knowledge that is in the Spirit."[91] Memra 3 claims that "those . . . who are in the Spirit are required by our Lord to be bound to him continually in thought (ܒܪܥܝܢܗ) in the sacrifice of the mind (ܬܐܪܬܐ), in thanksgiving, in prayer, and in lowliness, and once *they have thus been broken* while being set apart, to teach all people."[92] Where I have "broken" (ܟܕ ܡܫܚܩܝܢ), Kitchen and Parmentier translate "polished," nicely capturing the nuance of the phrase in this context, but it should be noted that the term here is again "to break" (ܫܚܩ). In this passage practices of inner mental humility merge with exterior lowliness and devotion in such a way as to refine a person via brokenness so that he becomes a fitting and competent teacher of others. Indeed, the labors of disciplined theological reflection on the teaching that one receives have a *breaking* or *wearing* effect that engenders personal growth: "and thus you will become adult inasmuch as you bear the burden of your soul and you *break your mind* with teaching and with questions of the word. As much as you are lowly, so you grow."[93]

For the *Book of Steps* the practices that correlate best with "breaking the mind" are ascetic practices. The interconnections that the author perceives between asceticism and excellent mental functioning become clear when seen against the backdrop of the narrative framework by which he interprets his experience. As Adam discovered, God teaches good and Satan evil.[94] Since

89. *BoS* 6.2.
90. *BoS* 14.3.
91. *BoS* 29.4.
92. *BoS* 3.14.
93. *BoS* 27.4.
94. *BoS* 21.1–2, 3.12.

knowledge always has a moral dimension and is never neutral, "let us be innocent in this world of evil, but wily in order to do all sorts of good things."[95] The ability to discern between the two requires recovering the mind's original spiritual orientation. Satan's mode of operation is to lure a person with visible, material things, captivating his mind with the promise of possessing and controlling, thereby causing a blockage of inner faculties that leaves him incapable of perceiving truth.[96] By obeying him people incur injuries to their interior organs of perception, much as a physical blow might damage exterior sense organs.[97] In this handicapped state a person remains insensible to the higher, invisible realities of God and his ways.[98]

God humbled himself in the incarnation precisely so that Adam's children could catch a glimpse of "their first image from which they had fallen," and thereby be drawn back to it.[99] Jesus's mind dwelt on heavenly things even while he walked the earth,[100] and his conduct exhibited a moral excellence congruent with his mind's heavenly orientation. He did not marry or possess property; he chose not to exercise control over things and persons; he avoided violence and retribution, but loved his persecutors. Recovering the ability to discern the truth involves imitating him, "the good tree," retraining the mind and body by emulating his renunciatory habits and focusing on the heavenly.[101] The extreme behaviors of renunciation that characterize the Perfect enable them to reclaim the angelic life and the discernment belonging to heavenly beings.[102] Yet the Upright also benefit from moderately ascetic practices. Even the simple routine of Sabbath-keeping will enhance the Upright's ability to "know his truth," whereas succumbing to the temptation of nonstop work for the sake of making more money will "prevent us gaining knowledge."[103]

95. *BoS* 27.7.

96. *BoS* 28.6–7, 25.1, 15.1–2; see Martikainen, "Böse in den Schriften," 45.

97. *BoS* 28.7.

98. *BoS* 28.6; see Stewart, *"Working the Earth,"* 165–66.

99. *BoS* 23.11.

100. *BoS* 21.5–7.

101. *BoS* 21.2, 2.6–7. "The 'imitation of Christ' is in fact the main Christological theme in the *Liber Graduum*" and a key to the text's soteriology, which Christians experience mainly in their exercise of humility; René Roux, "The Doctrine of the Imitation of Christ in the *Liber Graduum:* Between Exegetical Theory and Soteriology," in *Studia Patristica: Biblica Et Apocrypha, Ascetica, Liturgica,* edited by Elizabeth A. Livingstone and E. Peters, 30:259, 262 (Leuven: Peeters Publishers, 1997).

102. *BoS* 23.1, 21.3, 26.1. See the summary description in Juhl, *Askese im Liber Graduum,* 99–128.

103. *BoS* 7.19.

In spite of the striking "otherworldliness" of perfection, it is evident that its practices are not simply the consequences of matter-spirit dualism.[104] The ascetic disciplines are important not for negating or transcending corporeality, but for "attaining to a particular set of relational and communal virtues . . . as the primary means of attaining that perfection that was the goal of the Christian life. These virtues are many, yet they all involve active and concrete means of demonstrating love for other human beings."[105] The Perfect practice their asceticism within the context and for the benefit of a larger human community, rigorously avoiding "the economic and social structures of life in normal types of society . . . because they reflect the enmity and strife which resulted from the Fall."[106] The humility concretized in their asceticism emulates Christ's posture so that they lower themselves "in front of everybody on earth.[107] They acquire a remarkable empathy for others and are equipped for "an apostolic mission directed back towards the society they had forsaken."[108] By moving according to the rhythms set by their radical detachment from the world and their radical attachment to people—even outsiders—the role of the Perfect is to pray, serve as peacemakers, minister among the unrighteous, and mentor one another and the Upright by their teaching and paradigmatic lifestyle.[109] Ratcliff's study of this has been illuminating. He concludes, "While discipline of the body and separation from normal types of society did hold importance for the author's vision of the monastic life, they had no final value in themselves; they were important only in that they facilitated the relational virtues of forgiveness and reconciliation with other human beings which comprised the fundamental activities of the way of perfection."[110]

104. The inspiration for primitive Syrian asceticism owed more to Jesus's call to radical discipleship than to cosmological dualism; Brock, "Early Syrian Asceticism," 1–19; Murray, "Features," 53–77; Griffith, "Asceticism," 220–45; Jean Gribomont, "Monasticism and Asceticism: I. Eastern Christianity," In *Christian Spirituality: Origins to the 12th Century,* edited by Jean Leclercq, Bernard McGinn, and John Meyendorf, 1: 90–92, World Spirituality 16 (London: SCM, 1989). Susan Ashbrook Harvey notes the parallels between the striking artistry of these ascetics' bodily actions and the symbolism of Syriac poetic theology. Syrian ascetics sensed and embodied a pervasive interactivity between the divine and material realms; Harvey, "Creation and Asceticism: Syriac Christian Thought," in *Christian Thought: A Brief History,* edited by Adrian Hastings, Alistair Mason, and Hugh S. Pyper, 34–36 (Oxford: Oxford University Press, 2002); see Brown, *Body and Society,* 330–31.

105. Ratcliff, "Steps," 6.

106. Ratcliff, "Steps," 161.

107. *BoS* 1.2; 6.2.

108. Caner, *Wandering, Begging Monks,* 110–11.

109. Kitchen and Parmentier, *Book of Steps,* xxxix–xliv; Ratcliff, "Steps," 134–36.

110. Ratcliff, "Steps," 101. In his classic study of asceticism, Peter Brown sees the author of the *Book of*

God honors the offerings of ascetic sacrifices by granting practitioners the knowledge they seek.[111] Habits of lowliness enable a person to participate in a process of transformation, "breaking the mind," so that the person's mind comes increasingly to inhabit a spiritual environment.[112] Ascetics are engraining a Christocentric set of evaluative structures into their minds. People whose materialistic obsessions expose them as those of "an external mind, an exterior understanding, an exterior sense perception, an exterior taste, an exterior order and an exterior intelligence" are limited in what they can know, because their faculties are attuned to a very superficial dimension of reality.[113] "Fasting to the world"[114] remedies the toxic preoccupation with possessing and controlling, rehabituating the mind to resume its heavenly dispositions so that it can discern the voice of God from that of Satan, truth from falsehood.[115] For example, faculties so trained acquire the sensitivity to perceive that opportunities to injure others are not neutral tools, but swords of malice engineered by Satan, evil spirits bent on the destruction of the user's enemies as well as the user.[116] Using them makes one their slave, so that the continued practice of harmful behaviors blinds a person, making it impossible for him or her to perceive the truth about the devious nature of these implements.[117]

By contrast, increasing one's proficiency in the practice of self-emptying renunciation (ܡܣܪܩܘܬܐ; 1.2; 12.1) generates a proportional increase in spiritual maturity: "whoever lowers himself most, grows best."[118] This experience of im-

---

Steps as exemplifying those whose ascetic practices were linked to social concerns: "What these men felt they needed to explain was not so much the present weakness of the individual body; it was, rather, the tragic dislocation of society as a whole. . . . [Adam] had wished, through property, to replace God as Creator. He had set about creating economic wealth by labor, and had wished to pile up the physical wealth of progeny by intercourse. He had turned from the contemplation of God to build the society that we know" (Brown, *Body and Society*, 336–37).

111. *BoS* 1.2.

112. "While living in the flesh on earth, his mind daily dwells in Eden in the spirit. . . . Thus he grows daily and is fattened, delighting and rejoicing in the Spirit. . . . Then our Lord will come and take him away completely from this world, as he already took his mind and introduced it into Paradise"; *BoS* 6.2; see 14.2, 15.18.

113. *BoS* 28.6.

114. *BoS* 29.6; see also *BoS* 4.4, 15.6. For discussions of the source of the expression "fasting to the world," see Guillaumont, "ΝΗΣΤΕΥΕΙΝ ΤΟΝ ΚΟΣΜΟΝ (P.Oxy. 1, verso, l.5–6)," *Bulletin de l'Institut francais d'archeologie orientale* 61 (1962): 15–23; Dom Aelred Baker, "Fasting to the World," *Journal of Biblical Literature* 84 (1965): 291–94.

115. *BoS* 15.16–17.

116. *BoS* 7.7.

117. *BoS* 7.8–9.

118. *BoS* 3.1, 1.2, 8.2–3.

provement includes the development of deeper knowledge and more refined methods. For instance, it teaches one to be wary of making snap judgments about the accuracy or worth of particular truth claims or teachings. Instead, the seeker of truth should be patient, diligently examining all the claims, adjusting their evaluative processes to compensate for their own limitations—and remembering that some people know more than others: "Be careful until your knowledge is great enough and you know the whole truth as it is, until you break[119] the power of sin and until you are experienced and know everything. Distinguish one teacher from another and one educator from another until you know the way of our Lord and travel directly on it."[120]

In a passage showing the interrelationship of key virtues, the *Book of Steps* indicates that making progress entails knowing "the truth and love and lowliness."[121] Humility is associated with love, which is a foundation for knowledge: "With love a person will know everything."[122] Humility brings the awareness of one's commonality with others ("everyone is a child of Adam"), leading the humble person to love rather than judge, to treat sinners with respect, and even to honor one's persecutors.[123] The Spirit's presence within a person produces good thoughts, coloring one's perceptions according to the divine character so that he or she "thinks only good of all people, whether they are good or not."[124] Greeting people honorably and helping others resolve their conflicts—these are the ways of love that enable one's mind to reinhabit the heavenlies, so that it can attain complete knowledge.[125] In a very practical vein, abusing one's colleague will not do, since "perhaps the one whom you despise will know the truth and will explain [it] to you." Instead of sabotaging one's prospective source of knowledge through jealous and hateful behavior, one should "be humble and self-deprecating before God and all people."[126]

119. ܕܬܬܒܪ ܐܢܬ ܚܝܠܗ ܕܚܛܝܬܐ—the term here for "break" is ܬܒܪ.
120. *BoS* 30.10.
121. *BoS* 27.2.
122. *BoS* 17.1.
123. *BoS* 5.6–10, 12.3, 7.2.
124. *BoS* 3.12.
125. *BoS* 28.6, 29.10, 2.6, 30.3.
126. *BoS* 17.9.

"May Your Foot Tread on His Doorstep Every Day": The Role of Worthy Exemplars

The latter insight underscores a major virtue in the *Book of Steps*—the cultivation of appreciative interdependence in community.[127] The *Book of Steps* stands out in its unequivocal rejection of the individualistic and isolationist asceticism that would come to characterize so many movements, insisting instead that the aims of perfection can only be attained when the Perfect remain embedded within a larger community.[128] Practices of "breaking the mind" are largely communal in nature. Respectful discourse and collaboration will characterize a community devoted to ascertaining truth. Rather than grasping at the autonomy that tempted Adam, they will follow Jesus in pursuing concrete practices of dependence on others, not just for food and drink, but for knowledge, also. As a matter of epistemic practice, this pertains particularly to the habit of seeking out good teachers and worthy exemplars.[129] The author believes that knowledge has an essentially interpersonal dynamic. Good and bad teachings come through God and Satan, respectively.[130] The Paraclete is a personally indwelling vehicle of knowledge, establishing relationship between God and the human mind.[131] In memra 15 we read that Adam learned techniques of sexual intercourse by watching the cattle do it; he obviously chose poor exemplars and found himself drawn tragically into the imitation of bestial behavior.[132] The *Book of Steps* counsels the reader to choose models and teachers carefully. The chief mentor is Jesus. The incarnation was necessary

127. *BoS* 30.12. Portions of this section appear in Childers, "We Must Seek the Truth," 193–216.

128. See Ratcliff, "Steps," 115–30.

129. A principal function of the church is the formation and maturation of people; *BoS* 12.4–5. This requires that the community function as a family, in which "adults" nurture "children" and the diverse members are integrated into a mutually beneficial whole; see *BoS* 27.2–5. In one place, the author even admonishes, "No one should doubt the church or its priests, [for] from the catholic church all truth shall be known. Let us love even idolaters and infidels, while the catholic church is great in our eyes"; *BoS* 27.5. Although it has been suggested that the author overplays his endorsement of the institutional church for the sake of making peace politically, his affirmations are consistent with the communal vision he casts throughout the text; cf. Murray, *Symbols,* 35, 263; Guillaumont, "Situation et significance," 321; Kitchen, "Gattung," 174; Kitchen and Parmentier, *Book of Steps,* lv–lvi; and Ratcliff, "Steps," 53–57.

130. *BoS* 21.1–2.

131. For a study of the author's "sacramental conception of the indwelling presence of the Lord in the human person," see Stewart, *"Working the Earth,"* 216–23; see also Ratcliff, "Steps," 150–52.

132. *BoS* 15.2; see Martikainen, "Böse in den Schriften," 41.

partly due to the need for a suitable exemplar, and imitating him makes him one's teacher.[133] But one looks for exemplars within the community, as well, expressions of Jesus's character in the lives of those more knowledgeable than oneself. A basic premise of the division of the church into Upright and Perfect is the belief that not all minds are equal—some, by virtue of their inner dispositions and disciplined practices, are wiser or more mature than others.[134]

Virtuous people recognize their limitations and seek the communal resources they have in their mentors: "See who is reliable and straight, rational and orderly, loving and patient, and teaches the truth. Keep close to him and cleave to him. May your foot tread on his doorstep every day until you understand the truth and thoroughly learn the way of the Lord and his steps."[135] Some students need more doorstep-treading than others, but consistent mental growth always depends on long-term mentoring relationships. Rather than cultivating arrogant self-reliance in their search for truth and growth, both Upright and Perfect should manifest the humility that enables them to submit themselves to good teachers.[136] Students bear the responsibility of choosing their mentors discerningly.[137] The directive counsel of one's mentor might prove crucial in recognizing one's limitations and thereby avoiding possibly disastrous courses of action, or in appreciating the full range of options open to a person—for instance, a mentor can assist a person in discerning the call to join the path of the Perfect.[138]

For their part, exemplars must attend to the virtuous practices that will form them as responsible teachers and models.[139] Within the *Book of Steps* community, the Perfect are especially suited for this role.[140] Since their prac-

133. *BoS* 27.1; see also *BoS* 9.5–7. The author also often makes the point that the Perfect should imitate God, especially in his unconditional mercy and patience; see *BoS* 16.11, 23.6–8, 24.8.

134. *BoS* 30.1, 19.31. As Stewart maintains, "the twinned notions of distinction and discernment form the basis of the *Liber graduum*'s understanding of the Christian life"; Stewart, *"Working the Earth,"* 88.

135. *BoS* 30.13.

136. *BoS* 30.18. Some contexts imply that the Perfect have no need of instruction, since they are in direct communion with God (e.g., *BoS* 15.18), but many other contexts presume that even among the Perfect growth occurs, so that instruction and modeling are still needed.

137. *BoS* 30.10–11, 18.

138. *BoS* 15.18.

139. The author of the *Book of Steps* strongly discourages the Perfect from judging and reproving others; instead they are to teach positively and by example.

140. Kitchen and Parmentier contend that teaching and spiritual direction are the primary tasks of the Perfect; *Book of Steps,* xliii.

tices have honed their minds for maximum perception of truth, they become "distributors of the heavenly wealth." The Perfect person was once ignorant also, but was favored to have his craving "to know . . . the integrity of the world or how he was created and why he was created" satisfied; hence, he ought to take on the responsibility of bringing knowledge to others, both those among the Upright and those of the Perfect who are less adept.[141] The virtuous instructor should "teach . . . , be constant in prayer and intercession, in ministering and studying, in applying himself to the word of God's truth," so that by his ministry of instruction and modeling he becomes "a benefactor to all people and to himself also, in prayer and in counseling."[142] Sidney Griffith explains that in early Syrian Christian communities the status of the consecrated ascetic "seems to have been not so much a matter of spiritual elite . . . , or a matter of a church within the church. . . . Rather, the active stance that the ihidaya was expected to take in the community consisted principally in serving as a type for his own people."[143] In the *Book of Steps,* the Perfect are iconic exemplars, but they also take an active role in instructing and mentoring.

Even if people will not receive instruction, the good teacher carries on "humbly to teach all people, whether they are worthy or not, because our Lord wanted it this way."[144] Good teachers are also able to ascertain a student's maturity level and deliver specialized diets of learning that are properly suited to the student's abilities.[145] They practice humility and the service of others.[146] They understand their own limitations and recognize that they can acquire insight and wisdom from unlikely sources—such as little children or the insane.[147] They guard themselves against the arrogant condemnation of those with whom they disagree. The "morally rigid" person, instead of attending to his or her own conduct, is quick to criticize, compelled by the false belief that one's own justification and correctness hinge on the castigation of others' mistakes. This arrogance manifests itself in the mistreatment of those who are believed to be in error.[148] In contrast, virtuous practice involves peacemaking

141. *BoS* 15.18.

142. *BoS* 3.7.

143. Griffith, "Asceticism," 234; cf. Edmund Beck, *Dorea und Charis—Die Taufe: Zwei Beiträge zur Theologie Ephräms des Syrers,* Corpus Scriptorum Christianorum Orientalium 457 (Louvain: Peeters, 1984, 161); Murray, *Symbols,* 13–14.

144. *BoS* 3.8.

145. *BoS* 12.5, 30.13.

146. *BoS* 3.7–10.

147. *BoS* 16.6–7.

148. *BoS* 4.5.

and conflict resolution, not the exacerbation of divisions and contests.[149] Indeed, within the *Book of Steps* community love and respect for the outsider rather than love for one's own is the highest form of love, a trait exemplified by Jesus and most characteristic of the Perfect.[150] Shrewd discernment is necessary, but it must be conducted within the context of respectful and loving relationships: "One should not have to trust everyone, but his peace should be extended to everyone."[151]

Given the author's belief that knowledge has interpersonal dimensions, the community's diversity—complicating as it is—is not just to be tolerated as an inevitable hardship, but also to be welcomed. The interpersonal dynamics that arise between different classes of people within the community stimulate growth and help structure and guide the quest for truth.

Conclusion: "Know Truth and Love and Lowliness"

In addition to the cardinal virtues and key processes already discussed, the author calls his readers to embody a host of other epistemic virtues, as well, each grounded in a shared vision of reality and a fundamental commitment to humility.[152] For instance, they will guard their motives, striving genuinely to seek truth and avoid falsehood.[153] As the author brilliantly models in his deft handling of ostensibly contradictory biblical texts, they will diligently practice careful methods of research, facing the evidence squarely. He insists, "We must inquire into the words of our Lord one by one."[154] Under the tutelage of wise instructors and guided by their own experience, the readers will cultivate the wisdom needed for discernment and will practice submission to the necessary results of those researches. Seekers and mentors will remain optimistic about growth and learning, since the very nature of the Christian life is one of continued progress.

Furthermore, the seeker of knowledge will cultivate the integration of the inner and outer person. The *Book of Steps* stresses the need for behavior to match inner inclinations and for words to be consistent with actions.[155]

149. *BoS* 4.6–7.
150. *BoS* 22.2; Ratcliff, "Steps," 206, 209–12.
151. *BoS* 30.12.
152. Heading cites *BoS* 27.2.
153. *BoS* 1.1–2.
154. *BoS* 1.1.
155. *BoS* 10.3, 4, 8, 16.2.

Agreement between the inner and outer person invokes the presence of the Lord, effectively reinstating the mind to its proper place.[156] Practicing the congruence between the "visible church" and the "church of the heart" enables access to the "church on high." "Let us pray with our body as well as with our heart," the author enjoins.[157] Engaging in such practices as prayer[158] and ascetic habits will help conform the mind to the specific contours of Christian thought structure, while involvement in the sacraments will help engrain within them the narrative framework by which they can achieve coherent understanding.[159] Similarly, if we do what we know "by rote without passion," then "it is the same as if we do not know." Knowledge and understanding are not abstract and amoral objects. Knowledge and the quest to attain it necessarily have moral dimensions to which one must attend. When the knower is not experiencing integration, the knowledge he or she has is drained of its true power; "passion" and "interior understanding" are needed.[160] Related to the matter of integration is that of constancy. Constancy of discipline pays off in greater rewards, whereas erratic practices are not as beneficially formative.[161]

In all these areas the *Book of Steps* presumes the sort of connection between praiseworthy dispositions and cognitive processes that many virtue epistemologists find worthy of discussion today. Scholars conduct their work according to specific principles, as do practitioners of non-academic disciplines. Different means of regulating inquiry come into play that are evident in our classrooms, our laboratories, our publications, our conversations, and in the practice of various disciplines. The *Book of Steps* advances a particular

156. *BoS* 25.5.

157. *BoS* 12.1.

158. For a study of the Christocentric tendencies of the *Book of Steps'* prayer formulae, see Kowalski, "Die Gebete im Liber Graduum," *Orientalia Christiana Periodica* 55 (1989): 273–81.

159. Although the Perfect's full participation in Christ could be taken to preclude the need to participate in the sacraments, the *Book of Steps* insists that "one cannot separate the relational virtues which make up the way of *gamirutha* from participation in the visible church, its baptism, and its altar"; Ratcliff, "Steps," 151–53. For an explication of the sources and influences underlying the author's understanding of the role of liturgy in recovering paradise, see Alexander Golitizin, "Recovering the 'Glory of Adam': 'Divine Light' Traditions in the Dead Sea Scrolls and the Christian Ascetical Literature of Fourth-Century Syro-Mesopotamia," in *The Dead Sea Scrolls as Background to Postbiblical Judaism and Early Christianity: Papers from an International Conference at St. Andrews in 2001,* edited by James R. Davila, 285, 302–7 (Leiden: E. J. Brill, 2003).

160. *BoS* 29.3.

161. *BoS* 3.5, 10.9.

understanding of the mind and of knowledge, along with a set of interior and external practices, which also constitutes a manner of regulating inquiry. "Breaking the mind" involves rigorous and harsh habits, but they refine one's cognition and perfect one's humanity. According to the *Book of Steps,* virtuous inner dispositions, such as humility, a desire for truth, recognizing the moral dimensions of knowledge and knowing, and an awareness of one's own dependence, must cohere with virtuous practices, such as diligent research, achieving coherence, concrete habits of surrendering control or possession, the respectful treatment of others, and the cultivation of a collegial and appreciative learning environment. By the standards of contemporary epistemology the *Book of Steps* does not answer the question, "What is true knowledge?" but it does provide a compelling—though possibly idealized—picture of the way in which a community devoted to particular virtues can provide a hospitable and productive environment in which to conduct a search for truth.

Pablo Argárate

9. THE PERFECT AND PERFECTION IN THE *BOOK OF STEPS*

Since the publication of Michael Kmoskó's edition, the *Book of Steps* has puzzled scholars with its manifestation of an enigmatic form of Christianity.[1] Among many features, however, it is the profusion and variety of religious groups portrayed throughout its thirty memre that particularly drew attention to our anonymous work. Along with some more traditional functions, such as the leaders of the community, the priests, the "sick," and the "children," some mysterious sorts of Christianity enter into the picture, like the group of faith and the group of love.

Nevertheless, the most frequent and consistent ones are the Upright and the Perfect. This distinction is closely associated to the one between the major and minor commandments or between corporal and spiritual ministries. The origin of the separation between perfection and uprightness is traced by the *Book of Steps* to the very origin of humanity. Adam, created in perfection, by failing to keep God's commandments fell from that state, and uprightness was sanctioned until the coming of Christ, who would manifest in himself the true nature of Adam and perfection.

The *Book of Steps* portrays this perfection in a rather negative way by de-

1. For a *status quaestionis,* see Pablo Argárate, "Das *Ktābā dmasqātā*": Forschung und Bedeutung des syrischen Liber Graduum," in *Bibel, Byzanz und Christlicher Orient: Festschrift für Stephen Gerö zum 65. Geburtstag,* edited by E. Grypeou, A. Toepel, T. Sailors, and D. Bumazhnov, Orientalia Lovaniensia Analecta 187 (Leuven: Peeters, 2010).

nying the features of uprightness.[2] Whereas the Upright live in the world and care for it, working, possessing, and getting married, the Perfect are characterized by radical renunciation of the world (they "fast to the world"), neither working nor marrying nor having any tie with that world. On the contrary, they closely follow Christ by taking up his cross in complete poverty and lowliness. In doing so, according to the *Book of Steps,* they have succeeded in acquiring the status that Adam had in paradise before the fall.[3] Their functions within the community comprise of teaching to all the new life and the distinction between major and minor commandments. However, repeatedly, our book places the hallmark of perfection in unlimited love and forgiveness, in the footsteps of Jesus's Sermon on the Mount. The Perfect are thus required to love and forgive all without distinction: women, heretics, pagans, sinners, and even their own murderers. It is an in-depth research into this close association between perfection and love for enemies that forms the theme of this chapter.

The quest for perfection builds without any doubt the center of the *Book of Steps.* From its very outset, already in the first paragraph of memra 1, perfection and uprightness are brought into relation with the commandments of the Lord, which fall into two major categories: major and minor commandments. Furthermore, this distinction is closely related to what is the separation between perfection and uprightness. Indeed, memra 1 begins by summarizing its topic: "In which can be found an exposition of the commandments, showing for what purpose each single one has been given and to whom, why our Lord Jesus Christ gave major and minor commandments, and how one can distinguish Perfection from Uprightness, and that through the major commandments one becomes Perfect and through the minor ones Upright."[4]

2. This has led to believe that the *Book of Steps* might be addressed to the Upright rather than to the Perfect, the latter being more a theological category; see Robert A. Kitchen, "The Gattung of the Liber Graduum: Implications for a Sociology of Asceticism," in *IV Symposium Syriacum 1984,* edited by H. J. W. Drijvers, et al, 181, Orientalia Christiana Analecta 229 (Rome: Pontificium Institutum Studiorum Orientalium, 1987): "The Just, who undoubtedly are the majority of the *LG* community, are more concretely described and are the principal audience of the *LG.* The Perfect are not as clearly defined and in fact, represent more a school, not an individual. Its function as a canon for the community was the purpose for writing."

3. See Aleksander Kowalski, *Perfezione e giustizia di Adamo nel Liber Graduum,* Orientalia Christiana Analecta 232 (Rome: Pontificium Institutum Orientale, 1989); Gary A. Anderson, *The Genesis of Perfection: Adam and Eve in Jewish and Christian Imagination* (Louisville: Westminster John Knox Press, 2001); and Kitchen, "Syriac Additions to Anderson: The Garden of Eden in the Book of Steps and Philoxenus of Mabbug," *Hugoye: Journal of Syriac Studies* 6 (2003): 37–50.

4. *BoS* Preface, *LG* 12.1–5.

At this juncture the author identifies the rationale of the *Book of Steps* as teaching the fundamental discernment between the two types of commandments. In fact, the major commandments constitute the topic of memra 2,[5] where the author rehearses a long list of exhortations taken from the New Testament, mostly from the gospels, and especially from the sermons on the Mount and on the Plain. Curiously, among these there is no mention of the love of God, but chiefly the love of Christ, love among the disciples, and even love of one's enemies. In addition, it is worth noting that in the *Book of Steps* the major commandments do not primarily refer to the Decalogue, but to the new law proclaimed by Christ.[6]

The love of God is addressed in a general sense,[7] referred to as one of "the great commandments in the Torah" on account of their object. These are even called "the two great commandments of love,"[8] which are at the same time one.[9] One ought to point out here the variations in the rendering of these commandments. Traditionally couched as "Love the Lord your God with all your heart and with all your strength and with all your soul and with all your mind,"[10] following the biblical text, it also appears as "Love the Lord your God more than yourself and your neighbor as yourself."[11] In addition, this love of God is required to be deep and "with everything you have,"[12] even loving "God more than yourself."[13]

Nevertheless, this love of God does not usually appear without reference

5. *BoS* 2.1: "Now let us expound the major commandments, through which a person is made Perfect; that is to say, those commandments that were given by our Lord and his apostles to the Perfect, and distinguish them from the 'vegetables and milk.'"

6. *BoS* 2.1; and by the apostles.

7. *BoS* 7.13: "Then, let us deeply love our God and love and honor every person so that we may inherit the kingdom"; BoS 7.21: human persons "should treat one another well and love their Creator."

8. *BoS* 9.3: "Sometimes the Lord cast them down even below Uprightness, [the stage] that fulfills these two great commandments of love, because Uprightness does not curse or harm anyone."

9. *BoS* 11.1: "When the Law says, 'Love the Lord your God more than yourself and your neighbor as you' you should say, 'This commandment is mine.'"

10. *BoS* 30.26.

11. *BoS* 11.1.

12. Instead of "with all your soul."

13. *BoS* 22.23: "Know this, my friends, that all the beauty of the virtuous commandments, which you find in the Law or in the prophets, that is their sense, these commandments, which are called *iota* as our Lord said, 'You shall love the Lord God and the people who are all descendants of Adam, who are your neighbors, relatives, and family.' Therefore let us fulfill the Gospel and the *Iota,* which are one testament by which people conduct themselves in a new way."

to the love of the neighbors.[14] These are interpreted in a broad sense and entail "all people," or, expressed in another way, "all descendants of Adam."[15] It is this love of all fellow humans that takes the central position in the *Book of Steps.*

The quest for perfection is thus deeply linked to love more than to ascetical renunciation.

> But he is not able to attain Perfection unless he has abandoned the earth according to what our Lord has commanded him and has taken up the cross, has emptied and lowered himself and become celibate; and has become like a servant in his obedience, and not like a lord in his supervision. Let him have compassion on the sinners and the righteous; and let him love to give himself up for the evil ones, as [did] our Lord and his apostles. Then he will comprehend the height and the depth, the length and the width along with the saints, these who have understood the Holy One in everything he has shown them, with compassion and love and peace for all people, good and bad.[16]

That love takes such an important place is no wonder, given its role in Christianity. Particularly in the *Book of Steps,* love is regarded as a gift, the gift beyond all gifts.[17] A gift, however, that requires all our efforts. Indeed, it is acquired by means of the major commandments[18] and requires emptying oneself from the world, receiving the Paraclete and the indwelling of the Lord.[19] It fulfills the will of our Lord and accomplishes purity of heart and perfection.[20]

Without doubt, perfection is attained through perfect love, and this is produced by the Spirit when it fills a person.[21] First, it begins to drive out

14. *BoS* 30.26: "and love your neighbor as yourself."

15. *BoS* 22.23.

16. *BoS* 25.7.

17. *BoS* 19.36.

18. *BoS* 19.36.

19. *BoS* 15.9: "Therefore, those who empty themselves from the world, and give heed in heaven to their Lord and worship their God and love everyone, will become 'holy' and dwell with our Lord in the higher realm."

20. *BoS* 19.36; also *BoS* 20.7: "Therefore, when we have climbed these steps and have rooted up sin and its fruits from the heart, then we will be filled with the Spirit, the Paraclete, and our Lord will dwell in us completely. We will eat freely from that tree of life that is our Lord, from which we were separated by the transgression of the commandments; and then, we will be able to love and be merciful to all people, even our murderers, and be able to pray with love for all people and for our murderers. When we [are able to have] mercy upon and love everyone in this way, including our murderers, our heart being pure, then we will increase in Perfection and live according to that great, acceptable, and perfect will of our Lord."

21. *BoS* 3.12: "But whoever only does good works, empties himself, sanctifies himself, and loves all people—even those who are out to kill him—and he will not fail. He is made perfect by our Lord and filled with his Spirit, and whoever is full of the Spirit of Christ does all sorts of good works and thinks

sin,[22] and "those who travel on that perfect road will rejoice in the joy of our Lord and be glorified with him,"[23] they "will become 'holy' and dwell with our Lord in the higher realm,"[24] "inherit the kingdom," and eventually enter into the eternal bridal feast.[25]

Relevant is the protological and eschatological context of love provided by the *Book of Steps* in line with early Syriac theology. The centrality that our book attributes to paradise is well known. Love is one of the fruits of the Spirit,[26] of the spiritual fruits "on which the saints feed in Eden," and one of the trees of paradise, above the heavens and that Adam enjoyed before the fall.[27] It is worth noting that love is the only virtue that appears in both lists, among the fruits and trees of paradise. In sum, love is characteristic, if not the hallmark, of paradisiacal status (i.e., perfection). As such it has an eschatological function, as well. Given by the Lord, it is through it that we are granted reentrance into Eden.[28]

---

only good of all people, whether they are good or evil; in him there is not a single fault. But if he should find some fault in himself, he will fight it, eradicate it, and so rise above what is hateful, even though he is still in this world. When he departs this life as a Perfect one, he goes to live with our Lord and will see him face to face. . . . A Spirit-filled person is recognized by the following characteristics: he is obviously instructed by the Spirit, he loves all people—even his enemies and those who are out to kill him—and he prays for them diligently"; see also *BoS* 20.7, quoted in note 20.

22. *BoS* 16.9: "Look, when were you [more] contented—when you judged everyone, or now [when] you forgive everyone and love them? See, when did the power of sin begin to be driven from you? When you had enmity with your fellow believers and with [other] religious, or now when you love all people, good or bad, and have no enemy, except Satan, and have no strife with flesh and blood, descendants of Adam, but make war with evil spirits, the powers of sin? Abandon mammon and iniquity and all that passes away and distance yourself from it as an enemy. Every person, and our Lord, should be seen by you as friends, beloved ones, neighbors, fathers, and lords. You will be a servant to them by your love, and [like a] son and brother, friend and heir."

23. *BoS* 19.36.

24. *BoS* 15.9.

25. *BoS* 7.13: "Then, let us deeply love our God and love and honor every person so that we may inherit the kingdom—which is promised to us—whose rest does not pass away nor is its delight ever dissolved, neither is its feast ended nor do its wreaths wither, nor is its bridal feast done away with."

26. In *BoS* 1.1 the *Book of Steps* reads, "the fruits of the Spirit can be summed up as: goodness, lowliness, self-control, patience, gentleness and kindness, joy and peace with all people, and love for all people," rendering Gal 5:22–23. However, "for all people" does not appear in the Peshitta, but only ܚܘܒܐ. An English translation of the Peshitta renders, "But the fruit of the Spirit is love, joy, peace, long-suffering, kindness, goodness, faith, meekness, patience."

27. In *BoS* 2.6–7 it is said by the peacemakers that they eat, as Adam did before the fall, from the trees of spiritual paradise, i.e., faithfulness, abstinence, lowliness, love, hope, truthfulness, and holiness in our Lord. It is further stated that those who keep the major commandments eat from those trees.

28. *BoS* 20.6.

A fundamental pneumatological emphasis cannot be overlooked. Love is not only granted by the Spirit,[29] being the reception of the Paraclete *conditio sine qua non* for attaining perfect love, but also to some extent, love is even identified with the Spirit.[30] Furthermore, it is the possession of the Paraclete that distinguishes the Perfect from the Upright.

Having distinguished from the very beginning the major from the minor commandments as a key criterion and rationale for the *Book of Steps* and manifested the significance of the major commandments, the *Book of Steps* goes even further by maintaining the possibility of transcending those major commandments.[31] Moreover, this is explicitly linked to love. Memra 16 is "about how a person may surpass the major commandments in love."And this is explained through texts drawn from the gospels, chiefly from the Sermon on the Mount.[32] In a paradigmatic passage, the author renders in a clear fashion what is meant by transcending those commandments:

> Again he said to you: "Love your brother more than yourself. From here you shall understand what is love—whoever will put himself in the place of his friend. If my love is true for you, offer yourself in place of your brothers." However, if you love the evil ones, your despisers, more than yourself, you are much greater than he who [only] loves his neighbor more than himself and his despiser as himself. In this way, you will greatly surpass the major commandments and be glorified with our Lord. . . . Kiss the feet of your betrayers, and look, you will surpass one who [only] washes the feet of his betrayers.[33]

This text clearly transmits Christian maximalism, linking perfection to love of enemies and murderers. The logic of the Sermon on the Mount, rather than the call to holy war, appears at the core of the *Book of Steps*.[34] Indeed, I would like to draw attention to its usage of the first part of the section imme-

29. *BoS* 20.7.

30. *BoS* 24.2: "for people are baptized in the Spirit, which is love and truth."

31. *BoS* 2.8.

32. *BoS* 16.1–2. The same takes place in *BoS* 16.3–4.

33. *BoS* 16.4.

34. John H.Corbett, "They Do Not Take Wives, or Build, or Work the Ground: Ascetic Life in the Early Syriac Church," *Journal of the Canadian Society for Syriac Studies* 3 (2003): 16–17: "Semeio-structural analysis will clearly demonstrate how the Call to Holy War (with its associated themes of standing up, ascetic warfare, fasting and the single life—together, of course with the messianic banquet and the bridal chamber) generates the fundamental symbolic structure underlying the complex text of the Book of Steps."

diately following the Beatitudes in Luke.[35] In five places the *Book of Steps* refers to this passage expressed by the conjunction of the three verbs (i.e., bless, love, and pray, however, with some variants). While the text of Luke presents four verbs, the *Book of Steps* always omits "do good," placing "bless" before "love" and connecting "love" with those who "hate," and replacing "those who abuse you" by "those who (harm and) persecute (and deal harshly with) you."[36] As a result, the opposition between love and hate is stronger. In addition to this, the *Book of Steps* introduces the topic of persecution that was not explicitly present in the New Testament text.[37] This evidently has its own purpose in addressing the persecutions taking place in the community.[38] In the highly significant memra 19, which opposes road and paths, the author holds, "The Perfect road is this, 'Bless him who curses you and love him who hates you, and pray for whomever harms you and persecutes you.'"[39]

The relevance of this passage lies in identifying these three attitudes with the perfect road, (i.e., with perfection). In some other places, alongside the previously mentioned three verbs, forgiveness appears, as well.[40] Another significant passage in the same memra, conflating texts from Matthew and Luke, states in an even more persuasive fashion:

35. Luke 6:27–28.

36. Luke 6:27–28: "But I say to you that listen, Love your enemies, do good to those who hate you, bless those who curse you, pray for those who abuse you."

NT	*BoS*
Love—enemies	bless—curse
Do good—hate	
Bless—curse	love—hate
Pray—abuse	pray—(harm) persecute (deals harshly)

37. Although it was somehow present as a closing element in the previous Beatitudes, there is no explicit mention of persecution there. Nevertheless, this connection is made in Matt 6:43: "You have heard that it was said, 'Love your neighbor and hate your enemy.'"

38. See Shafiq Abouzayd, "Violence and Killing in the *Liber Graduum*," *ARAM* 12 (2000): 451–65; Kitchen, "Conflict on the Stairway to Heaven: The Anonymity of Perfection in the Syriac *Liber Graduum*," in *Symposium Syriacum VII: Uppsala University, Department of Asian and African Languages, 11–14 August 1996*, edited by René Lavenant, 211 (Rome: Pontificio Instituto Orientale, 1998).

39. *BoS* 19.12; see also *BoS* 2.2: "Love him who hates you, bless him who curses you, pray for the one who harms you and persecutes you"; and *BoS* 30.2: "Bless whoever curses you and love whoever hates you, and pray for whoever persecutes you and deals harshly with you. Have in your mind to become like lambs for the slaughter, just as it is written, 'Because of you, our Lord, we die every day and have become like sheep for the slaughter.'"

40. *BoS* 17.7: "These and such like them are the sufferings: If you bless whoever curses you and love whoever hates you and pray for whoever persecutes you and forgive whoever does you wrong seventy times seven in one day, all this because our Lord said, 'Never be angry against one who sins against you.'"

This is the Perfect road: If you love only the one who loves you and you greet only your brothers, what is your righteousness? Because even tax collectors and heathen and sinners act in this way. But love whoever hates you and persecutes you, and your peace will increase toward the good and the evil, and you shall be imitating the Father in heaven who makes his sun rise[41] and his rain fall upon them equally.[42]

Quotations and references are drawn here again from the sermons on the Mount and on the Plain. Yet the text is closer to Matthew 5,[43] with some variants, though, especially the substitution of reward with "righteousness"; even more importantly, in the last part of the quotation the author leaves aside prayer and greeting, concentrating everything on love for both those who hate and persecute. As a consequence of this action the *Book of Steps* introduces "peace toward the good and the evil," which in its turn produces the imitation of the Father's equal attitude toward those who hate and persecute. Luke 5 and the perfection of the Father are referred to by means of the perfect road, making explicit the theme of imitation.[44] The bottom line is that the attitude toward good and evil should be the same, an increasing peace. This idea is pivotal and occurs seven times throughout our work. In memra 3, the reference to love is evident:

This also applies to him who makes his love rise on the good and the evil as the Father's sun rises on all the good and evil.[45]

Or in the same vein:

A person is able to become a law of love for oneself, just as the ancient fathers became. They imitated God who makes his love rise upon the good and the bad, and makes his rain fall upon the just ant the unjust and they were not reproved by God, but were greatly glorified.[46]

41. Instead of Kitchen's "shine."

42. *BoS* 19.33.

43. Matt 5: 43–48, especially, 46–48. "You have heard that it was said, 'You shall love your neighbor and hate your enemy.' But I say to you, Love your enemies and pray for those who persecute you, so that you may be children of your Father in heaven; for he makes his sun rise on the evil and on the good, and sends rain on the righteous and on the unrighteous. For if you love those who love you, what reward do you have? Do not even the tax collectors do the same? And if you greet only your brothers and sisters, what more are you doing than others? Do not even the Gentiles do the same? Be perfect, therefore, as your heavenly Father is perfect."

44. Luke 5:48.

45. *BoS* 3.1.

46. *BoS* 22.10. This passage refers not only to good and bad but, following the NT text, to the just and the unjust.

On these grounds it follows that this love, "indifferent" to good and bad, just and unjust, constitutes the imitation of God,[47] of God's perfection. This love, which requires one not to judge, but to "love everyone as a saint of the Lord,"[48] is also identified as compassion.[49] This appears clear in the double reference to Abraham, when he is said to be an imitator of God because of his attitude toward the needy,[50] not discerning between those who deserve it and those who do not, but receiving "everyone as righteous people and as prophets."[51]

Connected to this "indifference" or lack of discernment, the *Book of Steps* introduces another topic that would prove very influential in later Byzantine and especially Russian traditions [the "holy fool" or the "fool for the sake of Christ" (*jurodivyj*)]: "Look at the fool who cannot distinguish good people from bad in his foolishness, and in the same way you should love the good and the bad while knowing them [for who they are]."[52]

Another text sheds even more light upon our theme while introducing new accents. First, the emphasis on loving the evil ones is stronger here, while the evil ones are described as "impious" and "enemies."

The disciples of love despise themselves, saying that they are impious while they are righteous, in order to love the impious and honor them and in order to love their enemies and pray for them. They are despised in [their] lowliness of mind so that

47. *BoS* 28.11: "He [Abraham] imitated God, who makes his love rise upon the good and the bad. For although everyone pities the good, one does not pity the bad, unless his love is great like our Lord's."

48. *BoS* 26.5: "Whoever seeks Perfection and loves holiness, out of these things will come the holiness of the heart; he will give everything he has to the needy and ascend above whatever is visible. There will be controversy against him, yet he will neither judge nor demand [anything] from anyone, but will love everyone as a saint of the Lord, for he makes his love rise on everyone like the sun, that the Father [causes to rise] upon all there is on the earth, whether good or evil, whether the just or the unjust."

49. *BoS* 24.7: "However, whoever rises his love upon each person is better than whoever does not even have compassion for a person."

50. *BoS* 3.1 and *BoS* 28.11.

51. *BoS* 3.1: "Then there is also the physical ministry that is practiced by the person who simply gives to the needy in the manner of Abraham, without inquiring who deserves it and who does not, but who receives everyone as righteous people and as prophets, though they may well be neither of the two."

52. *BoS* 16.7. The whole text reads, "The fools of the world, in their foolishness, are not able to distinguish between whoever is dishonoring them and whoever is honoring them, and they would be talking first thing in the morning with that one who struck them in the evening. Imitate them in this way. Enter [the home of] the people who are insolent to you as a fool and talk with them and honor those who honor you. Look at the fool who cannot distinguish good people from bad in his foolishness, and in the same way you should love the good and the bad while knowing them [for who they are]."

they might be fools for the sake of Christ and consider evil ones better than themselves. They become good servants through their love for everyone, and love and honor the evil ones as they would the good ones, just as our Lord became a good servant of the many, of the good and of the evil through his love, and suffered their insult and honored and prayed for them.[53]

Important also is that this lack of distinguishing appears here not as an imitation of the Father, as in the series of texts presented before, but chiefly as an imitation of Christ[54] through the introduction of the topic of the servant. His extreme love requires from us humility and becoming a servant for everyone. "Every person, and our Lord, should be seen by you as friends, beloved ones, neighbors, fathers, and lord's. You will be a servant to them by your love, and [like a] son and brother, friend and heir."[55]

It is worth it here to highlight again the emphasis on the Christological mediation. In order to imitate the Father we ought to imitate Christ, the perfect imitator of the Father,[56] who gave "himself for the evil ones."[57]

Throughout the *Book of Steps* we find repeatedly the emphasis on unlimited love. "God gave the authority to people to do good and virtuous things, as much as they desire and as it pleases them, because the limit for love and good deeds has not been set."[58] While our book stresses an unlimited love in its measure, more significant is, however, the lack of limits with regard to the addressees of that love. In this sense there is nobody that falls outside this love.[59]

From the outset of this chapter I have highlighted the variety of religious groups as one of the main characteristics of the *Book of Steps.* Among them the "sick" and the "children" were ranked within a basic degree, due mainly to their attitude toward evil people. This restriction of interaction with them

53. *BoS* 30.8.

54. On the imitation of Christ, see René Roux, "The Doctrine of the Imitation of Christ in the *Liber Graduum:* Between Exegetical Theory and Soteriology," in *Studia Patristica: Biblica Et Apocrypha, Ascetica, Liturgica,* edited by Elizabeth A. Livingstone and E. Peters, 30:259–64 (Leuven: Peeters, 1997).

55. *BoS* 16.9.

56. *BoS* 19.20: Christ "was a servant of everyone through his love and was struck and did not strike [anyone] and loved his murderers and prayed for them on account of his great mercy and his lowliness without limit to teach us to imitate him."

57. *BoS* 25.7: "Let him have compassion on the sinners and the righteous; and let him love to give himself up for the evil ones, as [did] our Lord and his apostles."

58. *BoS* 22.14.

59. Love to nonhuman creatures, however, is not explicitly thematized in our work.

hallmarks also to some extent the Upright and the so-called "disciples of faith,"[60] who probably are representatives of an "official" church. Unlike them, the Perfect and the "disciples of love" who are very close to the Perfect are freed from any sort of restriction in regard to their love. In consequence, it is the attitude toward the unrighteous that differentiates and characterizes "universal love" and perfection.

For this reason faith isolates its disciples from every brother who behaves wickedly, or from one who has something impure in him, until they grow up and are strong and securely established. Then they will become disciples of universal love, which is superior to faith, for [love] teaches its disciples something superior to faith, but is not useful to its disciples. . . . The commandments of love are more lowly than those of faith; they are all [things] to all [people]. But the commandments of faith are harder than those of love; they flee from being with evil ones.[61]

Due to "pedagogical" reasons, in the lower stages of spiritual growth the members of the different groups are precluded from universal love. The disciples of faith as well as the other "basic" Christians are characterized by their avoidance of evil. The passage cited refers also to an upgrade toward love, and this growth is caused precisely by the removal of limits. Consequently, core to the *Book of Steps'* understanding is the Pauline quote of becoming "all [things] to all [people],"[62] interpreted explicitly as love. This is manifested in the following text of memra 19 within the framework of the opposition between road and paths. Whereas the paths prevent us from attaining the major commandments of love and perfection,

[l]ove loves all, which the apostle extolled more than all [other] good gifts. It is acquired by the major commandments, and that Perfection, which our Lord said is like the angels, is accomplished on this difficult and narrow road. Now this road of the major commandments leads to the house of our Lord and enters his bridal chamber. . . . But those who travel on that perfect road will rejoice in the joy of our Lord and be glorified with him as it is written, "I will rejoice in your joy and be glorified also in your heritage."[63]

60. *BoS* 30.13: "But as long as you are young, you are not authorized to be all [things] with all [people] and to walk with everyone. That is, until you grow up you should not associate with licentious men and women, but with whoever admonishes you and hold you back from evil things, and teaches you [how] to become people who give honor and [are] not insolent ones, just as our Lord teaches you by his spirit and grace to become sheep among wolves and good ones among the evil."

61. *BoS* 30.1.

62. *BoS* 30.2.

63. *BoS* 19.36.

The universality of love is emphasized when the author of the *Book of Steps,* summarizing the Law and the Prophets, puts into the mouth of the Lord the double commandment, "You shall love the Lord God and the people who are all descendants of Adam, who are your neighbors, relatives, and family."[64] Obviously, this renders Matthew 22:37, 39. While the first part of the commandment is abbreviated, the second part is enhanced. It reads, "You should love your neighbor as yourself." The *Book of Steps* clearly elaborates on the understanding of "neighbor" by transcending a narrow comprehension. In other words, everybody is a neighbor. Every human being is a neighbor included in the supreme commandment of love. The emphasis of the *Book of Steps* is not placed, nevertheless, on overcoming ethnic differences, but on explicitly precluding any exclusion from these "descendants of Adam," any ethical exclusion. Allow me to cite here another text previously referred to: "Every person, and our Lord, should be seen by you as friends, beloved ones, neighbors, fathers, and lords. You will be a servant to them by your love, and [like a] son and brother, friend and heir."[65]

There is no limit for the disciple of love; he is urged to love "both fellow-countrymen and foreigners, . . . he honors them and regards them as better than himself."[66] In a further passage, this thought is made even clearer:

> In the same way, he comes to these great commandment in the Torah, upon which depend the whole power of the Law and the prophets and by which a person fulfills the whole Law and the prophets, [namely] "You shall love the Lord your God with all your heart and with all your strength and with everything you have"; and the one after it is similar to it, "You shall love your neighbor as yourself," which means all people. You should take care of them just as you would for yourself, in as much as you are able to assist them.[67]

Here the author reproduces the double commandment in a way closer to Matthew. Interesting, however, is how he glosses the second part of the commandment, "which means all people." Again the universality of love is highlighted. New here is the description by which this love is to be carried out. In a similar

64. *BoS* 20.23.

65. *BoS* 16.9: "Look, when were you [more] contented—when you judged everyone, or now [when] you forgive everyone and love them? . . . Every person, and our Lord, should be seen by you as friends, beloved ones, neighbors, fathers, and lords. You will be a servant to them by your love, and [like a] son and brother, friend and heir."

66. *BoS* 5.2.

67. *BoS* 7.2.

vein, the *Book of Steps* explains that, indeed, God commanded us to "love and honor them [our fellow human beings] deeply"[68] (i.e., the people who are all descendants of Adam, who are your neighbors, relatives, and family).

Having stated the absence of any restriction regarding those who are to be loved, the *Book of Steps* concentrates, nevertheless, on a special category: the unrighteous, evil, and even murderers. To some extent the difference between good and evil disappears in the Perfect. In fact, he "thinks only good of all people, whether they are good or evil,"[69] he forgives everyone and judges nobody.[70] Only having done so is he able to "pray with love for all people and for our murderers,"[71] to "be merciful to all people, even our murderers,"[72] and to love all people—even those who are out to kill him."[73] The *Book of Steps* goes so far in its requirements as to exhort the perfect to give themselves up for the evil ones and, by doing so, become perfect disciples of the Lord and the apostles. "Let him have compassion on the sinners and the righteous; and let him love to give himself up for the evil ones, as [did] our Lord and his apostles."[74]

Within the *Book of Steps'* understanding of the history of salvation, Christ reintroduces perfection, and this is understood as universal love toward everyone. Unlike the time of the prophets, when they were prevented from attaining perfection, "today God asks people to love one another."[75] Throughout the *Book of Steps* we have read the insistent exhortation to love all, but especially enemies, sinners, and murderers. Let us examine closely these three categories.

As already expressed, the context of the *Book of Steps* refers to internal and external persecutions taking place amid the community. Despite the limitation in the Old Covenant, the *Book of Steps* brings up some examples drawn from it. In fact, among the prophets, "Elisha also pursued Perfection when he fed and gave drink to his enemies as he wished that his enemies would do to him."[76] Perfection is here clearly connected to mercy toward the enemies. It is not affirmed, however, that Elisha had attained perfection, but merely that he pursued it. He could not have attained it before Christ, and this is manifest in the fact that this mercy is neither explicitly referred to as love nor is totally

68. *BoS* 7.6.
69. *BoS* 3.12.
70. *BoS* 16.9.
71. *BoS* 20.7.
72. *BoS* 20.7.
73. *BoS* 3.12. This phrase is repeated twice in this passage.
74. *BoS* 25.7.
75. *BoS* 9.4.
76. *BoS* 9.10.

disinterested. Indeed, it is not enough to be merciful to our enemies, but we ought to love them as the Lord did. "Even if we are merciful with them, we are still very much falling short of the kind of love our Lord had."[77] In loving who hates and persecutes us, we attain perfection, which consists in imitating the heavenly Father.[78] The disciples of love are therefore called to "love their enemies and pray for them."[79] Nevertheless, strictly speaking they do not have any enemy, but Satan, the evil spirits, and sin.[80]

The enemy's strategy consists precisely in introducing hate.[81] The saints, however, following in the footsteps of the Lord, love sinners and consider them as saints and, by doing so, destroy Satan's plan:

> When the Evil One sees you being so gentle to both the good and the bad, it will howl: "What shall I do? I have shown him impure and evil people, but he looks upon them as upon saints, and admonishes them as brothers! Alas, what shall I do? I now have nowhere to attack him, for my whole strategy is based on people hating each other, if only because of their sins! But this person loves sinners like our Lord! Alas, this person condemns me and destroys me just as He does! I had better quit and leave, rather than let him destroy me by a lowliness that resembles that of his teacher, Jesus!"[82]

77. *BoS* 5.3: "Scripture says, 'Do not rejoice at the destruction of your enemy,' lest God brings his destruction on you and has no mercy on you as you had no mercy on your brother. 'Whoever rejoices at misfortune will be his own ruin.' It is right that our Lord should die for sinners, but that we should hate them? Even if we are merciful with them, we are still very much falling short of the kind of love our Lord had. But if we hate them, we shall see him in eternity."

78. *BoS* 19.33: "This is the Perfect road: If you love only the one who loves you and you greet only your brothers, what is your righteousness? Because even tax-collectors and heathen and sinners act in this way. But love whoever hates you and persecutes you, and your peace will increase toward the good and the evil, and you shall be imitating the Father in heaven who makes his sun shine and his rain fall upon them equally."

79. *BoS* 30.8: "The disciples of love despise themselves, saying that they are impious while they are righteous, in order to love the impious and honor them and in order to love their enemies and pray for them. They are despised in [their] lowliness of mind so that they might be fools for the sake of Christ and consider evil ones better than themselves. They become good servants through their love for everyone, and love and honor the evil ones as they would the good ones, just as our Lord became a good servant of the many, of the good and of the evil through his love, and suffered their insult and honored and prayed for them."

80. *BoS* 16.8.

81. Here the author of the *Book of Steps* argues in a similar way to what Maximus Confessor will do later in his *Logos Asketikos*.

82. *BoS* 4.7.

By imitating Christ in his love to sinners, the saints succeed not only in defeating Satan, but also in entering into God's heart. In fact, for God, unlike Satan, there is no evil.

Also, here the eschatological love revealed by the Lord is foreshadowed in ancient times. This time it is Moses who "loved the sinners as himself and did not separate himself from them."[83] Again, progress is seen in regard to the ancient covenant. The Perfect one loves and considers sinners not as himself, but better than himself. Indeed, he "love(s) sinners, admonishes them and holds them to be good people—better than himself."[84]

After commanding the Perfect to love enemies and sinners, the *Book of Steps* attains its summit and climax in the requirement to love one's (own) murderers. This establishes the difference between the disciples of "faith" and those of "love" in the supreme act of martyrdom. Not having attained perfection, "[t]he martyrs of faith . . . are killed while not loving their murderers and their persecutors, condemning them while they are indeed dying on account of the Lord."[85] However, it is not enough not to hate the murderers, but we ought to love and bless them and pray for them.

Let us be careful. When the persecution of these martyrs of faith and of these martyrs of love is equal, and the murder of both is the same, these martyrs of love are much greater, not only than those martyrs who hate and despise their killers and persecutors, but also [greater] than those martyrs who do not hate their killers and persecutors, but do not love or pray for them nor condemn them. For when these martyrs of love were being killed, they prayed for their murderers and persecutors and blessed them with their love, just as our Lord and his apostles had done, [and] they will become very great and be glorified with our Lord.[86]

As a predecessor of Christ, the *Book of Steps* introduces the victim of the first murder in the biblical history.

Abel pursued Perfection when he submitted to his murderer and did not violate love and Uprightness by the striking [Cain], the thing that he hated lest someone should strike him. Adam demonstrated his [love of truth] when he did not require vengeance for Abel from the hands of Cain, because he wished that every person would forgive him whenever he would sin. Thus the Lord was content to forgive [Cain] on the day he went astray and did not kill him.[87]

83. *BoS* 21.12.

84. *BoS* 5.6.

85. *BoS* 30.4.

86. *BoS* 30.5.

87. *BoS* 9.11.

Also this time the example of the ancient economy points toward the perfect love revealed in Christ—however, falling short of it. While Abel does not hate Cain, neither does he love him. On the contrary, it is said from Christ himself that he "loved his murderers and prayed for them on account of his great mercy and his lowliness without limit to teach us to imitate him."[88]

After the Lord, we are called to imitate Stephen and the apostles as well in their love for their murderers.[89] Finally, let us express here that this supreme perfection is only granted by the reception of the Paraclete when we are filled with him and the Lord dwells in us.[90]

Let us conclude by saying that the Syriac *Book of Steps* is to be situated in the history of reception and interpretation of the Sermon on the Mount. Within this context it remains almost unparalleled in reflecting Jesus's uncompromised maximalism and radicalism.

> Therefore, when we have climbed these steps and have rooted up sin and its fruits from the heart, then we will be filled with the Spirit, the Paraclete, and our Lord will dwell in us completely. We will eat freely from that tree of life that is our Lord, from which we were deprived by the transgression of the commandments; and then, we will be able to love and be merciful to all people, even our murderers, and be able to pray with love for all people and for our murderers. When we [are able to have] mercy upon and love everyone in this way, including our murderers, our heart being pure, then we will increase in Perfection and live according to that great, acceptable, and perfect will of our Lord.[91]

The Perfect and perfection in the *Book of Steps* require an extreme asceticism that entails full renunciation of the world in all its forms.[92] Nevertheless, the goal of this tremendous asceticism is the configuration with the humble and suffering Christ and his all-embracing love.[93] In becoming servants not only

88. *BoS* 19.20: Christ "was a servant of everyone through his love and was struck and did not strike [anyone] and loved his murderers and prayed for them on account of his great mercy and his lowliness without limit to teach us to imitate him." Similarly, see *BoS* 20.14: Christ "loved those who hate him and his murderers and prayed for them with mercy."

89. *BoS* 30.4.

90. *BoS* 20.7.

91. *BoS* 20.7.

92. For asceticism in the *Book of Steps,* see Kitchen, "Becoming Perfect: The Maturing of Asceticism in the Liber Graduum," in *Journal of the Canadian Society for Syriac Studies* 2 (2002): 30–43; and Diana Juhl, *Die Askese im Liber Graduum und bei Afrahat: Eine vergleichende Studie zur frühsyrischen Frömmigkeit,* Orientalia Biblical et Christiana 9 (Wiesbaden: Harrassowitz Verlag, 1996).

93. See Antoine Guillaumont, "Situation et signification du 'Liber Graduum' dans la spiritualité

of the good, but also especially of the evil ones, the enemies, and even their own murderers,[94] The Perfect are called to reflect upon the world—like God's sun—the unlimited compassion of the Father.

syriaque," in *Symposium Syriacum 1972: Célébré dans les jours 26-31 octobre 1972 à l'Institut pontifical oriental de Rome: Rapports et communications,* edited by Ignacio Ortiz de Urbina, 313, Orientalia Christiana Analecta 197 (Rome: Pontificium Institutum Orientalium, 1974): "Les vertus du parfait sont avant tout l'humilité, le pardon, la douceur. Il s'applique à faire la paix parmi les hommes, à les enseigner avec humilité, à les corriger s'il le faut, mais en s'abstenant de les juger: aussi bien il s'estime inférieur à tous les hommes, bons ou pécheurs."

94. Argárate, "*Ktābā dmasqātā*": "Aus den 30 Mēmrē resultiert ein fazinierendes Bild einer asketisch charismatisch geprägten Gemeinde. Mitten in den verschiedenen und sogar komplexen Verfolgungen werden die Christen aufgerufen, ihren leidenden, armen und gedemutigten Herrn nachzuahmen. Auf diesem Weg werden sie durch die steigernde Präsenz und Wirksamkeit des Geistes zu einer mystique pneumatique bewegt. Ziel des Weges ist die Stadt Gottes, der Garten von Eden, die Wiedererlangung des verlorenen Paradieses."

Kelli E. Bryant

10. YOU ARE WHAT YOU EAT

Dietary Metaphors in the Syriac Book of Steps

Emerging from the milieu of the late-fourth-century, pre-monastic Christianity of the Persian Empire,[1] the Syriac *Book of Steps* provides a glimpse into the interactions of a peculiar community.[2] The author of this collection of thirty loosely connected memre[3] envisions the members of his community, at

1. Robert A. Kitchen, "Syriac Additions to Anderson: The Garden of Eden in the Book of Steps and Philoxenus of Mabbug," *Hugoye: Journal of Syriac Studies* 6 (2003): 38.

2. The community appeared to be so peculiar that it generated a lengthy scholarly dialogue as to whether it had connections with the so-called Messalian heresy. Associating the *Book of Steps* with Messalianism is problematic, particularly since there is little concrete evidence that the *Books of Steps* actually contains the allegedly Messalian doctrines; Arthur Vööbus, "*Liber Graduum:* Some Aspects of Its Significance for the History of Early Syrian Asceticism," in *Charisteria Iohanni Kopp octogenerio oblata,* 109–10, Papers of the Estonian Theological Society in Exile 7 (Stockholm: Estonian Theological Society in Exile, 1954); Columba Stewart, *"Working the Earth of the Heart": The Messalian Controversy in History, Texts, and Language to A.D. 431* (Oxford: Clarendon Press, 1991). While establishing that the *Book of Steps* derives from a heretical or Messalian community seems tenuous, the suggestion that this document belongs to a distinctive (perhaps sectarian) community is more helpful; see Robert Murray, *Symbols of Church and Kingdom: A Study in Early Syriac Tradition,* rev. ed. (London: T. and T. Clark; Piscataway, N.J.: Gorgias Press, 2004), 36; cf. Kitchen, "The Gattung of the Liber Graduum: Implications for a Sociology of Asceticism," in *IV Symposium Syriacum 1984,* edited by Han J. W. Drijvers, et al, 173–82, Orientalia Christiana Analecta 229 (Rome: Pontificium Institutum Studiorum Orientalium, 1987).

3. There have been attempts to outline the structure of the *Book of Steps.* Lionel Wickham suggests a complicated scheme, attempting to detect literary and thematic links between the memre; Wickham, "The *Liber Graduum* Revisited," in *VI Symposium Syriacum, 1992: University of Cambridge, Faculty of Divinity, 30 August–2 September 1992,* edited by René Lavenant, 180–84 (Rome: Pontificio Instituto Orientale, 1992). Kitchen distinguishes three sections: basic commandments, advanced perfection, and

their various levels of maturity, en route to the city of the Lord Jesus Christ, together arduously climbing the stairway to perfection. The author strives to assist his fellow sojourners by discerning the commandments of the Lord that correspond to the varying levels of discipleship within the community. The author distinguishes two basic categories of discipleship: the Perfect (those who renounce work, spouses, and possessions in order to dedicate themselves to the spiritual life and ministry) and the Upright (lay Christians who are married, have possessions, work, and engage in physical ministries).[4] The author navigates the tension between seemingly contradictory commandments in the New Testament by asserting that the scriptures "were not addressed to [only] one [type of] person."[5] He proposes that one group of instructions, the minor commandments, is given for the Upright, while the major commandments are those of the Perfect.

While the captivating image of an ascending journey provides inspiration for the title of this work,[6] another metaphor prominently recurs in its pages. A dietary metaphor designed to illustrate the distinction between the diverse commandments appears in nearly half of the memre.[7] The author detects people in his community who are "infants" requiring "milk," those who are "sick"

later period and redemption of the Upright; Robert A. Kitchen and Martien F. Parmentier, trans., *The Book of Steps: The Syriac Liber Graduum* (Kalamazoo, Mich.: Cistercian Publications, 2004), xxix–xxxviii. Determining the original order of the memre is difficult, because only three manuscripts approach completeness and one deviates in order from the other two; Kitchen and Parmentier, *Book of Steps,* xxix. Furthermore, there is no guarantee that the memre are arranged chronologically, making development over time difficult to substantiate.

4. It is the basic consensus of scholarship that there are two major categories of Christian discipleship in the *Book of Steps;* see Vööbus, *"Liber Graduum,"* 114. Beggiani agrees that there are two basic groups, the Just and the Perfect, and notes that the "spiritual life . . . consists of an indefinite number of degrees"; Seely J. Beggiani, *Introduction to Eastern Christian Spirituality: The Syriac Tradition* (London: Associated University Presses, 1991), 29–31. Kitchen has detected at least six different categories of Christian discipleship in the text; see Kitchen and Parmentier, *Book of Steps,* xxxviii.

5. This chapter references the text by the divisions in Kitchen and Parmentier's English translation of the *Book of Steps* rather than by the columns in Kmoskó's 1926 edition; see *BoS* 11.1.

6. Wickham notes that the journey metaphor is not consistently applied throughout the text, occurring most prominently only in memre 19 and 20, and he suggests that the original title of the *Book of Steps* was different—namely, that the first nine memre were collectively entitled, "On the mode of life of full maturity and the discrimination of Our Lord's commandments"; Wickham, "*Liber Graduum* Revisited," 179. The two themes of maturity and discrimination fit naturally with the dietary metaphors of milk, vegetables, and solid food. If a person is discriminating and eats the food corresponding to her spiritual state, she will grow, eventually attaining full maturity. While the journey metaphor actually haunts more of the background of the work than Wickham grants, it seems that the dietary metaphor may be nearly as prominent, if less striking. Both metaphors, journey and dietary, depict gradual growth along the road to perfection.

7. In many of the places where this metaphor occurs, it is simply applied, without much explication,

and in need of "vegetables" (or herbs), and "adults" who take in "solid food." The author expects that, by consuming the appropriate "food," each cohort will grow more toward perfection. The purpose of this chapter is to explicate the way in which the author creatively applies these traditional biblical images in order to vividly picture the status of different groups within his community. This dietary imagery allows the author to affirm each group, while distinguishing them and challenging them to grow further.

The Use of Dietary Images in the *Book of Steps*

Like most of the metaphors found in the *Book of Steps,* the author obtains the dietary metaphor from the rich imagery of the biblical text.[8] He creatively draws on two passages to detect a distinction between those who are young in the faith and those who are mature. Both 1 Corinthians and Hebrews use the images of milk and solid food to illustrate different levels of Christian maturity.[9] In the former, Paul explains that he fed the Corinthians "milk" because they were still spiritual infants, "people of the flesh" and not ready for solid food.[10] The passage from Hebrews has been especially influential in our author's use of this metaphor: "[F]or everyone who lives on milk, being still an infant, is unskilled in the word of righteousness. But solid food is for the mature, for those whose faculties have been trained by practice to distinguish good from evil."[11] This passage correlates directly with one of the larger purposes of the *Book of Steps,* which is to distinguish between the often contradictory commandments given to different groups corresponding to their spiritual maturity.[12]

---

as in *BoS* 2.1: "Now let us expound the major commandments . . . , and distinguish them from the 'vegetables and milk.'" The author expands the metaphor most notably in memre 4, 5, 11, 19, and 30.

8. Kitchen and Parmentier, *Book of Steps,* lxiii.

9. Direct quotations of 1 Cor 3:1–3 occur in *BoS* 11.5 and 19.5. Quotations of Heb 5:13–14 occur in *BoS* 5.8, 12.3, 19.5, and 19.10.

10. Paul goes on to say that as long as jealousy and quarreling occur in the community, the people are still of the flesh, behaving according to human inclinations. Like Paul, the author of the *Book of Steps* applies the dietary metaphors within a context addressing internal and external conflict. On the subject of conflict in the community of the *Book of Steps,* see Kitchen, "Conflict on the Stairway to Heaven: The Anonymity of Perfection in the Syriac *Liber Graduum,*" in *Symposium Syriacum VII: Uppsala University, Department of Asian and African Languages, 11–14 August 1996,* edited by René Lavenant, 211–20 (Rome: Pontificio Instituto Orientale, 1998).

11. All scripture quotations are from the New Revised Standard Version.

12. See Beggiani, *Introduction to Christian Spirituality,* 29. Scholars have proposed different purpos-

Romans 14:1–4 provides the biblical source for the "vegetables of the sick." In this passage Paul intervenes in a controversy over what kinds of food a Christian should eat. While Paul states that those who only eat vegetables are weak in faith, his pastoral advice is for everyone to refrain from judging one another based on diet.[13] Paul's advice for dealing with this controversy provides the author of the *Book of Steps* with another dietary image with which to play.[14] He employs and expands these dietary metaphors to make sense of the distinctions in his own community, and the metaphor thus takes on a life of its own. "Milk," "vegetables," and "solid food" correlate with the various types of commandments. [15] One way in which the *Book of Steps* describes the relationships between disparate groups is by identifying them according to the kinds of commandments they "eat," be it "milk for the Children," "vegetables for the Sick," or "solid food" for the mature.

Drawing on these dietary images from Hebrews, Corinthians, and Romans, the author creatively adapts them to fit the circumstances of his unique community.[16] While the first three memre of the collection merely hint at the identity of the sick and the children in contrast to the Perfect, [17] memre 4 and 5 take up this theme in earnest. In memra 4, "On the Vegetables for the Sick," the author identifies the sick as morally rigid people who, being unaware of

es for the *Book of Steps.* Vööbus suggests that the *Book of Steps* seeks to cling to ancient ideals in the face of encroaching Western monasticism; Vööbus, *"Liber Graduum,"* 126. If this were the case, one would expect more explicit references to Western monasticism and an explanation as to why the old ways are preferable. Stewart makes the constructive observation that the book seeks to show the way to perfection, persuading both the Upright and the Perfect to pursue this way; Stewart, *"Working the Earth,"* 92. Kitchen convincingly sees the distinctions between commandments as serving the larger purpose of igniting spiritual renewal in a community plagued by conflict; see Kitchen, "Conflict," 220. For a collection as large and diverse as the *Book of Steps,* there may be more than one operative purpose.

13. While the author of the *Book of Steps* uses Paul's concrete instructions in a metaphorical sense, he too insists that the members of his community "leave off judging altogether"; *BoS* 5.12.

14. The author anticipates objections to his use of "vegetables for the sick" in *BoS* 19.6. He has to explain, in light of Rom 14:2, why the Perfect fast from food, since Paul seems to say that those who refrain from eating certain foods are weak. He counters, "Is it not evident that Paul called 'sick' whomever is ill in his mind and whose understanding is little, but does not call 'sick' whoever fasts and eats bread and vegetables and salt?" Instead, the author insists that Paul really calls "sick" or "weak" whoever does not keep the major commandments.

15. That the various "foods" are commandments is made clear by memra 1: "[W]e do not know which commandments must be kept in order to receive the Paraclete, or which ones must be kept by a 'sick' person in order to be healed, or which ones a person must keep to 'grow like a child'" (*BoS* 1.2).

16. Heb 5:13–14; 1 Cor 3:1–3; Rom 14:1–4.

17. The Sick and the Children are usually grouped together; cf. *BoS* 2.1, 3.1, 11.1.

their own sinfulness, are "convinced they get contaminated by the sins of their neighbor, even though they do not sin along with him."[18] The sick feel compelled to admonish their brothers and sisters who have sinned, so the author claims that the Lord gave these instructions in Matthew 18 to help them heal from their moral rigidity:

If your brother sins against you, go and show him his fault, just between the two of you. If he listens to you, you have won your brother over. But if he will not listen, take one or two others along, so that "every matter may be established by the testimony of two or three witnesses." If he refuses to listen to them, tell it to the church; and if he refuses to listen even to the church, treat him as you would a pagan or a tax collector.[19]

The remainder of the memra outlines the way in which one may admonish a sinner in love. The author draws from the Beatitudes for apt responses to various situations in which one person might feel compelled to admonish another. For example, when one encounters an unmerciful person, the way to admonish her in love is to say, "Blessed are the merciful, for they will receive mercy."[20] The Beatitude is followed by exhortations urging the hearer to move toward perfection. The author follows the exhortation to be merciful with instructions on forgiveness. While each person should strive to forgive others, this is an action that especially characterizes perfection.[21] One might wonder whether the author intends these to be exhortations for the one being admonished or for the sick who feel compelled to admonish others. Perhaps such ambiguity is purposeful, since the sick person "does not observe the beam in his own eye, but condemns the person who is, in fact, just like himself"[22] and may need loving admonishment as much as the person whose sin he cannot ignore.

Memra 5, "On the Milk of the Children," naturally flows from the discus-

18. *BoS* 4.5

19. Matt 18:15–17.

20. *BoS* 4.4.

21. Compare *BoS* 11.3: "[O]ur Lord said, 'Forgive your brother seventy times seven, [even] if he does you wrong [that many times] in a single day.' Yet again he said, 'Think of him as a Gentile.' If these were spoken to [only] one [type of] person, which one would you choose? That one, 'Forgive him seventy times seven'; or that [other] one, 'Regard him as a Gentile and keep away from him'"? In this passage the author associates forgiveness with perfection and separation from the sinner with uprightness. Here the author has sorted out Perfect and Upright commandments that both occur in Matt 18, providing an excellent example of his distinct hermeneutic; see also Robert A. Ratcliff, "Steps Along the Way of Perfection: The *Liber Graduum* and Early Syrian Monasticism" (PhD diss., Emory University, 1988), 134–35.

22. *BoS* 4.1.

sion in the previous memra, providing an explanation of the commandments given to the children, whom the author frequently addresses alongside the sick. Whereas the sick cannot tolerate the presence of sinners, the children are not yet mature enough to be in the presence of sinners without being lured into their way of life. Because of their lack of discernment, the Lord gave commandments that they should separate themselves from sinners. Here the author applies a cluster of relevant passages from the gospels and the Pauline corpus. The author's first paraphrase is from 1 Corinthians: "Do not eat bread with adulterers, with violent people, with gluttons, with covetous people, or with people who swear."[23] Similar passages from Paul encouraging separation from sinners occur throughout the *Book of Steps,* as well.[24] The author also appeals to Jesus's instructions to the twelve when he sends them out in Matthew:[25]

> Neither go on the way of pagans nor inside the town of the Samaritans; instead go to the sheep who have wandered from the house of Israel. . . . When you enter a village, ask who is worthy in it, and stay with him. Do not greet anyone on the way. When anyone does not receive you, shake off the dust from your feet as you are leaving, and it will be easier for Sodom on the Day of Judgment than for that town.[26]

The author argues that the Lord instructed the disciples in this way because they were not yet mature. Being faithful Jews, the disciples were afraid to mix with sinners.[27] The author argues that these instructions were given to the disciples to protect them from stumbling blocks until they were full-grown, filled with the Spirit, and no longer susceptible to stumbling.[28] Throughout the *Book of Steps,* allusions to Matthew and these "separation" passages distinguish the ways of the children and sick from those of the Perfect.[29]

Who Are the Sick and the Children?

While some scholars have expressed uncertainty about whether to categorize the sick and children as a part of the Upright or as "fledgling Perfect

23. 1 Cor 5:11.

24. Similar passages include Rom 15:1, 2 Cor 6:17, and 2 Thess 3:14. References to 1 Cor 5 occur most often.

25. Matt 10:5–16, and the parallel in Luke 10:4.

26. *BoS* 5.4.

27. *BoS* 5.5–6.

28. *BoS* 5.7.

29. Matt 18:15–17.

ones,"[30] these two groups should usually be included among the Upright. Throughout the book, the author uses the metaphors of "vegetables" and "milk" as synonyms for the minor commandments, which are those addressed to the Upright.[31] "Vegetables and milk" is used interchangeably with "minor commandments" in many places. Memra 5 shows concern that the children will be outraged by sinners and treat them in a way that the children themselves would not want to be treated.[32] This would violate two of the four basic commandments of uprightness and cause one to fall from uprightness.[33] It follows that the "vegetables and milk" have been given to prevent one from falling from uprightness. In fact, the author suggests that the "vegetables and milk" are useful for the healing of one who has even fallen from uprightness.[34] Memra 19, the longest memra and the most nuanced exposition of the book,[35] contrasts the road of the Perfect with the paths of the sick and children. Some of the paths contrasted with the road of the Perfect deal with separation from sinners, while others concern issues that distinguish the Upright from the Perfect, such as marriage[36] or work.[37] Furthermore, memra 19 explains that the sick are unable to reconcile with their enemies—this is a step that they are not yet strong enough to take.[38] Since this is the first step of three that one must climb in order to become Perfect in memra 20,[39] the author cannot consider

30. Kitchen and Parmentier, *Book of Steps,* xl.

31. For example, see *BoS* 1.2, 11.1, and 19.5. The opening statement of memra 1 explains that the Upright keep the minor commandments, and 1.2 equates the "vegetables and milk" with the minor commandments.

32. See *BoS* 5.8–10.

33. There are four commandments that provide the basic framework for upright living. The upright person knows "the power of these commandments of Uprightness, 'Love the Lord your God with all your heart and people as yourself, and that thing that you hate, do not do to your neighbor, and as you wish that people do to you, so also you should do to them'"; *BoS* 15.15.

34. *BoS* 2.1.

35. Kitchen and Parmentier, *Book of Steps,* xxxiv.

36. *BoS* 19.14–15.

37. *BoS* 19.13, 16.

38. "Say to whoever is sick and is tormented and has not yet become strong, 'Go reconcile with your enemies, these who have treated you badly for no reason,' and see how he is confused and falls from this step if he goes to ascend it." The sick person may be unable to follow the command to go reconcile or may end up quarreling with the offender and thus fall from uprightness. "[This illness] causes him pain because he has not asked our Lord and has not received power from on high to reconcile by it his enemies"; *BoS* 19.37.

39. *BoS* 20.1–2: "There are three very difficult steps on this road leading to the city of our Lord Jesus. One is this: if a person has enemies, even though he does not offend or annoy anyone, he should go meet

the sick as a part of the Perfect. Additionally, the author makes clear that a leader of the church can only be upright because managing churches requires him to discipline and expel people according to the minor commandments.[40] In this case the necessity of judging and possibly expelling another person, thus keeping separate from him, is enough to keep a church leader from pursuing perfection. The sick and the children may one day seek perfection; indeed our author hopes to persuade them to grow in such a direction. However, such expectations of growth indicate that they have not arrived yet.

There are exceptions to the rule in which these two dietary metaphors and their corresponding social groups may not consistently refer to the Upright. In one case the image of being an infant or a child appears without the reference to feeding on milk. In memra 15 the author explains that before they sinned, Adam and Eve were innocent like infants (i.e., they were naked, but without lust).[41] Likewise, those who are growing in perfection will eventually turn from lust and become like little children, thus returning to the state of humanity before Adam and Eve fell from perfection. Along the same lines, in memra 16, the author urges his readers to become like infants who are humble and cannot perceive the evil of others.[42] Memra 16 explains that children are worthy of imitation when they show no concern for food or clothing, do not desire a spouse, cry at any time, and do not judge or perceive anyone as evil.[43] However, the author warns against imitating the way children lose their tempers, strike others, and naively follow evil instructions. The point of the child metaphor here is to illustrate innocence and purity, rather than levels of spiritual growth.[44] In this case certain aspects of childishness (but not all) are conducive to pursuing perfection, rather than "infancy" being a lesser spiritual state to outgrow. The lack of reference to "milk for the children" hints that the author is not concerned with delineating the commandments here, whereas elsewhere the metaphor is used to explain why different groups keep different commandments.

Another exception to the rule is more problematic. In memra 27, the met-

---

these enemies—and those who hate him for no reason—and reconcile with them. . . . Indeed, a person may climb that [first] step, in which one should humbly reconcile with his enemies who [hate him] for no reason through much fasting and powerful and lengthy prayer."

40. *BoS* 19.24; cf. *BoS* 19.31.

41. *BoS* 15.3.

42. *BoS* 16.5.

43. *BoS* 16.6.

44. The author relies on a different biblical passage for the metaphor here. Rather than drawing on the Pauline corpus or Hebrews, the author here reflects on the gospel accounts in which Jesus exhorts his disciples to be like little children (Matt 18:3 and parallels).

aphor of milk for children appears again, but this time the author seems to be addressing people who are youthful in age as well as in spiritual maturity. Rather than speaking to the Upright, the author gives pastoral advice to young Christians who aspire to become perfect. They are experiencing adversity from their non-Christian parents and are eager to leave home to engage in the lifestyle of a wandering ascetic. The trouble is, so it seems, that these young Christians are not as spiritually mature as they think they are. The author suspects that their eagerness has more to do with stubborn attitudes toward their parents.[45] They are too eager to enter the lifestyle of a Perfect one, and the author explains that they are still children who have not been weaned from milk and consequently still need a nurse.[46] If they leave home too soon, they may have to depend on a "foreign wet-nurse" who may not educate them thoroughly, leading them astray to become idolaters and pagans.[47] In this memra it becomes apparent that perfection cannot be systematically defined in the *Book of Steps* as embracing the ascetic disciplines. These young Christians are prepared to embark on a lifestyle of asceticism, but the author senses that they are not yet mature enough in the less concrete virtues of lowliness and love.[48] He advises his aspiring Perfect ones to view their life at home as a training ground for lowliness,[49] enduring harsh treatment from their parents as an appropriate way to suffer with Christ at this stage in their journey.[50] The author memorably quips, "In as much as you are lowly, so you shall grow."[51] In memra 27 the children are clearly aspiring Perfect ones, rather than the ordinary Upright, but they are not yet weaned from milk. It is still risky for them to be exposed to the world outside, lest they fall into idolatry and paganism. Yet remaining at home does not mean that the children are spiritually stagnant; this is a time for practicing humility in a safe environment, in preparation to leave home one day as physically and spiritually mature adults. This is the only use of the metaphor of "milk for the children" that does not directly correspond to the commandments of uprightness, but it still shows concern for gradual growth

45. *BoS* 27.3.

46. *BoS* 27.2.

47. *BoS* 27.2.

48. Ratcliff identifies these virtues as the centerpiece of the monastic life wherein the perfect seek to emulate Christ in every way; see Ratcliff, "Steps," 134–72. Celibacy, fasting, a life of prayer, and renunciation of possessions alone do not set apart the perfect from the upright. If one practices these disciplines without embodying love, forgiveness, and lowliness, one cannot attain perfection.

49. *BoS* 27.3.

50. *BoS* 27.1.

51. *BoS* 27.4.

in maturity and appropriate levels of interaction with the outside world.

If the most frequent use of "vegetables and milk" refers to the commandments of uprightness, what does the author mean by "solid food"? He seems to expect that the sick and children will one day become healthy and mature enough for it.[52] The *Book of Steps* does not mention solid food as often as one might expect. Perhaps the dietary metaphor is not as important to the author's conversation here. However, it does crop up in a few significant contexts. As one would expect, there is a clear association between "solid food" and the major commandments.[53] These major commandments are frequently contrasted with the "vegetables of the sick and the milk of the children."[54] When the author juxtaposes the major commandments or solid food with the "vegetables and milk," a cluster of biblical proof texts appear, representing the concerns of the Perfect. The following are among the most common: "Be all things to all people," "Forgive seventy times seven," and "Consider others better than yourself."[55] The author envisions the Perfect washing the feet of their enemies, as Jesus did to Iscariot, without exposing their enemies' sins.[56] The imitation of Jesus is central to the life of perfection, and washing the feet of Judas becomes a vivid picture of what the *imitatio Christi* entails. This is an action that distinguishes the Perfect from the sick and the children, who are unable to wash the feet of their enemies.[57] The life of perfection is centered on relational virtues of acceptance, forgiveness, reconciliation, and self-sacrifice.[58]

52. At least the author's rhetoric suggests that he expects such growth in perfection for everyone. It is more difficult to determine whether the author believes that everyone, even the sick and children, will one day become perfect.

53. *BoS* 1.2.

54. See table 10.1 for passages that explicitly contrast the "vegetables/milk of the Sick/Children" with the "solid food of the mature." The distinction between the two is fairly consistent.

55. Memra 19 demonstrates the prominence of these themes in contrast to the commandments for the sick and the children.

56. See *BoS* 17.3. The author is at pains to show that Jesus did not expose Judas as a sinner during the Last Supper. Memre 4 and 5 both show concern that by exposing the sinner a person would violate the Upright mandate: "Do not do to another what you would not have them do to you." Such a violation would make a person fall from uprightness. It would not fit with the vision of perfection the author espouses for Jesus to expose Judas as a sinner. Therefore, he anticipates the objections of a critical listener, and contends that Judas exposed his own sin; see also René Roux, "The Doctrine of the Imitation of Christ in the *Liber Graduum:* Between Exegetical Theory and Soteriology," in *Studia Patristica: Biblica Et Apocrypha, Ascetica, Liturgica,* edited by Elizabeth A. Livingstone and E. Peters, 30:261 (Leuven: Peeters, 1997).

57. *BoS* 19.37.

58. Ratcliff, "Steps," 172.

In this context of "solid food" for the Perfect, the dietary metaphors acquire a distinctive flavor. The author associates this dietary metaphor with the disobedience of Adam and Eve, which was, after all, related to a change in diet and with the reversal of those events in the work of Jesus Christ. As those who reconcile with their enemies and settle the disputes of others, the Perfect "obtain the trees of the spiritual paradise above the heavens."[59] The Perfect dine on the fruit of the trees of paradise from which Adam ate before he obeyed the Evil One. The fruits of these trees are "faithfulness, abstinence, lowliness, love, hope, truthfulness, and holiness in our Lord."[60] The Lord, whose lowliness the Perfect imitate, shares in this feast with them.[61] The Lord does not only share the feast with them; the good tree in the garden is, in fact, Jesus Christ himself.[62] Thus it is no surprise to find that this image has acquired a eucharistic sense in memra 12. The Perfect are those who "truly eat our Lord,"[63] for they "have the strength to train to comprehend what is the height and depth and length and width."[64] While everyone in the church partakes of the Eucharist,

59. *BoS* 2.6. The author's account of the story of Adam and Eve comes into play here. Prior to their downfall, Adam and Eve lived on earth with their minds in heaven (*BoS* 21.3). They sought to become like God in majesty (*BoS* 21.11) by eating from the tree of the knowledge of good and evil, and thus their minds descended from heaven and became engulfed in earthly preoccupations (*BoS* 21.10). Jesus enters the scene and makes it possible for human beings once again to attain their original state in the garden by imitating him in lowliness (*BoS* 21.11). Lowliness instead of pride is the key that unlocks the doors of paradise (*BoS* 21.12); see also Shafiq Abouzayd, *Ihidayutha: A Study of the Life of Singleness in the Syrian Orient, From Ignatius of Antioch to Chalcedon 451 AD* (Oxford: ARAM Society for Syro-Mesopotamian Studies, 1993), 45.

60. *BoS* 2.7. A similar passage occurs in *BoS* 21.3: "Everyone who imitates [our Lord] yields these fruits and becomes perfect. . . . [T]hese spiritual fruits are: 'Let us put on mercy, pity, harmony, peace, and the glory of our Lord'; that is, let us submit ourselves to one another through these spiritual fruits with love, patience, kindness, lowliness, endurance, moderation, and holiness without desire. These are the spiritual fruits on which the saints feed in Eden while separating these from the [commandments] that are hard for infants."

61. "These are the things they eat and enjoy with our Lord"; *BoS* 2.7.

62. *BoS* 21.2 reads, "Therefore, if you wish to be saved from the death of the Tree . . . , renounce and distance yourself from Satan. . . . The good tree . . . is our Lord Jesus. He is the tree of life who gives everything life by its fruits."

63. In the ancient world the choicest morsels of food are usually reserved for the social elite. It is interesting that those who are spiritually elite in the *Book of Steps* community, who "truly eat the Lord," are also those who have renounced sumptuous food and taken up a life of fasting. A subversive elitism is at work here. While both groups "eat" of Christ and both are following his commandments, the Perfect do so more completely—by means of receiving what is normally relegated to the poor and powerless on society's margins.

64. *BoS* 12.3. Eph 3:18 is one of the author's favorite passages for describing the spiritual knowledge of the Perfect.

the Perfect do so in a way that enables them to "reach that church on high" and continues to perfect them.[65] The result is that the Perfect "make their bodies temples and their hearts altars," communing simultaneously in the visible church and the heavenly church.[66] This language is reminiscent of the original state of humankind when Adam and Eve lived on earth with their minds in heaven.[67]

The Function of the Dietary Metaphors

Every time the author provides details about what the "vegetables and milk" are, they involve instructions about separating oneself from sinners. One might wonder, however, how the author made the connection between "vegetables and milk" and separation from sinners. At first glance these are not connotations that they have in the context of the biblical passages from which the author lifted these metaphors. Hebrews asserts that the mature who eat solid food have trained their minds to discern evil from good,[68] and therefore urges the reader to pursue perfection, leaving behind the basic teachings of the faith, which is defined in terms of repentance, baptism, resurrection, and eternal judgment.[69] In Hebrews these basic areas of catechesis are the "milk for the infants." The *Book of Steps,* on the other hand, typically identifies "milk" with separation from sinners. In both Romans and 1 Corinthians, Paul strives to navigate the differences between rival factions in the church.[70] The author of the *Book of Steps* seems to have made a hermeneutical leap in his application of the dietary metaphor to the discernment of the commandments for the Upright and the Perfect.[71] Such a leap indicates that the author was concerned to address the contradiction between the biblical instructions to separate oneself from sinners and commandments to consider others as better

65. *BoS* 12.3.

66. *BoS* 12.3. Memra 12 envisions the church existing on three different, yet interconnected levels: the visible church, the church of the heart, and the hidden, heavenly church.

67. *BoS* 21.3.

68. Heb 5:14.

69. Heb 6:1.

70. Rom 14:1–4; 1 Cor 3:1–4.

71. Or perhaps the author conflates these passages and their surrounding contexts; 1 Cor 3 does not mention separation from sinners, but 1 Cor 5 is dedicated to this topic of discussion. Either way, it seems that the tension between those who, like Paul, are "all things to all people" (1 Cor 9:22) and those who need to separate from sinners is a special concern of the author's. One could posit that a similar tension plagued the author's own spiritual community.

than oneself. This suggests the presence of serious conflict within the *Book of Steps* community regarding how one deals with sin and sinners.[72] The pastoral advice of the author makes it possible for factions to coexist peacefully in the community. However, the author is not satisfied just to see members of the community getting along with one another; he expects real progress to occur as people strive to keep the commandments corresponding to their state of spiritual maturity.

The author's pastoral concerns include the spiritual growth of the sick and the children. "Vegetables and milk" are a fine diet for those who cannot consume "solid food," but the author is concerned that some people are becoming too content with the diet of the sick and the children.[73] The author believes that if a person "eats" these too long, she will never grow up and be healed.[74] These commandments are meant to help one grow toward the major commandments. But how do the "vegetables and milk" heal the sick and help the children grow in maturity? What pedagogical function do these commandments perform? The function of these minor commandments is twofold: to prevent one from falling from uprightness and to help one progress in the road to perfection. The author shows concern that the sick and children might act harshly toward sinners. In memra 4 the author observes that a sick person may not be able to leave the sinner alone and may strike or expel the sinner, falling from uprightness because "he hates the fact that no one strikes the sinner, and therefore he strikes at [the sinner] himself."[75] Memra 5 similarly expresses the author's apprehension that the immature children will react violently, as the apostles did when they asked Jesus to allow them to call down fire on a village that would not receive them.[76] The author explains that Jesus's instructions to "shake off the dust and leave in peace" were given to prevent the apostles from being harsh and quarreling when they were immature. Violent reactions and quarreling would cause a sick person or an infant to fall from uprightness. The commandments also protect the children, who are in real danger of being de-

72. See Kitchen, "Conflict," 215.

73. Evidently, the author feared that people could become so satisfied with "vegetables and milk" that they would resist moving on to "solid food." The Evil One tricks people into thinking that it would be wrong for them to go beyond these commandments when it would actually be very good (*BoS* 2.7). In this way the minor commandments can also become a roadblock to further growth.

74. *BoS* 2.7.

75. *BoS* 4.2.

76. *BoS* 5.20.

ceived and seduced into sinful living.[77] Lashing out toward sinners or falling into their ways is not the only danger for the sick and the children, however. The instructions from Matthew must be tempered by the positive and negative formulations of the Golden Rule, which consists of two of the four basic commandments of uprightness.[78] If an upright person does to another person what she would not want another to do to her, then she has fallen from uprightness, including if she exposes the sin of another when she would not want someone to expose her sin.[79] The author seems to vacillate between whether one should judge and expose a person in front of the congregation as Matthew instructs,[80] or whether it is falling from uprightness to expose and judge a sinner.[81] The more central commandments to the Upright finally take precedent for our author, who advises the sick and the children to admonish a sinner only in a loving manner in private.[82]

The "vegetables and milk" are also prescribed to help one grow and mature for the journey toward perfection. Memra 19 describes them as training paths along the way of the road of perfection, allowing those who are "immature" or "sick" to continue exercising and gaining strength until they are strong enough to walk on the road. The author is not entirely clear on how keeping these commandments result in growth. At times he shows lofty ignorance about such things: "We . . . do not understand how, by the Paraclete, one person grows more than another, nor why by 'eating vegetables' one 'sick' person is healed more effectively than another, how why one person is blessed more than another when keeping the commandments that have been given to everyone."[83]

Ultimately, the author offers this observation: "[W]hoever lowers himself most grows best in the spiritual ministry."[84] Keeping the minor commandments prepares one to lower oneself. As to how a person would actually move from minor commandments to major, the author's advice is rather simple. For a person to outgrow the minor commandments, he must go beyond them.[85]

77. *BoS* 5.1, 5.16.

78. Matt 18:15–17.

79. *BoS* 5.8.

80. *BoS* 4.2.

81. *BoS* 5.8.

82. *BoS* 5.10.

83. *BoS* 1.3.

84. *BoS* 3.1.

85. *BoS* 2.7; see also *BoS* 11.5: "For a person will never rise up above that [commandment], 'Put your brother to shame before the church and regard him as a Gentile,' nor will he attain Perfection, unless he approaches that [commandment], 'Forgive him seventy times seven' and 'Think of him as better than

Fortunately one does not tread this road alone. Memra 12 takes pains to describe the church as a nurse who feeds the whole community according to their needs: "milk" for the thirty-day-old and "solid food" for the thirty-year-old.[86] Those who are healthy are encouraged to bear the illness of the sick, and the sick must go to the healthy for healing.[87] The author urges members of his community to seek out teachers in the way of perfection and to be cautious in their choice of mentors, choosing those who will teach with discernment.[88] Growth in maturity is not, of course, only a human endeavor, and perhaps this is why the author is so hesitant to explain how such growth occurs. God is also a part of this dynamic process. As the Lord helped the disciples "grow into knowledge step by step and he kept them from stumbling blocks until they were full grown and filled with the Spirit and would stumble no more," so the Lord will help the sick and children outgrow "vegetables and milk."[89] The Perfect are not finished products either; the Paraclete is at work, but does not make a person perfect all at once. Rather, by the Paraclete, the perfected person grows continually until the day of her death.[90] While the path to perfection certainly involves human effort, God is also at work, making the results less than predictable.

Conclusion

This exploration of the uses and functions of the dietary images in the Syriac *Book of Steps* has explicated the inner workings of a major device in the text. Drawing from the dietary metaphors and pastoral instructions of the Pauline corpus and Hebrews, the author of the *Book of Steps* vividly illustrates the distinctions between people of various levels of maturity in his community. His employment of "vegetables for the Sick" and "milk for the Children" versus "solid food" for the Perfect reveals that one's ability to interact well with sinners, within and without the community, is a significant indicator of one's position in the community. The author uses "vegetables and milk" as a meta-

you.'" To move beyond the major commandments, the author gives similar advice in *BoS* 16.1: "Our Lord said to you, 'Whoever strikes you upon your cheek, offer him the other.' Moreover, give him your whole body and, look, you will grow greater than him who only offers his cheek."

86. *BoS* 12.5.

87. *BoS* 11.4.

88. *BoS* 30.10–14.

89. *BoS* 5.7.

90. *BoS* 5.18.

Table 10-1. Identifying the Commandments: Vegetables and Milk vs. Solid Food

Memra	*Vegetables and Milk/Sick and Children*	*Solid Food/Mature or Perfect*
2.7	"Accuse your brother in court," "consider him as a Gentile."	"Judge not," "forgive him whenever he sins against you."
11.3	"Think of him as a Gentile," "do not associate with immoral people."	"Forgive your brother 70 x 7 times," "be all things to all people."
11.4	"Do not eat/associate with immoral people," "do not go to the sick but to the healthy."	"Do not be an obstacle to the sick," "make your soul lowly," "consider your brother better than yourself."
11.5	"Put your brother to shame and regard him as a Gentile"	"Forgive him 70 x 7," "think of him as better than yourself"
12.5	"Do not eat with adulterers nor have anything to do with prostitutes and gluttons and cursers and with any whose deeds are evil."	"Take up the misfortunes of the sick, and be all things to all people, and do not talk about anyone that he is a pagan or unclean or evil," "consider everyone better than yourself."
19.10	"If there is a brother who fornicates or curses, is greedy or drunken, do not even eat bread with him."	"Consider every person as better than yourself."
19.11	"Do not greet anyone on the road," "admonish the offenders."	"Blessed are those who make peace with everyone for they shall be called the children of God," "let your lowliness be known to all people."
19.12	"Consider whoever does not listen as a Gentile and as a tax-collector."	"Bless him who curses you and love him who hates, and pray for whoever harms you and persecutes you."
19.18	"Separate yourself from whoever [acts] this way, lest you get mixed up with him."	"Whoever forces you to go one mile, go with him two more and make peace with him."
19.26	"Do not eat bread with adulterers."	"Be all [things] with all people and teach everyone that you may win over everyone."
19.27	"If they do not receive you, shake off your dust against them in anger and ask who [else] is worthy? Enter and proclaim peace there."	"In every house you enter, proclaim peace over it and pray for its residents."
19.28	"Do not associate with fornicators."	"Do not call a person impure or defiled."
19.32	"Separate those who sin from being in the congregation, so that they may not stand among the wheat, in order that the infants may not imitate them and the ill not be scandalized by them."	"Leave tares growing with the wheat until I convert them in the harvest, lest you root up the wheat with the tares, because you do not know which are the tares, since the tares may be tranformed and become wheat."

Table 10-1 *(cont.)*

Memra	*Vegetables and Milk/Sick and Children*	*Solid Food/Mature or Perfect*
30.1–2	Faith separates the children and the sick from sinners until they grow up: "Distance [yourselves] from being with evil men and from every brother who behaves wickedly."	"Do not eat with adulterers, or with any brother who behaves wickedly." Love teaches its disciples to be all things to all people, to know how to give appropriate "food" to people at different levels of maturity, to bless those who curse them, to love whoever hates them, to pray for whoever persecutes them, and to become like lambs for the slaughter.
30.8[a]	Disciple of faith flees the company of evil people; his knowledge is immature.	Disciple of love, while recognizing those who are evil better than anyone else, does not make distinctions among them.

a. This passage does not clearly reference the metaphors of food or maturity and health, but separation from sinners seems to distinguish the disciples of faith from the disciples of love, as well.

phor for the minor commandments of the Upright. The sick and the children are generally (but not consistently) included among the larger cohort of the Upright rather than fledgling members of the Perfect. However, the author is not content that they remain stagnant. His descriptive use of "vegetables" and "milk" is also prescriptive; the "vegetables and milk" are temporary commandments to help a person grow until she is capable of taking in solid food. The author applies these metaphors in an unexpected way, one not necessarily suggested by their contexts in the New Testament texts, due to his need to address current problems in his own community. Such advice functions to urge people of all levels of maturity to continue to progress on the road to perfection, living peacefully with one another along the way.

Tera Stidham Harmon

11. FALLING FROM THE PATH OF PERFECTION

Sin in the Syriac Book of Steps

Reflection on the human predicament of sin abounds in both ancient and contemporary Christian literature. While Christian thought nearly unequivocally affirms that sin is responsible for human estrangement from God, major differences of opinion exist as to just what constitutes sin and how it works in human life. Does "sin" refer to a set of forbidden acts and dispositions that people can choose to engage or avoid, or to an outside force, such as slavery, that separates people from God? Is sin a weakened condition that humans have inherited since the beginning, or is it a legal state of guilt for which they are unable to compensate on their own? Each of the traditional models entails particular notions of atonement and implications for understanding human experience, but none are airtight categories. Many ancient Christian thinkers, including the author of the *Book of Steps,* make no attempt to systematize the topic, and instead pull from several images. While the *Book of Steps* exhibits interplay between various concepts of sin, a point of convergence is also visible. In the *Book of Steps* sin is primarily a problem with relationships, consisting of actions that disrupt relationships and characterized by consequences that further ruin relationships. Furthermore, the author's treatment of sin and the methods for overcoming it support his purposes of addressing conflict in the community and outlining a vision for the Upright and the Perfect to coexist peacefully.

The *Book of Steps* primarily concerns two groups of people, the Upright and the Perfect, who are situated in a community and are experiencing conflict as a result of their diversity. This community is decidedly different from the monastic communities that would later develop, being comprised of both laity and those who have devoted themselves to an ascetic lifestyle.[1] Caner aptly describes this community as "not so much a monastic community or even a single, unified ascetic elite as a reciprocal relationship that loosely binds spiritually advanced ascetics to other Christians."[2] While many details about the precise nature of this community remain elusive, it is evidently comprised of both ascetic and non-ascetic Christians with some degree of connection to one another.

Although a relationship exists between the two groups, their interactions are not always peaceful.[3] The *Book of Steps* itself suggests that its community

1. Robert A. Kitchen and Martien F. G. Parmentier, trans., *The Book of Steps: The Syriac Liber Graduum* (Kalamazoo, Mich.: Cistercian Publications, 2004), l–li.

2. Daniel Caner, *Wandering, Begging Monks: Spiritual Authority and the Promotion of Monasticism in Late Antiquity* (Berkeley and Los Angeles: University of California Press, 2002), 111. While scholars understand the community to which the *Book of Steps* was written with varying degrees of cohesiveness, most affirm that its membership is somewhat diverse; see Kitchen, "Conflict on the Stairway to Heaven: The Anonymity of Perfection in the Syriac *Liber Graduum*," in *Symposium Syriacum VII: Uppsala University, Department of Asian and African Languages, 11–14 August 1996,* edited by René Lavenant, 211–20 (Rome: Pontificio Instituto Orientale, 1998). What is more difficult to determine is the intended audience. Wickham, for example, understands this text as addressing different groups of people at various occasions. He mentions the following groups: "the literate Christianity of Syria . . . the theologically curious . . . the fellowship which shares in the pursuit of full maturity . . . a congregation in church where the common loyalty to mother church is affirmed despite different degrees of life . . . and the beginner who aspires to climbing the hill to the heavenly city"; Lionel Wickham, "'The *Liber Graduum*' Revisited," in *VI Symposium Syriacum, 1992: University of Cambridge, Faculty of Divinity, 30 August–2 September 1992,* edited by René Lavenant, 177–87 (Rome: Pontificio Instituto Orientale, 1992). Some, however, have a different understanding of the *Book of Steps'* community; Baker says, "our authors [of which the *Book of Steps* is one] are writing or preaching only for or about dedicated ascetics," and, "The *Liber Graduum* and Macarius were originally intended for a more specialized audience"; Dom Aelred Baker, "Early Syriac Asceticism," *The Downside Review* 88 (1970): 393–409.

3. Kitchen categorizes the conflicted parties into three groups: "conflict and violence among several groups in the *Liber Graduum* community and from outside sources; a spiritualizing or quietistic tendency from within the Church; and a perception of spiritual malaise and loss of higher standards within the *Liber Graduum* elite"; Kitchen and Parmentier, *Book of Steps,* lii; see also Caner, *Wandering, Begging Monks,* 154–57; and Kitchen, "The Gattung of the Liber Graduum: Implications for a Sociology of Asceticism," in *IV Symposium Syriacum 1984,* edited by Hendrik J. W. Drijvers, et al, 173–82, Orientalia Christiana Analecta 229 (Rome: Pontificium Institutum Studiorum Orientalium, 1987).

is entrenched in conflict to the point that some members in the community are persecuting and even killing others: "The disciples of faith confront the disciples of love, ignorantly persecuting them, [while] the disciples of love endure . . . the martyrs of love are persecuted and killed by the members of the household of faith."[4] In the midst of this the author strives to resolve some of the conflict that plagues his community. He writes, "Thus God desires that all humanity act, each one according to the stage on which he stands. They should treat one another well and love their creator,"[5] and again, "let us submit ourselves to one another through these spiritual fruits with love, patience, kindness, lowliness, endurance, moderation, and holiness without desire."[6]

The author casts a vision in which he pictures the community as pilgrims on a steep and arduous path that "leads to the house of our Lord and enters his bridal chamber."[7] This path is difficult, however, and only the Perfect will be able to ascend it fully. But for those who are unable to climb it, deviating trails offer less strenuous options: "But these paths that travel near this road are the minor commandments, which are given to the infants as milk and to the ill as vegetables, because as long as they are immature in their intelligence and ill in their minds, they are not able to come to these major commandments of love and Perfection."[8] In situating the whole community on paths that share a basic direction but vary in difficulty and detail, the author casts a vision of mutual effort and striving, carefully noting that the deviating paths are "not despicable."[9] The paths provide ample space for all in the community to travel, but the author has a definite preference for the path of the Perfect, encouraging all who can to "seek a nurse" to help them become Perfect.[10] The author's imagery pictures everyone in the community on the same trajectory, yet also allows for differences in the levels of spiritual maturity. By encouraging the path of the Perfect while defending the position of the deviating paths, the author advocates a more peaceful and accepting attitude between the two groups.

4. *BoS* 30.4.

5. *BoS* 7.21.

6. *BoS* 21.3.

7. *BoS* 19.36. The most extensive discussion of the path metaphor is in memra 19.

8. *BoS* 19.35.

9. *BoS* 19.2.

10. *BoS* 19.38.

Sin in the *Book of Steps*

As the community travels upward, all members face pitfalls of sin that threaten to cause them to "fall into the great deep that takes [them] down to Sheol."[11] The author employs a variety of images to explain the human tendency for sin: an implanted inclination,[12] the loss of the original inbreathing of the Holy Spirit,[13] and sin personified as an adversarial being[14] each illustrate why people sin. Other images, such as sin as an obstacle,[15] a diversion,[16] and a disease,[17] depict the effects of sin. Piecing together the images and descriptions of sin in the *Book of Steps,* it becomes clear that human beings are in a weakened condition as a result of sin, and if left to its own devices, sin will prevent people from intimate communion with God.

From the beginning, notions of ruptured relationships surrounded the actions and consequences of sin: Adam and Eve culpably sinned by disobeying the commands of God[18] and trying to become equal to God.[19] Upon doing this, the connection that existed between heaven and earth was severed, and Adam and Eve no longer dwelt on earth physically while remaining in heaven spiritually.[20] Although they had been in communion with God, "God closed the doors of Paradise before him," causing a rift between them.[21] This disobedience would cause injury to human relationships, as well: God warns

11. *BoS* 19.2. The author makes an exception to allow for those elite few who have defeated sin; see *BoS* 18.1, 20.3–8.

12. *BoS* 5.14, 16.6, 20.3. *BoS* 5.14 reads, "For there is no one among the sons of Adam, who has not in the first place sinned and subsequently been justified. This inclination was implanted in Adam on the day he transgressed the command. From then on it was implanted in all of his offspring from their mother's womb." According to the *Book of Steps,* it is not sin itself that is implanted, but rather a tendency to sin. Persons are not deserving of judgment based on this inclination to sin, but rather they must battle sin or else be conquered by it. It is significant that this very inclination can be uprooted in the final stages of perfection (*BoS* 20.3).

13. *BoS* 28.4.

14. *BoS* 7.19, 18.3, 20.4, 20.9.

15. *BoS* 1.2.

16. *BoS* 25.4.

17. *BoS* 17.7, 28.6–7.

18. The author takes care to show that while Satan taught and tempted Adam, Adam was responsible for his own choice (*BoS* 21.10). In the *Book of Steps,* sin is frequently described as breaking or transgressing the commands of God; see *BoS* 7.8, 15.2, 15.3, 15.8, 20.1, 20.4, 20.16.

19. *BoS* 21.10–11, 23.7.

20. *BoS* 21.8, 21.17. For more on the anthropological doctrine in the *Book of Steps,* see Michela Aveta, "Ad instar angelorum: Per un'analisi storico-religiosa dell'antropologia del *Liber Graduum,*" *Christianesimo nella storia* 8 (1987): 481–500.

21. *BoS* 21.12.

in memra 21 that listening to Satan would ultimately cause them to "slay one another."[22] Following their sin, God took pity on them and made for them the way of the Upright, allowing them to marry and work.[23] Following the introduction of sin into the world, some were able to attain Uprightness and some had inclinations toward Perfection,[24] but "no one among human beings was perfected until our Lord was perfected before them";[25] that is, none were able to attain the communion with God in which Adam and Eve had lived.[26]

In the incarnation, Jesus reversed the effects of Adam by emptying himself rather than grasping for equality with God (as Adam did) "so that he might show us how a person becomes a brother and a son and an heir and a neighbor, for [God] desired ungrudgingly that the earthly ones dwell with him."[27] In the present era the path to Perfection has been opened by the example of Christ, but Uprightness remains an option for Christians. The Perfect are ascetics who renounce marriage, work, and property[28] and follow Jesus's example of forgiveness, lowliness, and nonretaliation. With respect to sin they are eligible to attempt to uproot all sin and live in the pre-fallen state of Adam and Eve—that is, in intimate relationship with God, a state that is often described as the bridal chamber of the Lord.[29]

The Upright do not follow the ascetic ideal, but minister to the physical needs of people[30] and follow the Golden Rule.[31] With respect to sin the

22. *BoS* 21.1.

23. *BoS* 15.8.

24. See especially memra 9.

25. *BoS* 30.24.

26. For more on the sin of Adam and Eve in the *Book of Steps,* see Kitchen, "Syriac Additions to Anderson: The Garden of Eden in the Book of Steps and Philoxenus of Mabbug," *Hugoye: Journal of Syriac Studies* 6 (2003): 37–50; Robert A. Ratcliff, "Steps Along the Way of Perfection: The Liber Graduum and Early Syrian Monasticism" (PhD diss., Emory University, 1988), 136–39; Peter R. Brown, *The Body and Society: Men, Women, and Sexual Renunciation in Early Christianity* (New York: Columbia University Press, 1988), 336–37; Alexander Golitzin, "Recovering the 'Glory of Adam': 'Divine Light' Traditions in the Dead Sea Scrolls and the Christian Ascetical Literature of Fourth-Century Syro-Mesopotamia," in *The Dead Sea Scrolls as Background to Postbiblical Judaism and Early Christianity: Papers from an International Conference at St. Andrews in 2001,* edited by James R. Davila, 282 (Leiden: E. J. Brill, 2003); and Columba Stewart, "*Working the Earth of the Heart*": *The Messalian Controversy in History, Texts, and Language to A.D. 431* (Oxford: Clarendon Press, 1991), 88.

27. *BoS* 21.11; see Kitchen, "Syriac Additions," 6.

28. *BoS* 15.3.

29. *BoS* 20.14, 19.36.

30. *BoS* 3.2.

31. *BoS* 7.1. For further discussion on the Perfect and the Upright, see Kitchen and Parmentier, *Book of Steps,* xxxviii–xliv; and Kitchen, "Becoming Perfect: The Maturing of Asceticism in the Liber Graduum," *Journal of the Canadian Society for Syriac Studies* 2 (2002): 30–45, particularly 31–32.

Upright are in a more tenuous position than the Perfect, being closer to the boundary of unacceptable behavior, and are therefore harassed more by evil and are in more danger of falling into Sheol.[32] The Upright also are not eligible to uproot sin completely and return to the original state of humanity because of their entanglements with marriage, labor, and anxiety, which "happened to Adam on account of sin" and are therefore hallmarks of the post-fall era.[33] The position of the Upright is further described as "sanctified from the evil of the earth, but not from its possessions, its benefits or its fellowship."[34] While they are excluded from some of the practices and rewards of the Perfect, they are expected to perform virtues and are promised salvation.[35]

The story about the origins of sin and the prescriptions for overcoming it in the *Book of Steps* suggests why relations within the community are strained and provides a strategy by which to foster harmony in the community. The author does this by (1) providing the group with a shared story, thereby creating common identity while allowing diversity along the path and making room for all in the community, and (2) presenting methods for overcoming sin that encourage reciprocity between the groups. Because all in the community share the same story of salvation history and all have at some point sinned,[36] they share a common identity. The author, however, realizes that people experience sin and its effects differently, depending upon their position on the path, and directs his communal prescriptions at healing sin in a way that anticipates the restoration of creation to its original state.

Diversity on the Path

The discussion about sin in the *Book of Steps* assists the purpose of promoting peace in the community. Although the Perfect and Upright have different positions with respect to sin, evil, and temptation, the author allows them to

32. *BoS* 25.9.

33. *BoS* 20.6; see also *BoS* 3.2.

34. *BoS* 14.1.

35. For further description of the distinctions between the Upright and the Perfect, see Arthur Vööbus, *History of Asceticism in the Syrian Orient: A Contribution to the History of Culture in the Near East,* Corpus Scriptorum Christianorum Orientalium 500 (Louvain: Peeters, 1988), 3:1–18; Seely J. Beggiani, *Introduction to Eastern Christian Spirituality: The Syriac Tradition* (London: Associated University Presses, 1991), 32–33.

36. *BoS* 24.2.

live in their various positions while pursuing the same basic trajectory. The text at times clearly favors the Perfect, but there is also a strong message of acceptance of the Upright into the community throughout, although this is more evident in some memre than others.[37] In some memre, while noting that Upright people will inherit the kingdom, the author seems more grudging in his acceptance of them, emphasizing that the inheritance of the Perfect is to be preferred.[38] Other memre emphasize the proximity of the Upright to Perfection; for example, memra 25.8 reads, "If they desire to leave behind the earth, as our Lord commanded, and journey in the footsteps of his lowliness, they will quickly ascend to Perfection, for they are not very far from it."

Memra 3 expresses the diversity of the community by using the metaphor of a pledge. Each person has a pledge of the Spirit and/or a pledge of sin.[39] People exist with various amounts of these pledges, which correspond to the degree one listens to and obeys the Spirit or sin. On one end of the scale, some of the Perfect have emptied themselves completely of the pledge of sin and are

37. Kitchen has suggested, and it seems probable, that the author shows increasing support of the Upright in memre 25 through 30, which he characterizes as a move "from the idealization of the Perfect to justification and approval of the Upright"; Kitchen and Parmentier, *Book of Steps,* lxxix.

38. *BoS* 3.2–3.

39. The notion of the pledge of the Spirit and the pledge of sin is important for the discussion of Messalianism in the *Book of Steps.* The concept of the pledge of sin dwelling in a person is one reason some understood the *Book of Steps* as being associated with the Messalian heresy. In more recent years, scholarly consensus has appropriately turned its focus away from purported heretical connections in an attempt to understand the *Book of Steps* community as distinct. For discussions regarding the "pledge," see Stewart, *"'Working the Earth,'"* especially 198–203; Antoine Guillamont, "Les 'arrhes de l'Esprit' dans le Livre des degrés," in *Mémorial Mgr Gabriel Khouri-Sarkis (1898–1968): Fondateur et directeur de l'Orient syrien, 1956–1967,* edited by François Graffin, 107–13 (Louvain: Imprimerie Orientaliste, 1969); Kitchen and Parmentier, *Book of Steps,* xlvii–xlix; and Juoko Martikainen, "Das Böse in den Schriften des Syrers Ephrem, im Stufenbuch und in Corpus Macarianum," in *Makarios-Symposium über das Böse: Vorträge der Finnisch-Deutschen Theologentagung in Goslar 1980,* edited by Werner Strothmann, 36–46, Göttinger Orientforschungen 1, Reihe: Syriaca 24 (Wiesbaden: Harrassowitz Verlag, 1983). For general discussions on Messalianism and the *Liber Graduum,* see Vööbus, "*Liber Graduum:* Some Aspects of Its Significance for the History of Early Syrian Asceticism," in *Charisteria Iohanni Kopp octogenerio oblata,* 108–28, Papers of the Estonian Theological Society in Exile 7 (Stockholm: Estonian Theological Society in Exile, 1954); Vööbus, *Celibacy: A Requirement for Admission to Baptism in the Early Syrian Church,* Papers of the Estonian Theological Society in Exile 1 (Stockholm: Estonian Theological Society in Exile, 1951), 178–84; Caner, *Wandering, Begging Monks,* 83–125; Kitchen, "Gattung," 173–82; Robert Murray, *Symbols of Church and Kingdom: A Study in Early Syriac Tradition,* rev. ed. (London: T. and T. Clark; Piscataway, N.J.: Gorgias Press, 2004), 35–36; Beggiani, *Introduction to Eastern Christian Spirituality,* 32–33; Wickham, "Teachings About God and Christ in the Liber Graduum," in *Logos: Festschrift für Luise Abramowski zum 8. Juli 1993,* edited by Hanns Christof Brennecke, Ernst Ludwig Grasmück, and Christoph Markschies, 486–98 (New York: Walter de Gruyter, 1993).

full of the pledge of the Spirit. These are the ones in whom the Paraclete has come to dwell, causing them to "belong to our Lord continually."[40] On the other end are those who continually do evil and whom the author describes as devoid of the pledge of the Spirit. Being indwelled fully by the pledge of sin, they are ultimately rejected. Others, however, live with partial pledges of sin and of the Spirit, sometimes heeding the pledge of the Spirit and doing good and sometimes heeding the pledge of the sin and doing evil. By choosing to act in accordance with sin or the Spirit, one can increase or reduce the amount of her pledge. Although experiencing the influences of temptation and of the Spirit in different levels, all on the path aim toward a fuller pledge of the Spirit that in turn leads to increased relational virtue, since "a Spirit-filled person is recognized by the following characteristics: he is obviously instructed by that Spirit, he loves all people—even his enemies and those who are out to kill him—and he prays for them diligently."[41]

While some memre note the differences between the groups, others focus on the common trajectory of both Upright and Perfect. Memra 24.7 states, "Whoever has compassion upon everyone, whether good or evil, is a blessed one," and memra 26.1 emphasizes the same theme, stating to the Upright, "If you keep this law of Uprightness and pursue love and Perfection, at the end of the ages of this world I will be revealed and will perfect you and all who pursue love and Perfection and you will enter the spiritual Paradise that you left." Although perfection is still the ideal, the emphasis is on affirming the position of the Upright. In memra 30 the author gives the examples of Abraham and Zacchaeus as two people who faithfully lived an upright life. He lists their virtues and states, "Whoever acts in this way will dwell in my tent and reside on my holy mountain that is the comfort to come for the Upright, says the Lord Omnipotent."[42] Although the Upright are in a more fragile position on the path with regard to sin and its entanglements, the author creates space for them to live into the possibility of eschatological perfection.

40. *BoS* 3.11.
41. *BoS* 3.12.
42. *BoS* 30.29.

Overcoming Sin

Perhaps the most significant way in which the view of sin in the *Book of Steps* contributes to the purpose of promoting peace in the community is found in the instruction of the author regarding how to overcome sin. The *Book of Steps* is, at its heart, a practical text exhorting its readers to live holier lives. The result of sin is broken relationships, and in order to overcome sin, the author prescribes virtues aimed at healing relationships between people, their fellow humans, and their God.

Using *imitatio Christi* as the basis for his appeal that each traveler battle with sin,[43] the author gives specific examples of ways to overcome sin that illustrate the attempt of the author to repair damaged relationships. In order to do this, the author repeatedly stresses lowliness, nonretaliation, and forgiveness, all of which are virtues that serve as correctives to conflict. For the Upright this manifests itself in instructions to follow the Golden Rule and to provide for all who are needy equally, with no regard for a person's moral standing. The Perfect are then instructed to refrain from judging and to forgive and love enemies to the extent that they are disqualified from any positions that would require church discipline. Ratcliff relates these virtues to the imitation of Christ, saying, "By refusing to judge, by forgiving the fallen, by loving and suffering on behalf of one's enemies as Christ had done, individuals will be caught up in the redemptive power of Christ's victory over evil as well."[44]

Evidence of an appeal for harmony is further found in memra 4, in which the author advises the readers to treat well those who have sinned. He instructs them to admonish one another gently and in private, rather than in front of the whole community. The latter part of the memra gives specific examples about how to be diplomatic and admonish people gently in ways that will not promote defensiveness. For example, the author instructs, "When you meet people who are at enmity with one another, say, 'Brother, blessed are the peacemakers, for they shall be called sons of God.'" He goes on to tell the read-

43. Roux correctly identifies the imitation of Christ as "the main Christological theme in the *Book of Steps*"; René Roux, "The Doctrine of the Imitation of Christ in the *Liber Graduum:* Between Exegetical Theory and Soteriology," in *Studia Patristica: Biblica Et Apocrypha, Ascetica, Liturgica,* vol. 30, edited by Elizabeth A. Livingstone and E. Peters, 259 (Leuven: Peeters Publishers, 1997).

44. Ratcliff, "Steps," 8–9.

er to "transform their harmful words into harmless ones" in order to mediate the conflict.[45] In addition to being peaceable, the person also becomes a peacemaker, setting an example for the quarreling parties as Christ set an example and, in turn, participating in the reversal of Adam and return to humanity's original state.

In order to further mend relationships, the author recommends ascetic discipline, the goal of which is increased love for others. Although the ascetic ideal is located in the Perfect and some ascetic disciplines, such as virginity,[46] are upheld by the Perfect alone, the text makes a strong appeal for Perfect and Upright alike to involve themselves in physical ascetic disciplines in order to combat sin. Memra 10 argues for the importance of physical disciplines (against those who would spiritualize them): "When our Lord and the apostles emptied themselves, they emptied themselves completely and fasted fully with [both] their bodies and their souls . . . may no one turn away from the ascetic discipline of our Lord and his apostles."[47] The author states that disciplines such as fasting provide gradual remedy to the person practicing them[48] and "restrain a person from evil things and encourage him to do good things"[49]—namely, humility, acceptance, and forgiveness. Memra 29.1 states, "I will subdue myself in order to honor everyone as a servant and in order to stand before and greet everyone before me, bowing [my] head before everyone. I will make [my body] run on foot like a servant in order to reconcile with its enemies while not offending them, and to bow its head before whoever is less than it." Ratcliff has assessed that, for the author of the *Book of Steps*, ascetic disciplines were a means to relational virtues: "One engaged in the dis-

45. *BoS* 4.6.

46. See Sebastian P. Brock, *The Luminous Eye: The Spiritual World Vision of St. Ephrem the Syrian* (Kalamazoo, Mich.: Cistercian Publications, 1992), 131–41. The ascetic ideal in the *Book of Steps* is not against marriage per se, but against sinful marriage—namely, that which comes from the fall of Adam and Eve. Ascetics aim for holy marriage of themselves to Christ, the bridegroom; see Shafiq Abouzayd, *Ihidayutha: A Study of the Life of Singleness in the Syrian Orient, from Ignatius of Antioch to Chalcedon 451 AD* (Oxford: ARAM Society for Syro-Mesopotamian Studies, 1993), 273.

47. *BoS* 10.10. Harvey notes that an emphasis on the physical is characteristic of Syriac Christianity: "The physical mattered in Syriac Christianity in all its aspects: the body, its actions, the world we inhabit, both civic and natural"; Susan Ashbrook Harvey, "Creation and Asceticism: Syriac Christian Thought," in *Christian Thought: A Brief History*, edited by Adrian Hastings, Alistair Mason, and Hugh S. Pyper, 33–37 (Oxford: Oxford University Press, 2002).

48. *BoS* 10.9.

49. *BoS* 29.6.

ciplines of self-denial because they freed one from concern with one's physical desires so that one might better attend to loving others. Discipline of the body was thus only a secondary means to monastic perfection."[50] Upright and Perfect alike participate in physical disciplines that will allow them to defeat sin by cultivating habits that are the opposite of sin (that is, healing relationships instead of breaking them) and thus imitating Christ's reversal of Adam's sin.

Finally, the *Book of Steps* suggests a reciprocal relationship between Upright and Perfect that allows both parties more fully to live out their respective callings. Like the practice of ascetic disciplines, pursuing a reciprocal relationship between Upright and Perfect fosters behaviors that establish rather than disintegrate relationships. The nature of the reciprocal relationship between the Upright and the Perfect was such that the Upright provided for the physical needs of the Perfect (as the Upright are expected to provide for any person in need, whether good or evil),[51] while the Perfect ministered to the spiritual needs of the Upright. In memra 25 the author exhorts the Perfect not to be anxious, because the Lord will "tell the Upright who work the earth to nourish and clothe you and they will live the life of the new world on account of you, and they will do for you these things by their labor while not treating anyone badly."[52] The Perfect, in return, are "ministers of word and prayer," and can be spiritual mentors, or "nurses."[53]

The author of the *Book of Steps* sounds his exhortations into a community experiencing conflict to the point of persecution, hoping to alleviate the tension. The deepest threats to the well-being of this community are those that would fracture and dissolve it from within, an observation that leads the author of the *Book of Steps* to conceive of sin as essentially those actions and patterns that disrupt relationships. His depictions of ideal community, his explanation of sin, and his prescriptions against it are intended to guard against the effects of sin so conceived. The *Book of Steps* community consists of indi-

50. Ratcliff, "Steps," 117.

51. *BoS* 25.7.

52. *BoS* 25.3.

53. *BoS* 3.15, 19.38; see also *BoS* 10.6. For more on the reciprocal relationship of the Upright and the Perfect, see Kitchen and Parmentier, *Book of Steps,* li; Caner, *Wandering, Begging Monks*, 110–12; Nancy Khalek, "Methods of Instructing Syriac-Speaking Christians to Care for the Poor: A Brief Comparison of the Eighth Memra of the Book of Steps and the Story of the Man of God of Edessa," *Hugoye: Journal of Syriac Studies* 8 (2005): 13–25. It is important to note that the author does not suggest that there must always be Upright in order for the Perfect to survive. Rather, he contends that if all were Perfect, God would provide their physical needs; see *BoS* 25.3.

viduals poised for a journey with a steep ascent ahead. Different paths upward lie before them, and although the author prefers the more steep and arduous path, he provides allowances within the community for those who choose a more gradual slope. As they ascend, all travelers must contend with sin and attempt to overcome it by engaging in ascetic disciplines of fasting, prayer, and ministry. In working to overcome their own sin, they participate with their exemplar, Christ, to reverse the effects of Adam's sin and return to the pristine state of original humanity, in which humanity dwelt in communion with God. The shared story, room for diversity, the common disciplines, and the reciprocal relationship all advance an ideal vision of a cooperative community, in which "there is quiet and peace and harmony between the great and the small, making a joyful noise together, and there is no one there who is superior to one smaller than him, nor one who despises someone greater than him, so pray that all people may become like this."[54]

54. *BoS* 21.2.

PART 5

PRACTICES OF ASCETICISM IN THE *BOOK OF STEPS*

Robert A. Kitchen

12. DISTURBED SINNERS

In Pursuit of Sanctity in the Book of Steps

There are no saints, no holy men or women, in the late-fourth-century *Book of Steps,*[1] no hagiography in the classical modes, though plenty of exegesis and reinterpretation of the biblical narratives and personalities. Where there is holiness, it is *qaddishutha* (ܩܕܝܫܘܬܐ), a term overwhelmed by ascetical insistence on the renunciation of sexual relations—a most insistent requirement in the *Book of Steps* for an Upright one to enter the realm of the Perfect ones.

While I do not want to contest or deny the critical function of celibacy in the author's perception of the Christian life, I do wish to bracket it for the moment and examine another critical aspect of holiness—the spiritual state denoting an intimate relationship with and transformation by the divine. Just what is it that makes someone's "soul" holy, when, and how? And most importantly for our moment, is anyone holy in the *Book of Steps?*

The *Book of Steps* has been long recognized as an oddly heterodox collection of ascetical texts, but not ascetical in the fashion to which readers of fourth-, fifth-, and sixth-century desert literature and the lives of the saints were accustomed. The anonymity of the author extends to his original sub-

1. Michael Kmoskó, ed., *Liber Graduum,* Patrologia Syriaca 1.3 (Paris: Firmin-Didot, 1926); Robert A. Kitchen and Martien F. G. Parmentier, trans., *The Book of Steps: The Syriac Liber Graduum* (Kalamazoo, Mich.: Cistercian Publications, 2004).

jects and audience—no one in the community to which the author is pastor is named or identified. Neither is the community. Except for biblical characters, no model of appropriate or inappropriate behavior and holiness is presented with a name, location, or *Sitz im Leben.*

Holiness may be scarce, but there is perfection (ܓܡܝܪܘܬܐ). Perfection, especially in the *Book of Steps,* does not by necessity equal holiness; and it is not necessarily what most of us understand as perfection. Translation is the first act of interpretation, so there have been more than a few who have wanted to retranslate the "Perfect ones" (ܓܡܝܪܐ) as the "Mature ones." I resisted the temptation, largely in light of how the term appears in other important Syriac ascetical and spiritual authors. John the Solitary of Apamea employed the term as a state attained eschatologically; that is, one achieves perfection only in the next world in the kingdom of heaven.[2] I maintained the translation "perfection," and "perfect ones" in the *Book of Steps* as an anticipation of the *eschaton,* or in language characteristic of the *Book of Steps* as "a pledge" (ܪܗܒܘܢܐ) of Eden and a "taste of eternal life." The author persistently urges the Perfect ones to continue growing in perfection, for "there is yet more truth and light to issue forth from God's holy word."[3] The perfect or mature ones are not hagiographical literary constructs, so the purpose here is to understand the ways in which they are and are not yet holy.

I have been immersed in the Upright and the Perfect for a good while and have tried to make sense of their ordinariness or "profanity," realizing that this ordinariness is how things and people operate and are perceived in the non-theologically imagined world. Surprised to hear echoes and murmurs of the Upright and Perfect in all manner of places, I am proposing to examine several contemporary theological interpretations of holiness in order to acquire insight into the conundrums of the *Book of Steps.* While one has to be cautious not to squeeze late antiquity phenomena into twentieth-century concepts, the conversation between the disciplines of early Christian studies and modern systematic theology bodes fruitful possibilities for both.

2. "It is not in this world that [God] perfects these things for us. Indeed, we see that error is still found [in us], and everyone is enslaved to the servitude of sin. . . . But the abolition of these things takes place in the new person in the New World"; *Briefe von Johannes dem Einsiedler*, edited by Lars Gösta Rignell, 33*:2–4, 11–12 (Lund: Håkan Ohlssons Boktryckeri, 1941).

3. John Robinson's reputed farewell message to the members of his Puritan congregation based in exile in Leiden as some—"the Pilgrims"—set sail on the *Mayflower* for New England in 1620.

Holiness: Theological Reality and Social Construct

Peter Brown's article "The Rise and Function of the Holy Man in Late Antiquity" has engendered a generation of studies on the holy man, particularly from the perspective of social interaction and power.[4] Renewed interest in the theological substance and character of holiness *per se* has been emerging, particularly with regard to the so-called attributes of God and the Trinity. One starting point is the voluminous thought and writings of the Swiss Reformed theologian Karl Barth (1886–1968), reputedly called "the last of the Church Fathers" by Pope Pius XII.

As is typically the case in his magnum opus, *Church Dogmatics,*[5] Barth has a number of things to say about holiness and holy people in a number of widely dispersed contexts. In volume 1, part 1, Barth's initial comments concern the nature of the "religious man"—a term that, while much broader than "holy man," includes this type as a specific and singular case. Barth emphatically declares that there is no such thing as a "religious man." That is, a person is not able to retain under his own power the holiness received from God. One's holiness is an event, received only at each and every moment that God alone initiates. No one should think that by means of various religious disciplines one could become "permanently (ontologically)" holy or religious.

In a wonderful sentence, Barth surprises us:

> But tell them that this epistemological order applies also and particularly to the religious man, that he also and particularly has no possibility, not even a received possibility, but can only receive the possibility of experience of God's Word, can use it only as it is conferred in the actuality of reception, tell them that this possibility is and remains God's possibility, and does not pass out of His hands into any other hands, tell them this and at once bitter and irreconcilable controversy breaks out.[6]

4. Peter R. Brown, "The Rise and Function of the Holy Man in Late Antiquity," *Journal of Roman Studies* 61 (1971): 80–101; see also Brown, *Society and the Holy in Late Antiquity* (Berkeley and Los Angeles: University of California Press, 1982), 103–52.

5. Karl Barth, *Church Dogmatics,* edited by G. W. Bromiley and T. F. Torrance, 14 vols. (Edinburgh: T. and T. Clark, 1936–1969); Barth, *Kirchliche Dogmatik* (Zollikon-Zurich: Evangelischer Verlag, 1932–1970).

6. Barth, *Church Dogmatics,* 1:1, 213.

This "possibility" creates problems for those who study "the Holy Man" utilizing historical, sociological, or literary methodologies. The studies that identify the social and political roles of the holy man—patron, arbiter, intercessor, exemplar, mediator, and teacher—seldom examine whether the "holy man" is authentically holy in the theological sense. Are Barth and Brown describing the same person, utilizing different methodologies, or are their holy men different people?

There are important intersections. Brown's characterization of the holy man as "a stranger"—both socially and as a wholly other kind of human—has been affirmed and challenged, depending upon the holy man under discussion. Patricia Cox Miller has presented the difficult image of "the body from nowhere" and "the body on the horizon." This kind of holy man is not a native son whom everybody knows.[7] The Syriac term ܝܚܝܕܝܐ, "solitary," "single one," one who imitates Christ "the Only Begotten One," registers a similar strangeness.[8]

Barth readily admits, "Holiness also has unquestionably the meaning of strange; God comes to men, but not to be at home with them."[9]

John Webster refines this concept in his lectures on *Holiness,* paraphrasing, "It is no longer I who live, but Christ who lives in me"; "The Christian's sanctity is in Christ, in the Spirit, not *in se; it is always and only an alien sanctity.* Sanctification does not signal the birth of self-sufficiency, rather it indicates a 'perpetual and inherent lack of self-sufficiency.'. . . It is a matter of the externality of *sanctitas christiana,* the saint being and acting *in another.*"[10]

Part of that strangeness, Barth insists, is that God works in and through "very specific men."

All this signifies that when the Bible gives an account of revelation it means to narrate history, (i.e., not to tell of a relation between God and man that exists generally in every time and place and that is always in process), but to tell of an event that takes place there and only there, then and only then, between God and certain very specific men. The divine self-unveiling which it records, with the holiness which it

7. Patricia Cox Miller, "Desert Asceticism and 'The Body from Nowhere,'" *Journal of Early Christian Studies* 2 (1994): 137–53.

8. Cf. Sidney H.Griffith, "Monks, 'Singles,' and the 'Sons of the Covenant': Reflections on Syriac Ascetic Terminology," in *Euloghema: Studies in Honor of Robert Taft, S.J.,* edited by E. Carr, 141–60, Studia Anselmiana 110 (Rome: Pontificio Ateneo S. Anselmo, 1993).

9. Barth, *Church Dogmatics,* 1:1, 322.

10. John B. Webster, *Holiness* (Grand Rapids: Eerdmans, 2003), 83–84.

ascribes to God in this act, is not imparted to man but to such and such men in very definite situations. It is a very specific event and as such it is incomparable and cannot be repeated.[11]

Holy men, like John the Baptist emerging out of the wilderness, catch us totally unprepared, startling us. But not only for the audience, those who observe the holy man, is this eventful gift of God's holiness to one such person startling. Barth concludes:

In many callings this resistance is not especially stressed, though neither is there in any instance a preparation for the call. What the Bible is trying to say here is obviously that there is no disposition in man at all. Calling is a nonderivative fact or derivative only from election. The prophets and apostles are not portrayed as heroes. *They stand there in their utter humanity.* Yet for all that they have, as it were, come from heaven as prophets and apostles. *They are no less astonishing to themselves than to those around them.*[12]

The author of the *Book of Steps* appears to comprehend this revelatory event, for he takes pains to point out how the Old Testament prophets had received different kinds of commands from God, especially in memre 9, as well as admitting that his own Perfect ones at times function less than perfectly. We reflect God's holiness only when God is with us; we are not capable of manufacturing our own versions. Yet, as with innumerable mentor-disciple relationships throughout the Egyptian and Syrian deserts, is not the author attempting to teach, to train and educate his Upright and Perfect disciples in the science of holiness? Was the author a poor teacher, or were the Perfect poor students, or is God's revelation unteachable?

In his chapter on "The Sanctification of Man" Barth picks up the Reformed debate on justification and sanctification that had frequently become stalemated in terms of which event and status has priority and final authority.[13] "[God] has introduced him in the new form of existence of a faithful covenant-partner who is well-pleasing to Him and blessed by Him. 'I will be your God' is the justification of man. 'Ye shall be my people' is his sanctification."[14]

11. Barth, *Church Dogmatics,* 1:1, 326.

12. Barth, *Church Dogmatics,* 1:1, 331.

13. Webster, *Holiness,* speaks of "mortification" and "vivification" as more modern Reformed equivalents, reflecting a death on the cross/resurrection dichotomy; cf. esp. 88–92.

14. Barth, *Church Dogmatics,* 4:2, 499.

Barth does not consider the two as separate conditions or events, but simultaneous aspects of the one event, neither identical nor interchangeable concepts. He resists the attempts to reduce justification to merely the beginning of sanctification, or to reduce sanctification to merely a paraphrase of justification.[15] The fact of the matter is that "*even in his best works the sanctified man still stands in continual need of justification before God.*"[16]

This is precisely the situation in the *Book of Steps,* where the author struggles to lead his disciples toward sanctification. He tells them that they are already justified, but it is in the living out and failing to live out their callings that problems ensue. The Perfect never arrive or achieve a final condition: they are always in the process of *becoming holy.*[17] Memra 6, "On Those Who Are Made Perfect and Continue to Grow," and memra 16, "On How a Person May Surpass the Major Commandments," make it clear that the attainment of the status of perfection is ever in process, not an end. And for the Upright, sanctification is a much longer road.

What exactly is a saint? Barth's definition is both phenomenological and spiritual.

> To describe their sanctity—in view of the fact that they are undoubtedly still sinners—we must first use a very modest and restrained, yet significant expression. They are *disturbed sinners* (*gestörte Sünder*).[18] Their sleep as such is broken. Their activity as such is hemmed in by qualifications and doubts. They are no longer happy in the cause that they have espoused. . . . The unreconciled man, the man to whom the reconciliation of the world with God, which comprehends his own sanctification, is concealed, is an undisturbed sinner (*ungestörter Sünder*). . . . The direction of the Son of Man, the work of the Holy Spirit, is needed if he is to be disturbed in a way which cannot be overcome. The saints are sinners who are disturbed in this way.[19]

This is not the sainthood of hagiography, but it depicts saints alive in a living community of faith. One does not read of the Perfect performing any healings or miracles, but one does hear of their struggles and imperfections. Contrary to popular mythology, an authentic saint is not perfectly carefree

15. Barth, *Church Dogmatics,* 4:2, 504.

16. Barth, *Church Dogmatics,* 4:2, 504.

17. "It is characteristic of the kind of creature that we are that we discover our identity by fulfilling a vocation through time; we *become* holy"; Webster, *Holiness,* 104.

18. Barth, *Church Dogmatics,* 4:2, 593.

19. Barth, *Church Dogmatics,* 4:2, 524.

in his goodness and holiness. That is the happier fate of the undisturbed sinner. "The limitation which thus comes to him is his sanctification. It is not at all the case, then, that the being of saints is compromised by their being as sinners. On the contrary, their being as sinners, their life in the flesh, is overwhelmingly and totally compromised by their being as saints."[20] Compromised by being a saint, a holy person, appears to be the condition of the Upright and the Perfect.

Despite such a large text there are several significant gaps in our knowledge of the *Book of Steps.* There are no indications regarding how the Upright and the Perfect were selected or recruited or entered their particular level. It is apparent, however, that the Upright live a consecrated lifestyle that distinguishes them from those who are "below Uprightness." The emphasis upon the importance and absolute necessity of the visible church with its visible sacraments (memra 12) inclines one to believe that entry, qualification, and the process of sanctification occur within the local church. But despite the insistence upon the visible church as the base for the hidden church and church of the heart, the life of that visible church is revealed only in shadows. Unlike most other ascetical and hagiographical works, we hear only the voice of the author. Only biblical personalities are permitted a speaking role, though as with many other texts, the author frames what they say. Of the activities of the Perfect ones, we hear only mumblings in the disappointed sermons of the author.

Toward Holiness and Perfection in the *Book of Steps*

The author seldom mentions saints. *Qaddishutha* (ܩܕܝܫܘܬܐ) and *qaddishe* (ܩܕܝܫܐ) are the Semitic terms translated usually as "holy," "set apart," which, in Syriac and Mesopotamian culture and in the majority of their occurrences in the *Book of Steps,* is holiness dominated by sexual renunciation and celibacy. The frequent use of the phrase "the saints in the city of Our Lord" in the *Book of Steps* is simply reflecting the Pauline term for the undifferentiated collective inhabitants of the kingdom of heaven.[21]

20. Barth, *Church Dogmatics,* 4:2, 526.

21. "The phrase 'holy people' is an obvious one, but it is used with astonishing infrequency in the canonical Old Testament"; Barth, *Church Dogmatics,* 4:2, 511. "Yet rather strangely no individual Christian

The author does use *qaddishe* on a few scattered occasions to indicate not just those engaged in physical and sexual renunciation, but those striving for an interior spiritual attainment, as well. The most striking expression in a single occurrence is "holiness of the heart."

Whoever seeks Perfection and *loves holiness,* out of these things will come *the holiness of the heart;* he will give everything he has to the needy and ascend above whatever is visible. There will be controversy against him, yet he will neither judge nor demand [anything from] anyone, *but will love everyone as a saint of our Lord,* for he makes his love shine on everyone like the sun which the Father [causes to shine] upon all there is on the earth, whether good or evil, whether the just or the unjust.[22]

The author appears to have adapted this phrase from his "Church of the Heart" (memra 12) and perhaps more directly from Paul's "circumcision of the heart."[23] Holiness of the heart is something different than physical holiness (i.e., renunciation and celibacy). Attaining this holiness of the heart and the way of living this holinesss generates controversy and antipathy toward the holy person, a circumstance noted several times by the author. Nonetheless, the one with a holy heart loves everyone as if she were a saint, not as a celibate individual, but as one who shares and cherishes a similar interior holiness of soul and spirit.

On the Steep Steps to the City of Our Lord

The author reserves his only use of "steps" (ܡܣܩܬܐ) for memre 19 and 20, but his image of the steep road becoming steeper with all sorts of gentler side-paths—whereby one can be undisturbed and never return to the main road—does fit well in his movement through justification toward full sanctification of the Perfect. He deals with two levels of justified Christians: undisturbed and disturbed. What convinces the reader that this is not an imagined or theoretical construct of a community is his witness to the practical complexity

is ever called a saint. . . . The saints of the NT exist only in plurality. Sanctity belongs to them, but only in their common life, not as individuals. . . . Indeed, in 1 Corinthians 14:33 the congregations are generally referred to as 'churches of the saints.' Yet we must not imagine that their holiness derives from that of the individual members who constitute them, for as we have seen these are not called 'saints' as individuals"; Barth, *Church Dogmatics,* 4:2, 512–13.

22. *BoS* 26.5, *LG* 765:3–13.

23. Rom 2:17–29.

found in the two levels—the Perfect are anything but perfect, while the Upright sometimes are almost perfect.

Yet much of his detailing of the shape of the life of perfection and uprightness (ܟܐܢܘܬܐ) is theoretical, theologically driven, and in some instances painfully naive.[24] It is in his sermons (memre 10, 25, 29) that the human foibles surface. The final memra, 30, on which several recent studies have rightly focused on the violence, murder, and internal conflict between the levels, functions as well as a "starting again from the beginning" (to borrow one of Barth's favorite phrases) in order to detail how one ascends that steep road to perfection. The audience seems to have shifted and appears to be dominated by the Upright. Yes, they must still renounce marriage and embrace celibacy, but there is a different tone of encouragement and enticement this time.

Perfect Holiness

The author presents a consistent portrait of what constitutes an authentic Perfect and holy person.

(1) Renunciation or "emptying" (ܡܣܪܩܘܬܐ). The renunciation of the world, its possessions and of its culture. The Semitic root ܣܪܩ "*s-r-q*" is primarily used, and (at Fr. Alexander Golitzin's suggestion) the translation "to empty" mirrors Christ's emptying himself of his divinity.[25] Renunciation here is not only physical—emptying oneself of wealth, property, employment, family—but also renunciation of secular culture and worldview, epitomized in his phrase "fasting to the world" also found in the Gospel of Thomas.[26]

(2) Celibacy (ܩܕܝܫܘܬܐ, *qaddishutha*). The familiar requirement to renounce sexual relationships is the most troublesome boundary line for those considering ascending from uprightness to perfection. The author does not

24. Cf. Memra 13 in its prescriptions to the Upright; note *BoS* 15.7, *LG* 349:23–52:3: "When you become a celibate without lust you will see that these members are for urinating and not for intercourse. Because when you become a celibate, lust will never ascend again upon your heart, and you will no longer desire intercourse just as a dead person whose soul is removed does not desire it."

25. Phil 2:7.

26. *Gospel of Thomas 27,* trans. Thomas O. Lambdin, in *The Nag Hammadi Library in English,* edited by James M. Robinson and Richard Smith, 129, 3rd ed. (San Francisco: Harper and Row, 1988). John Calvin describes mortification as self-abandonment: "Let this therefore be the first step, that a man depart from himself"; cited in John Webster, *Holiness,* 90–91.

mention any inner conflict or regression to noncelibate activities among the Perfect, but repeatedly he is found insisting upon celibacy for entry into the higher level, then pleading with some of the more talented Upright candidates to take just this one extra step—perhaps after midlife responsibilities are completed. Memra 15, "On Adam's Marital Desire," exhibits the author's frustration as he argues passionately for celibacy, attempting to demonstrate that celibacy is the natural state for a human being, as evidenced by the lustlessness of Adam and Eve in the Garden of Eden before Adam sinned. Sexual lust was not at the root of Adam's disobedience to God's commandment; it was his desire to become equal to God. Sexual intercourse came about as a result of disobedience—they had watched the animals perform and wanted to imitate—and not as the cause.[27] Many have argued, of course, that sexuality is a natural part of the human makeup and so not sinful or inhibiting of spiritual growth.[28] For the author and other early Syriac ascetics, sexuality is not obviously natural, and is the consequence of a sinful disobedience; therefore, a Perfect one is doing what originally is natural by not engaging in sexual activities.

Nevertheless, knowing this to be a tough sell, the author describes how marriage came about as an inferior institution, grudgingly blessed by God. Certainly, a primarily Upright audience would not have found this presentation gracious.

Renunciation and celibacy are demanding physical negations that require tremendous maturity and spiritual development.

(3) Lowliness or "humility" (ܡܟܝܟܘܬܐ). This is the primary locus of authentic perfection and holiness—as close to the substance of "the holiness of heart" as the author appears to come. Lowliness consists of a constellation of oft-mentioned characteristics and attitudes. The first is "Consider everyone

27. "[F]or Adam desired intercourse as a result of the teaching of the Evil One who had plotted to make him fall from the sanctity of the angels and imitate wild beasts"; *BoS* 15.1, *LG* 336:10–13; "There did not exist in them any lust to desire intercourse; but they greatly desired it because the Evil One had directed their gaze [to it] through cattle"; *BoS* 15.2, *LG* 337:19–21; A person watched the animals and desired to become like them, and hated the celibacy of the angels; that is, in the hope that he will become greater than the angels and be like their Lord"; *BoS* 15.7, *LG* 352:15–18.

28. "But Adam did not know that if they had kept the commandment they would have been fruitful and multiplied, as he had made Eve fruitful by the word of our Lord without lust. Although they would not have been able to do a thing without the word of the Lord, still they believed that without our Lord what the Evil One had said would come to be"; *BoS* 15.6, *LG* 348:18–24.

better than yourself,"[29] which means that one has renounced personal power and a sense of superiority over anyone. "Lower yourself from the commandments of love and teach a young mind the commandments of faith which are lower than love. Once you have taught him how to walk resolutely in faith, go [back] up to Perfection and consider him better than you, and place him in front of you and greet and bow down to him, since you are inferior to him."[30]

All one is left with is his or her status as a child of God whose primary action is love. The implications of this universal inferiority are seen in the second characteristic, the author's persistent call to love and serve your enemies, even your murderers.[31] Jesus kissing the feet of Judas his betrayer, while not betraying him, is our ultimate model.[32]

The third characteristic proceeds from the second: one never judges another person and definitely does not use violence and power to subject others to judgment, no matter how righteous. Abel is considered to have pursued perfection because he did not strike back at his brother Cain as he was being murdered.[33] The judges of this world are considered evil, cruel, and dishonest, but necessary to control the wanton sinfulness of much of humanity. But it is their potential for violence against citizens about which the author warns his Perfect ones. If you are in the government, get out before you are complicit in doing violence and murder to a person under your jurisdiction.[34] Even a bish-

29. Phil 2:3.

30. *BoS* 30.2, *LG* 865:17–25.

31. "Kiss the feet of your betrayers, and look, you will surpass one who [only] washes the feet of his betrayers"; *BoS* 16.4, *LG* 396:21–22.

32. "[Here is] another [form of] suffering: when our Lord submitted himself and washed the feet of the person who was going to sell and deliver him to death, becoming a neighbor to his murderers. Our Lord made him sit and [then] stood before him like a servant and washed the feet of the one who hated him before he washed [the feet of] his friends. [For example, here was, on one hand,] the dreg of the disciples, that is, [Judas] Iscariot the thief; and [on the other], Simeon the chief [disciple]; but he began with Iscariot and finished with Simeon. Therefore, if you know who are your betrayers and your sellers and the companions of your murderers, control your tendency [to strike out] and make them sit down and wipe their feet, before [going on to] the feet of your loved ones, and do not make [it] known that they are your enemies, just as our Lord did not expose Iscariot"; *BoS* 17.3, *LG* 420:14–21:1.

33. *BoS* 9.11, *LG* 228.13–21.

34. "The Perfect do not come near to the positions of leadership, but if they are [in] leadership positions and are pursuing Perfection, they should leave these positions. Then they can be perfected because the Perfect teach everyone with lowliness and are not able to coerce a person like the rulers [do]"; *BoS* 19.24, *LG* 493:10–15.

op wields too much potentially violent power, so the author flatly declares that bishops cannot be Perfect![35]

Since holiness is always God's holiness, which human beings may reflect in the event of revelation, the model for a human manifestation of holiness is to be seen in Jesus. Jesus, however, is not exactly doing something new; Jesus's gospel is in fact the life lived by Adam and Eve in the Garden of Eden before Adam had sinned. Perfection was the status and reality of Eden; uprightness was devised as a second law afterward so that Adam and his descendants might not utterly perish. The evangelical perfection of the Perfect ones (ܓܡܝܪܐ) is a reenactment of the creation in the microcosm of Eden, a reentering the garden.

Coming out of Eden, Adam and humanity bear three burdens or marks of unholiness or profanity, according to the author: toil (ܥܡܠܐ), anxiety (ܪܢܝܐ), and marriage, each of which are the consequences and byproducts of disobedience and the desire to be equal to God. These burdens are punishments and marks of the struggle of uprightness, and so a deficiency in holiness.

Toil or labor issues from God's condemnation of Adam and descendants to work the land in order to eat and survive.[36] Not to work is thus the characteristic or "pledge" of Eden, providing the author's rationale for the Perfect's renunciation of work. Many have perceived this refusal to work to be of Messalian influence, but the author understands this prohibition simply from a rigorous biblical exegesis pointing to one aspect of the way of life of perfection. Again, such holiness creates conflict between the two levels when the Upright work for the Perfect, who are above work. Labor is deemed, if not unholy, then at the least profane activity that does not contribute to holiness.[37]

Anxiety does not derive directly from Eden—unless Adam's hiding from God counts—yet obviously is a universal bane of human existence, Jesus's call to non-anxiety[38] in the Sermon on the Mount being the source. Recalling Barth's characterization of saints as "disturbed sinners," what is this "disturbance," if not anxiety, the causeless emotion that tells you somewhere, somehow, something is not right and you are at fault? A disturbed sinner is bothered by the

35. "But as long as [the rulers—ܪܫܢܐ] have authority they remain apart from Perfection"; *BoS* 19.17, *LG* 480:13–15.

36. Gen 3:17–19.

37. "And since the Perfect lack clothing and food, and God sends no manna at all down to them, the Upright can give [them] alms in order to be saved in this way"; *BoS* 28.11, *LG* 801:24–27.

38. Matt 6:25–33.

holy act she has not committed, while ironically it is the undisturbed sinner who lacks precisely this kind of anxiety and does not recognize the deeper nature of his sinfulness. The author's paradigm places anxiety in a state lacking grace, yet from his descriptions, the Perfect ones are not allowed to escape from the anxiety that they might become greater and more perfect.

As for the punishment of marriage, not too much needs to be said. The author makes it clear that marriage and its sexuality are inferior alternatives to the higher level. Married people are certainly able to perform good deeds, but they themselves cannot become holy as long as they remain in that status. Celibacy (ܩܕܝܫܘܬܐ) and marriage are mutually exclusive conditions.

The pursuit of perfection and holiness consists in unloading and reversing these burdens, all three through a certain *via negativa:* not performing work, not being anxious, not having conjugal relations or the inhibitions of family. The last and most difficult step is the one the author dramatically describes on the threshold of the City of Our Lord: the recognition of all our sins, certainly cause for tremendous anxiety and disturbance, and such recognition frequently causes the long-suffering pilgrim to shrink back on the brink of paradise and not enter.[39] The challenge of this last step cannot be taken lightly or in stride even after all his ascetic labor, for a desperate wrestling match occurs on the threshold, with a successful outcome never guaranteed.[40]

What the author never spells out explicitly is whether one of the Perfect ones in his church has had to cross that terrible threshold before or after his being recognized as a Perfect one in the church. The description of the road to the City of Our Lord carries an eschatological tone, yet on several occasions he observes that the Perfect, while standing with their feet on the earth, find their eyes and minds existing in heaven. The boundaries of perfection and holiness, of anxiety and distractedness, of labor and ascetic toil, are indefinite, if not fuzzy and vague—alas, just as long as you are not married! Perfect ho-

39. "Therefore, the entire difficulty of this step lies in that a person uproots the hidden death, which Adam experienced in the transgression of the commandment, [as well as] all the [evil] thoughts of sin, everything which is considered spiteful in a person. . . . Within and without, this sin entices him, for it is that [same] death which our parents Adam and Eve experienced in the transgression of the first commandment"; *BoS* 20.4, *LG* 536:2–7, 10–12.

40. "Because of this even an athlete, who sees [sin] standing menacingly before him preventing him from crossing over to the place our Lord promised him, battles desperately, struggling with sin"; *BoS* 20.4, *LG* 533:6–10.

liness is not a destination to be reached, but a pilgrimage that theoretically is completed in this life and world.

Holy Men?

The *Book of Steps* is not a treatise of systematic theology, so let us gather the disparate pieces together and come back to the original question: are there holy men and women in the *Book of Steps?* Quickly one can write off the judges and those who practice divination and cast magic spells. Surprisingly, bishops typically fall below uprightness, as do many of the Old Testament prophets. If the prophets performed their less than perfect deeds of violence and harsh judgment at the command of God, then they would be perfected after the apostles and the Perfect ones of contemporary times, according to the author's interpretation of Hebrews 11:39–40 in memra 9.[41] As for the bishops, their status depends upon the source of their decisions, for it is sobering to remember that the author declared several times that God no longer makes such demands on his followers and subsequently excuses and vindicates them.[42] Now everyone is judged by his own actions and merits.

The author flashes a glimpse of a quintessential holy man, though supplying neither name nor location nor situation, an individual one might label "a fool for Christ" or "holy fool." "Let me describe for you a crazy person (ܫܢܝܐ), so that when you see a crazy one who treats himself with contempt and does not own a house or a wife and any property, not even [extra] garments beside his clothes, nor food apart from a day-to-day [supply], say, 'these are my [ways of life] and I should imitate them.'. . . 'These are mine, this is the madness of the Apostles.'"[43]

Crazy and holy are often confused, since both exist on terms outside this world's configuration of what is normal and profane. A more sedate model, but someone described with apparent affection, is given in the final memra.

And we say, "We will drink like so and so"; and what is the difference between so and so and me who eats and drinks, enters among the evil ones or speaks to and

41. Cf. Kitchen, "Making the Imperfect Perfect: The Adaptation of Hebrews 11 in the 9th Mēmrā of the Syriac Book of Steps," in *Reading and Interpretation of the Bible in Late Antiquity: Charles Kannengiesser Festschrift* (Leiden: E. J. Brill, 2008), 227–51.

42. *BoS* 22.4, *LG* 641.3–44.15.

43. *BoS* 16.7, *LG* 401:18–23, 404:3–4.

teaches women [who knows] how many times? Because you observe him today eating or drinking or being able to speak with everyone, be aware that while you were sucking milk by night and by day, he was truly fasting and praying day and night, and he struggled with and crucified his body from all desires.[44]

Are the Perfect holy? Yes, as long as they remain "disturbed," for once they lose that disturbance—holy anxiety, perhaps—and take for granted their status and power, then they fall undisturbed down to uprightness at the minimum. The author expresses his dismay at some of the Perfect who have allowed unwittingly their discipline to slide away with good intentions.

[The Evil One] deluding the Perfect one, says the following, "It is virtuous that you should acquire a little [wealth] through Uprightness, sufficient for your own comfort and for whomever comes to you. Build for yourself a dwelling which is just adequate for strangers to come and rest in it. Plant a little crop and make for yourself a vegetable garden which will be for the healthy and the sick." Under the pretext of the comfort of the afflicted [the Evil One] schemes to make [a Perfect] one fall from that major commandment which [Jesus] directs to the Perfect, "Do not be anxious even about yourself," and by that [other] commandment, "Think about what is above and not of what is on the earth.[45]

The author's concern appears more focused on the undisturbed sinner whose laxity toward the regimens of faith leads him or her astray without knowing it. "But there are people who lower themselves to a certain degree only; they do not do it in front of everybody and they do not subdue/break their mind. For this reason, they do not know what the truth is. There are others who do subdue their mind, but who do not lower themselves in front of everybody on earth. For this reason, they too are ignorant of the truth."[46]

Can the Upright be holy? The potentiality is always there, and the author becomes increasingly convinced that they are on the verge of perfection, if only something could be done about that burden of marriage and sexuality. This is the realm of speculation, but does not the author say that his most virtuous Upright ones have virtually attained "the holiness of heart"?[47]

44. *BoS* 30.19, *LG* 908:10–19.

45. *BoS* 25.5, *LG* 741:21–44:6.

46. *BoS* 1.2, *LG* 13:12–17.

47. "Therefore, the Lord reviled these false people who fraudulently fasted and lowered themselves falsely, and said, 'I will not accept a deceitful lowliness and a false fast. It would be better for a person to eat and drink and wear white [clothes] than to do evil things while fasting and wearing sackcloth and causing everyone to wail through the evil things he does'"; *BoS* 29.12, *LG* 844:11–17.

Finally, another unanswerable question: is the author a holy man? It is only his voice we hear—or more precisely, only his words we read—and besides not telling us his name, he mentions no details whatsoever about his own life, except ironically about the things for which he is passionate. The recent work of Derek Krueger on writing and holiness[48] opens wider perhaps the most important perspective on the author: his writing. His asceticism is revealed through his text, and like the true Perfect one he depicts, the author's primary task has been to instruct and discipline and mediate those who listen to him. Indeed, the author does not describe himself doing anything else. One of the most common traits in hagiographical writing is the protests of the author's humility and lack of skill. Sometimes it appears disingenuous, but Krueger notes that "rather than a rhetoric of false modesty, it might be more accurate to speak of a rhetoric of longed-for humility."[49] Except for the enigmatic preface, the author's self-effacement, his lowliness and humility, is so thorough and effective that we really do not know who he is, yet. Without taking the analogy too far, the author is "the Man of God of the Lesser Zab."

We gather that he is a pastor, a spiritual director and mentor, a talented biblical exegete and preacher by the things he writes about. His social power is implicit—that he can actually preach such things—prescriptive as well as challenging—though apparently not with complete success. All that remains is his passion for the gospel and his writings describing a unique community of faith he has worked to shape and mold. By his own standards, the author of the *Book of Steps* would seem to be a saint, a holy man. Even Peter Brown would take him in.

48. Derek Krueger, *Writing and Holiness: The Practice of Authorship in the Early Christian East,* Divinations: Rereading Late Ancient Religion (Philadelphia: University of Pennsylvania Press, 2004); cf. chap. 5, "Hagiography as Asceticism: Humility as Authorial Practice," 94–109.

49. Krueger, *Writing and Holiness,* 98.

Sergey Minov

13. MARRIAGE AND SEXUALITY IN THE *BOOK OF STEPS*

From Encratism to Orthodoxy

When one looks at the history of Christianity, it is the fourth century that by right wins the title of "axial age" when compared to other historical periods. This period of rapid sociocultural and religious changes saw an exceptional outburst of intellectual creativity. The shift of paradigms during the transition from ancient to medieval Christianity was marked by questioning and reevaluation of a wide variety of ideas and practices. Among the most important questions that were problematized and hotly debated during this period were those focused on the place of asceticism in Christian life, including closely related issues of marriage and sexuality. It was the rise of institutionalized monasticism during the fourth century that contributed greatly to these debates, one of the most noticeable manifestations of which was the proliferation of writings concerned with virginity.[1]

I would like to express my gratitude to Rev. Craig Morrison and Serge Ruzer for their help and comments on an earlier draft of this paper as, well as to Sarah Contrucci for improving my English style.

1. See Peter R. Brown, *The Body and Society: Men, Women, and Sexual Renunciation in Early Christianity* (New York: Columbia University Press, 1988); Ton H. C. Van Eijk, "Marriage and Virginity, Death and Immortality," in *Mélanges patristiques offerts au Cardinal Jean Daniélou,* edited by Jacques Fontaine and Charles Kannengiesser, 209–35 (Paris: Beauchesne, 1972). On the fourth-century literature on virginity, see P. Thomas Camelot, " Les traités 'De virginitate' au IVe siècle," in *Mystique et continence: Travaux scientifiques du VIIe Congrès international d'Avon,* 273–92 (Bruges: Desclée de Brouwer, 1952).

Syriac-speaking Christians had a role in contributing to this trend, as well, as one can see from the writings of Aphrahat and Ephrem.[2] However, while many scholars dealt with how these two great Syriac writers treated varied issues pertaining to marriage and sexuality, relatively less attention in this regard has been paid to another important composition, the *Book of Steps,* an anonymous ascetic work that was composed in East Syria somewhere in the late fourth century.[3]

This masterpiece of Syriac ascetic literature provides rich material for scholars interested in the development of Christian anthropological thought.[4] In what follows I intend to explore how the author of the *Book of Steps* handles various issues related to the institution of marriage. I shall start my investigation with an analysis of how he promotes his understanding of these issues through a consistently ascetical reading of scripture, especially of the book of Genesis. The second part brings into focus his views on the origins of matrimony and of sexual desire. Finally, the practical and pastoral aspects of the *Book of Steps'* marriage-related rhetoric shall be considered.

One of the central objectives of this article is the examination of how the views on marriage and sexuality espoused by the author of the *Book of Steps* fit into the wide context of fourth-century Syrian Christianity. For this purpose I shall compare him with Aphrahat and Ephrem, as well as with some other Syrian writers. Of special importance will be the investigation of the *Book of Steps'* relation to the ideology of Encratism, an Early Christian movement that particularly stressed asceticism and sexual renunciation.[5] On Syrian soil

2. See Arthur Vööbus, *History of Asceticism in the Syrian Orient: A Contribution to the History of Culture in the Near East,* vol. 3, Corpus Scriptorum Christianorum Orientalium 500 (Louvain: Peeters, 1988); Shafiq AbouZayd, *Ihidayutha: A Study of the Life of Singleness in the Syrian Orient, From Ignatius of Antioch to Chalcedon 451 AD* (Oxford: ARAM Society for Syro-Mesopotamian Studies, 1993).

3. For general information on this document, see the introduction in Robert A. Kitchen and Martien F. G. Parmentier, trans., *The Book of Steps: The Syriac Liber Graduum* (Kalamazoo, Mich.: Cistercian Publications, 2004). All the quotations from the *Book of Steps* in this chapter are from this edition. Syriac text is that of Michael Kmoskó, ed., *Liber Graduum,* Patrologia Syriaca 1.3 (Paris: Firmin-Didot, 1926).

4. On asceticism of the *Book of Steps,* see Vööbus,"*Liber Graduum:* Some Aspects of Its Significance for the History of Early Syrian Asceticism," in *Charisteria Iohanni Kopp octogenerio oblata,* 108–28, Papers of the Estonian Theological Society in Exile 7 (Stockholm: Estonian Theological Society in Exile, 1954); Antoine Guillaumont, "Liber Graduum," in *Dictionnaire de spiritualité ascétique et mystique: Doctrine et histoire,* 9:749–54 (Paris: Beauchesne, 1976); Kitchen, "Becoming Perfect: The Maturing of Asceticism in the Liber Graduum," in *Journal of the Canadian Society for Syriac Studies* 2 (2002): 30–45.

5. On Encratism in general, see Henry Chadwick, "Enkrateia," in *Reallexikon für Antike und Chris-*

this movement was represented first by Tatian, the *Acts of Thomas,* and the followers of Marcion. As I intend to demonstrate, in comparison with other fourth-century Syriac writers, our author stands particularly close to the ascetical ideology typical for this sector of early Christianity. In this respect it would also be important to address the question of how the views expressed in the *Book of Steps* are related to the prevalent fourth-century Christian discourse on marriage, where approval of this institution's fundamental goodness became one of the touchstones of nascent orthodoxy.

Ascetic Reading of Scripture in the *Book of Steps*

One of the main tasks pursued by the author of the *Book of Steps* in his work was to reinterpret scripture in order to make it agree with his general ascetic vision, where sexuality is regarded not as an original and integral part of human nature, but as a development that belongs to the fallen world. For that purpose he resorts to a variety of exegetical and rhetorical strategies, many of which are known to us from the writings of other Christian ascetical readers of scripture in antiquity. This rich exegetical repertoire has been closely examined recently by Elizabeth Clark.[6] Following her lead, one can better appreciate the particular way our author interpreted the authoritative text while trying to cope with the challenges presented to his ascetic vision by several scriptural passages, especially those where the goodness of marriage is affirmed.

A particular exegetical challenge to the ascetic vision of primeval history promoted by the *Book of Steps* was posed by Genesis 1:28, where God himself blesses Adam and Eve and commands them to procreate *before* the fall.[7] It is by struggling with this biblical verse that our author demonstrates with full force

tentum, edited by Theodor Klauser, 5:343–65 (Stuttgart: Hiersemann, 1962); Robert C. Cecire, *Encratism: Early Christian Ascetic Extremism* (PhD diss., The University of Kansas, 1985); Gilles Quispel, "The Study of Encratism: A Historical Survey," in *La tradizione dell'enkrateia: motivazioni ontologiche e protologiche. Atti del Colloquio Internazionale, Milano 20–23 aprile 1982,* edited by Ugo Bianchi, 35–81 (Roma: Ateneo, 1985).

6. See Elizabeth A. Clark, *Reading Renunciation: Asceticism and Scripture in Early Christianity* (Princeton: Princeton University Press, 1999), 104–52.

7. For a useful overview of Christian exegesis of this verse, see Jeremy Cohen, *"Be Fertile and Increase, Fill the Earth and Master It": The Ancient and Medieval Career of a Biblical Text* (Ithaca: Cornell University Press, 1989), 229–70.

his ingenuity as an exegete, while trying to lower the pro-marriage "weight" of this passage.

First, it is remarkable how the author of the *Book of Steps* completely ignores this blessing of procreation through the whole of his work. He never quotes this scriptural verse—even in those contexts where it might be appropriate. Likewise, he totally ignores the biblical account of Eve's creation in Genesis 2:20–24, with its manifestly pro-marriage message. He also turns a blind eye to those passages in the New Testament, especially in the (Deutero-) Pauline epistles, where the goodness of marriage and childbearing is stressed.[8] This is not surprising, since these scriptural loci would undermine completely his view of marriage and sexuality as the negative features of the postlapsarian human existence.

Another, more resourceful exegetical strategy to neutralize the positive message of Genesis 1:28 is found in several passages that relate the story of Satan seducing the first couple: "The evil one had taught Adam and Eve, 'In this way you shall become as great as God,' and then 'There is a way for you to be fruitful and multiply (ܦܘܪܣܐ ܕܬܦܪܘܢ ܘܬܣܓܘܢ), and to do everything you desire, as does the Creator.'"[9] "In this way he also seduced Adam with deceit and approached him as someone concerned [for him] and a bearer of [his] burden and he counseled Eve to advise Adam and commanded her to speak to Adam so that he might acquire wealth and become a king. 'Look, gold and silver are on the earth and all sorts of pleasures. Possess and enjoy yourself; rule, increase, and multiply (ܘܐܬܡܠܟܘ ܘܦܪܘ ܘܣܓܘ),' the evil one counseled."[10] In the first case, which illustrates the general ascetic principle held by our author that "food and pleasures do not allow us to stand before God," Satan schemes to separate man from his Creator by persuading Adam and Eve to choose the way of earthly pleasures. In the second example he again pushes the first couple to the way of material self-gratification in order to gain mastery over the earth. In both of these cases Satan seduces Adam by offering him wrong means to gain the goods that otherwise would be provided freely by God. In what concerns procreation, Satan tricks him to choose the way of animal intercourse instead of the miraculous asexual way of reproduction intended originally by God. It is remarkable that in both passages we see masked, but nevertheless unmistak-

8. Cf. 1Tim 2:15, 3:2–5, 5:10, 14; Titus 2:4.

9. *BoS* 15.6.

10. *BoS* 21.9.

ably recognizable allusions to Genesis 1:28.[11] By putting the key words of the verse—"be fruitful and multiply" (ܦܪܘ ܘܣܓܘ)—into Satan's mouth, our author in a subtle way subverts its positive message while strengthening even more the association of sexuality with Satan, an idea reiterated by him through the whole *Book of Steps.*

An important and original approach used by our author in order to deal with some pro-marriage scriptural passages is his introduction of the theory of the two laws—the one of perfection (ܓܡܝܪܘܬܐ) and the one of uprightness (ܟܐܢܘܬܐ). The first one is the original law that governed human life before the fall, while the second one has been introduced by God only after the fall. It is only according to this inferior law that God permitted Adam to marry.[12] These two laws correspond directly to the two ways of life open for Christians to pursue. On the way of perfection an ascetic in his ultimate quest for the primeval state of Adam's holiness devotes himself totally to God and renounces all worldly bonds, including familial and marital ones. On the other hand, for those believers who are not able stand up to the highest standards of this vocation, the way of uprightness is open to follow in order to be saved:

If a person does not have work in heaven, he is not able to cease from earthly labor. Therefore, after he saw that Adam loved such things, [God] allowed him to be married and to become Upright in this world which he loved and to be saved and not utterly perish. Because of his compassion our Lord, even if we desired something through sin, effected that we might be [involved] in it without sins, if we become Upright.[13]

Therefore, because the Upright have not separated themselves from everything there is on earth, nor from marriage and anxiety and toil, they are still eating from the same tree from which Adam ate and have many faults [separating] them from Perfection. But our Lord desired through his mercy to give them [the opportunity] to keep Uprightness, which is lower than Perfection, so that while they are married and [involved] in these visible things they will be in good condition on the day of our Lord.[14]

11. Jansma, Taeke, and Marinus D. Koester, eds., *The Old Testament in Syriac according to the Peshitta Version,* part 1, fasc. 1, *Preface; Genesis–Exodus* (Leiden: E.J. Brill, 1977), 2: ܘܒܪܟ ܐܢܘܢ ܐܠܗܐ ܘܐܡܪ ܠܗܘܢ ܐܠܗܐ. ܦܪܘ ܘܣܓܘ ܘܡܠܘ ܐܪܥܐ ܘܟܘܒܫܘܗ̇. ܘܫܠܛܘ ܒܢܘܢܐ ܕܝܡܐ ܘܒܦܪܚܬܐ ܕܫܡܝܐ ܘܒܒܥܝܪܐ ܘܒܟܠܗ̇ ܚܝܘܬܐ ܕܪܚܫܐ ܥܠ ܐܪܥܐ. Cf. also *BoS* 15.8.

12. *BoS* 15.1: ܗܘ ܕܝܢ ܗܘ ܒܢܡܘܣܐ ܐܦܣ ܠܗ ܕܢܙܘܓ; cf. also *BoS* 15.8.

13. *BoS* 25.2; cf. *BoS* 13.5.

14. *BoS* 20.6.

Needless to say, in the eyes of our author these two options do not possess an equal value, and the way of perfection for him is much superior to that of uprightness.[15]

Each of these ways is regulated by its own law—the "minor" and "major" commandments, in the terminology used by the *Book of Steps:* "In order that the whole world not be afraid of this effort, and fall short through fear and perish, our Lord compassionately lowered himself and gave other lesser commandments [that] were not very difficult and inferior to that major commandment. People are able to perform them while they are in their homes with their wealth and their wives and children, and [still] be saved."[16] "Understand from this that people are saved if they do as they were commanded—[following] that precept that is lower than that perfect and superior precept, [even] while they are married and possessing wealth."[17]

This hermeneutical move of dividing all commandments and precepts that appear in the Bible into the two hierarchically differentiated categories allows our author to cope with many difficult pro-marriage passages from the New Testament. He successfully limits their prescriptive authority by interpreting them as addressing not those who follow the way of perfection, but only the regular "upright" Christians.

For instance, he resorts to this strategy in the case of Matthew 19:6, a part of Jesus's argument from the dispute with the Pharisees about the permissibility of divorce and an important pro-marriage passage, in which Jesus declares the indissolubility of marriage as an institution inaugurated by God himself. First our author diminishes the authority of these words by avoiding any mention of the fact that they belong to Jesus. Second, and more important, he recontextualizes them by contrasting them with a paraphrase based loosely on Matthew 10:37 and 22:30, where the superiority of the celibate lifestyle enjoyed by the Perfect is affirmed, thus making the previous passage relevant only for those Christians who fail to live up to these high standards: "This is the Perfect road: 'Men who do not take wives and women who do not belong

15. Cf. *BoS* 20.6: "If a person compares the deeds of the Upright with those of the Perfect, they amount to very little in his eyes. Even if the Upright defeat evil, prevailing over sin and purifying their heart of evil thoughts, yet some of the fruits of sins are still living in them, since their heart was not purified from anxiety, toil, and marriage."

16. *BoS* 30.25.

17. *BoS* 30.27; cf. also *BoS* 19.34–36.

to men are like angels and cannot die. Whoever does not leave his wife and his children and his family and everything he has in the hand, is not worthy of me.' However, the path that leads you away from it is this: 'Whatever God has joined together do not separate.'"[18]

In the same way the author of the *Book of Steps* deals with Hebrews 13:4, another significant passage from the New Testament in which the purity and blessed nature of marriage are asserted. Again, as in the case of Matthew 19:6, this pro-marriage apostolic dictum is confronted with other words of Paul's, a paraphrased version of 1 Corinthians 7:32–34, which promote celibacy as the only viable option for those who wish to devote themselves to the Lord. Consequently, the saying's potential threat to the author's ascetic project is well defused through restriction of its intended audience only to those believers who go astray from the road of perfection:

> This is the Perfect road: "A virgin who does not marry a man and a man who does not take a wife are pleasing to our Lord in body and in spirit, while those who do marry please one another." However, the path that leads you away from it is this: "Marriage is [held] in honor and their bed is pure." This, again, is written for whoever does not subdue his body from food and is [not] constant in fasting and in prayer.[19]

Another noteworthy hermeneutical strategy applied by the author of the *Book of Steps* to the New Testament in order to promote his ascetic agenda consists of putting the message of celibacy directly into the mouth of Jesus through the forging of scriptural quotations that are not actually found in the gospel text. One instance occurs when he weaves together Matthew 19:21 and John 15:19 into a new quasi-scriptural unit, introduced as a saying by Jesus himself, where particular emphasis is laid on the repudiation of sexuality: "When our Lord said, 'Lower yourselves and separate yourselves and become celibate from the world and from intercourse (ܐܬܡܟܟܘ ܘܐܬܦܪܫܘ ܘܐܬܩܕܫܘ ܡܢ ܥܠܡܐ ܘܡܢ ܫܘܬܦܘܬܐ), love everyone and follow me. Do not be of the world as I am not of it and do not labor in it, but follow me and become Perfect ones.'"[20]

In a similar vein he combines Matthew 10:37, 19:29, and Luke 14:26 into a single quasi-Dominical saying while adding a general demand to "rise above

18. *BoS* 19.14.
19. *BoS* 19.15.
20. *BoS* 24.4.

marriage" to the list of the earthly commitments to be renounced by the true disciples of Jesus:

That great and acceptable and perfect will of our Lord is this: all people should maintain their virginity (ܢܛܪܘܢ ܦܓܪܝܗܘܢ ܒܒܬܘܠܘܬܐ) and empty themselves and sanctify their hearts from all hateful thoughts of sin, and imitate our Lord, lifting up his cross and following him and becoming perfect through his universal love that makes peace with all, as he had said, "Whoever does not leave everything he has and everything he possesses on the earth and [leave] his father and his mother, his brothers and his sisters, his sons, and his family, and rise above marriage (ܘܢܬܥܠܐ ܡܢ ܙܘܘܓܐ), is not worthy of me."[21]

Once again, as in the previous case, the technique of composite quotation is employed by our author in order to take the ascetic and anti-familial message of Jesus's original words to extremes. An immediate goal of these ascetically oriented rewritings of scriptural text is to present Jesus himself as the teacher of sexual renunciation and, as a consequence, to lend the ultimate authority to this practice.

The author of the *Book of Steps* shares with the majority of ancient Christian interpreters of Genesis the notion of Adam and Eve as virgins in paradise and of sexuality as belonging to the fallen word.[22] This idea is one of the foundation stones of his anthropological system, and it is of the foremost importance for our author to demonstrate that the prelapsarian state of Adam and Eve excluded any possibility of sexual intercourse. He employs various strategies to accomplish this goal.

First of all, he likens the condition of Adam and Eve before their transgression with that of children. He substantiates this comparison by appealing to the nakedness of the first couple before the fall, taking Genesis 2:25 and 3:7 as the scriptural proof-texts:

It is written, "Adam and Eve were naked, but they could not see their own nakedness," that is, like milk-sucking infants who are bare (ܐܝܟ ܝܢܩܐ ܕܚܠܒܐ ܕܡܥܪܛܠܝܢ) and do not know what nakedness is. In this, they did not have a despicable thought, but

21. *BoS* 30.25 (translation slightly modified).

22. See Hendrik S. Benjamins, "Keeping Marriage out of Paradise: The Creation of Man and Woman in Patristic Literature," in *The Creation of Man and Woman: Interpretations of the Biblical Narrative in Jewish and Christian Traditions,* edited by Gerard P. Luttikhuizen, 94–106, Themes in Biblical Narrative, Jewish and Christian Traditions 3 (Leiden: E. J. Brill, 2000). For Syriac milieu, cf. Aphrahat, *Demonstration* XVIII.9; *Cave of Treasures* V.17–18.

if they had known, they would have put on clothes. . . . Before Adam and Eve had sinned, they were naked like the milk-sucking infants (ܥܪܛܠܝܢ ܗܘܘ ܐܝܟ ܝܠܘ̈ܕܐ ܕܚܠܒܐ), but since the lust (ܪܓܬܐ) in their heart was not aroused they were not ashamed, just as infants are not ashamed. Once they had sinned, and sin existed in their heart, directing them to desire intercourse, [then] "They saw that they were naked"; that is, they knew the shame they had not known.[23]

Since shame was generally thought to be an indispensable component of sexual experience, its absence emphasized in Genesis 2:25 proves that Adam and his wife led a celibate way of life. In view of that notion a Perfect who strives to arrive at the pre-fallen state of freedom from sexual desire should look at children as his model: "When you see him (i.e., a child) not desiring a wife and capable of crying at any time, say, 'These are mine, I will become without desire and cry at any time.'"[24]

Depiction of Adam and Eve in paradise as children appears in the writings of several Christian writers during the second and third centuries.[25] Later on it gained some currency in the Syriac milieu, as well.[26] It is remarkable, however, that Ephrem seems to be directly opposed to exactly the kind of interpretation of the protoplasts' nakedness that we find in the *Book of Steps*. In his commentary on Genesis 2:25, he ascribes such an exegetical stand to "outsiders" and argues that in what concerns their age Adam and Eve were not "children" (ܫܒܪ̈ܐ), but "young adults" (ܥܠܝ̈ܡܐ).[27] One might explain this exegetical disagreement as stemming from the difference in importance ascribed by these two authors to the notion of "the garments of glory/light"—the splendid attire that

23. *BoS* 15.3 (translation slightly changed); cf. also *BoS* 21.8.

24. *BoS* 16.6.

25. Cf. Theophilus of Antioch, *Ad Autol.* II.25; Irenaeus, *Adv. haer.* III.22.4, III.23.5; Clement of Alexandria, *Protr.* XI.1.

26. See Robert Murray, *Symbols of Church and Kingdom: A Study in Early Syriac Tradition,* rev. ed. (London: T. and T. Clark; Piscataway, N.J.: Gorgias Press, 2004), 304–6; Aleksander Kowalski, "Adam i Ewa jako dzieci w egzegezie syryjskiej," *Roczniki Teologiczno-Kanoniczne* 30, no. 1 (1983): 117–22; Alison Salvesen, "Infants or Fools in the Garden of Eden? An Ambiguity in Early Syriac Tradition," in *Hamlet on a Hill: Semitic and Greek Studies Presented to Professor T. Muraoka on the Occasion of His Sixty-Fifth Birthday,* edited by Martin F. J. Baasten and Wido T. van Peursen, 432–40, Orientalia Lovaniensia Analecta 118 (Leuven: Peeters, 2003), and Salvesen, "Without Shame or Desire: The Pronouncements of Jesus on Children and the Kingdom, and Early Syriac Attitudes to Childhood," *Scottish Journal of Theology* 59, no. 3 (2006): 307–26.

27. Ephrem, *In Gen.* II.14.1, in *Sancti Ephraem Syri in Genesim et in Exodum commentarii,* edited by Raymond-Marie Tonneau, 33, Corpus Scriptorum Christianorum Orientalium 152, Syr. 71 (Louvain: L. Durbecq, 1955).

covered Adam in paradise.[28] While to Ephrem and many other ancient Syriac authors this motif serves as one of the key images in their reflections on Adam, his fall, and redemption, it is almost completely absent from the *Book of Steps.*[29]

Another, and by far the most important, strategy in service of the author's vision of the virginal life led by the first humans in paradise is that he consistently represents Adam and Eve as enjoying a quasi-angelic status before the fall: "God first commanded Adam to become a perfect saint (ܩܕܝܫܐ ܓܡܝܪܐ), just like the watchers and angels in heaven (ܥܝܪܐ ܘܡܠܐܟܐ ܕܒܫܡܝܐ), so that while living physically on the earth, being stripped of everything in it, he might dwell spiritually in heaven with the angels while his mind is clothed with the glory of his Creator (ܫܘܒܚܐ ܕܒܪܘܝܗ) and the earth is not seen by him."[30] "But because Adam and Eve had gone astray in transgressing the commandment concerning the heavenly ministry (ܦܘܩܕܢܐ ܠܬܫܡܫܬܐ ܫܡܝܢܝܬܐ), which they used to fulfill like angels and together with the angels (ܐܝܟ ܡܠܐܟܐ ܥܡ ܡܠܐܟܐ ܡܫܡܫܝܢ ܗܘܘ), God gave them the visible ministry on earth (ܠܬܫܡܫܬܐ ܕܡܬܚܙܝܐ ܒܐܪܥܐ) in the likeness of that heavenly one, so that they might not all perish together."[31]

That this theme was of crucial importance for the anthropological conception of the author of the *Book of Steps* is seen from the fact that he continues to reiterate it throughout the work.[32]

The roots of this notion of angelomorphic humanity might be traced back ultimately to some Jewish protological and eschatological speculations on re-

28. On this motif in Syriac literature, see Sebastian P. Brock, "Clothing Metaphors as a Means of Theological Expression in Syriac Tradition," in *Typus, Symbol, Allegorie bei den östlichen Vätern und ihren Parallelen im Mittelalter: Internationales Kolloquium, Eichstätt 1981,* edited by Margot Schmidt and Carl F. Greyer, 11–38, Eichstätter Beiträge 4 (Regensburg: Friedrich Pustet, 1982); Alexander Golitzin, "Recovering the 'Glory of Adam': 'Divine Light' Traditions in the Dead Sea Scrolls and the Christian Ascetical Literature of Fourth-Century Syro-Mesopotamia," in *The Dead Sea Scrolls as Background to Postbiblical Judaism and Early Christianity: Papers from an International Conference at St. Andrews in 2001,* edited by James R. Davila, 275–308 (Leiden: E. J. Brill, 2003).

29. See on this Kowalski, *Perfezione e giustizia di Adamo nel Liber Graduum,* Orientalia Christiana Analecta 232 (Rome: Pontificium Institutum Orientale, 1989, 76). Although the imagery of Adam's "glory" does occasionally appear in the *Book of Steps* (cf. *BoS* 21.2, 28.11), it does not constitute an important part of the author's anthropological discourse.

30. *BoS* 21.2.

31. *BoS* 28.9.

32. Cf. *BoS* 9.12, 21.10, 17, 26.1, 30.24. On this motif in the *Book of Steps,* see Michela Aveta, "Ad instar angelorum: Per un'analisi storico-religiosa dell'antropologia del *Liber Graduum,*" *Christianesimo nella storia* 8 (1987): 481–500; Kowalski, *Perfezione e giustizia,* 81–85.

lations between humans and angels from the Second Temple Period, especially those found in the writings from Qumran.[33] Taking into consideration a growing body of research on various connections between Qumran and Syriac Christianity, it seems worthwhile to pursue the possibility of the Jewish background for this tradition in the *Book of Steps*.[34]

However old the idea of angelomorphic humanity might be, by the fourth century it was widely spread through the Christian world in the understanding and representation of ideal ascetic life as *vita angelica*.[35] Such understanding of the ultimate goal of ascetic praxis was by no means alien to Syriac-speaking Christians, among whom it had deep roots and was shared by the majority of the fourth-century Syriac writers.[36] Our author is no exception to that trend. The ideal of *imitatio angeli* lies at the core of his ascetical program: "For the Perfect are like angels, as our Lord said, 'Those who are worthy of that resurrection are not able to die, but are like angels.' From then on they become like angels. Whoever wishes to be perfected should imitate the angels."[37]

33. See John J. Collins, "In the Likeness of the Holy Ones: The Creation of Humankind in a Wisdom Text from Qumran," in *The Provo International Conference on the Dead Sea Scrolls: Technological Innovations, New Texts, and Reformulated Issues,* edited by Donald W. Parry and Eugene Ulrich, 609–18, Studies on the Texts of the Desert of Judah 30 (Leiden: E. J. Brill, 1999); Collins, "The Angelic Life," in *Metamorphoses: Resurrection, Body, and Transformative Practices in Early Christianity,* edited by Turid K. Seim and Jorunn Økland, 291–310, Ekstasis 1 (Berlin: Walter de Gruyter, 2009); Devorah Dimant, "Men as Angels: The Self-Image of the Qumran Community," in *Religion and Politics in the Ancient Near East,* edited by Adele Berlin, 93–103, Studies and Texts in Jewish History and Culture (Bethesda: University Press of Maryland, 1986); Crispin H. T. Fletcher-Louis, *All the Glory of Adam: Liturgical Anthropology in the Dead Sea Scrolls,* Studies on the Texts of the Desert of Judah 42 (Leiden: E. J. Brill, 2002).

34. For a general discussion of how Jewish apocryphal material had been transmitted in the late antique Near East, see Reeves, "Exploring the Afterlife of Jewish Pseudepigrapha in Medieval Near Eastern Religious Traditions: Some Initial Soundings," *Journal for the Study of Judaism* 30, no. 2 (1999): 148–77. For Jewish influences upon Syriac angelology, see Murray, "Some Themes and Problems of Early Syriac Angelology," in *V Symposium Syriacum, 1988: Katholieke Universiteit, Leuven, 29–31 août 1988,* edited by René Lavenant, 148–52, Orientalia Christiana Analecta 236 (Rome: Pontificium Institutum Studiorum Orientalium, 1990); Stephen E. Robinson, "The Testament of Adam and the Angelic Liturgy," *Revue de Qumrân* 12 (1985): 105–10.

35. See Karl S. Frank, *Angelikos Bios: Begriffsanalytische und Begriffsgeschichtliche Untersuchung zum "Engelgleichen Leben" im frühen Mönchtum* (Münster: Aschendorffsche Verlagsbuchhandlung, 1964); Ellen Muehlberger, "Ambivalence about the Angelic Life: The Promise and Perils of an Early Christian Discourse of Asceticism," *Journal of Early Christian Studies* 16, no. 4 (2008): 447–78.

36. Cf. Aphrahat, *Demonstration* VI.1, 6, XVIII.12; Ephrem, *De virg.* I.8; Ephrem, *De Nativ.* XXI.4; Ephrem, *Commentary on the Diatessaron* XVI.22; see Vööbus, *History of Asceticism,* 2:298–307.

37. *BoS* 25.8.

Therefore, once they have emptied and lowered themselves, as they were exalted in the beginning, the instinct of lust (ܡܚܫܒܬܐ ܕܪܓܬܐ) is uprooted from them. . . . So today—when they have abandoned the earth and all in it, and have given heed to our Lord in heaven, and attained that thing that Adam had lost, . . . —they will be freed from the instinct of lust. God will sever it from them and they will become like the angels in heaven who do not lust.[38]

It is noteworthy that the author of the *Book of Steps* encourages the practice of celibacy first and foremost on the basis of protological reasoning. Although we do find the notion of *imitatio Christi* in the *Book of Steps,* no particular stress seems to be laid on Jesus's celibate lifestyle in the author's panegyrics to virginity.[39] In that sense he stands close to Aphrahat, for whom the virginity of the Bnay Qyama is not based on the celibacy of Jesus, nor on the virginity of Mary, his mother.[40] In the soteriological perspective of the *Book of Steps* the principal goal of Jesus's mission is to bring fallen humanity back to the primeval state of perfection that Adam and Eve enjoyed in paradise: "After Jesus revealed himself, he revealed to whoever wishes to become like the creation of the first Adam (ܐܝܟ ܒܪܝܬܗ ܕܐܕܡ ܩܕܡܝܬܐ)."[41] Since, in the view of our author, virginity was the fundamental characteristic of the prelapsarian human existence, it is consistently promoted by him as a *conditio sine qua non* for anyone who aspires to pursue the way of perfection: "The Perfect road is this, 'Whoever does not leave his family is not capable [of walking on this road].'"[42]

Using the general hermeneutic principle that "the last things shall be as the first,"[43] he reads the biblical story of Adam and Eve before their fall through the lens of Jesus's words about the angelic-like state of resurrected humanity transmitted by the Synoptics (Matthew 22:29–30; Mark 12:24–25; Luke 20:34–36). It is the Lukan version of the pericope that was of special impor-

38. *BoS* 15.9.

39. Cf. *BoS* 1.2, 3.10, 10.10, 14.2. On *imitatio Christi* in the *Book of Steps,* see René Roux, "The Doctrine of the Imitation of Christ in the *Liber Graduum:* Between Exegetical Theory and Soteriology," in *Studia Patristica: Biblica Et Apocrypha, Ascetica, Liturgica,* vol. 30, edited by Elizabeth A. Livingstone and E. Peters (Leuven: Peeters, 1997).

40. On this aspect of Aphrahat's thought, see Shafiq Abouzayd, "Virginity in Aphrahat," in *V Symposium Syriacum, 1988: Katholieke Universiteit, Leuven, 29–31 août 1988,* edited by René Lavenant, 131–32, Orientalia Christiana Analecta 236 (Rome: Pontificium Institutum Orientalium Studiorum, 1990).

41. *BoS* 15.7 (translation slightly modified).

42. *BoS* 19.9; cf. also *BoS* 3.3, 15.13, 13.5, 9, 20.6, 24.7, 29.5–6, 13, 30.25–26.

43. Cf. *Letter of Barnabas* VI.13: ποιῶ τὰ ἔσχατα ὡς τὰ πρῶτα.

tance for the ascetically minded readers of the scripture in antiquity, since it lent itself with a particular ease to interpretations that presumed abstinence from marriage to be not only a characteristic of human existence in the anticipated eschatological consummation, but a necessary *condition* for having part in it that could and should be attained here and now.[44] The author of the *Book of Steps* also belongs to this tradition of ascetical reading of the New Testament when he makes use of these verses in order to support his claim that the true believers should imitate angels.[45]

Finally, the idea of the *vita angelica* led by Adam and Eve before the fall is closely related to the author's other major strategy to promote his vision of the virginal paradise—his claim that the institution of marriage was introduced only after the fall and, therefore, is one of its negative consequences. Accordingly, it has only a temporary and insubstantial significance in the history of salvation.

In antiquity many ascetically oriented Christian interpreters, who wanted to support the idea that sexuality does not constitute an integral part of human nature, resorted to the technique of "close reading" of scripture.[46] Of foremost importance for many of these exegetes was the argument based on "chronology" of events in the first chapters of the book of Genesis, when the observation that, according to the sequence of the biblical narrative, Adam "knew" Eve only after they were expelled from Paradise (Genesis 4:1) was taken to prove that no carnal relations between them existed before that.[47] The author of the *Book of Steps* is no exception to this trend; he too employs the chronological argument and explicitly quotes Genesis 4:1 in order to illustrate his point that sexual desire took place in humans only after the fall: "Then the lustful instinct of marriage (ܡܚܫܒܬܐ ܕܪܓܬܐ ܕܙܘܘܓܐ) came to exist in Adam and in

44. For a helpful discussion of ascetical aspects of this pericope, see Ugo Bianchi, "The Religio-Historical Relevance of Luke 20:34–36," in *Studies in Gnosticism and Hellenistic Religions Presented to Gilles Quispel on the Occasion of His 65th Birthday,* edited by Roelof van den Broek and Maarten J. Vermaseren, 31–37 (Leiden: E. J. Brill, 1981); see also David E. Aune, "Luke 20:34–36: A Gnosticized Logion of Jesus?" in *Geschichte-Tradition- Reflexion: Festschrift für Martin Hengel zum 70. Geburtstag,* edited by Hubert Cancik, Hermann Lichtenberger, and Peter Schäfer, 3:187–202 (Tübingen: Mohr Siebeck, 1996), who puts it in the context of early Syrian Christianity.

45. Cf. *BoS* 15.4, 25.8.

46. For a discussion of this exegetical strategy, see Clark, *Reading Renunciation,* 118–22.

47. Cf. Irenaeus, *Adv. haer.* III.23.5; Tertullian, *De monog.* 17.5; Jerome, *Ep.* 22.19; Gregory of Nyssa, *De virgin.* 12.4; John Chrysostom, *Hom. in Gen.* 18.

Eve, and then, at the end of all his folly, he had intercourse (ܐܫܬܘܬܦ). For it is written that after God had indicted Adam and allowed him to acquire that thing he had desired, Adam departed from Paradise and worked the soil from which he was taken, and knew Eve (ܝܕܥ ܠܚܘܐ) and she gave birth to Cain."[48] This appeal to chronology serves as a foundation upon which our author builds his argument that not only sexual desire, but the institution of marriage as such, should be considered as coming into existence only after the fall and thus as belonging to the postlapsarian world: "So God permitted them to marry (ܢܙܕܘܓܘܢ) and to labor after he had cursed them. Lust and the procreative instinct (ܪܓܬܐ ܡܙܪܢܝܬܐ ܘܙܪܥܐ) was in them because they have sinned and violated his commandment. They hated holiness (ܩܕܝܫܘܬܐ) and loved intercourse (ܫܘܬܦܘܬܐ)."[49] "Then the lustful instinct of marriage (ܡܙܪܢܝܬܐ ܪܓܬܐ ܕܙܘܘܓܐ) came to exist in Adam and Eve, and, because of all their transgressions, they were married."[50] "For these [three] things happened to Adam by the counsel of sin, and on account of this these are its fruits. For when Adam listened to sin and neglected the word of his creator, [God] gave him toil, anxiety and marriage (ܥܡܠܐ ܘܪܢܝܬܐ ܘܙܘܘܓܐ). While he did not have need of these things, he had great need after he had sinned."[51]

It must be noted at this point that there might be some opposition to the kind of ascetic interpretation of Genesis 1–3 practiced by the author of the *Book of Steps*. Thus, in the fifteenth memra, he counters several arguments that could be posed as a challenge to his views. While these arguments may be considered as merely a rhetorical construction used by our author in order to expound his views, one may also recognize here some echoes of real opposition to his ideas.

One such argument in defense of sexuality as constituting an integral part of human nature belongs to the realm of anatomy—namely, the assertion that the authentic function of genital organs intended by God would be that of sexual reproduction. The answer given by our author is that these organs were originally formed exclusively for the purpose of excretion: "If you say, 'Look, the [genital] members were meant for intercourse' (ܗܐ ܗܕ̈ܡܐ ܐܬܥܒܕܘ ܗܘܘ ܐܝܟ ܕܠܗ ܠܫܘܬܦܘܬܐ), but you [really] do not desire intercourse, [you should say] that the Creator made them in order for you to urinate."[52]

48. *BoS* 15.8 (translation slightly modified).
49. *BoS* 15.2.
50. *BoS* 15.8.
51. *BoS* 20.6.
52. *BoS* 15.6.

This theoretical claim can be authenticated by the actual ascetic experience, which in this way serves as the ultimate authority, where the author's anthropological speculations find their basis and corroboration: "When you became a celibate without lust (ܩܕܝܫܐ ܕܠܐ ܪܓܬܐ) you will see that these members are for urinating and not for intercourse."[53]

Another more serious challenge to the author's view of angelic humanity is the argument based on the fact of humanity's division into two sexes. The central question in this respect is why God created human beings as male and female:

If you say, "Why did he make male and female?"—Go and blame him because he created male and female, and he shall say to you: "It would do no harm to you, if you did not desire to become like the beasts or like the angels." "But the man watched the animals and desired to become like them, and hated the celibacy of the angels—that is, in the hope that he will become greater than the angels and be like their Lord."[54]

Unfortunately, the syntax of this passage is not immediately clear, possibly due to textual corruption,[55] which makes it difficult to fully grasp the logic of the author's answer. It seems to imply that the sexual difference would play no role in human life if Adam and his wife had not fallen from the state of primeval perfection by choosing to imitate animals instead of angels.[56]

Origins of Marriage: Encratite Legacy

As has been mentioned previously, in Christian tradition the idea that sexuality is an extraneous and thus expendable component of human nature could be traced back to Jesus's words about resurrected humanity. This notion has been taken for granted by the majority of fourth-century Syriac-speaking writers. Thus Aphrahat, in one of his references to the world-to-come, states, "In that age there [will be] no female sex, just as also in heaven there is no female sex nor childbearing, nor use of sexual desire (ܢܩܒܘܬܐ ܘܡܘܠܕܐ ܐܘ ܚܘܫܚܐ ܕܪܓܬܐ)."[57] In

53. *BoS* 15.7.

54. *BoS* 15.7 (modified).

55. It might be that the double appearance of the same phrase (ܕܥܠ ܡܛܠ ܥܒܕ ܕܟܪܐ ܘܢܩܒܬܐ) is a result of dittography.

56. For more on this important motif, see further.

57. Aphrahat, *Demonstration* XXII.13, in *Aphraatis Sapientis Persae Demonstrationes,* edited by Jean Parisot, Patrologia Syriaca 1.1 (Paris: Firmin-Didot, 1894), 1017; Murray, *Symbols*, 304.

a similar way, Ephrem, while describing the eschatological paradise, stresses the absence of sexual desire (ܪܓܬܐ) there.[58]

While searching for the ultimate origins of this notion in Syriac Christianity, one may turn to the early Jewish traditions in addition to the canonical texts. One of its earliest attestations comes from the Syriac *Apocalypse of Baruch,* a Jewish pseudepigraphical text composed originally in Greek and translated quite early into Syriac. In this work sexual instinct is listed alongside the rest of the negative aspects of human existence that began to have an effect on the human race after Adam's transgression: "For when he (i.e., Adam) transgressed, untimely death came into being, mourning was mentioned, affliction was prepared, illness was created, labor accomplished, pride began to come into existence, the realm of death began to ask to be renewed with blood, the conception of children came about (ܘܢܣܒܐ ܕܒܢ̈ܝܐ ܗܘܬ), the passion of the parents was produced (ܘܪܬܚܐ ܕܐܒܗ̈ܐ ܐܬܬܥܒܕ), the loftiness of men was humiliated, and goodness vanished."[59]

There exists a virtual scholarly consensus that the phrase "ܪܬܚܐ ܕܐܒܗ̈ܐ" should be translated as "the passion of the parents," and what is meant here is most probably sexual desire.[60] However, another sentence, "ܘܢܣܒܐ ܕܒܢ̈ܝܐ ܗܘܬ," is more problematic. While Albertus F. J. Klijn has translated it as "the conception of children came about," thus making it agree logically with the following phrase, his understanding of the noun "ܢܣܒܐ" as "conception" does not have a firm lexical ground. As has been recently argued by Eugen J. Pentiuc, this noun should be translated as "taking," and it does not refer to sexuality at all.[61] Accordingly, one can understand the sentence as referring to such an affliction as the untimely death of children. Additional support for Pentiuc's proposal comes from the Arabic version of 2 Baruch, where the problematic Syriac sentence is translated

58. *De Parad.* XIV.11, in *Des heiligen Ephraem des Syrers Hymnen de Paradiso und Contra Julianum,* edited by Edmund Beck, Corpus Scriptorum Christianorum Orientalium 175, 176 (Louvain: Peeters, 1957).

59. 2 Bar 56.6, in *The Old Testament in Syriac according to the Peshitta Version,* part 4, fasc. 3, *Apocalypse of Baruch; 4 Esdras,* edited by Sven Dedering and Raphael J. Bidawid, 32 (Leiden: E. J. Brill, 1973); Albertus F. J. Klijn, trans., "2 (Syriac Apocalypse of) Baruch," in *The Old Testament Pseudepigrapha,* edited by James H. Charlesworth, 1:641 (New York: Doubleday, 1983, 1985).

60. See John R. Levison, *Portraits of Adam in Early Judaism: From Sirach to 2 Baruch, Journal for the Study of the Pseudepigrapha,* Supplement Series 1 (Sheffield: JSOT Press, 1988), 141.

61. See Eugen J. Pentiuc, "'Renewed by Blood': Sheol's Quest in 2 Baruch 56.6," *Revue Biblique* 114, no. 4 (2007): 558–59.

as "and the offspring were taken away" (وقبض الذرية).[62] In addition, the notion of infant mortality as one of the calamities that were brought upon the world as a result of Adam's sin is attested in writings of several Syriac authors.[63]

All this demonstrates that at the time of the *Book of Steps'* composition, the general notion of sexuality and procreation being counted among those negative aspects of human existence in the fallen world order that shall be eliminated from the world-to-come enjoyed wide popularity among the Syriac-speaking Christians. And it is against this background, shared by our author and his contemporaries, that one can better appreciate his originality as a thinker and his contribution to the development of anthropological and theological discourse in Syria-Mesopotamia.

In order to situate the *Book of Steps* adequately in the theological landscape of fourth-century Syriac Christianity, particular attention should be paid to the way its author understands the fall, since it has a direct bearing on his views about the origins of sexuality and marriage. In that respect, most serious attention should be given to a crucial aspect of his anthropological thought: the extraordinary importance ascribed by him to the idea of Satan as the principal instigator of sexual desire. According to the *Book of Steps,* the whole idea of sexual procreation is nothing but a trap that was laid by Satan in order to bring down Adam and Eve. For example, after Adam's transgression God turns to him with the words, "Look, the marriage (ܙܘܘܓܐ) that you sought through the advice of the evil one (ܒܝܫܐ) has been given to you."[64] This idea is repeated more than a few times throughout the book: "They had not had any desire of the instinct for [sexual] union (ܡܪܓܪܓܬܐ ܕܙܘܓܬܐ) until they had been persuaded by the evil one to become earthly people and to acquire earthly toil and wealth."[65] "It was then that carnal desire (ܡܪܓܪܓܬܐ ܕܙܘܓܬܐ) came to exist in him, for Adam desired intercourse (ܫܘܬܦܘܬܐ) as a result of the teaching of the evil one."[66]

One of the results of Adam's transgression was that he "became an earthly being" (ܗܘܐ ܐܪܥܢܐ).[67] It is important to note here that this notion in the *Book*

62. Fred Leemhuis, Albertus F. J. Klijn, and Geert J. van Gelder, eds., *The Arabic Text of the Apocalypse of Baruch: Edited and Translated with a Parallel Translation of the Syriac Text* (Leiden: E. J. Brill, 1986), 88.

63. Aphrahat, *Demonstration* VI.6: ܥܘܠܠ̈ܐ ܒܢ̈ܝ ܝܘܡܐ ܚܢܢܐ ܘܡܫܡܫܢܐ ܠܡܘܬܐ, in *Aphraatis Sapientis,* col. 265, edited by Parisot; cf. also Ephrem, *In Gen.* II.30.2 (on Gen 3:16); *De Parad.* VII.22.

64. *BoS* 26.2.

65. *BoS* 15.2.

66. *BoS* 15.1.

67. *BoS* 26.4.

of Steps is not identical with the doctrine of "double creation," espoused by some Christian theologians influenced by Platonism, who claimed that Adam was created first as a purely spiritual being, and that only after the fall had he acquired a material body.[68] According to the *Book of Steps,* Adam and Eve do have material bodies even before their transgression, which is understood primarily as the act of turning their minds from the contemplation of heavenly realms to earthly concerns.[69]

The strong connection between Satan and the origins of human sexuality that we observe in the *Book of Steps* is not an invention of its author, but seems to be inherited by him from his predecessors. There is enough evidence that demonstrates deep roots of this notion in the early Syrian Christian tradition, especially in its Encratite segment.

The earliest proponent of this idea in Syria seems to be Saturninus (or Satornil), an early second-century Gnostic teacher, whose views are known to us only from the later reports of heresiologists.[70] Among other things, it is reported that he taught that marriage and procreation come from Satan.[71] Another second-century Syrian teacher, Tatian, while interpreting Paul in one of his lost works, *On Perfection according to the Savior,* claims that even those who practice intercourse within lawful marriage "would serve license and fornication and the devil."[72] Later, in the third century, this idea appears in the *Acts of Thomas,* where the apostle laments the destructive effects of sexual desire and calls it "the work of the serpent" (Gr. ἔργον ὄφεως).[73]

68. On this concept, see the articles in *La "doppia creazione" dell'uomo negli Alessandrini, nei Cappadoci e nella gnosi,* edited by Ugo Bianchi, Nuovi Saggi 70 (Roma: Ateneo and Bizzarri, 1978).

69. Cf. *BoS* 21.2, 8, 10.

70. See on Saturninus John J. Gunther, "Syrian Christian Dualism," *Vigiliae Christianae* 25, no. 2 (1971): 81–93.

71. Irenaeus, *Adv. haer.* I.24.2: τὸ δὲ γαμεῖν καὶ γεννᾶν ἀπὸ τοῦ Σατανᾶ φησιν εἶναι, in *Irénée de Lyon: Contre les hérésies; Livre I,* edited by Adelin Rousseau and Louis Doutreleau, 2:325, Sources Chrétiennes 253–64 (Paris: Éditions du Cerf, 1979); cf. also Hippolytus, *Adv. haer.* VII.28.7; Epiphanius, *Panar.* I.23.2. This notion reappears in some later Gnostic systems, as well. Thus, according to such a popular Gnostic work as the *Apocryphon of John,* it was the serpent or the demonic cosmic ruler Yaldabaoth who planted sexual desire in Adam and Eve; cf. NHC II 21:12–15; BG 58:4–7 or NHC II 24:26–29; BG 63:2–9 respectively.

72. Clement of Alexandria, *Strom.* III.81.1–2, in *Tatian: Oratio ad Graecos and Fragments,* edited by Molly Whittaker, 80–81 (Oxford: Clarendon Press, 1982). It is unclear whether Tatian held the institution of marriage itself to be invented by Satan. This is, however, the way he was understood by Clement; cf. *Strom.* III.80.3–81.1.

73. *Acts of Thomas* §52, in *Acta Thomae: Graece partim cum novis codicibus contulit partim primus*

Ideas of this sort retained their attractiveness even later, during the fourth and fifth centuries, when orthodoxy had begun to hold sway in the region. Thus, in addition to our author, one can mention the anonymous Syriac *Commentary on Job,* attributed incorrectly to John of Apamea. According to this work, translated from Greek into Syriac during the fifth century, it was Satan "who reported Adam's transgression to this world and introduced the sensual intercourse of men and women" (ܘܗܘܝ ܫܘܬܦܘܬܐ ܡܪܓܫܬܐ ܕܓܒܪ̈ܐ ܘܢܩ̈ܒܬܐ).[74]

The idea of Satan as the instigator of sexual desire was not at all foreign to the Jewish exegetes during late antiquity. Traditions of this kind are found in the Babylonian Talmud, where we find a claim that only the giving of Torah at Mount Sinai freed Jews from being enslaved to the power of lust that was implanted into human nature by Satan.[75] There is no place to discuss it here, but one might wonder how this parallelism might be explained in light of the growing awareness among scholars about the importance of Syriac Christianity for an adequate understanding of sociocultural background of the Talmud of Babylonia.[76]

It is now that we come to one of the most significant aspects of how the author of the *Book of Steps* understood the fall—namely, his depiction of this "event" as the process of humanity's degradation from the sexless quasi-angelic state to the sexualized animal-like one. According to his view, it was one of the most dramatic results of Satan's trickery that instead of reproducing in an asexual, spiritual way, the first couple fell into the animal-like mode of procreation. The stratagem used by the envy-driven Satan in order to bring down Adam was "to make him fall from the sanctity of the angels and imitate wild beasts."[77] There are several references to Adam's fall in the *Book of Steps,* where

edidit, edited by Max Bonnet, 37, Latine recensuit, Supplementum Codicis Apocryphi 1 (Leipzig: H. Mendelssohn, 1883). This phrase is absent from the Syriac version of the Acts.

74. 6 [Syr.], 10 [tr.], in "An Ascetic Reading of the Book of Job: Fragments from a Syriac Commentary Attributed to John the Solitary; Ms. London, British Library, Add.18814, f. 91r–95r," by Lucas Van Rompay, *Le Muséon* 119, no. 1–2 (2006): 1–24.

75. See *b.Shabbath* 146a; *b.Yebamoth* 103b, for the story about Satan infecting Eve, and through her the whole human race, with "lust" (Aram. זוהמא).

76. Cf. the recent case studies by Shlomo Naeh, "Freedom and Celibacy: A Talmudic Variation on Tales of Temptation and Fall in Genesis and Its Syrian Background," in *The Book of Genesis in Jewish and Oriental Christian Interpretation,* edited by Judith Frishman and Lucas van Rompay, 73–89, Traditio Exegetica Graeca 5 (Louvain: Peeters, 1997); Burton L. Visotzky, "Three Syriac Cruxes," *Journal of Jewish Studies* 42, no. 2 (1991): 167–75.

77. *BoS* 15.1.

the motif of *imitatio animalis* understood primarily as sexual imitation plays the crucial role:

There did not exist in them any lust to desire intercourse (ܪܓܬܐ ܕܢܪܓܘܢ ܠܡܫܘܬܦܘܬܐ), but they greatly desired it because the evil one had directed their gaze [to it] through cattle (ܐܚܝܪ ܐܢܘܢ ܒܝܕ ܒܥܝܪܐ). That is why David said, "A person who has not taken notice of his honor," because he was holy like the angels and peaceful like the heavenly ones. But he saw an animal (ܚܙܐ ܚܝܘܬܐ) and wished to imitate it in the marriage of intercourse (ܙܘܘܓܐ ܕܡܫܘܬܦܘܬܐ).[78]

"Adam wanted to rebel and consented to imitate the intercourse of animals (ܡܫܘܬܦܘܬܐ ܕܚܝ̈ܘܬܐ).[79]" "They were separated from the angels and the great hosts. . . . They went on to desire [conjugal] union (ܠܡܪܓܓ ܠܡܫܘܬܦܘܬܐ) and to give birth like the animals (ܠܡܐܠܕ ܐܝܟ ܚܝ̈ܘܬܐ)."[80]

While thinking about the origins of this peculiar understanding of the fall, one might recall the exegetical motif based on Genesis 2:19–20 about Adam learning his need for a sexual partner from the animals, which is known to us from the Jewish tradition.[81] However one may assess this parallel, it is more important that we do find a similar idea in some early Christian circles. Thus a scenario of the fall corresponding very closely to that of the *Book of Steps* appears in the third book of Clement of Alexandria's *Stromata,* devoted mainly to anti-Encratite polemic and defense of marriage. At one point, in the course of developing his argument against Cassian, Marcion, and Valentine, for whom "humanity became like cattle in coming to sexual intercourse,"[82] Clement offers the following summary of his opponents' views on the origins of sexuality: "That the snake took the practice of sexual union from the irrational animals, and prevailed on Adam to come to an agreement on sexual intercourse with Eve, and that the first created humans did not naturally prac-

78. *BoS* 15.2 (slightly modified), citing Psalms 49:12.

79. *BoS* 15.6.

80. *BoS* 21.10.

81. Cf. Josephus, *Ant.* I.35; in its most explicit form this tradition is attested in a medieval composition, *Midrash ha-Gadol* on Gen 2:20; see on this Gary A. Anderson, "The Garden of Eden and Sexuality in Early Judaism," in *People of the Body: Jews and Judaism from an Embodied Perspective,* edited by Howard Eilberg-Schwartz, 52 (Albany: State University of New York Press, 1992).

82. *Strom.* III.102.3, in *Clement of Alexandria: Stromateis; Books One to Three,* translated by J. Ferguson, 321, The Fathers of the Church: A New Translation 85 (Washington, D.C.: The Catholic University of America Press, 1991). In what concerns the Valentinian tradition, cf. the *Gospel of Philip* (NHC II 71:22–28), where it is said about Adam that he had eaten from "the animal tree."

tice this."[83] The striking similarity between this description of the fall and the passages from the *Book of Steps* quoted above in assigning such an important role to the sexually understood motif of *imitatio animalis* betrays indebtedness of our author to the Encratite theological matrix.

For the author of the *Book of Steps,* the whole drama of human existence unfolds in the context of a sharp opposition between the angelic and animal modes of being. This anthropological position, where animals play an extremely important role as the negative point of reference, might be considered as another feature that brings our author close to the Encratite segment of Early Syrian Christianity.[84] For example, we know that such a prominent representative of this "movement" as Tatian had composed a whole treatise, *On animals,* now unfortunately lost, where he followed a similar line of thought. As Tatian himself reports, in this work he expounded his anthropological ideas, while using as a conceptual framework the radical opposition between "one who acts like animals" and "one who has advanced far beyond his humanity towards God himself."[85] A fundamental characteristic of this anthropological scheme that connects it with the *Book of Steps* is the absence of "middle ground," since both of them presuppose only the two radically opposite possibilities for human condition—animal-like and God- or angel-like, paying no attention to human nature as *sui generis.*

In this respect it is also noteworthy that through the whole of his work, the author of the *Book of Steps* does not refer even once to such a cornerstone of biblical anthropology as the idea of humans having been created in God's image. Surprisingly, notwithstanding all his anthropological concern, he never quotes those scriptural verses where this notion appears.[86] In fact he verges on the brink of endorsing an alternative opinion—namely, that man was created in "the image of angels." Thus in one instance he presents God as telling Adam after the fall that "you were created like watchers (ܒܪܝܐ ܗܘܝܬ ܐܝܟ ܥܝܪ̈ܐ)."[87] In an-

83. *Strom.* III.102.4, in *Clement of Alexandria,* trans. Ferguson, 321.

84. On some developments of this theme in Early Christianity, see Ingvild S. Gilhus, *Animals, Gods and Humans: Changing Attitudes to Animals in Greek, Roman and Early Christian Ideas* (London: Routledge, 2006), 205–26. I leave aside an intriguing question of whether the well-attested practice of vegetarianism among the Encratites might be rooted in the notion of *imitatio Dei* or *imitatio angelorum,* as opposed to *imitatio animalis.*

85. Tatian, *Or.* 15, in Whittaker, *Tatian,* 31.

86. Gen 1:26–27, 5:1, 9:6.

87. *BoS* 26.1.

other place it is said about Adam that he fell short of "the holiness in which he was created in the image of angels (ܕܐܝܟ ܕܕܡܘܬܐ ܕܡ̈ܠܐܟܐ ܒܪܐ ܗܘܐ).[88]" These formulations of angelocentric anthropology set our author apart from the mainstream Christian speculations on the meaning of the scriptural notion of *imago Dei,* since they seem to imply not just the kind of functional resemblance between humans and angels that we have already seen in some of his speculations on the first humans, but their ontological sameness. Yet the author of the *Book of Steps* was not the only ancient reader of scripture who understood Adam's original state in this way. Thus one comes across it in Rabbinic literature, where one of the rabbis interprets God's words "like one of us" of Genesis 3:22 as referring to "the ministering angels."[89] Similar images appear also in ancient Christian writings. In the Gnostic *Apocalypse of Adam,* the first humans "resembled the great eternal angels."[90] In the Coptic version of the *Apocalypse of Paul* the apostle during his heavenly journey meets Adam, represented as an "angel who was taller than they all, and who was exceedingly fair to behold."[91] That this idea enjoyed certain popularity among Christians even after the time of the *Book of Steps* testifies of Severus of Antioch, who in one of his pastoral letters refutes opinions of certain Alexander, denying the future bodily resurrection on the basis of man to be "in the form of angels" (ܕܒܕܡܘܬܐ ܕܡ̈ܠܐܟܐ ܐܡܪ ܠܒܪ̈ܢܫܐ).[92]

Another remarkable aspect of our author's anthropological speculations that distinguishes him among the most of his Syriac predecessors and contemporaries is the idea that if Adam and Eve had not sinned, the human race would reproduce itself in an alternative nonsexual way. There are several instances where he speaks about this subject: "Adam did not know, however, that if they had kept the commandment they would have been fruitful and

88. *BoS* 30.24.

89. *Genesis Rabbah* 21.5; cf. also *Genesis Rabbah* 8.11. One can mention in this relation a relatively late Samaritan tradition, saying about Adam that "his form was as the form of the angels"; trans. by John Bowman,"The Malef," *Abr-Nahrain* 20 (1981–1982): 6.

90. *Apocalypse of Adam,* NHC V 5:64.14, trans. G. W. MacRae in *Nag Hammadi Codices V, 2–5 and VI with Papyrus Berolinensis 8502, 1 and 4,* edited by Douglas M. Parrott, 157, Nag Hammadi Studies 11 (Leiden: E. J. Brill, 1979).

91. Ernest A. W. Budge, *Miscellaneous Coptic Texts in the Dialect of Upper Egypt,* Coptic Texts 5 (London: British Museum, 1915), 1077.

92. Severus of Antioch, Letter no. 27, in *A Collection of Letters of Severus of Antioch from Numerous Syriac Manuscripts,* edited by Ernest W. Brooks, 1:248, Patrologia Orientalis 12.2, 14.1 (Paris: Firmin-Didot, 1915, 1920).

multiplied (ܘܦܪܝܢ ܗܘܘ ܘܣܓܝܢ), as he had begotten Eve by the word of our Lord without lust (ܐܝܟ ܕܐܦܪܝܗ̇ ܗܘܐ ܠܚܘܐ ܒܡܠܬܗ ܕܡܪܢ ܕܠܐ ܪܓܬܐ)."[93] "And so our Lord would have made for them children as he had made Eve from Adam, without lust and without marriage (ܕܠܐ ܪܓܬܐ ܘܕܠܐ ܙܘܘܓܐ), or if he had wanted he could have made children by the hairs of their heads or by their finger nails, and the people would have become the images of angels (ܐܝܟ ܕܡܘܬܐ ܕܡܠܐܟܐ)."[94] "If all people desire to become holy (ܕܢܬܩܕܫܘܢ ܟܠܗܘܢ ܒܢܝ̈ܢܫܐ), I would create for them children just as I made a daughter for Adam from himself, without marriage and without lust (ܕܠܐ ܙܘܘܓܐ ܘܕܠܐ ܪܓܬܐ)."[95] If the first couple in their rebellion against their Creator had not chosen the animal sexual mode of procreation, it would be God's responsibility to provide them with an appropriate way to multiply the human race—be it cloning or budding. The key image around which our author's thought revolves is the act of Eve's creation from Adam's side.[96] This biblical account serves as a precedent and thus the proof that asexual reproduction is in principle possible for humankind.

Our author by no means was the first Christian thinker whose thought moved in this direction. By the time of the *Book of Steps'* composition, ideas of this sort had already gained some currency among the Greek-speaking theologians. Thus Gregory of Nyssa, an older contemporary of our author, also speculates about a prelapsarian angelic mode of reproduction in his treatise *On the Creation of Man.*[97] However, it seems unlikely that the author of the *Book of Steps* was directly influenced by the Cappadocian father, since there are no recognizable traces of Greek Christian influence upon his theology. Moreover, in distinction from the *Book of Steps,* Gregory does not resort to the image of Eve's creation in his speculations about asexual reproduction. Our author thus stands out as the first proponent of this peculiar idea in the Syrian milieu.[98]

In connection with that observation, it is interesting to compare the po-

93. *BoS* 15.6. I have slightly modified the English translation, following the argument of Aleksander Kowalski, who suggested that the verb ܐܦܪܝ in the last clause of this passage bears the meaning "to generate" and not "to make fruitful"; see Kowalski, *Perfezione e giustizia,* 69n98.

94. *BoS* 21.7.

95. *BoS* 25.3.

96. Gen 2:21–23.

97. Gregory of Nyssa, *De hom. opif.* 17. For an analysis of Gregory's view of human sexuality espoused in this work, see recently John Behr, "The Rational Animal: A Rereading of Gregory of Nyssa's *De hominis opificio,*" *Journal of Early Christian Studies* 7, no. 2 (1999): 219–47.

98. Later this notion appears in the writings of Severus of Antioch; cf. his *Letter to Eupraxius the Chamberlain,* no. 65 in Brooks, *Collection of Letters,* 2:45–46.

sition of the author of the *Book of Steps* with that of Ephrem, since the latter was also aware of the biological possibility of asexual procreation and did not hesitate to use this concept on some occasions. For example, Ephrem resorts to it in his *Hymns on Nativity,* while referring to the virginal conception of Jesus: "The Spirit spoke a parable in the worm, for it reproduces without sexual union."[99] Nonetheless, he never makes use of this or similar imagery in order to refer to the prelapsarian condition of Adam and Eve. Moreover, Ephrem takes an opposite stand when, in his commentary on Genesis 3:16, he speaks positively about the possibility of sexual reproduction before the fall: "Even though she (i.e., Eve) would have given birth because she had received the blessing of birth (ܒܘܪܟܬܐ ܕܡܘܠܕܐ) along with all the animals, she would not have given birth to many, for those to whom she would have given birth would have remained immortal. She would have been preserved from the pangs of their births, from the ignominy of having to raise them, and from wailing over their deaths."[100] The difference between Ephrem and the *Book of Steps* on that issue could be accounted for by their different backgrounds. The manner in which the author of the *Book of Steps* interprets primeval history, especially the fall, is deeply rooted in the set of ideas usually associated with Encratite ideology that closely associates sexuality and marriage with Satan, while to Ephrem such a radically negative view of sexuality is rather alien.

Another aspect of the *Book of Steps* that might help us to appreciate better the peculiar character of this work's anthropological stance is the way its author conceptualizes "lust" or "desire" (Syr. ܪܓܬܐ). On the one hand, he is an heir to the Pauline notion of desire (ἐπιθυμία). Scriptural origins of this important category of Paul's ethics can be traced back to the Tenth Commandment, especially as it was interpreted by the apostle, who, by omitting the list

99. *De Nativ.* I.10, in *Ephrem the Syrian: Hymns on the Nativity, Hymns Against Julian, Hymns on Virginity and on the Symbols of the Lord,* translated by Kathleen E. McVey, The Classics of Western Spirituality (New York: Paulist Press, 1989), 64.This image is also used by Ephrem in order to illustrate the begetting of the Son by the Father in *De Fide* XLI.1.

100. *In Gen.* II.30.2, in *Sancti Ephraem Syri in Genesim et in Exodum commentarii,* edited by Raymond-Marie Tonneau, 43, Corpus Scriptorum Christianorum Orientalium 152, Syr. 71 (Louvain: L. Durbecq, 1955); Edward G. Matthews and Joseph P. Amar, trans., *St. Ephrem the Syrian: Selected Prose Works,* The Fathers of the Church 91 (Washington, D.C.: The Catholic University of America Press, 1994), 119. However, Gen 1:28 is interpreted by Ephrem in the sense that the commandment to procreate, which God gave to Adam and Eve, was meant to be fulfilled not in paradise, but on earth—that is, only after the fall; cf. *In Gen.* I.30.1–2, in Tonneau, *Sancti Ephraem,* 24.

of the objects forbidden to covet, added a new psychological dimension to the biblical ethical principle.[101] Similar to its use in Paul's writings, the use of this concept in the *Book of Steps* is not restricted only to the area of sexual mores. Thus, in memra 15.8, a distinction is made between "the lust of intercourse" (ܪܓܬܐ ܕܡܫܘܬܦܘܬܐ) and the lust to possess, derived from the prohibition of Exodus 20:17. However, our author takes the whole notion of desire in a completely new direction when he connects its origins with the malicious activity of Satan, an idea that is absent from Paul. As has been demonstrated earlier, one of the distinctive characteristics of the *Book of Steps* that brings it close to the Encratite approach to sexuality and marriage is the view that these were invented by Satan.[102] Given that, it is no wonder that in the worldview of the *Book of Steps* a married person in some fundamental sense goes against God's will, since marriage is nothing but an unwilling concession that God made grudgingly to humanity: "[If] your freedom listened to the evil one and you desired [intercourse] like Adam, your Creator will angrily (ܒܚܡܬܐ) give it to you as he had to Adam. [God] is angry (ܪܓܙ) because we renounce the celibacy of the angels (ܩܕܝܫܘܬܐ ܕܡ̈ܠܐܟܐ) and imitate the beasts. [God,] however will have compassion upon you as he had upon Adam and you will observe Uprightness and be alive while you [are involved] in intercourse (ܐܦ ܒܡܫܘܬܦܘܬܐ)."[103] "Just as when their mind loved the earth and all in it—God allowed lust to be in them (ܐܦܣ ܠܗܘܢ ܐܠܗܐ ܕܢܗܘܐ ܒܗܘܢ ܪܓܬܐ)."[104]

In another passage the author of the *Book of Steps* puts an additional stress on the irredeemable sinfulness of sexual desire, even when it is practiced within lawful marriage: "Since even the intercourse [permitted to] Uprightness is infused with evil (ܒܡܫܘܬܦܘܬܐ ܕܟܐܢܘܬܐ ܡܚܠܛܐ ܒܝܫܬܐ), as a result of this [evil], adultery and fornication have increased and something more evil than fornication—something that God hated, which makes the descendants of Adam fall even from Uprightness."[105]

It would be helpful to compare the Encratite rhetoric found in the *Book*

101. Ex 20:17; Deut 5:21; cf. Rom 7:7, 13:9. On Paul's conception of ἐπιθυμία, see Kathy L. Gaca, *The Making of Fornication: Eros, Ethics, and Political Reform in Greek Philosophy and Early Christianity,* Hellenistic Culture and Society 40 (Berkeley and Los Angeles: University of California Press, 2003),152–57.

102. In addition to the Syrian sources quoted previously, cf. Clement of Alexandria, *Strom.* III.49.1; Epiphanius, *Panar.* II.47.1.6; Theodoret, *Haer.* I.20.

103. *BoS* 15.7.

104. *BoS* 15.9.

105. *BoS* 15.9 (slightly modified).

of Steps with one of the most outstanding instances of how the notion of sexual desire in the Syrian milieu could be developed in a strikingly non-Encratite way. The example comes from the Pseudo-Clementine *Homilies,* an anonymous fourth-century work written in Greek in Syria. There, after Simon Magus inquires of Peter concerning the rationale of such negative facilities of the human soul as lust, anger and grief, the apostle answers him in the following way:

Yes, these belong to the things that are accidental (συμβαινόντων ἐστίν), not to those that always exist (οὐ τῶν ἀεὶ ὄντων), and it will be found that they now occur with advantage to the soul (χρησίμως δὲ τῇ ψυχῇ συμβαίνοντα νῦν εὑρεθήσεται). For lust (ἐπιθυμία) has, by the will of Him who created all things well, been made to arise within the living being, that, led by it to intercourse (κοινωνίαν), he may increase humanity, from a selection of which a multitude of superior beings arise who are fit for eternal life. But if it were not for lust, no one would trouble himself with intercourse with his wife; but now, for the sake of pleasure, and, as it were, gratifying himself, man carries out His will. Now, if a man uses lust for lawful marriage, he does not act impiously; but if he rushes to adultery, he acts impiously, and he is punished because he makes a bad use of a good ordinance.[106]

What draws attention in this passage is that its author, while acknowledging that lust does belong to the realm of the fallen world, maintains that it was introduced by God himself in order to guarantee the propagation of the human race. It is not by accident, perhaps, that such a relatively positive assessment of sexual desire comes from the Jewish-Christian circles with which the Pseudo-Clementine writings are usually associated.[107] It would be enough to recall here the ambivalent notion of "the evil inclination" (Heb. יצר הרע) current in Judaism, which constitutes the closest counterpart to Syr. ܪܓܬܐ. This

106. *Hom.* XIX.21.2–5, in *Die Pseudoklementinen. I: Homilien,* edited by Bernhard Rehm, 264, Die griechischen christlichen Schriftsteller der ersten drei Jahrhunderte 42 (Berlin: Akademie Verlag, 1953); Thomas Smith, Peter Peterson, and James Donaldson, trans., "The Clementine Homilies," in *Ante-Nicene Christian Library: Translations of the Writings of the Fathers down to A.D. 325,* edited by A. Roberts and J. Donaldson, 17: 306–7 (Edinburgh: T. and T. Clark, 1800); cf. also *Hom.* XX.4.4: "Wherefore God is not evil, who has rightly placed lust within man (ὁ καλῶς θεὶς τὴν ἐπιθυμίαν), that there may be a continuance of life, but they are most impious who have used the good of lust badly"; Rehm, *Pseudoklementinen,* 270; Smith, Peterson, and Donaldson, "Clementine Homilies," 315.

107. See Frederick S. Jones, "Jewish Christianity of the *Pseudo-Clementines,*" in *A Companion to Second-Century Christian "Heretics,"* edited by P. Luomanen and A. Marjanen, 315–34, Supplements to Vigiliae Christianae 76 (Leiden: E. J. Brill, 2005); Graham Stanton, "Jewish Christian Elements in the Pseudo-Clementine Writings," in *Jewish Believers in Jesus: The Early Centuries,* edited by O. Skarsaune and R. Hvalvik, 305–24 (Peabody, Mass.: Hendrickson, 2007).

anthropological concept, known to us primarily from the rabbinic literature, conveys the idea of sexuality as an indispensable part of human nature, notwithstanding all the negative effects it happens to bring about.[108]

Contrary to the position of the Pseudo-Clementines, the author of the *Book of Steps* construes sexual desire as an integral factor in the fall's unfolding, so that it provides him with a key for understanding the inner logic of this process. In a sense the acquisition of sexual desire by the first humans is a culmination of their transgression and not just one of the negative side effects whose purpose is to facilitate its negative results, as in the Pseudo-Clementines. In my opinion, this difference in understanding of the etiology of human sexuality and its role in the fall may serve as a useful criterion that allows us to distinguish between Encratite and non-Encratite anthropological approaches.

As has been already said, the negative view of matrimony found in the *Book of Steps* is deeply rooted in the author's speculations about demonic origins of this institute. In that sense it has no parallels in the writings of his predecessors Aphrahat and Ephrem, who, all their ascetic proclivities notwithstanding, would never indulge themselves in this kind of rhetoric. What is even more significant, both these Syriac writers provide us with positive references to matrimony of the kind that we never find in the *Book of Steps.* For an example, one could turn to Ephrem's *Hymns on Nativity,* where he describes the relationship between marriage and celibacy in the following way: "But intercourse is not defiled, / nor is marriage accursed (ܠܘ ܕܝܢ ܡܣܝܒܐ ܫܘܬܦܘܬܐ ܐܦ ܠܐ ܙܘܘܓܐ ܗܘ ܠܝܛܐ). // Chastity's wings are greater and lighter / Than [the wings of] marriage. // Intercourse, while pure, is lower (ܫܘܬܦܘܬܐ ܕܝ ܕܟܝܐ ܡܟܝܟܬܐ ܗܝ). / Its house of refuge is modest darkness. // Confidence belongs entirely to chastity, / which light enfolds."[109] Likewise, in his *Hymns on Virginity,* Ephrem weaves the following sophisticated imagery around oil, while asserting again the purity of marriage:

108. On this subject, see Johann Cook, "The Origin of the Tradition of the יצר הרע and יצר הטוב," *Journal for the Study of Judaism* 38, no. 1 (2007): 80–91; Daniel Boyarin, *Carnal Israel: Reading Sex in Talmudic Culture* (Berkeley and Los Angeles: University of California Press, 1993), 61–76; Pieter W. Van Der Horst, "A Note on the Evil Inclination and Sexual Desire in Talmudic Literature," in *Jews and Christians in Their Graeco-Roman Context: Selected Essays on Early Judaism, Samaritanism, Hellenism, and Christianity,* Wissenschaftliche Untersuchungen zum Neuen Testament 196 (Tübingen: Mohr Siebeck, 2006), 59–65; Ishay Rosen-Zvi, *Demonic Desires: Yetzer Hara and the Problem of Evil in Late Antiquity,* Divinations: Rereading Late Ancient Religion (Philadelphia: University of Pennsylvania Press, 2011).

109. *De Nativ.* XXVIII.3, in *Des heiligen Ephraem des Syrers Hymnen de Nativitate (Epiphania),* edited by Edmund Beck, 141, Corpus Scriptorum Christianorum Orientalium 186, Syr. 82 (Louvain: Secrétariat du Corpus SCO, 1959); trans. McVey, *Ephrem the Syrian,* 215.

Therefore, [oil is] like God, Who loves virginity: / the daughter of the symbol of the house of Michael and kinswoman of the house of Gabriel. / [Oil] consoles the barren women like Sarah and Rebekah and Rachel. / It also strengthens those who bring forth [children] / like Leah, Zilpah and Bilhah, since to [oil] marriage is pure (ܕܕܟܝܐ ܗܘ ܠܗ ܫܘܬܦܘܬܐ), / since [marriage] is a vine planted on earth, and like fruits the babes hang on it.[110]

This pro-marriage attitude of Ephrem is not surprising in view of the vehement polemic that he waged against those Christians who disparage matrimony, such as the followers of Marcion, who "despises marriage" (ܡܣܠܐ ܠܙܘܘܓܐ).[111] In contrast, it is hard to imagine the author of the *Book of Steps* using the Ephremian language of "purity" in relation to sexual activity.

Neither does one find in the *Book of Steps* such an unambiguous assertion of the goodness of marriage or acknowledgment that this institute was introduced by no one else but God himself as the following one made by Aphrahat, where marriage is listed among other "good" things created by God in the beginning:

Far be it from us that we should attribute anything shameful to marriage which God has placed in the world, for thus it is written, "God saw all that he had made, and it was very good" (Gen. 1:31). But there are some things which are better than others. God created heaven and earth, and they are very good, but the heaven is better than the earth. . . . He created marriage, worldly procreation (ܘܒܪܐ ܫܘܬܦܘܬܐ ܡܘܠܕܐ ܕܥܠܡܐ), and it is very good (ܛܒ ܫܦܝܪܐ); but virginity (ܒܬܘܠܘܬܐ) is more excellent than it.[112]

Finally, in distinction from both Aphrahat and Ephrem, our author refrains from ascribing to marriage even such iconic value as the ability to symbolize the mystery of Christ's union with the church.[113] Only faint echoes of

110. *De virgin.* V.14, in *Des heiligen Ephraem des Syrers Hymnen de Virginitate,* edited by Edmund Beck, 20, Corpus Scriptorum Christianorum Orientalium 223, Syr. 94 (Louvain: Peeters, 1962); trans. McVey, *Ephrem the Syrian,* 285; cf. also *De Parad.* VII.6–8, where both virginity and marriage find their place in Eden.

111. *De fid.* LXV.4, in *Des heiligen Ephraem des Syrers Hymnen de Fide,* edited by Beck, 201, Corpus Scriptorum Christianorum Orientalium 154, Syr. 73 (Louvain: L. Durbecq, 1955); cf. also *De virgin.* I.6, in Beck, *Hymnen de Virginitate.*

112. Aphrahat, *Demonstration* XVIII.8, in Parisot, *Aphraatis Sapientis,* 836–37; *Aphrahat and Judaism: The Christian-Jewish Argument in Fourth-Century Iran,* trans. Jacob Neusner, Studia Post-Biblica 19 (Leiden: E. J. Brill, 1971), 81.

113. First formulated by Paul (Eph 5:22–32), this notion made a deep impact on the later Christian theology of marriage. On the use of this symbolism by Syriac authors, including Ephrem and Aphrahat, see Murray, *Symbols,* 131–58.

this important ecclesiological conception could be found in the *Book of Steps,* mainly in the form of the imagery of "the bridal chamber" (ܓܢܘܢܐ). In the conceptual framework of realized eschatology typical of our author, this image indicates the state of highest closeness to God, which is the ultimate goal and reward on the road of the major commandments pursued by the Perfect.[114] Sometimes it is referred to as "the bridal chamber of glory" (ܓܢܘܢܐ ܕܫܘܒܚܐ) or "the bridal chamber of the Kingdom" (ܓܢܘܢܗ ܕܡܠܟܘܬܐ).[115] This symbolism has deep roots in Syriac Christian tradition and appears already in the *Acts of Thomas* (§124), where the corrupt and transitory marriage of this world is opposed to the "everlasting bridal chamber" (ܠܗܘ ܓܢܘܢܐ ܕܠܥܠܡ ܡܩܘܝܐ), in which believers are united with Jesus, the true bridegroom.[116] Later on this imagery is used by Aphrahat and Ephrem, as well.[117]

It should be noted, however, that in spite of all his antipathy toward the institution of marriage, our author does make an effort to distance himself from the radical anti-marriage attitudes known to us from the earlier stages of Syrian Christianity. It can be seen, for example, in the fact that he never allows himself to slip into extremely negative rhetoric of the kind found in the early Encratite tradition.

As an example of the latter's anti-marriage attitude, one might refer to Tatian, who considered marriage to be "corruption and fornication" (φθορὰν καὶ πορνείαν).[118] This language was taken to its extremity by the author of the *Acts of Thomas,* where the following repertoire of derogatory expressions is used to refer to spousal relations: "filthy intercourse" (ܫܘܬܦܘܬܐ ܕܛܢܦܬܐ),[119] "hateful inter-

114. Cf. *BoS* 19.36.

115. *BoS* 19.36, 20.6.

116. *Apocryphal Acts of the Apostles, Edited from Syriac Manuscripts in the British Museum and Other Libraries,* edited by William Wright, 1:294 (London: Williams and Norgate, 1871).

117. Cf. Aphrahat, *Demonstration* VI.1; Ephrem, *De virgin.* XXXIII.3; *De Parad.* VII.15, XIII.3, 10. For more on this subject, see Murray, *Symbols,* 131–42; Brock, "The Bridal Chamber of Light: A Distinctive Feature of the Syriac Liturgical Tradition," *The Harp* 18 (2005): 179–91.

118. Cf. Irenaeus, *Adv. haer.* I.28.1, in *Irénée de Lyon,* edited by Rousseau and Doutreleau, 2:357. A useful discussion of Tatian's views on marriage and sexuality could be found in Gaca, *Making of Fornication,* 221–46; Emily J. Hunt, *Christianity in the Second Century: The Case of Tatian* (London: Routledge, 2003), 144–75. For the sake of justice, it should be noted here that for Tatian the problem was not the institution of marriage as such, but rather sexual relations that it implied. It seems that he would hardly argue against "spiritual marriage"—that is, the kind of arrangement where the institution originally blessed by God would be purified from the satanic leaven of lust; see on this Hunt, *Christianity in the Second Century,* 154.

119. Wright, *Apocryphal Acts,* §12, 51, 88; 1:181, 220, 257.

course" (ܫܘܬܦܘܬܐ ܣܢܝܬܐ),"[120] "harlotry" (ܙܢܝܘܬܐ),[121] "corruption" (ܚܒܠܐ),[122] "unclean couch" (ܡܫܟܒܐ ܕܛܢܦܘܬܐ),[123] etc. This kind of vocabulary, characteristic of the Encratite-minded Christians, whose goal according to Giulia Sfameni Gasparro "was not so much to extol the virtues of sexual continence as to denounce the sinful nature of *gamos*,"[124] is certainly foreign to our author.

Marriage in Practice: Orthodox Mainstream

However preoccupied by the theological aspects of the origins of marriage the author of the *Book of Steps* might seem, he does not confine himself exclusively to those issues. One should remember that his work had a practical goal to address the needs of his community, especially those of its largest segment, comprised of the Upright—that is, of the married Christians.[125] Accordingly, it was important for him to present his audience with a particular vision of this social institution.

There are not many straightforwardly prescriptive attempts to regulate sexual or nuptial mores in the *Book of Steps*. In that respect our author rarely goes beyond the general rhetoric aimed against polygamy and licentiousness, as illustrated by these words of God to Adam: "Look, the marriage that you sought through the advice of the evil one has been given to you, only do not desire the wife of your neighbor and do not take two wives and do not allow your sons to commit fornication nor let your daughters to become harlots."[126]

An interesting singular matter of practical concern for our author was the manner in which the weddings were celebrated by his flock. Thus he promotes the ideals of modesty and temperance by recommending to the Upright that

120. Wright, *Apocryphal Acts*, §84; 1:254.

121. Wright, *Apocryphal Acts*, §13; 1:182.

122. Wright, *Apocryphal Acts*, §124 ,103; 1:270, 294.

123. Wight, *Apocryphal Acts*, §84; 1:254.

124. Giulia Sfameni Gasparro, "Asceticism and Antropology: *Enkrateia* and 'Double Creation' in Early Christianity," in *Asceticism*, edited by V. L. Wimbush and R. Valantasis, 128 (Oxford: Oxford University Press, 1995).

125. On this aspect of the *Book of Steps*, see Kitchen, "The Gattung of the *Liber Graduum:* Implications for a Sociology of Asceticism," in *IV Symposium Syriacum 1984*, edited by Han J. W. Drijvers, et al, 174–82, Orientalia Christiana Analecta 229 (Rome: Pontificium Institutum Studiorum Orientalium, 1987).

126. *BoS* 26.2; cf. also *BoS* 13.6 (monogamy) and 14.1 (prohibition of adultery).

they should take "[only] one wife without songs, foul language, and commotion."[127] Such pastoral unease about nuptial customs was shared by other church leaders contemporary with him, as, for example, by John Chrysostom, who attempted to reform the wedding habits of his Antiochene parishioners along similar lines.[128]

One might wonder how these projects of teetotaling wedding celebrations might have been met by their potential addressees. Despite the understandable difficulties posed to historical questions of this sort by the limited character of our data, there is some evidence that allows us to suggest that the most likely reaction to this kind of pastoral exhortation was one of resistance. For instance, we have a story about Rabban Bar ʿIdtā, a sixth-century East-Syrian monastic leader, who, while being in the district of Margha, had tried to prevent the supposedly pagan custom of singing at a wedding. He intended to replace it with the singing of appropriate Christian texts by the clergy. However, as the story tells us, the groom's family refused to give up the age-old custom, in spite of all the Rabban's efforts.[129]

Another, more efficient strategy used by the author of the *Book of Steps* to promote his vision of Christian marriage is an indirect one, which makes creative use of biblical material. For this he turns to the figures of the Old Testament patriarchs, such as Abraham, Isaac, Job, and Enoch. Their principal purpose is to serve as role models for the Upright. In this quality they supply our author with an essential hermeneutical tool that allows him to find a positive meaning for marriage by anchoring this institution firmly in the framework of God's providential care for humanity. In order to do that it is important for him to dispel any doubt that might be raised about whether their lifestyle was approved by God: "If anyone should ask, 'So those prophets and righteous people who lived before the advent of our Lord, who were either married or had possessions, were they under the curse (ܬܚܝܬ ܠܘܛܬܐ)?' [Then he should know that] one should not say anything against them; they did as the Lord had told them during their whole lives."[130]

127. *BoS* 10.3.

128. See *Hom. in Gen.* XLVIII.30. On this aspect of Chrysostom's pastoral care, see Brown, *Body and Society,* 313–14.

129. See Budge, ed., trans. *The Histories of Rabban Hôrmîzd the Persian and Rabban Bar-ʿIdtâ,* 1:178–79 [Syr.], 2.1: 271–73 (London: Luzac, 1902).

130. *BoS* 28.11.

The married way of life led by the forefathers was regarded by our author as first and foremost grounded in a conscious act of obedience to the will of God, who deliberately held them back from the way of perfection in order to offer a paradigm of virtuous behavior for those Christians who currently chose the way of uprightness: "But all whom the Lord held back from renunciation (ܣܘܪܩܐ) and from physical celibacy (ܩܕܝܫܘܬܐ ܕܦܓܪܐ) were to become an example to all who are married in this world, so that they might live like them."[131] Abraham and Sarah are chosen as a most suitable example of the ideal marriage, where sexual desire is controlled in complete obedience to God's will: "Consider Abraham and Sarah. After they had ceased carnal intercourse and their bodies were dead to desire (ܡܢ ܕܒܛܠܘ ܡܢ ܫܘܬܦܘܬܐ ܘܡܝܬܘ ܦܓܪܝܗܘܢ ܡܢ ܪܓܬܐ), they obeyed the word of God and returned to having intercourse. In the same way, if God had told Abraham when he was young that he should keep himself holy from his wife (ܕܢܬܩܕܫ ܡܢ ܐܢܬܬܗ), he would have kept himself holy."[132] This description of the patriarchs' compliance with God's will in the matters of reproduction reminds one of the ideal of marriage found in the works of Clement of Alexandria, where sexual desire is not only subordinated to reason, but eliminated entirely.[133]

On the path of setting Old Testament figures as paradigms for his audience, our author faces a particular exegetical challenge: the biblical stories about the doubtful behavior of Abraham and Isaac toward their wives when the patriarchs tried to pass them off as their sisters for the sake of personal safety while sojourning among the strangers.[134] He solves the problem by interpreting this behavior as stemming from the forefathers' peacefulness and readiness to give up their wives in order not to avoid conflict with other people, and sets it as an example of reliance on God's help only for the Upright.[135]

One might recognize in this defense of the patriarchs residual traces of anti-Marcionite polemic in the *Book of Steps.* Marcion, a second-century

131. *BoS* 9.19.

132. *BoS* 28.11.

133. Cf. *Strom.* III, 57–58; see on this Elaine H. Pagels, "Adam and Eve, Christ and the Church: A Survey of Second Century Controversies Concerning Marriage," in *The New Testament and Gnosis: Essays in Honour of Robert McL. Wilson,* edited by A. H. B. Logan and A. J. M. Wedderburn, 172–73 (Edinburgh: T. and T. Clark, 1983).

134. Gen 12:11–20, 26:6–11.

135. *BoS* 15.9; cf. also *BoS* 9.8.

Christian teacher, saw the law as opposed to the gospel and attributed the difference to different deities. In his system the righteous figures of the Old Testament were fulfilling not the will of the highest God, who sent Jesus, but the will of the inferior deity, and thus are damned. Marcion's treatment of Abraham is of particular relevance for us. According to Irenaeus's report Marcion considered him to be cursed and, as a consequence, eliminated all positive references to this biblical figure from his version of the New Testament.[136] It is noteworthy that in memra 28.11, after making a general statement about the patriarchs' pious way of life, our author uses Abraham as an illustration of his thesis about their obedience to God and freedom from curse. We know that in Syria Marcionism enjoyed special popularity and was perceived as a serious rival by the emerging orthodoxy, whose representatives waged fierce polemic against it.[137] In fact, in the Syrian countryside, this movement survived well into the fifth century.[138] It seems reasonable to take this particular background into consideration for a better understanding of the context in which our author's view of the Old Testament develops.

The author of the *Book of Steps* also makes an effort to win at least some of the Old Testament characters who were married to his ascetic cause by laying stress on their readiness to leave the way of uprightness for that of perfection, including the embracement of celibacy. For example, he chooses for that purpose the figure of Enoch. According to our author, the ideal choice for an Upright, who has already fulfilled the duty of procreation and is in his middle years, would be to renounce worldly possessions, accept celibacy, and become holy "like Enoch, who after he had begotten Methuselah, became holy (ܐܬܩܕܫ) and did not taste death."[139]

136. On the curse of Abraham, cf. Irenaeus, *Adv. haer.* I.27.3; IV.8.1. On Marcion's treatment of the New Testament passages relating to Abraham, see John J. Clabeaux, "Abraham in Marcion's Gospel and Epistles: Marcion and the Jews," in *When Judaism and Christianity Began: Essays in Memory of Anthony J. Saldarini,* edited by A. J. Avery-Peck, D. J. Harrington, and J. Neusner, 69–92, vol. 1, *Christianity in the Beginning,* Supplements to the Journal for the Study of Judaism 85 (Leiden: E. J. Brill, 2004).

137. On Marcionism in Syria, see David Bundy, "Marcion and the Marcionites in Early Syriac Apologetics," *Le Muséon* 101, nos. 1 and 2 (1988): 21–32; Han J. W. Drijvers, "Marcionism in Syria: Principles, Problem, Polemics," *The Second Century* 6, no. 3 (1987–88): 153–72; Jean-Maurice Fiey, "Les Marcionites dans les textes historiques de l'Église de Perse," *Le Muséon* 83, nos. 1 and 2 (1970): 183–88.

138. Cf. Theodoret's account of his crusade against Marcionite villages in the vicinity of Cyrrhus in *Hist. relig.* 21.15–21, 22.1.

139. *BoS* 13.4.

The connection between the virginity of Enoch and his ascent to heaven stands in close parallel with the traditions about virginity of Elijah that appear in the writings of several Syriac fathers.[140] In both these instances we see at work an exegetical strategy often employed by ascetical readers of the Old Testament, when they come across certain characters whose "wives" are not explicitly mentioned in the text. Its main goal is to retrieve such biblical figures from Hebrew "carnality" by representing them as exemplars of Christian asceticism.[141]

This tradition about Enoch, as well as the story about Abraham and Sarah quoted previously, promotes a particular scenario of marriage—the one where sexuality is totally subjugated to the goal of reproduction and whose logical culmination is the acceptance of celibacy. Such a vision of ideal marriage had currency in various ascetic circles during late antiquity. As an example of a similar approach, one can mention the *History of the Rechabites,* also known as the *Journey of Zosimos,* an anonymous composition from the fourth century, written originally in Greek and translated into, among other languages, Syriac.[142] In this work an ideal ascetic community is described as where the naked "Blessed Ones" live a simple life in constant prayer and in harmonious communion with angels. Among other things, its author presents us with a remarkable description of sinless marriage that takes place between those who withdraw from sexual activity as soon as they have fulfilled the duty of procreation: "Nor are there any of us taking wives for themselves, (except) until they produce two children. And after they produced two children, they separate from each other and are in chastity (ἐν ἁγνείᾳ), not knowing that they were once in the intimacy of marriage (ἐν συνηθείᾳ τοῦ γάμου); but as if from the beginning being in virginity (ἐν τῇ παρθενίᾳ)."[143]

140. Cf. Aphrahat, *Demonstration* VI.1; Ephrem, *De Parad.* VI.24. Although Elijah does figure in the *Book of Steps* (*BoS* 9.9) as the one who "pursued Perfection," there is no explicit mention of his virginity. On Elijah in Syriac tradition, see Craig E. Morrison, "The Recasting of Elijah in Aphrahat's VI Demonstration," *The Harp* 20 (2006): 325–40.

141. See on this Clark, *Reading Renunciation,* 106–7.

142. A developed argument in favor of Christian provenance for this work has been recently made by Ronit Nikolsky, *The Provenance of "The Journey of Zosimos"* (PhD diss., The Hebrew University of Jerusalem, 2003) [in Hebrew], who suggested that it was composed during the fourth century in monastic circles of Byzantine Palestine.

143. *History of the Rechabites* 11.6–8, in *History of the Rechabites,* edited and translated by John H. Charlesworth, vol. 1, *The Greek Recension,* 66–67, SBL Texts and Translations 17 (Chico: Scholars Press, 1982).

One might still recognize in these imaginary attempts to infuse the established social custom of matrimony with a new ascetic flavor distant reverberations of the institution of "spiritual marriage," an archaic practice that on Syrian soil survived until as late as the last quarter of the fourth century.[144] In this direction points the use of the root *qdš,* "to make holy" or "to separate," by the author of the *Book of Steps* in order to describe Abraham's possible and Enoch's actual ascetic behavior. Several derivatives of this root (ܩܕܝܫܘܬܐ, ܩܕܝܫܐ) are attested through a variety of early Syriac writings as referring to nonvirginal celibacy of this sort.[145]

Still, all the positive references to the God-pleasing way of life led by the married forefathers notwithstanding, the author of the *Book of Steps* does not forget to establish the hierarchical difference between them and the New Testament saints. He does that while measuring one against another the two major segments within his community, for whom these scriptural figures serve as respective role models—the Upright and the Perfect. Since the former group is relegated to a position of inferiority vis-à-vis the latter, the corresponding relationship of subordination is assigned to the Old Testament patriarchs, who are thus much inferior by their rank than the apostles and martyrs: "There are many who have wives, are involved in business, and [possess] male and female servants like Abraham and Job. The apostle did not say that they do not gain a thing, but that they are much inferior to the martyrs who emptied themselves and are humble like our Lord, resembling the apostles and Stephen."[146] In another place our author describes hierarchical relationships between the married and celibate believers in a more nuanced and dynamical way, putting a particular stress on the importance of the spiritual dimension for both of these vocations. However, even here he remains faithful to the ascetic scale of values and gives preference to celibacy:

144. Cf. the story about an ascetic couple living in this kind of arrangement told by Jerome, who met them during his stay in the Syrian desert of Chalcis; *Vita Malchi* 2; *Jérôme: Trois vies de moines: Paul, Malchus, Hilarion,* edited by Pierre Leclerc and Edgardo M. Morales, 184–88, Sources chrétiennes 508 (Paris: Cerf, 2007). For general information on this practice in ancient Christianity, see Hans Achelis, *Virgines subintroductae: Ein Beitrag zum VII. Kapital des 1. Korintherbriefs* (Leipzig: J. C. Hinrichs, 1902).

145. See Brock, "Early Syrian Asceticism," *Numen* 20 (1973): 10–11; Naomi Koltun-Fromm, Yokes of the Holy-Ones: The Embodiment of a Christian Vocation," *Harvard Theological Review* 94, no. 2 (2001): 211–15.

146. *BoS* 8.4.

If marriage sanctifies (ܐܢ ܡܩܕܫ ܙܘܘܓܐ) and lowers itself more than physical virginity (ܒܬܘܠܘܬܐ ܕܦܓܪܐ), it will be superior to it, but if it is only a little ahead of [virginity] in lowliness, it will [only] be equal to it (ܙܥܘܪ ܠܗ ܡܢܗ ܘܐܢܗܘ ܡܟܝܟ ܩܕܡ ܠܗ ܒܡܘܟܟܐ ܗܘܐ ܐܫܘܝܗ). If, however, physical virginity becomes spiritual (ܒܬܘܠܘܬܐ ܕܦܓܪܐ ܠܗܘܐ ܪܘܚܢܝ) and empties and lowers itself more than everything, there is nothing surpassing it among people. Yet, marriage, which, like it, has lowered and sanctified itself spiritually, can reach it while still being inferior to it (ܐܬܐ ܠܘܬܗ ܟܕ ܒܨܝܪ ܡܢܗ).[147]

It should be emphasized at this point that the modern notion of "lay spirituality" was alien to the worldview of the *Book of Steps.* First of all, our author readily endorses Paul's view of marriage to be nothing more than a palliative measure meant to protect from the danger posed by sexual desire those believers who are not able to live up to the highest standards of Christian calling: "Because [Paul] knows that the person who builds up his body and is void of spiritual work is overcome by desires; it is better for him to marry and not be licentious and corrupt."[148] In that sense his argumentation is similar to that found in the Syriac *Didascalia* (chap. XXII), with its advice to parents to get their children married in order to keep them from fornication, as well as to that of the author of the Pseudo-Clementine *Homilies* (III.68), who admonishes his audience to inculcate marriage upon both the young and advanced in years in order to protect them and the whole community from the dangers of sexual misbehavior.

Furthermore, according to the *Book of Steps,* the married state is incompatible with a full-fledged spiritual life, and the renunciation of marriage is a necessary condition for the gifts of the Holy Spirit conferred upon every Christian in baptism to be actualized:

If there is a person who is in the conjugal state (ܒܙܘܘܓܐ) while he is in the Uprightness of the Upright, a pledge of the Holy Spirit (ܪܗܒܘܢܐ ܕܪܘܚܐ ܕܩܘܕܫܐ) exists in him. . . . If he has elevated himself above marriage, he will elevate himself above intercourse to the way of life of the apostles, [then] quickly he will be perfected and receive the Paraclete (ܦܪܩܠܛܐ) and hear the voice of God.[149]

The Upright are not able to do all the will of our Lord, unless they come to holiness (ܩܕܝܫܘܬܐ) and empty themselves; but the Perfect do these things and live with our Lord.[150]

147. *BoS* 15.19.
148. *BoS* 19.15; cf. 1 Cor 7:9, 36.
149. *BoS* 15.19. On the "pledge of Spirit," see also *BoS* 1.3, 28.2; cf. Acts 2:38, 10:45.
150. *BoS* 14.2; cf. also *BoS* 13.9.

This position reminds us of that of Aphrahat, who in a rather peculiar exegesis of Genesis 2:24 interprets the "leaving of father and mother" as the abandonment of God and the Holy Spirit by a man upon entering the married state, implying as a consequence that no true closeness to God is possible for married Christians.[151]

All this does not mean that the author of the *Book of Steps* has no good words to say about marriage. For example, at one point he articulates a very positive vision of this institution as the place where disagreement between the sexes is overcome and where reign harmonious relationships of mutual love, which are put to the service of those in need: "And a woman bestows her love upon a man, and he bestows [his love] upon her (ܘܦܪܢܐ ܐܢܬܬܐ ܠܓܒܪܐ ܚܘܒܗ ܘܗܘ ܦܪܢ ܠܗ); and they comfort everyone who is troubled and a stranger in whatever they can; and a man and a woman are equal, or a man and a man, or a woman and a woman."[152]

However, this positive mention of marriage is by no means able to outweigh the numerous negative references to this institution scattered throughout the *Book of Steps.* Such pronounced emphasis on sexual renunciation as an indispensable condition for those who want to lead a truly spiritual life is another trait that betrays our author's indebtedness to the archaic Encratite mentality. As an example of the latter approach, one might mention the *Acts of Thomas,* where the apostle proclaims, "Whoever indulges in filthy intercourse (ܫܘܬܦܘܬܐ ܛܢܦܬܐ), especially in that of adultery, has not life with this God whom I preach."[153]

Such a negative approach to lay spirituality by no means went unchallenged among Syrian Christians. One of the earliest examples of reaction against this ascetical exclusiveness appears in the Syriac *Didascalia,* a product of the third-century Syrian Christianity that reflects a milieu where Jewish Christianity still played an important role.[154] The author of the *Didascalia,*

151. *Demonstration* XVIII.10–11, in Parisot, *Aphraatis Sapientis,* col. 840.

152. *BoS* 13.3 (slightly modified).

153. Wright, *Apocryphal Acts,* §51, 1:220; Klijn, trans., *The Acts of Thomas: Introduction, Text, and Commentary,* 2nd ed., Supplements to Novum Testamentum (Leiden: E. J. Brill, 2003), 127.

154. Written originally in Greek, the *Didascalia* has been preserved as a whole only in a Syriac translation. For a convincing reconstruction of its *Sitz im Leben,* see Charlotte E. Fonrobert, "The *Didascalia Apostolorum:* A Mishnah for the Disciples of Jesus," *Journal of Early Christian Studies* 9, no. 4 (2001): 483–509.

while retelling the Apostolic Council (Acts 15), wages polemic against different groups, the most prominent among which are Judaizing and Encratite Christians. The latter group is referred to as those who "were observing holiness (ܩܕܝܫܘܬܐ).[155] The author proceeds further with the supposed apostolic decree that dissuades Christians from Judaizing practices and urges them to marry, while quoting Proverbs 19:14, Matthew 19:4–6, and Genesis 2:24 as the scriptural proof-texts. In conclusion, he brings out the following argument against those among his opponents who practiced ritual ablutions: "For through baptism they receive the Holy Spirit who is always with those that work righteousness, and does not depart from them by reason of natural fluxes and the intercourse of marriage (ܪ̈ܕܝܐ ܕܟܝܢܐ ܘܫܘܬܦܘܬܐ ܕܙܘܘܓܐ), but always perseveres with those who possess Him, and keeps them."[156] This argument has particular significance for our discussion, since, although being directed primarily against the Judaizing Christians,[157] it seems to be aimed against the Encratite believers, as well. One can easily recognize here the typical Encratite notion of sexual intercourse making impossible any real presence of the Holy Spirit in the lives of married believers. While the former group resolved the problem of incompatibility between sexuality and spiritual life through the ritual practice borrowed from the Jewish matrix, the latter endorsed a much more radical approach by trying to eliminate completely this whole area of human life. The author of the *Didascalia,* who opposes both of these options, provides us with one of the earliest attempts coming from the Syrian milieu to defend marriage against ascetically minded radicals, an approach that would constitute one of the distinctive features of the nascent orthodoxy in this region during the fourth century and even later.

As we have seen, there is some inconsistency in the position taken by the author of the *Book of Steps* on marriage. On the one side, he presents this institution as one of the negative outcomes of the fall, only grudgingly tolerated by God. On the other side, he does acknowledge its legitimacy, even under the new dispensation of return to the angelic state of perfection inaugurat-

155. *Didasc.* XXIV, in *The Didascalia Apostolorum in Syriac,* edited and translated by Arthur Vööbus, 231 [Syr.], 214, Corpus Scriptorum Christianorum Orientalium 401–2, 407–8, Syr. 175–76, 179–80 (Louvain: Secrétariat du Corpus SCO, 1979). Some mss. add ܟܕ ܣܒܪܝܢ ܠܗ ܛܡܐܐ ܠܙܘܘܓܐ, "thinking marriage defiled."

156. *Didasc.* XXVI, in Vööbus, trans., *Didascalia Apostolorum,* 255 [Syr.], 238.

157. See on this Fonrobert, *Menstrual Purity: Rabbinic and Christian Reconstructions of Biblical Gender,* Contraversions: Jews and Other Differences (Stanford: Stanford University Press, 2000), 166–85.

ed by Christ. This contradiction stems from the fact that the author tried to reconcile an "archaic" Encratite notion of marriage as the "work of the devil" with the idea of it being divinely ordained, an idea that by the fourth century became one of the touchstones of nascent orthodoxy in Syria and elsewhere. The presence of archaic features in the *Book of Steps* is similar to the case of Aphrahat, in whose demonstrations some scholars discerned the traces of an ancient Syrian baptismal liturgy that required the vows of celibacy to be taken as a necessary condition.[158]

While giving its due to the original character of Syriac Christianity, it should always be kept in mind that it was by no means isolated from what was going on in the Greek-speaking West. Accordingly, in order to understand better the position of the *Book of Steps* on marriage one has to take into consideration that the fourth century was the time when the process of readjustment of Syriac-speaking Christians to the emerging norms of Western Christian orthodoxy had started.[159] This "westward turn" of Syriac Christianity had many dimensions, one of which was reassessment of the meaning and place of marriage in the life of believers. It is significant that, in the middle of the fourth century, the Council of Gangra took place, the primary concern of which was rebuttal of the radical anti-marriage views current in some ascetic circles of Asia Minor and Armenia.[160]

The ambivalent character of marriage-related rhetoric in the *Book of Steps* agrees well with the theory of the transitional character of the Christian community to which our author belonged. This aspect of the *Book of Steps* has been noted by Arthur Vööbus, who, while discussing the peculiarities of ecclesiology and community structure in this work, came to the conclusion that it reflects "the reorientation and consolidation of the spiritual forces in a Christianity which could not keep the archaic past any longer."[161] The inconsistent

158. See Vööbus, *Celibacy: A Requirement for Admission to Baptism in the Early Syrian Church,* Papers of the Estonian Theological Society in Exile 1 (Stockholm: Estonian Theological Society in Exile, 1951); Murray, "The Exhortation to Candidates for Ascetical Vows at Baptism in the Ancient Syrian Church," *New Testament Studies* 21 (1974–75): 58–79.

159. See on this Vööbus, *Celibacy,* 38–44.

160. See O. Larry Yarbrough, "Canons from the Council of Gangra," in *Ascetic Behavior in Greco-Roman Antiquity: A Sourcebook,* edited by Vincent L. Wimbush, 448–55, Studies in Antiquity and Christianity (Minneapolis: Fortress Press, 1990).

161. See Vööbus, "*Liber Graduum:* Some Aspects of Its Significance for the History of Early Syrian Asceticism," in *Charisteria Iohanni Kopp octogenerio oblata,* 123, Papers of the Estonian Theological Society in Exile 7 (Stockholm: Estonian Theological Society in Exile, 1954).

position of the *Book of Steps* regarding marriage gives additional strength to this hypothesis and exposes our work as an invaluable witness that reveals how the uncompromising Encratite ideal of Christian life was modified and adapted to serve the needs of a community in transition.

The Western influence upon Syriac Christianity aside, there were also some internal driving forces behind this transition. One of them was the process of Christianization, which had started in Syria in the late fourth century and continued well into the fifth and even sixth centuries.[162] A necessary condition for the success of Christian mission was the fashioning of a more positive approach to family and marriage. As has been pointed out by Peter Brown, "It was through the validation of conception and childbirth that the hand of the holy man reached into the Christian family."[163] Moreover, it should be remembered that the fourth century was a time of strong confrontation between Judaism and Christianity in the region, and the issues of marriage and sexuality played an important role in the polemic between the two religious communities. In that respect the case of Aphrahat is particularly revealing, but there are additional examples of Syrian writers who had to deal with Jewish arguments against the Christian view of marriage and celibacy.[164] These factors, I believe, contributed as well to the development of a new "orthodox" consensus on marriage in which the author of the *Book of Steps* participates, notwithstanding his Encratite leanings.

Conclusion

In the course of our examination it has been shown how the author of the *Book of Steps* dealt with the variety of issues related to marriage and sexuality. While some of the opinions expressed by the author on these subjects have parallels in the works of early or contemporary Syrian writers, many of those were developed in an original way or have no precedent at all. This fact characterizes him as an independent thinker who creatively adopted and modified

162. See John H. W. G. Liebeschuetz, "Epigraphic Evidence on the Christianisation of Syria," in *Akten des XI. Internationalen Limeskongresses*, 485–508 (Budapest: Akadémiai Kiadó, 1981).

163. Brown, *Body and Society*, 325.

164. Cf. Aphrahat, *Demonstration* XVIII.12; see on this Koltun-Fromm, "Sexuality and Holiness." Ephrem, or one of his students, confronts the Jewish anti-ascetic viewpoint in the *Commentary on the Diatessaron* XVI.22.

current ideas in order to convey his own theological and anthropological views.

Fundamental for understanding of our author's position on marriage is the peculiar version of anthropology developed by him. At the core of his ascetically oriented anthropological system stands the idea of angelomorphic humanity. Working in the general framework of realized eschatology, the author of the *Book of Steps* establishes close correspondence between the protological and eschatological state of humanity. On this base he promotes restoration of human nature to the state of the angelic-like perfection of Adam before his fall as the ultimate goal of Christian life. Marriage, while allowed for the ordinary believers, is not compatible with this high vocation.

While pursuing his agenda the author of the *Book of Steps* resorts to a variety of strategies, many of which appeal to the authority of scripture. As a result he emerges as one of the most sophisticated and original among the ascetical readers of the Bible in late antique Syria. On the hermeneutical level our author's approach to scripture exhibits both the affirmation of continuity and the establishment of difference. The former strategy is pursued through appropriation of several key figures from the Old Testament as the role models for the believers, while the latter finds its most distinct expression in the theory of the two laws that govern the lives of the two separate groups of Christians—the Perfect and the Upright.

It has been demonstrated that the negative rhetoric directed by the author of the *Book of Steps* against sexual desire in general and the institute of marriage in particular goes well beyond the limits of what one might find in the writings of his contemporaries Aphrahat and Ephrem. Thus dissociation of marriage from the biblical commandment to procreate undermines effectively the positive meaning of this social institution. Furthermore, by ascribing the origins of sexuality and marriage to the malevolent activity of Satan, our author, much like Tatian before him, "undercuts the biblical tenet that sexuality and fertility belong in God's absolute power."[165] This tendency sets the author of the *Book of Steps* apart from the majority of fourth-century Syrian writers and betrays his indebtedness to the Encratite tradition, where, according to Peter Brown, "sexuality was presented less as a drive than as the symbol of ineluctable process, the clearest token of human bondage."[166]

165. Gaca, *Making of Fornication,* 241.

166. Brown, *Body and Society,* 99.

Thomas Kollamparampil

14. "HIDDEN WORK" OF THE HEART AND SPIRITUAL PROGRESSION IN THE *BOOK OF STEPS*

The Syriac *Book of Steps,* generally considered to be written in the fourth century, is a product of the Syriac pre-monastic vision of the spiritual life and spiritual growth in Christian life. Beyond the stratification of the spiritual life, the *Book of Steps* explains the dynamics of this life as a way, a journey in progress, to Perfection that needs the constant activity of the heart.[1] The *Book of Steps* describes the Syriac spirituality of the heart as well as the necessary "work of the heart" (which is unseen) at all levels of the spiritual life. This invisible working of the heart is the starting point, the means and medium of growth in Christian life and Perfection.

Semitic Syriac View of the Heart and Spiritual Growth

In the Semitic Judeo-Christian understanding, the heart is the seat of both the intellect and the emotions. The heart stands as the sense of senses. It is the heart that governs all the orientations of our intellectual pursuits, the patterns of our moral behavior, and the integration or disintegration or our emotions.

1. *BoS* 6.

For Syriac writers the "heart" means the center of one's being. In this respect Syriac writers integrate the role of the physiological heart and the central controlling power of the intellect, will, and emotions. There is a tendency to locate intellect, thought, and will in the head, and, as a consequence, there emerges the dichotomy of the heart versus head, or feeling versus reason. In the Platonic and neo-Platonic view the heart has a lower place in the spiritual geography. According to such viewpoints, more importance is accorded to intellect and reason; hence, head rather than heart. Thus the heart is reduced to be merely the seat of emotions. But in the Semitic Eastern culture the heart is the seat of the intellect, reason, and will. The heart functions as the center of one's being and as the controlling factor of all actions. This is closer to biblical anthropology. For the Hebrews in the Semitic culture, any dichotomy is baseless, because the heart is the seat of feelings, emotions, intellect, reason, and will. This basic perception makes a substantial difference to the spiritual outlook, especially in the Syriac Christian spiritual vision.

Spirituality of the heart, in which the heart is viewed as the center of all acts of the inner person, describes a more biblical outlook. Paul calls it the center of one's inner self.[2] The heart is also, at the same time, the focal point of our physical existence. In general the heart acts as the focal point of our two modes of existence—namely, our physical and spiritual modes. Thus the heart governs our inner and outer person. Our body, as Paul teaches, serves as the "temple of the Holy Spirit." This is a holistic approach that the *Book of Steps* presupposes in its spiritual vision.

Purity of the Heart and Spiritual Growth in the *Book of Steps*

In the words of the *Book of Steps,* "We do not understand what our Lord meant when he said, 'In my Father's house there are many places.'"[3] We also do not know fully why "one 'sick' person is healed more effectively than another, or why by 'milk' one 'child' becomes more beautiful than another, or why one person is blessed more than another when keeping the commandments that

2. Rom 7:22.
3. *BoS* 1.4, citing John 14:2.

have been given to everyone."[4] All these depend on one's own decision and the state of one's heart,[5] while the state of one's heart, whether obedient or hard, is expressed in one's actions. The Lord gave the gospel to all those who want to become Perfect. The actions of "good works" are the means to ascend on the steps of spiritual life.[6] "Good works" issue out of the internal decisions of the heart, which are the first steps for any good work. Adam obeyed the evil one and thus defiled his heart, and hence lost the purity of his heart.[7]

One's purity of the heart determines whether one goes up or down in the spiritual life, in the levels of Uprightness and Perfection. So memra 14 describes:

> Everyone is exalted according to his manner of life and according to his rank, his wearied mind, and the lowliness of his soul. As for the rest, everyone is rewarded in that world, whether good or bad, according to what he has done—whether good or bad—in this world. As the apostle said, "We must all stand before the tribunal of Christ in order that each one of us may be rewarded [for] whatever he has done in his body."[8]

In the heart of every Christian there are deposits (*'urbānā:* literally, a pledge) of the Holy Spirit and of sin.[9] Adam came to this state when he disobeyed and brought in a mixture of sin into himself. These deposits, or pledges, of the Holy Spirit and of sin are in different degrees and levels in different human beings (e.g., Martha's position was lesser than that of Mary).[10] Growth in spiritual life depends on the eradication of the faults from the heart, or, in other words, it depends on the purification of the heart.[11] One has to internally increase the deposit of the Holy Spirit and decrease the deposit to sin in one's heart. Adam obeyed the evil one and was thus defiled in his heart, thereby losing the purity of his heart.[12] One has to purify the heart, and such inner purification of the heart is possible through taking up the concealed or hidden cross (*sliba kasia*).[13] Even before carrying the visible cross, the carrying of the hidden cross in our heart has to take place. This hidden work of the heart has to take place before every external or visible bearing of the cross. Just as one is

4. *BoS* 1.3.
5. *BoS* 1.3.
6. *BoS* 2.1.
7. *BoS* 2.6.
8. *BoS* 14.3, citing 2 Cor 5:10.
9. *BoS* 3.11.
10. *BoS* 3.13
11. *BoS* 3.4.
12. *BoS* 2.6.
13. *BoS* 3.10.

bound to the visible cross physically, one has to be initially bound in spirit to the concealed cross in an invisible or spiritual manner.

The repentance of the publican, Zacchaeus, Rahab, the Samaritan woman, and others are due to the hidden work of the heart. Education in the visible church is necessary for making our body a temple and our heart an altar. So states memra 12 of the *Book of Steps:* "For our Lord and his first and last preachers did not erect in vain the Church and the altar and baptism, all of which are visible to the physical eye. It is through these visible things, however, that we shall be in these heavenly things, which are invisible to eyes of flesh, our bodies becoming temples and our hearts altars."[14]

As our body becomes a temple and our heart an altar in all purity, a new vision and perception emerge in us.[15] By such a vision we see our enemies and murderers in another light and attain a new understanding as to who our neighbor is. This new vision enables one to be all things to all at all times.

Spiritual Journey and Progress in the *Book of Steps*

As is evident, the spiritual life is an engagement between the divine and the human. At each level this journey is from the physical to the spiritual—from the visible to the invisible space and time. There is a transition from the physical topography to the spiritual topography. The journey seems to start in the physical realm, but has a spiritual and invisible beginning in the decisions of the heart: as the heart decides in an invisible manner, the person journeys from the external observances, with a pure conscience and unshakable faith, toward the truth and purity of the heart. This journey is taken in sacred space and time, through which only the heart can travel and work.[16]

The journey that starts with faith leads to observance, which in turn leads one to Uprightness. From Uprightness, through the exercise of love, one reaches the level of Perfection.[17] Through faith and observance one uproots one's faults and investigates the road to travel diligently toward Perfection.[18]

From the unbelieving stage to the believing stage, the journey is through a road of signs. Our Lord performed signs and wonders to bring people to be-

14. *BoS* 12.2; Heb 11:3.
15. *BoS* 7.2.
16. *BoS* 16.9–10.
17. *BoS* 17.1.
18. *BoS* 19.1.

lief. Once somebody starts believing, he has to suffer with the Lord so as to be glorified with the Lord.[19] There is internal suffering in controlling the tendency to strike back at one's enemy. More than that, our Lord actually washed the feet of his enemies, in the case of Judas, before washing the feet of his friends like Simon Peter and others.

As there are several levels for the spiritual journey,[20] there are different commandments and scriptural teachings. The instructions of Jesus may seem contradictory if one does not understand the levels of application and observances required at different stages of the spiritual life.[21] The scriptures are not addressed only to one type of people.[22] There are commandments that are of "milk and vegetables," which are minor and meant for children and the sick. There are commandments that are major—that of "solid food," meant for the grownups. There is the commandment "Do not associate with the immoral people."[23] Again, the same scripture instructs, "Be all things with all people."[24] If the "infants" and "sick" in faith associate with the immoral people, they will be negatively affected and perish, whereas the grownup ones in faith, if they become all things with all people, including immoral people, instead of perishing themselves, will gain and redeem the immoral and sick ones. Thus in the teachings of our Lord and in the scriptures we have to distinguish between different levels of spiritual life and growth.[25] Therefore, while reading the scriptures and understanding the teachings of the Lord, each person has to distinguish his level and discern the commandments.

As the journey progresses, the mind of the person transcends the place of evil and reaches the place of peace where our Lord resides.[26] The journey upward is steep and narrow. It is a journey through fire and water. Hence, if one falls from the steep level he may be crushed. If he falls to one side, there is fire that burns, and on the other side is the water that drowns all.[27] Every step is a covenant with Christ, and brings refreshment from the Kingdom's table.[28] If you turn back from the covenant, you will fall (from the steep height) down to Sheol. If you transgress the commandment, you will go to *Gehenna,* where

19. *BoS* 17.1.
20. *BoS* 9.13–14.
21. *BoS* 11.
22. *BoS* 11.1.
23. 1 Cor 5:9.
24. 1 Cor 9:22.
25. *BoS* 11.1–3.
26. *BoS* 15.18.
27. *BoS* 19.2.
28. Luke 22:30.

there is fire. If you renounce Christ, you will be drowned in the hidden waters that are the teachings of the evil one.[29]

On the onward journey the infants and the immature have to be strengthened and the sick have to be cured. Only the valiant and brave ones travel on the road to Perfection.[30] There are three difficult steps to the city of our Lord: (1) Be reconciled with all enemies of one's life; (2) Do not work for one's own self or out of selfishness; and (3) Raise up one's pure hands and heart to the Lord.[31] At such a stage one is externally (by the works of hands) and internally (by the work of the heart) staying pure so as to reach up to the abode of the Lord. In order to reach up to the Lord, one needs to uproot all evil thoughts and sins from the heart. This is a very difficult step, because sin stands up in front of any valiant athlete. Either the sin should be killed or it kills you. One has to battle with the internal death that Adam experienced when he transgressed the commandments. Instead of getting killed as Adam, like a brave athlete, one has to battle with evil thoughts in the heart and, if needed, as the scriptures advise, encounter bloodshed and murder against sin internally.[32] By this, one can uproot the "hidden death" that Adam suffered.[33]

Even if one becomes Perfect, he has to go further still. This is made clear from the imageries of palace building and chest making for the king. Good palace builders and good chest makers, after having built the required structure in perfect form, request the king to inhabit the palace and to fill the chest with pearls and valuables.[34] Once the heart is purified, it becomes a palace or a chest that has to be filled with the riches of virtues and the treasures of a good life leading to Perfection. As one grows in Perfection the entry into the bridal chamber of the Kingdom becomes an apt image for depicting the crowning step of spiritual life.[35]

Spiritual Progress through the Work of the Heart

In every human deed there are hidden or invisible as well as manifest and visible elements. As human beings have both body and soul, all spiritual jour-

29. *BoS* 19.2.
30. *BoS* 19.4–5.
31. *BoS* 20.1.
32. Heb 12:4.
33. *BoS* 20.4.
34. *BoS* 6.2.
35. *BoS* 20.6.

neys have to seriously take into account all external works. In the words of the *Book of Steps,* nobody should dispute, saying, "In our soul we shall be justified and shall heal our own illness."[36] Such disputes are from the evil one. Hence the author of the *Book of Steps* writes:

> Evil teaches us all these things, so that we might falter and not be diligent in our body and in our soul. But just as evil makes us believe that we work in our hearts, it makes us work neither in our heart nor in our body. For there is no one who accomplishes righteousness with his heart and does not also accomplish righteousness in his body, because, from the fullness of the heart, lips speak and, after the thought of the heart, the body moves. As the heart is humble, so the body will also be humble.[37]

The Lord and all his prophets fasted completely with both their bodies and their souls.[38] There was perfect conformity between their inner and outer works. Since their heart was integrated with their body, they had hidden fasting, hidden prayer, and hidden renunciation in their body that was a hidden temple and their heart, a hidden altar.[39] Corresponding to the visible baptism in the water, there is the invisible baptism of fire and spirit.[40] Much hidden work of the heart is required for the realization of this "baptism of fire and spirit." One who is childish in spirit needs more visible work to integrate the body and the soul. But the adult in spirit knows the hidden work of the heart, and he advances in the spiritual life.[41] Adam desired food, which means that he desired luxury and pleasures. Against such desires the true fasting described by Isaiah has to be observed in order to "break the bonds of iniquity and cut the burden of deceit."[42] This is a spiritual sacrifice and a true fasting,[43] which are done by the invisible work of the heart.

Corresponding to our visible garment, we need the invisible garment that is acquired through the hidden work of the heart.[44] There are people who are externally satisfied and clothed. Yet they may be internally naked and thirsty because they do not have the "light," "life" and "Kingdom."[45] The wedding garments of the kingdom are made out of good works. The proper wedding garment to wear for the Lord's feast is the purified heart.[46] For such a state of

36. *BoS* 10.7.
37. *BoS* 10.8.
38. *BoS* 10.10.
39. *BoS* 12.1.
40. *BoS* 12.4.
41. *BoS* 12.6.
42. Isa 58:5–6.
43. *BoS* 29.1, 2, 12.
44. *BoS* 3.9.
45. *BoS* 3.9.
46. *BoS* 20.14–17.

the heart we need to be afflicted internally in prayer with the Lord and shed tears for purification of the heart. Our hidden sins and evil thoughts will be removed and our hearts will be purified only by the hidden work done in the heart.[47]

Our Lord became human and assumed our sinful nature and showed us how to climb the difficult steps like an athlete.[48] We have to pass through the steps of Uprightness and Perfection. In our journey, imitating our Lord, we have to be watchful, fasting, observing lowliness and crying out with many tears with supplication and with sweat of afflictions, as our Lord suffered. At such a point we will be filled with the Spirit, the Paraclete, and the Lord will come and stay with us. All these things will happen only through the working of the heart. As the angel appeared and strengthened our Lord at the end of his sufferings, the Lord himself will come and save us.[49] At such a level the "inbreathing" that was taken away from Adam, causing his death, will be reversed, and life will be abundant.[50] The perfect integration of the exterior and the interior will take place, and the truth of the biblical text, "if two of you agree on earth and keep my words, whatever you ask in prayer and believe, while keeping my words, you will receive" will be accomplished.[51] According to the author of the *Book of Steps,* these "two of you" are the "interior" and "exterior" of the person who perfectly agree in keeping the commandments. When these two realms of the person ask in agreement for the gifts of the Holy Spirit, they will be added to them as a pledge, and that person will be established as a trinity and live.[52] This will be the fruit of the "living sacrifice"[53] involving our whole person,[54] and in which the working of the heart is crucial.

Journey of Self-Realization through Self-Denial and Humility to Perfection

The true self of every creature is found in relationship with the creator Lord. If any creature turns away from the Creator it is an act of self-negation and self-destruction. Only if the creature negates or denies its own self-centeredness and remains related to its Creator can there be proper self-realization.

47. *BoS* 18.4.
48. *BoS* 20.8.
49. *BoS* 20.8.
50. *BoS* 28.4.
51. Matt 18:19, 21:22; Mark 11:24.
52. *BoS* 28.5.
53. Rom 12:2.
54. *BoS* 29.4.

Adam wanted to taste from the tree of the knowledge of good and evil. This means he tasted from good and evil. He is a mixture of both, not at all perfect in goodness.[55] Adam had vanity, and he thought that he would become like God. He was proud, and he placed his own self first, instead of the commandments of God. So he experienced the fall. He was expelled from the spiritual or invisible paradise to the earthly paradise.[56] So the author of the *Book of Steps* writes:

For nothing brought down Adam on the day that he fell, except the pride by which he desired to become the equal of God in his majesty. Too much pride forced him to depart from the paradise of the Kingdom and humbled him down to earth. My brothers, let us flee from pride lest we become salt whose flavor is lost, for it is not useful even for fertilizer (Matthew 5:13), because it does not have any taste in order to salt from it offerings (Leviticus 2:13) and no field is fertilized by it nor is any wheat produced by it as our Lord said, "Whoever exalts himself—like Jesus—will be exalted, just as he was exalted."[57]

As Adam took for himself the image of majesty, so Christ took the image of the servant, which is the perfect model of self-denial.

In the spiritual journey envisaged in the *Book of Steps,* there are three levels of self-realization. The visible church teaches infants for growth, the church of the heart fortifies the sick, and the higher church perfects all.[58] This is the path of self-realization from the stage of "child in spirit" to the stage of "adult in spirit." The adult in spirit has more powerful hidden or invisible works of the heart.[59]

The Upright should abandon everything and thus attach themselves to the Lord. Like the Lord, they have to suffer. All forms of sufferings with the Lord are for self-denial, through which all our external and internal sins are washed away. Such a process of purification happens through the prayer of tears and groans,[60] which will bring us closer to the Lord. When we are close to the Lord, the Lord suffers with us in an invisible manner. There will be corporate suffering with the Lord. This, in other words, means walking in the "image of the Lord."[61] At such a stage one becomes a law unto himself.[62] All these

55. *BoS* 21.1.
56. *BoS* 21.11.
57. *BoS* 21.11, citing Matt 23:12 and Luke 14:11.
58. *BoS* 21.3.
59. *BoS* 12.6.
60. *BoS* 18.3.
61. *BoS* 17.8.
62. *BoS* 22.10, 18.5, 25.2.

developments are brought about through changes in the heart. Then the true reconciliation of the heavenly and earthly takes place through the work in the heart that is hidden or invisible.[63]

Conclusion

In conclusion, as far as I understand, the *Book of Steps* provides a realistic and holistic picture of the spiritual life of Christians at different levels. The requisite work of the heart at all levels is treated and practically described. The pendulum of the Christian spiritual life and ascetical practices seen in the *Book of Steps* swings in a balanced manner to the right and left, to the divine and human, to the visible and invisible, to the external and internal activities of a person. Thus the *Book of Steps* gives holistic and practical spiritual guidance with adequate insight for the journey to Perfection.

The due importance given to the visible order of the church, its altar, and the sacraments in the *Book of Steps,* refutes the accusation of it having Messalianism tendencies and contempt for the external order and observances in the church. The *Book of Steps,* while focusing on the higher steps of spiritual life and dealing with the inner levels of the heart, may seem to be disregarding the externals. In fact, the author of the *Book of Steps* is concerned with the higher levels of spiritual life that concentrate on the invisible internal levels of the heart that presuppose the realization of earlier steps.

The *Book of Steps,* when it deals with the higher levels of the hidden work of the heart and the purity of the heart in the Perfect, speaks with a tone of high spiritualizing tendency. At the same time, when it comes to the case of belief and practices of the Upright, the *Book of Steps* is very down to earth. It sheds light on the required purity of the work of hands. Thus we find the instructions to blend the works of hands (external) and the work of the heart (internal) in the *Book of Steps.* This is done with the view of joining with the Lord with pure hands and pure hearts so that our offerings might be pure and acceptable spiritual sacrifices.

In general, the *Book of Steps* deals with all grades of spiritual life and provides concrete instruction to all levels of Christians. This Syriac treatise on

63. *BoS* 25.2.

Christian spiritual life is quite relevant to the world of plurality and diversity in Christian understanding of spiritual life and progress. The teachings of the *Book of Steps* need to be approached and explained to the modern Christian society with a certain hermeneutical sensitivity. Yet its relevance is clear. Social life in general, at present, is full of much evil, imperfection, and ill will. Love of one's neighbor, in its wider and horizontal dimensions, is ignored in the world of globalization, commercial mentality filled with consumerism and egoism. All such evils are actually issuing from the heart. Hence a true purification of the heart and a pilgrimage to Perfection through different steps demanded by the *Book of Steps* are all the more relevant in the church and in society today. Here the teaching of our Lord is doubly meaningful: "Not what goes into the mouth defiles a person, but it is what comes out of the mouth, this defiles. . . . But what comes out of the mouth proceeds from the heart, and this is what defiles. For out of the heart come evil intentions, murder, adultery, fornication, theft, false witness, slander."[64] Hence the *Book of Steps* advocates purity of the heart and further progress by filling the heart with riches of virtues and treasures of good works of life.

64. Matt 15:11, 18, 19.

Aryeh Kofsky and Serge Ruzer

15. READING THE ASCETIC IDEAL INTO GENESIS 1–3

Hermeneutic Strategies in the Book of Steps *Memra 21*

The Syriac late-fourth or early-fifth century *Book of Steps*[1] reflects the transition from pre-monastic Syrian asceticism to the subsequent phase influenced by Egyptian and Basilian monasticism.[2] Thus the *Book of Steps* still reflects proto-monastic ascetic patterns—primarily familiar to us from the early Syriac fathers Aphrahat and Ephrem—though there was already also a significant development of anchoritic and coenobitic monasticism in Syria at that time.[3] The treatise is characterized by its sharp division of Christian society into the Upright—representing the mass of ordinary believers—and the Perfect ascetics. The former are those not detached from the world. They deal with the "mi-

1. For the Syriac edition of the text, see Michael Kmoskó, ed., *Liber Graduum* (*LG*), Patrologia Syriaca 1.3. Paris: Firmin-Didot, 1926. For an English translation, see Robert A. Kitchen and Martien F. G. Parmentier, trans., *The Book of Steps: The Syriac Liber Graduum* (BoS) (Kalamazoo, Mich.: Cistercian Publications, 2004).

2. See Sidney H. Griffith, "'Singles' in God's Service: Thoughts on Ihidaye from the Works of Aphrahat and Ephraem the Syrian," *The Harp* 4 (1991): 145–59; Griffith, "Monks, 'Singles,' and the 'Sons of the Covenant': Reflections on Syriac Ascetic Terminology," in *Euloghema: Studies in Honor of Robert Taft, S. J.,* edited by E. Carr, A. A. Thiermeyer, and E. Velkovska, 141–60, Analecta Liturgica 17 (Rome: Pontificio Ateneo S. Anselmo, 1993); Kitchen and Parmentier, *Book of Steps,* xlix–l.

3. See Theodoret of Cyrrhus, in *Histoire des Moines de Syrie,* edited and translated by Pierre Canivet and Alice Leroy-Molinghen, Sources Chrétiennes 234, 257 (Paris: Éditions du Cerf, 1977, 1979).

nor commandments" pertaining to the charities of active life, while the latter are those that deal with the "grand commandments" of detachment from the world, become "strangers to the world," "leave the earth," and thus take up the cross in imitation of Christ.[4] Within this socioreligious division, the Upright are further perceived as those in whom—unlike the Perfect—a demonic presence persists alongside the activity of the Holy Spirit.[5] This trait—mentioned also by Ephrem—is reminiscent of Messalianic tenets, though the author of the *Book of Steps* never suggests that Satan dwells substantively in the soul of the Upright, who is regarded as a full member of the liturgical community, destined for the final triumph of the Spirit and redemption.[6]

The treatise contains thirty chapters, or memre (sing. memra), our focus being on memra 21, which portrays the original setting of Adam and Eve in paradise as essentially an ascetic situation and Adam and Eve before the fall as models of perfect ascetics.[7] This seems to be a peculiar trait of the *Book of Steps,* especially highlighted in memra 21, compared both to early monastic writings and to early Christian literature at large. The special emphasis on Adam and Eve in this context thus provides an additional theological dimension to the ascetic discourse in the *Book of Steps.* The insistence on the primordial biblical foundation for asceticism also determines the centrality of the hermeneutics of Genesis 1–3.

Relying on earlier scholarship on this topic, notably Aleksander Kowalski's pioneering work,[8] we intend to analyze some of the core motifs employed in this memra. We hope, inter alia, to clarify the uncommon hermeneutic strategies of the author, still belonging to an early, unapologetically indepen-

4. *BoS* 3.11, 5.16, 5.18; Antoine Guillaumont, "Les 'arrhes de l'Esprit' dans le Livre des degrés," in *Mémorial Mgr Gabriel Khouri-Sarkis (1898–1968): Fondateur et directeur de l'Orient syrien, 1956–1967,* edited by François Graffin, 107–13 (Louvain: Imprimerie Orientaliste, 1969).

5. See, e.g., *BoS* 3.11; Guillaumont, "'Arrhes de l'Esprit,'" 107–13.

6. See Ephrem, *Hymns on Faith* 6.3–4, in *Des heiligen Ephraem des Syrers Hymnen de Fide,* edited by Edmund Beck, CSCO 154–55, Syr. 73–74 (Louvain: Peeters, 1955); Kitchen and Parmentier, *Book of Steps,* 48–49; Columba Stewart, *"Working the Earth of the Heart": The Messalian Controversy in History, Texts, and Language to A.D. 431* (Oxford: Clarendon Press, 1991).

7. The ascetic portrayal of the protoplasts' existence in paradise stands in contrast to the biblical motif of the richness of paradise expressed in the *Book of Steps* as "heavenly wealth" (ܥܘܬܪܐ ܫܡܝܢܐ; see *BoS* 21.11, *LG* 613.22); cf. *BoS* 21.10, *LG* 612.21–23. On this motif, see Aelred Baker, "The Gospel of Thomas and the Syriac Liber Graduum," *New Testament Studies* 12 (1965–66): 52.

8. Aleksander Kowalski, *Perfezione e giustizia di Adamo nel Liber Graduum,* Orientalia Christiana Analecta 232 (Rome: Pontificium Institutum Orientale, 1989).

dent phase of Syriac Christianity. We do not aim here to provide a comprehensive analysis of the memra, but rather to focus on its explicit and implicit exegetical devices.

The author of the *Book of Steps* entertains a concept of a dual paradise—an earthly physical and a heavenly spiritual—as the setting of Adam and Eve's life before the fall. Their physical existence takes place in the earthly paradise, while their mind dwells in the spiritual one.[9] Various concepts of such a dual paradise were common in early Christian thought.[10] The collation of this perception with the concept of paradise as *locus asceticus,* however, seems to constitute a peculiar trait of the *Book of Steps* and determines the different aspects of its discourse. One of the core aspects of the theme is the nature of primordial sin and, correspondingly, the ascetic way of restoring the "paradise lost," propagated by the author.

Adam and Eve's state before the fall is portrayed as perfect innocence and ignorance of evil, since when God created them he taught them only good (ܕܛܒܬܐ ܗܘ ܒܠܚܘܕ ܐܠܦ ܐܢܘܢ ܐܠܗܐ).[11] This innocence signifies the total spiritual preoccupation with heavenly things in immortal existence. Yet, in the *Book of Steps,* this blissful state is not identical to the final consummation of man's destiny: man is called upon to choose—out of the freedom granted to him by the Creator—to resist temptation and remain in heavenly bliss or, in the words of the author, to "eat our Lord (ܘܢܐܟܘܠܝܘܗܝ ܠܗ ܠܡܪܢ) and live and become great and be perfected (ܘܢܬܓܡܪܘܢ) through him."[12] "The consummation of the Lord" refers to the spiritual consummation of the tree of life—identified by the author with Christ[13]—that would have been Adam's lot had he

9. *BoS* 21.7, *LG* 600–604.

10. See Jean Daniélou, "Terre et paradis chez les Pères de l'Église," *Eranos Jahrbuch* 22 (1953): 433–72; Andrew Louth, "Paradies: IV Theologiegeschichtlich," in *Theologische Realenzyklopädie,* edited by Gerhard Müller, 25:714–19 (Berlin and New York: Walter de Gruyter, 1995).

11. *BoS* 21.1, *LG* 585.1–2. According to Martikainen, the *Book of Steps* differs here from Ephrem, for whom the twofold knowledge of Adam of good and evil exists unconditionally, already in the state of bliss; see Juoko Martikainen, "Das Böse in den Schriften des Syrers Ephrem, im Stufenbuch und in Corpus Macarianum," in *Makarios-Symposium über das Böse: Vorträge der Finnisch-Deutschen Theologentagung in Goslar 1980,* edited by Werner Strothmann, 36–46, Göttinger Orientforschungen 1. Reihe: Syriaca 24 (Wiesbaden: Harrassowitz Verlag, 1983).

12. *BoS* 21.1, *LG* 588.8–9.

13. *BoS* 21.2, *LG* 589.3–5.

not sinned. We will return later to the peculiarity of this understanding of the consummation of the Lord and its eucharistic connotations. Had the above reality been fulfilled, it would have led in turn to the final transformation of human existence, when its physical and spiritual aspects would have united in the heavenly paradise.[14]

Like Ephrem in his commentary on Genesis, the author of the *Book of Steps* perceives the primordial sin as essentially an act of free will, which could therefore have been avoided: "However, in the end, Adam had a will, and if he had not so desired, the evil one would not have oppressed him [during] the thousand years he lived on the earth."[15] But whereas in Ephrem the sin is conceived of in general terms of disobedience, according to the *Book of Steps,* it is portrayed as a shift in the inner intellectual focus from heavenly to earthly concerns, "the thought of transitory things by which Adam and Eve tasted death. For through it they came to know evil (ܒܝܫܬܐ), that they had not known. . . . After they obeyed the evil one (ܒܝܫܐ) and observed the earth and saw this thing on [the earth] and loved it, evil (ܒܝܫܬܐ) had power over them and they knew it."[16] Earthly concerns are in fact equated here with both evil and death and are introduced by Satan through Adam and Eve's voluntary decision.[17] Their own decision thus constituted a precondition for their submission to Satan's power and to earthly concerns. Consequently, his role in the paradisiacal narrative is substantially marginalized; he merely performs a supporting role in the pivotal drama of the ascetic psyche—the author's concept of the heavenly paradise being thus primarily metaphorical, as distinct from many other early Christian and Jewish traditions.[18] This is further manifested in the internalization of evil by Adam and Eve as a psychological entity dis-

14. *BoS* 21.7, *LG* 604.1–3.

15. *BoS* 21.10, *LG* 612.9–14; see Aryeh Kofsky and Serge Ruzer, "Justice, Free Will and Divine Mercy in Ephrem's Commentary on Genesis 2–3," *Le Muséon* 113 (2000): 315–32.

16. *BoS* 21.1, *LG* 584.4–12; cf. *BoS* 21.10, *LG* 612.12–24; *BoS* 21.17, *LG* 625.20–26.

17. *BoS* 21.20, *LG* 632. In Syriac literature, free will is often identified with celibate and ascetic life, in opposition to Satan; see, e.g., Aphrahat, *Demonstration* 7.25, in *Aphraatis Sapientis Persae Demonstrationes,* edited by Jean Parisot, Patrologia Syriaca 1.1 (Paris: Firmin-Didot, 1894); Paolo Bettiolo, "Adamo in Eden e la liturgia celeste: Temi della meditazione cristiana nella Siria del IV secolo, tra Afraate e il Liber Graduum," *Rivista di Storia e Letteratura Religiosa* 37 (2001): 3–27, esp. 4.

18. For a discussion of the figure of Satan in the context of the biblical account of paradise in early Christian and Jewish sources, see Gary A. Anderson, *The Genesis of Perfection: Adam and Eve in Jewish and Christian Imagination* (Louisville: Westminster John Knox Press, 2001), 21–42.

tinct from Satan; it is this psychological entity (ܒܝܫܬܐ) rather than Satan as the "evil one" (ܒܝܫܐ) that is said to overpower the protoplasts.

Satan, however, is still regarded by the *Book of Steps* as the epistemic source of evil, identified peculiarly with the tree of knowledge—another sign of his metaphorical devaluation.[19] This notion is presented in tandem with the more traditional identification of Christ with the tree of life.[20] It should be noted that, somewhat unexpectedly, Augustine's view here is akin to that of the *Book of Steps.* In line with his generally negative appraisal of free will, he identifies the tree of knowledge with the exercise of free will as disobedience.[21] The *Book of Steps,* however, seems also to perceive free will as a source for the underlying principles guiding the Upright in their mundane existence and thus to discern certain positive aspects of the tree.[22] But its author claims that knowledge of good was taught to the protoplasts by God himself prior to the fall, and according to his idiosyncratic interpretation the tree of knowledge signifies in fact the additional ungodly knowledge of evil:

> Because God had only taught what is good (ܒܠܚܘܕ ܛܒܬܐ) to Adam and Eve when he created them. . . . Because of this Satan is called the "Tree," through which Adam and Eve knew evil and good (ܝܕܥܘ ܒܗ ܒܝܫܬܐ ܘܛܒܬܐ). They learned good from God (ܝܠܦܘ ܛܒܬܐ ܡܢ ܐܠܗܐ) and evil from Satan. They became "knowers of good and evil," and from there the enmity of impiety (ܣܢܐܬܐ ܕܪܫܝܥܘܬܐ) bound Adam and his children.[23]

19. *BoS* 21.1, *LG* 585.5. Unlike Ephrem, however, who also devalues the original status of Satan before his fall, our author retains Satan's original heavenly status; see Martikainen, "Böse in den Schriften," 38. The question as to whether the tree of knowledge is Satan appears in ps. Macarius, although his own concept is different; see Hermann Dörries, *Die Theologie des Makarios/Symeon,* Abhandlungen der Akademie der Wissenschaft, Philologisch-historische Klasse, Series 3, no. 105 (Göttingen: Vandenhoeck and Ruprecht, 1978), 42.

20. *BoS* 21.2, *LG* 589.3–6; Ephrem, *Hymns on Paradise* 3.2.15, in *Des Heiligen Ephraem des Syrers Hymnen de paradiso und contra Julianum,* edited by Edmund Beck, CSCO, vol. 175–76 (Louvain: Peeters, 1957); Augustine *De Civ. Dei* 13.21; Louth, "Paradies," 716.

21. For Augustine's general concept of free will, see, e.g., *De spiritu et littera* 5; *Ep.* 217 (To Vitalis); *De correptione et gratia* 34–38. His negative view of free will is also similar in principle to that of Evagrius Ponticus; see, e.g., Evagrius, *Chapters on Prayer* 31, Patrologia Graeca 79, cols. 1165–1200; English translation Robert E. Sinkewicz, *Evagrius of Pontus: The Greek Ascetic Corpus* (Oxford: Oxford University Press, 2003). On Augustine's identification of the tree of knowledge with free will, cf. *De Civ. Dei* 13.21; Louth, "Paradies," 716. For additional patristic views on free will, see Kowalski, *Perfezione e giustizia,* 124.

22. *BoS* 21.8, *LG* 604.17–25.

23. *BoS* 21.1, *LG* 585.4–9.

According to our author, earthly concerns are a general category of thought of what he terms "transitory" things (ܥܒܘܪ̈ܝܬܐ)—such things as labor and anxiety regarding food, property, beauty, honor, clothes and sex—namely, concerns alien to the ascetic ideal, all branded as lust (ܪܓܬܐ). It deserves notice that, though undeniably belonging to the story of Adam and Eve, sex is here no more than one aspect of the human yearning for mundane existence.[24] The very concept of primordial sin as an act of free will and its inescapable consequences encompasses the list of transitory interests, reflecting the *Book of Steps'* ascetic perception of paradise. This approach allows the *Book of Steps* to entertain a twofold understanding of the commandment not to eat from the tree as symbolically representing a general prohibition of lust for material possessions, as well as literally sanctioning against the "lustful anxiety" for food.[25] The latter emphasis appears as also applying to the rest of earthly concerns, in a sense encapsulating the concept of primordial sin. This approach is strikingly reminiscent of similar attitudes prevalent in early Egyptian monasticism—as highlighted by Peter Brown—where it was widely believed that the first sin of Adam and Eve had been lust for food rather than for the sexual act.[26]

Thus, in a number of contexts in the *Book of Steps,* the act of eating functions as an allegorical representation of sin—namely, of the fateful change in spiritual and intellectual orientation. The sin is thus perceived essentially as being of a spiritual character.[27] This is explicit, inter alia, in the following passage: "But after they ate from the tree, that is, after they had abandoned heaven and loved the earth, their mind came from heaven to their bodies (ܠܘܬ ܦܓܪ̈ܝܗܘܢ ܐܬܐ ܪܥܝܢܗܘܢ ܡܢ ܫܡܝܐ), [and] then they saw that they were naked."[28] Therefore, the result of the initial attention they paid to earthly desires or—

24. *BoS* 21.1, *LG* 584.5; *BoS* 21.4, *LG* 596.1; *BoS* 21.7, *LG* 600.25–26; see also Robert A. Kitchen, "Syriac Additions to Anderson: The Garden of Eden in the Book of Steps and Philoxenus of Mabbug," *Hugoye: Journal of Syriac Studies* 6 (2003): 37–50.

25. *BoS* 21.7. In this context the *Book of Steps* also uses the idiom "fasting to the world" (ܨܘܡܘܗܝ ܠܥܠܡܐ), otherwise attested in Oxyrhynchus papyrus (*Oxy.* I.2) and the *Gospel of Thomas* 27; see Antoine Guillaumont, "ΝΗΣΤΕΥΕΙΝ ΤΟΝ ΚΟΣΜΟΝ (P. Oxy. 1, verso, l.5–6)," Bulletin de l'Institut francais d'archeologie orientale 61 (1962): 15–23; Aelred Baker, "Fasting to the World," *Journal of Biblical Literature* 84 (1965): 291–94.

26. Peter R. Brown, *The Body and Society: Men, Women, and Sexual Renunciation in Early Christianity* (New York: Columbia University Press, 1988), 220–21.

27. See Kowalski, *Perfezione e giustizia,* 206–7.

28. *BoS* 21.8, *LG* 605.8–12.

according to the *Book of Steps'* imagery—the initial *consummation* is humanity's enslavement to those desires. This is in contradistinction to the spiritual food—namely, the "life-giving words of our Lord," represented by the tree of life. Had Adam and Eve chosen this latter path, it would have allowed them to realize their potential immortality and "be bound up" with the Lord (ܢܬܐܣܪܘܢ ܒܡܪܢ ܗܘܘ ܠܚܝܐ ܕܠܝܬ ܒܗ ܡܘܬܐ).[29] One may discern here an interesting parallel, *mutatis mutandis,* to Ludwig Feuerbach's famous interpretation of an old dictum: "Der Mensch ist, was er ißt" (One is what one eats).[30] In Feuerbach's context, the *consumption* relates not to food, but rather to the particularities of man's sociocultural environment that define his world outlook.

In light of his perception of the dual paradisiacal reality, the author of the *Book of Steps* distinguishes between the spiritual and allegorical nourishment and the material sustenance of the physical body of Adam and Eve in their pre-fall existence. The material food is referred to as heavenly bread (ܠܚܡܐ ܫܡܝܢܐ), identical with that of the angels (ܠܚܡܐ ܕܡܠܐܟܐ).[31] This heavenly bread—apparently referring to Psalm 78:24-25—is associated with the manna that is the food both of the primordial state in paradise and of the perfect ascetic.[32] In contrast to the notion that the physical food in paradise came from the various trees—as implied by the biblical verse (Genesis 2:16, "And the Lord God commanded the man, saying, you may freely eat of every tree of the garden") and endorsed by common Christian exegesis, including Ephrem[33]—the *Book of Steps'* author, focusing exclusively on the manna, gives no indication of the fruit trees in paradise being a source of physical nutrition. In the blissful prelapsarian state, Adam is fully absorbed in the contemplation of heaven, while his physical needs are supplied by God: "He looked into heaven and not on earth and rejoiced with the heavenly angels without anxiety and pains, and

29. *BoS* 21.1, *LG* 588.5–9; cf. this peculiar idiom with the biblical verse that later became a Jewish liturgical formula expressing the soul's immortality: "To be bound up in the bundle of life"; 1 Sam 25:29; the prayer for the dead "*El male rachamim*" (merciful God).

30. Ludwig Feuerbach, *Das Wesen des Christentums,* in *Essence of Christianity,* translated by George Eliot 67–93 (Leipzig: Otto Wigand, 1904).

31. *BoS* 21.7, *LG* 601.1–2; Kowalski, *Perfezione e giustizia,* 103–5.

32. *BoS* 25.8, *LG* 752.24–53.4. This idea differs from the understanding of manna as spiritual food, as suggested in 1 Cor 10:3.

33. See Ephrem, *Gen. Com.* 2.8, in *Sancti Ephraem Syri in Genesim et in Exodum commentarii,* edited by Raymond-Marie Tonneau, CSCO 153 (Louvain: L. Durbecq, 1955); Kofsky and Ruzer, "Justice," 321–22.

was concerned neither about clothing nor about food. But God fed him, as was appropriate to the wealth of his kindness (ܥܘܬܪܐ ܕܒܣܝܡܘܬܗ) with heavenly bread."[34]

The author emphasizes, in this context as elsewhere in the treatise,[35] that the heavenly bread is gained by Adam and the perfect ascetics without toil (ܒܥܡܠܐ ܠܐ ܗܘܝܢ ܗܘܘ),[36] denoting his radical anti-labor ascetical concept, where labor is regarded essentially as an impediment to a truly spiritual existence and hence on a par with the rest of earthly concerns: "However, Adam chose labor, that is the opposite of perfection, and through his own choice he bore anxiety—something that stifles those who seek to ascend to the higher realm."[37]

This concept is manifestly distinct from the more common monastic approach, where labor is considered essential to the monk's ideal of autarky. Moreover, since the need for material nourishment is common to both the pre-fall and the post-fall modes of existence, it is precisely the exigency of labor that determines the essential difference between the two types of material food—namely, the heavenly and the earthly. The author of the *Book of Steps* thus associates the cessation of heavenly bread with the fall and the beginning of the need for human toil to produce food: "They saw that the heavenly bread was withheld (ܐܬܟܠܝ) and went on to labor (ܠܡܦܠܚ) on the earth for food."[38]

The exegetical strategy here is founded upon two biblical passages employed to define both the nature of the ideal physical existence—be it of the protoplasts in paradise or the perfect ascetics—and the consequences of the fall. The first is obviously the verdict: "In the sweat of your face you shall eat bread,"[39] while the second is the Exodus description of the divine gift of manna in the desert and its abuse by the Children of Israel, expressed in the exaggerated care for the food and the consequent punishment.[40] From the *Book of Steps'* perspective, this misconduct might have been interpreted as excessive attention to earthly concerns and a lack of spiritual focus.

34. *BoS* 21.7, *LG* 600.23–1.2; see also *BoS* 23.1, *LG* 692.11–13. The motif of contemplation of heaven before the fall has antecedents and parallels in Greek Christian literature; see Kowalski, *Perfezione e giustizia,* 54n55. The angelic state of Adam and Eve is an old motif found already in Jewish Pseudepigrapha and early Christian literature; see Kowalski, *Perfezione e giustizia,* 84n144.

35. See, for example, *BoS* 25.8, *LG* 752.1–53.8.

36. *BoS* 21.7, *LG* 601.3–4.

37. *BoS* 21.20, *LG* 632.7–11.

38. *BoS* 21.10, *LG* 613.10–11.

39. Gen 3:19.

40. Ex 16:14–27.

This anti-labor stance may be perceived as contradicting the dictum in Genesis 2:15, "The Lord God took the man and put him in the Garden of Eden to *work* it and keep it." It may not be accidental that our author, in the whole of his lengthy work, does not relate to this verse. On the other hand, it is plausible that he is relying on an old and common exegetical tradition, that interpreted "to work it" not literally as physical labor, but rather as either intellectual contemplation of divine truths and the performing of the celestial liturgy or as generally observing God's commandments. These patterns of exegesis—ignoring the literal sense of the verse, which implies physical labor—are found already, for example, in Philo,[41] in later rabbinic tradition,[42] and in Ephrem, who combines the interpretation of "work" as observing the commandment not to eat from the tree with its identification as Adam's priestly ministry.[43]

As noted, the idea of real material paradisiacal nourishment is complemented in the *Book of Steps* by the notion of spiritual sustenance—an idea that in itself was widely known both in the Jewish Hellenistic and in the Christian traditions. An early example is found in Philo's elaboration on the spiritual food consumed by the elect among the Children of Israel on Mount Sinai. Relating to Exodus 24:11 ("And he did not lay his hand on the chief men of the people of Israel; they beheld God, and ate and drank"), Philo interprets beholding God (ויחזו את האלהים) as seeing God with the keen-sighted eyes of the mind; this vision is, according to him, the food of souls, of which a true partaking results in immortality. Thus the ascent to Mount Sinai is perceived as a heavenly ascent to the tree of life, to a holy and divine place identified as God's logos. In Philo's context, the sacrificial meal of the biblical narrative is entirely

41. Philo, *Legum Allegoria* 1.14.

42. *Tg. Neofiti, Tg. Yer., Tg. Frag.* ad locum; see also Tryggve Kronholm, *Motifs from Genesis 1–11, in the Genuine Hymns of Ephrem the Syrian with Particular Reference to the Influence of Jewish Exegetical Tradition* (Upsala: Almqvist and Wiksell, 1978), 76n96; *Gen. Rab.* 16.15; Judah Theodore and Chanoch Albeck, ed., *Midrash Bereshit Rabbah* (Jerusalem: Wahrmann, 1965).

43. *Hymns on Paradise* III.2, 3, 5, 13–14, 16; II.10–13; see also Ignacio Ortiz de Urbina, "Le Paradis eschatologique d'aprés Saint Ephrem," *Orientalia Christiana Periodica* 21 (1956): 467–72; Nicholas Séd, "Les Hymnes sur le Paradis de Saint Ephrem et les Tradition Juives," *Le Muséon* 81 (1968): 455–501; Tryggve Kronholm, "The Trees of Paradise in the Hymns of Ephraem Syrus," *Annual of the Swedish Theological Institute Leiden* 1 (1978): 48–56; Sebastian P. Brock, *St. Ephrem the Syrian: Hymns on Paradise* (New York: St. Vladimir's Seminary Press, 1990), 52–53; Kronholm, *Motifs*, 76–77; see also the discussion in Kofsky and Ruzer, "Justice."

spiritualized and replaced by an ecstatic vision of God that provides "food for the soul" without any physical food consumed! Sacrificial cult is thus replaced by ecstatic vision. All this is connected in Philo to Israel's privileged status, recognized in their divine gifts of "seeing" God (a Philonic pseudo-etymology of the name Israel) and later enjoying the heavenly manna.[44]

The general concept of spiritual food as the true nourishment of the human soul appears in the *Book of Steps* in the peculiar form of a spiritual consummation of the tree of life. Unlike Philo, for whom the Sinai revelation is intrinsically connected to the tree of life, for the Syriac author the archetypal metaphor of spiritual sustenance is grounded in the pre-cosmic reality of the heavenly paradise. Moreover, the primordial tree of life is perceived as a purely spiritual entity identified in the context of Christian theological discourse with the eternal Messiah-Christ. According to the *Book of Steps,* then, the spiritual food is in fact the "words of our Lord (Jesus)," tantamount here to the Lord himself and to the tree of life: "In that world in that there is no death, where they will eat the life-giving words of our Lord (ܡܠܘ̈ܗܝ ܕܡܪܢ ܕܐܟܠܝܢ ܚܝ̈ܐ ܡܚܝ̈ܢܐ). They shall eat our Lord (ܘܐܟܠܘܢ ܠܗ ܠܡܪܢ) and live. . . . The good tree, in that world of light invisible to the eyes of flesh, is our Lord Jesus. He is the tree of life (ܗܘܝܘ ܐܝܠܢܐ ܕܚܝ̈ܐ) who gives everything life by its fruit wherever the perfect will of God is."[45] This logos-centered interpretation is reminiscent of Philo, though here, as noted, it is clearly part of the Christian discourse. Moreover, both traditions seem to refer to the biblical dictum "man does not live by bread alone, but . . . by everything that proceeds out of the mouth of the Lord."[46] This may have served as a scriptural foundation for the *Book of Steps'* concept of the double nourishment in paradise, the spiritual one being identified with the words of the Lord or even with the divine logos symbolically

44. See Philo, *Quaestiones et solutiones in Exodum* to Exod 24:11–12, in *Philo: Questions on Exodus,* translated by Ralph Marcus, 80–83, Loeb Classical Library 401 (Cambridge, Mass.: Harvard University Press, 1953). Various noetic nourishment traditions according to which angels do not consume material sustenance are attested in rabbinic, patristic, and pseudepigraphic writings. Manna and ecstatic vision as both sources of divine knowledge and angelic sustenance are attested also in Jewish Hellenistic writings; for discussion, see Andrea Lieber, "Jewish and Christian Heavenly Meal Traditions," in *Paradise Now: Essays on Early Jewish and Christian Mysticism,* edited by April D. DeConick, 313–39, esp. 315–20, SBL Symposium Series 11 (Atlanta: Society of Biblical Literature, 2006).

45. *BoS* 21.1–2, *LG* 588.6–89.7. The appellation "our Lord" (ܡܪܢ) is a regular title for Jesus among Syriac writers; see Kowalski, *Perfezione e giustizia,* 47.

46. Deut 8:3.

represented by the tree of life. The identification of the tree of life with Christ, albeit without the consummation motif peculiar to the *Book of Steps,* was apparently a common feature of early Syriac thought, as evident in Ephrem.[47]

The purely spiritual interpretation suggested here for the "eating of the Lord" is complemented by the negative spiritual alternative of eating from the tree of knowledge, identified with Satan: "Because of this Satan is called the 'Tree' (ܡܠܦܢܐ ܣܟܠܐ ܐܝܠܢܐ) through which Adam and Eve knew evil and good. They learned good from God, and evil from Satan. . . . Because of this, God said to them: 'Do not eat from the tree of the knowledge of good and evil,' that is, do not listen to it because it will teach you all sorts of evil things and take you away from heavenly things (ܫܡܝܢܝܬܐ) and from the kindness of your Creator."[48] It seems that this elaboration of the paradisiacal spiritual consummation of the tree of life, understood as the consummation of the Lord, has implicit eucharistic connotations.[49] In other words, the spiritual nourishment in the heavenly paradise is identified with the eucharistic communion. Consequently, in this emphasis on the equation of "eating the Lord" with hearing his words, one may see how the general focus of the *Book of Steps* on the inner intellectual preoccupation with heavenly things is further enhanced by symbolic understanding of the Eucharist, an understanding rather common in early Christianity that coexisted peacefully with "literal" interpretations.[50] It is worth noting that such clearly metaphorical usage of the idiom "eating the Messiah" is not restricted to Christian sources, but is also found in a contemporaneous rabbinic tradition, albeit in a different context and with a different meaning. According to this tradition, "Israel has no Messiah, because they have consumed him already in the days of Hezekiah" (אין להם משיח לישראל שכבר אכלוהו בימי חזקיה).[51]

47. See Ephrem, *Hymns on Paradise* 3.2.15 (see note 20); *Hymns on Faith* 6.14.9–11, 29 (see note 6); see also Robert Murray, *Symbols of Church and Kingdom: A Study in Early Syriac Tradition,* rev. ed. (London: T. and T. Clark; Piscataway, N.J.: Gorgias Press, 2004), 113–29, 320–24; Kronholm, *Motifs,* 74. This identification is also found in Augustine, *De Civ. Dei* 13.21; see also Louth, "Paradies," 716.

48. *BoS* 21.1, *LG* 585.4–15.

49. It is noteworthy that for Ephrem it is rather the tree of knowledge that bears eucharistic connotations. According to him, the Eucharist is a form of eating from the tree of knowledge; see Ephrem, *Hymns on Paradise* VI.7–8; XII.7; XII.15; Kofsky and Ruzer, "Justice," 328.

50. Johannes Betz, *Eucharistie in der Schrift und Patristik,* Handbuch der Dogmengeschichte IV (Freiburg: Herder, 1979).

51. Babylonian Talmud, tractate Sanhedrin 98b.

The perception of the consequent earthly existence of humanity as virtual death, in contrast to the paradisiacal one, corresponds to the ascetic imperative, where death to the world constitutes true life. This informs the *Book of Steps'* idiosyncratic interpretation of Genesis 2:17: "But of the tree of the knowledge of good and evil you shall not eat, for in the day that you eat of it you shall surely die." God, then, according to the *Book of Steps*—in contradistinction to a common Jewish and Christian exegetical pattern[52]—does not inform Adam here about an impending punishment of death at the end of human life span, but simply warns him of the inevitable transformation ensuing immediately after the change of inner disposition. We can further notice here the hermeneutical aspect of the *Book of Steps'* elaboration of the subject, expressed in its idiosyncratic interpretation of the story of paradise in Genesis, according to the general ascetic paradigm.

Memra 21 also links the protoplasts' enchantment with earthly concerns with their desire—either triggered or enhanced by Satan's instigation—to "become like God,"[53] a desire branded by the *Book of Steps* as silly and infantile (ܫܒܪܝܢ) and in fact perceived as a manifestation of the sin of pride.[54] In this the author further unfolds the uncommon parallelism between Adam's sin and Satan's earlier sin and fall, reflected in his notion that in Adam, Satan was looking for a soul mate of a sort.[55]

The Genesis narrative itself[56] contains an inherent tension between the divine proclamation that man is created in God's image followed by the clear mandate to rule over the natural world and multiply—this dominion is understood by Ephrem as the ultimate expression of being in God's image—and Satan's/the serpent's enticement to become like God.[57] The author of the *Book*

52. See Anderson, *Genesis of Perfection,* 155–76.

53. Gen 3:5.

54. *BoS* 21.11, *LG* 616.2–5, 25. For a discussion of the nuances of the terms ܫܒܪܐ and ܫܒܪܘܬܐ in the context of early Syriac traditions about the state of Adam and Eve before the fall, see Alison Salvesen, "Infants or Fools in the Garden of Eden? An Ambiguity in Early Syriac Tradition," in *Hamlet on a Hill: Semitic and Greek Studies Presented to Professor T. Muraoka on the Occasion of His Sixty-Fifth Birthday,* edited by Martin F. J. Baasten and Wido T. van Peursen, 433–40, Orientalia Lovaniensia Analecta 118 (Leuven: Peeters, 2003). Salvesen notes that though childhood is elsewhere used as a simile of humanity's perfect innocence before the fall, in the *Book of Steps* Adam's state of perfection is contrasted with ܫܒܪܘܬܐ in its meaning of immaturity and foolishness, regardless of his actual age.

55. *BoS* 21.18, *LG* 628.20–23; see also Kitchen, "Syriac Additions," §7.

56. Gen 1:26–27.

57. Gen 3:4–5.

of Steps is manifestly aware of this inherent tension, due inter alia to the centrality of the rejection motif vis-à-vis the earthly world. He highlights this tension by further adapting Satan's speech to God's proclamation: "The evil one (ܒܝܫܐ) counseled: Possess and enjoy yourself; rule, increase, and multiply. Cast off from yourself asceticism (ܫܕܝ ܡܢܟ ܚܣܝܘܬܐ) and renunciation (ܡܣܪܩܘܬܐ) and holiness, also lowliness (ܐܦ ܡܘܟܟܐ), and know evil as well as good things and grow and become like God who created you."[58] The call to "rule, increase, and multiply" deliberately echoes the divine mandate in Genesis 1:26–28.

According to the author, Adam perceived earthly paradise as the realm of his dominion, where he could hide from God, who was restricted, as it were, to his heavenly domain.[59] The author suggests that the way to dominion lies not in the pursuit of earthly wealth and power—advocated by Satan—but in renunciation of the world in imitation of Christ's *kenosis.* Namely, the possibility of *imitatio Dei* is here restricted to an imitation of Christ in his condescending state and not in his function as creator and *Pantokrator.* The idea of deification, common in Ephrem and in Greek patristic literature, is totally unknown to the author; according to him, it is impossible—a vain, childish arrogance—to aspire to be like God and act like God the King and Creator.[60]

Moreover, God's commandment in Genesis 1:28 is idiosyncratically reinterpreted as a law given "for the aid of his soul *lest he let go off heaven and inherit the earth.*"[61] Thus the desire to be like God signifies a total rebellion against God and a rejection of his will regarding certain precepts of ascetic perfection, following the earlier revolt of Satan.[62] Yet in the *Book of Steps,* the achievement of a limited degree of *imitatio Christi* is in fact tantamount to a deification of sorts, where humanity is able to be a true image of God or to "become like God" and partake in his dominion.[63]

58. *BoS* 21.9, *LG* 609.7–12.

59. *BoS* 21.17, *LG* 625.3–15. Kitchen sees here a comic element introduced by the author into the biblical narrative; see Kitchen, "Syriac Additions," §25.

60. On the idea of deification in Ephrem, see *Hymns on the Church* 45.32.1, in *Des heiligen Ephrem des Syrers Hymnen de Ecclesia,* edited by Edmund Beck, Corpus Scriptorum Christianorum Orientalium 198, 117 (Louvain: Peeters, 1960); *Carmina Nisibena* 69.12.1, in *Carmina Nisibena,* edited by Edmund Beck, CSCO 240, 112 (Louvain: Peeters, 1963).

61. *BoS* 21.8, *LG* 604.26–5.1; see also Paolo Bettiolo, "Confessare Dio in perfetta spogliazione: La via del discernimento dei comandamenti nel *Liber graduum,*" *Cristianesimo nella storia* 19 (1998): 631–51.

62. See Kowalski, *Perfezione e giustizia,* 206–7.

63. A "low" notion of deification—alongside "higher" deification concepts—is also common in

This is how the treatise resolves the inherent tension, retaining both the ascetic imperative and the state of dominion from Genesis 1 or, as the *Book of Steps* restates it elsewhere:

> Thus people would have been on earth physically and in heaven spiritually until it pleased their Creator to elevate them to on high. Nothing on earth would have harmed them: neither reptile, nor wild beast, nor Satan. . . . For he said to them on the day he created them, "I will throw the fear and dread of you upon all that exists on the earth." The hand of the Lord was on Adam and the hand of Adam tamed (ܡܟܒܫܐ ܗܘܬ) all there was on the earth beneath him by the power of our omnipotent (ܐܚܝܕ ܟܠ) Lord.[64]

Another conspicuous motif in the Genesis 1:26–28 divine call to humanity involves the mandate to procreate and multiply. This maxim seemingly contradicts the manifest ascetic program of the author, forcing him to adapt his exegesis correspondingly.[65] His hermeneutical solution is the claim that, had the protoplasts kept God's commandments, they would have multiplied in the earthly paradise in a nonsexual mode of procreation, one resembling the creation of Eve from Adam's rib: "But if they had kept the commandments of our Lord and made supplication to him . . . our Lord would have made (ܥܒܕ) for them children as he had made Eve from Adam, without lust (ܪܓܬܐ) and without intercourse (ܙܘܘܓܐ), or if he had wanted he could have made children by the hairs of their heads or by the fingernails, and the people would have become the image (ܕܡܘܬܐ) of angels."[66] This mode of procreation, then, somewhat resembles the natural vegetative mode of reproduction, or even a primitive form of the idea of cloning. The absence of lust is emphasized as characterizing this neutral mode of procreation.[67] In propagating this nonsexual, quasi-angelic form

Greek patristic literature; see, e.g., Norman Russel, *The Doctrine of Deification in the Greek Patristic Tradition* (Oxford: Oxford University Press, 2005).

64. *BoS* 21.7, *LG* 604.1–12; Gen 9:2.

65. The difficulty regarding the existence of male and female genitalia—similarly contradicting the ascetic agenda of the author—is also addressed by him; see Kowalski, *Perfezione e giustizia,* 63, 68.

66. *BoS* 21.7, *LG* 601.11–19. For Adam's similarity to angels in his pristine state, see also *BoS* 23.1, *LG* 692.11–13. Gregory of Nyssa also expresses the idea of an angelic mode of procreation, which Adam and Eve lost; Gregory of Nyssa, *De hominis opificio* 17, Patrologia Graeca 44, col. 189.

67. Cf. *BoS* 25.3, *LG* 737.26–40.2, where the author refers to Eve as Adam's daughter, who was created out of him in a nonsexual way. The idea that Adam generated Eve and hence has a kind of parental relation to her has some equivalent in Aphrahat, who says that Adam "gave birth" (ܐܘܠܕ) to Eve

of reproduction, the author deliberately avoids the common verb ܐܘܠܕ, which is for him connected with sexual and animal procreation that Adam and Eve engaged in only after the fall.[68] Adam and Eve, in fact, sin sexually after *watching* the animals.[69] Before that, concupiscence did not enter their hearts, as they were like children. The motif of the ideal innocence of childhood is combined here with that of nudity.[70] It should be noted that Eve's role in the sin and fall is not developed in the *Book of Steps* beyond repetition of the biblical details. She is not the actual cause of Adam's sin—in sharp contrast to Aphrahat and Ephrem, where Eve plays a major role in the fall.[71]

All of this is in line with the author's concept of the parallel dual existence, when the mind is totally absorbed in its heavenly contemplation and the body exercises its biological functions without sensation. This undoubtedly reflects the ascetic agenda of the author, espousing the idea of a passionless physical existence in paradise without abolishing, however, the literal aspect of procre-

(*Demonstration* 18.9, edited by Jean Parisot, Patrologia Syriaca 1.1 [Paris: : Firmin-Didot, 1894], col. 837.15), whereas Ephrem explicitly denies that Eve was Adam's daughter (*Commentary on the Diatessaron*, Arm. 19.5, in *Saint Éphrem: Commentaire de l'évangile concordant,* in Scriptores armeniaci I, edited by Louis Leloir, CSCO 137, 277 (Louvain: Imprimerie Orientaliste L. Durbecq and Peeters, 1954); see Kowalski, *Perfezione e giustizia,* 69. See also *BoS* 15.6, *LG* 348.18–21, where this ideal form of reproduction seems to be restricted to Eve and hence to the female sex, and is initiated by a divine word: "he (God) would have made Eve fruitful by the word of our Lord without lust" (ܘܐܦܪܝ ܗܘܐ ܠܚܘܐ ܒܡܠܬܐ ܕܡܪܢ ܘܠܐ ܪܓܬܐ). This seems to connote Mary's conception of Jesus without lust or intercourse; cf. John 1:13, where it is applied to the believers at large; see also *BoS* 25.3. The concept of heavenly bliss without lust was known also to Aphrahat (*Demonstration* 22.12–13) and Ephrem (*Hymns on Paradise* 7.5.4, 14.11.3).

68. Kowalski, *Perfezione e giustizia,* 71; cf. Philo, who regards Adam before the creation of Eve as an ascetic, imitating the solitary asceticism of God; Philo, *De opificio mundi* 151, 153, in *Philo Volume 1,* translated by Francis H. Colson and George H. Whitaker, Loeb Classical Library 226 (London: Heinemann, 1929); Bettiolo, "Adamo in Eden," 6. For an overview of Jewish and Christian traditions regarding the possibility of sexual relations between the protoplasts in paradise, see Gary A. Anderson, "Celibacy or Consummation in the Garden? Reflections on Early Jewish and Christian Interpretations of the Garden of Eden," *Harvard Theological Review* 82 (1989): 121–48.

69. *BoS* 21.10, *LG* 613.15–19. The idea that Adam and Eve and their first descendants learned basic human functions by observing the animal world is found also in Ephrem, as well as in rabbinic and early Muslim sources; see Ephrem, *Hymns on Faith* 34.2–4; Martikainen, "Böse in den Schriften," 41–42; Gerald Friedlander, trans., *Pirke de Rabbi Eliezer: The Chapters of Rabbi Eliezer the Great according to the Text of the Manuscript belonging to Abraham Epstein of Vienna* (New York: Hermon Press, 1965), 156; Quran 5:31; Abraham Geiger, *Judaism and Islam,* translated by F. M. Young (Madras, India: Zohar Books, 1898), 80–81.

70. *BoS* 15.3, *LG* 341.1–6. For a discussion of this motif, see Kowalski, *Perfezione e giustizia,* 64, 74–77.

71. See Kofsky and Ruzer, "Justice," 325–28; Anderson, *Genesis of Perfection,* 99–116; Kowalski, *Perfezione e giustizia,* 208–9.

ation.[72] We suggest that this balancing act is derived from the hermeneutical framework of harmonizing Genesis 1:26–28 with the author's ascetic ideal.

The description of Adam's paradisiacal existence and of the nature of his fall provides the author of the *Book of Steps* with the necessary backdrop for his portrayal of the Messiah-Christ (ܡܫܝܚܐ) as one who fulfills the original perfection of the Adamic ascetic ideal. This is clearly an idiosyncratic elaboration of the Pauline motif of Jesus as the second Adam, where Paul seems to relate to the two phases in the creation of Adam depicted in Genesis 2:7—namely, his formation from the dust of the earth, followed by the breathing of the spirit of life into him.[73]

In the *Book of Steps,* Adam's sin is posited as the opposite of Christ's achievement. What failed in Adam succeeded in the Messiah: God wanted that Adam should not transgress his commandment, and that wish was fulfilled in the Messiah. Christ and Adam both started from the same point—that is, both were made according to the image (ܕܡܘܬܐ) of God. Moreover, Christ is clearly presented as created in the image of the "true primitive Adam before the fall."[74] But from the moment of sin, their paths diverged dramatically. Adam betrayed his original state of perfection in his foolish hope to

72. See Kowalski, *Perfezione e giustizia,* 63–67.

73. Rom 5:14–19. In the *Book of Steps* there is no first creation of Adam in the Origenian sense of a double creation. On the distinction between the "first" and "second" Adam in Paul, and its possible midrashic setting, see Menahem Kister, "'In Adam': 1 Cor 15:21–22; 12:27 in Their Jewish Setting," in *Flores Florentino: Dead Sea Scrolls and Other Early Jewish Studies in Honour of Florentino García Martínez,* edited by A. Hilhorst, É. Puech, and E. Tigchelaar, 687–90 (Leiden: E. J. Brill, 2007); Kister, "'First Adam' and 'Second Adam' in 1 Cor 15:45–49 in the Light of Midrashic Exegesis and Hebrew Usage," in *The New Testament and Rabbinic Literature,* edited by Reimund Bieringer, Florentino García Martínez, Didier Pollefeyt, and Peter J. Tomson, 351–62 (Leiden: E. J. Brill, 2010). The motif of a "second Eve," common among Syriac authors, does not appear in the *Book of Steps;* see Kowalski, *Perfezione e giustizia,* 209. According to the *Book of Steps,* in addition to the created spirit, God also breathed into Adam something of the non-created Holy Spirit, the same spirit that Christ gave the apostles on the day of his resurrection; *BoS* 28.1. This was already a traditional Syriac motif found in various stages of development in Tatian, the *Acts of Judas Thomas,* Aphrahat, and Ephrem; see Antoine Tanghe, "Memra de Philoxène de Mabboug sur l'inhabitation du Saint Esprit," *Le Muséon* (1960): 39–71. Here, too, the author of the *Book of Steps* has in mind the identity between the primordial state of Adam and the state of the Perfect. The Holy Spirit dwells in a person only as long as he follows the right ascetic way; *BoS* 28.1.

74. *BoS* 21.11, *LG* 616.2–24, based on Phil 2:6–7; see André Louf, "Une Ancienne exégèse de Phil 2:6 dans le Ketaba DeMasqata (Livre des Degrés)," in *Studiorum paulinorum congressus internationalis Catholicus 1961,* 2:523–33, Analecta Biblica 17–18 (Rome: Pontificio Instituto Biblico, 1963).

become like God, whereas Christ adhered to it. The difference between the two consists in their relation to God: Christ assumed Adam's existential situation and was able—by adopting a different stance than Adam—to realize via his *kenosis* God's plan for the state of ascetic perfection.[75] Christ, in fact, came to show people their original nature and teach them how to return to their original form; this seems to be the major purpose of the incarnation.[76] Indeed, there seems to be no special emphasis in the *Book of Steps* on the death of Christ as a redeeming sacrifice; rather, it is on his crucifixion as an ultimate ascetic example of the detachment of the Perfect from earthly existence.[77] We shall return to this ideal of self-crucifixion later.

The author of the *Book of Steps* is distinguished by his uncommon elaboration of the comparison between Jesus and Adam, based mainly on the description of the temptation in Matthew 4:1–11.[78] Jesus's temptation by Satan is in fact presented as a replay of Adam's temptation. This hermeneutical choice presents itself as ideally befitting the *Book of Steps'* agenda. In addition to the ascetic setting of the scene in the desert, two of the temptations relate to food and dominion over the world, the latter being explicitly exploited in our treatise. Thus according to the *Book of Steps:*

> "He approached and was tempted [by Satan]" in order to show us how Adam was tempted (ܐܬܢܣܝ) in the first place. It is written, "He defeated Satan" in order to show us how if Adam had wished by a [single] word (ܒܡܠܬܐ), he would have been able to demolish (ܡܫܟܚ ܗܘܐ ܠܗ) [Satan] . . . by that word (ܒܗܝ ܡܠܬܐ) to which he (Christ) did not listen when [Satan] cajoled him to look out over the earth like Adam so that he might lust (ܢܪܓܝ) for the wealth of the earth and its transitory beauty (ܫܘܦܪܗ ܥܒܘܪܐ) as Adam and Eve had yearned for.[79]

This hermeneutical device recurs further on in the memra, where the seduction of Adam—and here also Eve—by Satan is paralleled by his attempt to seduce Jesus: "But when the deceitful one (ܢܟܠܐ) approached Eve and Adam . . . he seduced (ܛܥܝ) them as he would have seduced Jesus, and said to the Creator of

75. See Louf, "Ancienne exégèse," 523–33; Kowalski, *Perfezione e giustizia,* 139–41; cf. Aphrahat, *Demonstration* 23.51.

76. *BoS* 21.3–4, 23.1, 26.1; cf. Eph 1:10.

77. See *BoS* 21.3, *LG* 593.7–9.

78. *BoS* 21.4, *LG* 593–96. On the pre-Nicene motif of comparison between Adam and Christ, see Kowalski, *Perfezione e giustizia,* 127n20; cf. Mark 1:12–13; Luke 4:1–13.

79. *BoS* 21.4, *LG* 593.19–96.2; see Matt 4:3 and Matt 4:10–11.

the universe, 'Look, see how the earth is attractive with its possession and its kingdoms. Listen to me and take possession (ܩܢܝܢܝ ܘܩܢܝ) and rule (ܐܡܠܟ) and you will not become *poor* (ܘܠܐ ܬܬܡܣܟܢ) and *empty yourself* (ܬܬܣܪܩ) and become a *stranger* (ܬܗܘܐ ܢܘܟܪܝܐ) on the earth.'"[80] This parallel contains more than a shred of irony, since Christ who is being tempted by earthly possessions is emphatically called here "the Creator of the universe" (ܒܪܘܝܐ ܕܒܪ̈ܝܬܐ ܟܠܗܘܢ),[81] demonstrating the absurdity of Satan's scheme. We may also note here the ascetic terminology of Satan's temptation, such as "become *poor,*" "*empty yourself,*" and "become a *stranger* on the earth."[82] In Christ's victory over Satan through his unwavering humility, crowned by the crucifixion, he had broken down "the fence of enmity (ܣܝܓܐ ܕܒܥܠܕܒܒܘܬܐ) and 'everything is made new again in Christ,' as [God] had wanted Adam to become, and as he had been created before he transgressed."[83] In other words, Christ carries out God's eschatological (last) will, which is identified by the author with God's original will envisioned for human paradisiacal existence but rejected by Adam, who "had done away with [it] at creation."[84]

The Christ-Adam opposition—integral to their parallelism—is further accentuated by the radical contrast in their perception of the vocation of humanity, created in God's image. Adam's misinterpretation of the nature of his divine image as one of majesty is contrasted with Christ's adherence to the original ascetic virtue of humility as the only avenue open for humans to "become like God." In other words, the only way to *imitatio Dei* is that of humility and *kenosis.* This is exegetically linked in the *Book of Steps* to the famous passage in Philippians 2:6, depicting Christ's semi-divine status as derived from

80. *BoS* 21.9, *LG* 608.19–24.

81. In *BoS* 21.11, *LG* 616.4–5, Christ is similarly described as "that one who is the Creator and who is our Lord Jesus Christ." The Trinitarian identification of Christ as the creator of the universe was not self-evident in earlier Syriac theology, as is clearly attested by both Aphrahat and Ephrem; see Aryeh Kofsky and Serge Ruzer, "Logos, Holy Spirit and Messiah: Aspects of Aphrahat's Theology Reconsidered," *Orientalia Christiana Periodica* 73 (2007): 347–78. Thus the *Book of Steps* may be regarded as an early instance of adapting to Greek Nicene Trinitarian theology, albeit in an undeveloped form; see also Kowalski, *Perfezione e giustizia,* 115, 201–3.

82. On the ascetic virtue of *xeniteia,* see Antoine Guillaumont, "Le dépaysement comme form d'ascèse dans le monachism ancient," in *Aux origines du monachisme chrétien: Pour une phénoménologie du monachisme,* 89–116, Spiritualité Orientale 30 (Bégrolles-en-Mauges, France: Abbaye de Bellefontaine, 1979); Brouria Bitton-Ashkelony, *Encountering the Sacred: The Debate on Christian Pilgrimage in Late Antiquity* (Berkeley and Los Angeles: The University of California Press, 2005), 146–60.

83. *BoS* 21.3, *LG* 592.14–20; see Eph 1:10.

84. *BoS* 21.8, *LG* 605.15–16.

his humility. Contrary to Adam, who desired to become equal to God, Christ "took the example of a servant while he was in the image of that creation of the first human being. . . . He took the image of servant so that he might obey his father like a servant—not in the way Adam took the image of majesty in order to be the opposite and adversary to his Lord and Creator."[85]

In line with his general view of Christ's death, as an ultimate ascetic example of detachment from earthly existence rather than as an atoning sacrifice, the author states that the Messiah showed the way up to the Perfect; as he dwells in the upper heavens, they also should strive to achieve this goal through humility, ascetic detachment, and obedience.[86] In other words, the perfect ascetic faces the same challenge: to die in his thoughts to earthly things (ܢܡܘܬ ܡܢ ܐܪܥܐ ܒܪܥܝܢܗ) and the way is open for him here and now to follow Christ and not Adam.[87] This apparently explains the lack of eschatological emphasis on Christ's second coming, since the ascetic imperative is now envisioned as the ultimate avenue for salvation.[88]

The ideal of ascetic humility as the vehicle for *imitatio Dei* is further enhanced by the notion that a chain of Old and New Testament figures had exemplified this virtue, including Noah, Moses, Job, Daniel, Mary, Paul, and the apostles. Moses and Paul, in fact, were willing to sacrifice their lives for the sake of their brethren.[89] It is significant that the author here changes the biblical attribute of Noah in Genesis 6:9 and 7:2 from "righteous" (ܙܕܝܩ) to "humble" (ܡܟܝܟ) and calls him "the most humble of all the earth" (ܡܟܝܟ ܡܢ ܟܠܗ ܐܪܥܐ).[90] The *Book of Steps* seems to discern an exegetical link between Noah and Moses

85. *BoS* 21.11, *LG* 616.14–23; see also Louf, "Ancienne exégèse," 523–33; cf. Phil 2:6.

86. *BoS* 21.4, *LG* 596.13–17; *BoS* 21.11, *LG* 616.16–17.

87. *BoS* 21.5, *LG* 597.

88. According to Naeh, one may discern in certain Talmudic traditions a "messianic dimension of celibacy" influenced by Syriac early asceticism; see Shlomo Naeh, "Freedom and Celibacy: A Talmudic Variation on Tales of Temptation and Fall in Genesis and Its Syrian Background," in *The Book of Genesis in Jewish and Oriental Christian Interpretation,* edited by Judith Frishman and Lucas van Rompay, 80n28, Traditio Exegetica Graeca 5 (Louvain: Peeters, 1997). On sexuality in general in rabbinic literature, see Daniel Boyarin, *Carnal Israel: Reading Sex in Talmudic Culture* (Berkeley and Los Angeles: University of California Press, 1993).

89. *BoS* 21.12–16, 21.15. On Moses's plea for his brethren in Jewish and Christian literature, see Anderson, *Genesis of Perfection,* 168–70; see Ex 32:33 and Rom 9:3.

90. *BoS* 21.13, *LG* 620.21–21.

in the verb "to blot out," ܡܚܐ, used in both Genesis 6:7 and Exodus 32:33, denoting God's readiness to annihilate the rest of humanity or the people of Israel.[91] Our composition thus attributes a similar status to Noah as that of Paul and Moses, as an advocate for the sinners.[92]

According to the *Book of Steps,* Moses was chosen precisely because he was the humblest. God weighed Moses against all the other 600,000 Israelites and their families, who sinned in pride, and in his lowliness and humility he outweighed them all.[93] A similar motif—the scales of pride versus humility—appears in connection with Noah, whose lowliness outweighed all the rest of humanity.[94] This type of humility is represented in various generations, so that a clear shift of emphasis from the biblical virtue of righteousness to the ascetic virtue of humility can be discerned.[95] Moreover, the author also singles out Mary's humility as the prime motive for her election as the mother of the Messiah, going so far as to state that "if there had been another woman who was more humble (ܡܟܝܟܐ) than Mary, Christ would have been given birth to by her!"[96] The ascetic ideal of perfection through humility, then, is expanded to include outstanding figures from the whole range of pre-monastic sacred history and thus relativized in preparing the ground for contemporary ascetics.[97]

The contemporary notion of ascetics as a spiritual elite is molded into the author's paradigm of the dual division of Christian society between the Perfect and the Upright—compatible with his idea of a dual paradise.[98] The Upright represent the situation of Adam after the fall and in the physical paradise, whereas the Perfect achieve in their lives Adam's original state of existing in the earthly paradise while dwelling spiritually in the heavenly one. The double existence of Adam and Eve—mind in heaven, body on earth—is thus

91. *BoS* 21.12, *LG* 620.8–10; *BoS* 21.13, *LG* 620.23–24.

92. *BoS* 21.13, *LG* 620.19–21.6. The motif of Noah's negotiation with God for the sake of humanity is manifestly adopted from the story of Abraham and Sodom (Gen 18:23–36).

93. *BoS* 21.12, *LG* 617.23–20.6; for this motif, see Syriac Acts of Thomas 9, in *Apocryphal Acts of the Apostles, edited from Syriac Manuscripts in the British Museum and Other Libraries*, edited and translated by William Wright, 2 vols. (London: Williams and Norgate, 1871).

94. *BoS* 21.13. Noah's humility vis-à-vis the contempt and abuse of his contemporaries as he was building the ark is also found in rabbinic midrash; see *Midrash Tanhuma* Noah 5, edited by Solomon Buber (Warsaw: 1878).

95. For the application of this motif to Job and Daniel, see *BoS* 21.14.

96. *BoS* 21.16, *LG* 624.22–25.4.

97. See also *BoS* 21.3, *LG* 592.22–93.3.

98. *BoS* 21.1, *LG* 584–85.

likened to "spiritual people" of today—namely, ascetics (ܐܝܟ ܕܝܘܡܢܐ ܕܐܝܬ ܐܢܫܐ ܕܒܪ̈ܘܚ)—whose mind is "with our Lord in heaven."[99] According to this conceptual framework, Satan harms the Upright because they are tied to transitory things. The Perfect, by contrast, are bound spiritually to the world of light. Thus a perfect ascetic liberates himself from Satan in this life through asceticism, perceived as following the way of Jesus:

Therefore . . . [if] you do not wish to die, renounce and distance yourself from Satan and his teaching: that is, from Satan, from everything evil, from the world, from its anxiety, and from everything that Jesus had said to abandon through lowliness, prayer, and fasting, while keeping the commandments. Moreover . . . the teaching of the evil one . . . who harms the Upright ones because they are held fast in this world by transitory things and are far removed from the Perfect.[100]

The ideal of *imitatio Christi* is exemplified by a number of basic images—living like angels in the upper heaven as Adam did before the fall, and as the Messiah did[101] and, more prominently, the self-crucifixion of the ascetic as representing his or her dying to all things earthly: "Whoever does not get far away from the evil one and abandon everything on earth and look into heaven while being crucified (ܘܚܙܐ ܒܫܡܝܐ ܟܕ ܙܩܝܦ) will not attain that thing that Adam lost."[102] This ideal of self-crucifixion is in fact presented by the author as a cardinal commandment given by Christ to the apostles and is further enjoined by them to all future believers.[103] Self-crucifixion is perceived as the ultimate expression of humility. It would appear, then, that it was achieved by the biblical paragons of humility, though the author attributes it explicitly only to Paul.[104] Here too we may discern the relativization of the ideal of ascetic perfection, preparing the ground for its realization by contemporary ascetics. The author even goes a step further and claims that there is a handful of ascetics in his own generation who are closer to the full achievement of the ideal than their biblical predecessors.[105]

These contemporary ascetics, however, might also, like Adam and Eve, fall

99. *BoS* 21.8, *LG* 605.22–8.8–9.

100. *BoS* 21.2, *LG* 588.10–21.

101. *BoS* 21.4, *LG* 596.26–97.4; *BoS* 21.7, *LG* 601.18–19; cf. *BoS* 21.17, *LG* 625.10–11.

102. *BoS* 21.3, *LG* 593.6–9.

103. *BoS* 21.3, *LG* 592.16–93.1; *BoS* 21.5, *LG* 597.5–17. According to *BoS* 9.13, 28.1, the restoration of the original perfection of Adam begins, following Christ, with the apostles; see also Stewart, *"Working the Earth,"* 91; Bettiolo, "Adamo in Eden," 25.

104. *BoS* 21.6.

105. *BoS* 21.14, *LG* 621.15–24.4.

into the sin of pride and "return to the earth in order to possess and use it . . . and the door will be closed in their faces. They will depart from the heavenly Jerusalem just like Adam from the spiritual Eden, that is the spiritual Jerusalem, the city of God."[106] Nevertheless, the way of return through repentance (ܬܝܒܘܬܐ, lit. "return"—cf. the Hebrew תשובה) is still open to the ascetic—a manifestation of God's mercy—as it was originally open to Adam and Eve.[107] This possibility was further facilitated by a law (ܢܡܘܣܐ) that God "established . . . for them *on earth* (ܒܐܪܥܐ), for if a person does it he will be saved thereby."[108] This auxiliary law thus differs from the sublime law given to the protoplasts in paradise consisting of the epitomizing commandment to abandon all earthly concerns. This duality of the law apparently corresponds to the socioreligious division of Christian society espoused by the author, the second law destined to govern the conduct of the Upright.[109]

It is according to this perception of the perfect ascetics, whose will and desires are entirely focused on heaven, in imitation of Christ, that the author interprets the Lord's Prayer. In the prayer the ascetic should ask that "He might dwell spiritually in heaven with the angels while his mind is clothed with the glory of his Creator and the earth is not seen by him. . . . wherever the perfect will of God is, as our Lord said: 'Pray so that the will of God might be on earth as it is in heaven.'"[110] It seems that the hermeneutical choice in this context was influenced no less by the earth-heaven duality found in the Lord's Prayer than by the motif of God's will. The prayer is thus turned into a petition for achieving the ideal mode of human existence, existing in heaven according to God's initial will with regard to Adam while dwelling on earth. Doing so is facilitated by the divine glory that constitutes an existential buffer between the perfect ascetic and earthly reality; in other words, it blinds the Perfect from seeing that reality (ܘܠܐ ܡܬܚܙܝܐ ܠܗ).[111]

106. *BoS* 21.8, *LG* 608.9–15. Paradise as the spiritual and heavenly Jerusalem of the perfect signifies the identity of the primordial and eschatological reality in contradistinction to the tradition deriving from the Apocalypse of John—apparently unknown to or rejected by the early Syriac church—that does not associate it with paradise; see Murray, *Symbols,* 261–62.

107. According already to certain ancient midrashic traditions, Adam and Eve have repented; see, e.g., *The Life of Adam and Eve* 9, 30, trans. Marshall D. Johnson, in *The Old Testament Pseudepigrapha,* edited by James H. Charlesworth, vol. 2 (New York: Doubleday, 1985); *Gen. R.* 22.13; cf. *Num. R.* 13.3.

108. *BoS* 21.18, *LG* 628.23–29.1.

109. See also Kitchen, "Syriac Additions," 30–32; Kowalski, *Perfezione e giustizia,* 210–11.

110. *BoS* 21.2, *LG* 589.1–9, citing Matt 6:10.

111. The emphasis here differs from the common ascetic interpretation of giving up one's will in or-

A further means of reaching and maintaining ascetic perfection is an imitation of Adam's consumption of the Lord identified as the tree of life and interpreted as consumption of the "life-giving words of Christ," with its clear eucharistic connotations. The existential alternative would be eating from the tree of knowledge of evil identified with Satan and the transitory world:

> Today the children of Adam still eat with the hardness of their heart from this tree, which makes known [to them] evil and teaches them to be bound on the earth by transitory things. . . . Neither do they learn from God nor from a person of God how they may be bound up with our Lord in that world in that there is no death where they will eat the life-giving words of our Lord (ܡܠܘܗܝ ܕܡܪܢ ܕܐܟܠܘܢ ܚܝ̈ܐ ܡܚܝܢ̈ܐ). They shall eat our Lord and live and become great and be perfected through him.[112]

This imagery of the "life-giving words" of Christ as the spiritual fruits of the tree of life is complemented by perceiving the ascetics themselves as those who in turn yield these fruits as part of their perfection: "Everyone who imitates [our Lord] yields these fruits and becomes perfect."[113] Thus the *imitatio Christi* of the perfect ascetics not only restores in their lifetime the lost status of Adam in paradise, but in fact transcends his original state, becoming as it were a branch for diffusing the spiritual gifts of the tree of life.

Conclusion

The author of the *Book of Steps* harbors the concept of a dual paradise as the setting of Adam and Eve before the fall. The perception of paradise as *locus asceticus* constitutes a peculiar trait of the *Book of Steps* and determines the various aspects of its discussion. Core aspects here are the nature of primordial sin and the ascetic way of restoring the "paradise lost." In the *Book of Steps,* primordial sin is peculiarly portrayed as a shift in the inner intellectual focus from heavenly to earthly concerns, epitomized by the lust for food. The author is also distinguished by his radical anti-labor ascetic concept. Earthly concerns are equated with evil and death and are introduced through the protoplasts' voluntary decision; consequently, Satan's role in the paradisiacal narrative is substantially marginalized. Moreover, the primordial tree of life and tree of knowledge are

der to follow God's will; see Aryeh Kofsky, "The Renunciation of Will in the Monastic School of Gaza," *Liber Annuus* 56 (2006): 321–46; cf. *m. Avot* 2.4: "Do His will as if it was your will, that He may do your will as if it was His will."

112. *BoS* 21.1, *LG* 585.20–87.9; cf. John 6:53–58.

113. *BoS* 21.3, *LG* 589.18–20.

perceived as purely spiritual principles, identified respectively with Christ and Satan. The spiritual existence in paradise is tantamount to the consummation of the tree of life—namely, the Lord; it thus has implicit eucharistic connotations.

The description of Adam's paradisiacal existence and of the nature of his fall provides the author with the backdrop for his portrayal of the Messiah-Christ as Adam's corrective, as the one who fulfills the original ideal of Adamic ascetic perfection. Though Christ is identified with the tree of life and the logos, his primary function in the redemption of the ascetic is to show the way to the restoration of that perfection—this seems to be the major purpose of the incarnation. There is no special emphasis in the *Book of Steps* on the death of Christ as a redeeming sacrifice; rather, it is on his crucifixion as an ultimate example of the detachment from earthly existence. In other words, the only way to *imitatio Dei* is that of humility and *kenosis.* The way is open for the perfect ascetic here and now to follow Christ and not Adam. Hence the lack of eschatological emphasis on Christ's second coming.

The ideal of ascetic humility as the vehicle for *imitatio Dei* is further enhanced by the notion that a chain of pre-monastic Old and New Testament figures exemplified this virtue; it is thus relativized as preparing the ground for contemporary ascetics. The contemporary notion of ascetics as a spiritual elite is molded into the author's paradigm of a dual Christian society—a society divided between Perfect and Upright—compatible with his idea of a dual paradise.

This chapter has focused on the way the ascetic agenda of the *Book of Steps* informs its author's hermeneutical approach to the biblical narrative on the Garden of Eden. Whereas some particularities of the narrative fit readily into this mold, others clearly contradict it and demand creative, idiosyncratic, exegetical solutions. These include the author's interpretation of both the dominion over the earth and human procreation in Genesis 1:26–28 as relating to kenotic humility and nonsexual procreation. A major hermeneutical key for interpreting the story of the fall is provided by Satan's temptation of Jesus; the latter's ascetic elements are projected backward to Adam's temptation. The author also invokes the Lord's Prayer, a central liturgical text of the community, as epitomizing his ascetic existential vision of overcoming the cosmic spiritual dichotomy. It is precisely because the *Book of Steps* is not an exegetical treatise, but an ascetic manifesto, that its hermeneutical strategies stand out as an illuminating example of exegetical "acts of power."

Jason Scully

16. LOWERING IN ORDER TO BE RAISED, EMPTYING IN ORDER TO BE FILLED

The Ascetical System of the Book of Steps

Many scholars have emphasized the peculiarity of the *Book of Steps'* asceticism. Though the peculiar qualities of the *Book of Steps* are undeniable, the basic ascetical system of this work shares certain qualities with other ascetical writings of the fourth century.[1] Since recent scholarship tends to focus on the *Book of Steps'* distinction between the Upright and the Perfect as the final breath of a dying form of asceticism in a changing society, many of the more subtle aspects of the ascetical system outlined in the *Book of Steps* have not yet been examined. By explaining some of the components of the ascetical

I owe special thanks to Right Rev. Alexander Golitzin and Dr. Deirdre Dempsey for their help on this paper. I am also grateful for suggestions given by members of the "Jewish Roots of Christian Mysticism" seminar at Marquette University.

1. The most succinct summary of this system is found in memra 6: "When a person has lowered himself from all things that are on earth, has broken his mind in the night and in the day, has considered everyone else as more excellent than himself, has emptied himself of everything he has, and has kissed the feet of his enemies, then our Lord will look upon his lowliness and send him the Spirit—Paraclete—and he shall know the whole truth"; *LG* 141.7–14. Column and line numbers refer to *Liber Graduum,* ed. Michael Kmoskó, Patrologica Syriaca 1.3 (Paris: Firmin-Didot, 1926). All translations in this chapter are my own, although I have consulted the English translation in Robert A. Kitchen and Martien F. G. Parmentier, trans., *The Book of Steps: The Syriac Liber Graduum* (Kalamazoo, Mich.: Cistercian Publications, 2004).

terminology in the *Book of Steps* in more detail, I hope to open the door to more comparative studies between the *Book of Steps* and other ascetical texts of antiquity. I also intend to address a position proposed by Diana Juhl, who says that the *Book of Steps'* emphasis on the imitation of Christ's humility *limits* the need for the grace of God through Christ. I will argue that the author of the *Book of Steps* does not intend to limit the role of Christ in salvation, because the ascetical activities he describes are meant to be understood as ways in which one can become mystically united to Christ. As with Aphrahat, the author of the *Book of Steps* saw mystical union with Christ as the end goal of the ascetic's attempt to imitate Christ's lowliness.

Ascetical Terminology in the *Book of Steps:* The Negative Aspect

One of author of the *Book of Steps'* main reasons for writing these sermons is to explain how one comes to understand the commands of Jesus Christ contained in the scriptures. He begins memra 1 with statements such as the following: "It is fitting for us to look into the words of our Lord one by one" and "We must seek the truth, for as our Lord said, the truth will set us free."[2] In beginning the memre this way, the author intends to show that living the Christian life is a matter of knowledge—that is, one must understand the commands of Christ before one can do them. He also indicates that a correct understanding of scripture comes only through the Spirit. Continuing in the first memra, he says, "No one is able to comprehend Scripture or distinguish the commandments unless he is a man who partakes of God in the Spirit."[3] Therefore, one of the author's main purposes for writing the *Book of Steps* is to explain how the Christian ascetic arrives at a state of being capable of understanding the scriptures through inspiration from the Spirit. In doing so he describes an ascetical system containing a number of technical terms within the Syriac ascetical tradition.

After noting the importance of seeking the truth within the scriptures, the author begins to describe the ascetical actions required in such a task. Two exhortations are given right away: the ascetic must lower himself, (ܡܟܟ ܢܦܫܐ) and

2. *LG* 12.2–3; *LG* 13.7–8.
3. *LG* 13.26–16.1.

the ascetic must break his mind (ܪܥܝܢܐ ܡܥܟ).[4] The author's subsequent suggestion that these two actions serve as sacrifices to God implies that he derived his terminology from the Peshitta version of Psalm 51:17, which praises the lowly and broken person in the context of sacrifice: "The sacrifices of God are a lowly spirit (ܪܘܚܐ ܡܟܝܟܬܐ), for God does not reject a broken heart (ܠܒܐ ܡܥܝܟܐ)."[5] The phrase "breaking one's mind" (ܪܥܝܢܐ ܡܥܟ) is especially poignant in the context of a text concerned with acquiring knowledge. For the author of the *Book of Steps,* the phrase appears to have a technical meaning, as can be demonstrated from the way he consistently uses a different Syriac word, ܬܒܪ, when he wants to speak of the "breaking" of sin or the "breaking" of one's body in an ascetical context.[6] In this latter use of breaking the author of the *Book of Steps* is consistent with Aphrahat, who connects ܬܒܪ with its biblical roots when he refers to the "broken sting of death" from 1 Corinthians 15:55–56 and the "yoke of iron that is broken from the neck of men" from Jeremiah 28:14.[7] Both citations are in the context of "breaking" the power of sin that afflicts human beings and reflect the way the word ܬܒܪ was used in fourth-century Syriac writing.

The word ܡܥܟ, on the other hand, is used quite differently in the *Book of Steps.* While ܬܒܪ means to break in the sense of destroy or defeat, the connotation of ܡܥܟ is often closer to "wearing out," "troubling," or "disturbing."[8] Thus when the author of the *Book of Steps* uses ܡܥܟ in relation to the mind, he understands that breaking one's mind means the "wearing away" of useless knowledge so that Christian teaching can fill its place. In fact the author explicitly suggests that the activity of "breaking one's mind" is accomplished "with instruction (ܡܠܦܢܐ) and inquiry (ܒܥܘܬܐ) of the Word."[9] One breaks his

4. *LG* 13.9.

5. The author also alludes to this verse in memra 3 (*LG* 76.26), and he quotes this verse directly in memra 30 (*LG* 900.5–6).

6. See, for example, *LG* 885.17–20, where the author uses ܬܒܪ in reference to the destruction of sin: "Take care so that your understanding is increasing and you know the whole truth as it is, so that you *break* the power of sin, and so that you are learned and know everything"; cf. *LG* 716.23–25: "They *break* the heart of the penitents, when we are all penitents, and we all have sins."

7. Aphrahat, *Demonstration* VI.6 (PS 268.23) and V.16 (PS 216.20). Column and line numbers refer to *Aphraatis Sapientis Persae Demonstrationes,* ed. Jean Parisot, Patrologia Syriaca (hereafter PS) 1.1 (Paris: Firmin-Didot, 1894).

8. Jessie Payne Smith, *A Compendious Syriac Dictionary: Founded Upon the Thesaurus Syriacus of R. Payne Smith, DD* (Oxford: Oxford University Press; Eugene: Wipf and Stock, 1999), 572 and 604. Citations are to the Wipf and Stock edition.

9. See *LG* 776.5–6. Presumably the author means Christian instruction and inquiry into the Word

mind, therefore, so that he can make room for a proper understanding of scripture.

We turn now to the author's use of the Syriac verb ܡܟܟ and its corresponding noun form (ܡܟܝܟܘܬܐ). "Lowering oneself" and "lowliness" appear regularly throughout the memre, and the importance of this terminology has already been noted by several commentators.[10] In order to substantiate the importance of lowliness within the Christian life, the author quotes Isaiah 66:2, which states that God will look to "the peaceful and lowly (ܡܟܝܟ) in spirit." His main focus, however, is on imitating the lowliness of Christ, who consciously lowered himself as a model for future Christians. In memra 21 he says, for example, "The whole reason Christ came and lowered himself is so that he might teach us how to lower ourselves."[11] In order to illustrate God's favor toward those who reach a state of lowliness, the author rehearses a list of historical figures who received God's favor based on their lowliness. Moses, for example, was chosen by God because he "was the lowest of all people."[12] The author goes on to explain that "lowliness was compared with everything and it weighed heavy [in God's mind]."[13] Mary, likewise, was chosen to give birth to Christ based on her lowliness. He says, "If there had been another woman

of God, as Kitchen, *Book of Steps,* 308, renders in his translation: "Wear out your mind with [Christian] teaching and with questions of the Word [of God]."

10. See for example, Columba Stewart, *"Working the Earth of the Heart": The Messalian Controversy in History, Texts, and Language to A.D. 431* (Oxford: Clarendon Press, 1991), 88; see also Diana Juhl, *Die Askese im Liber Graduum und bei Afrahat: Eine vergleichende Studie zur frühsyrischen Frömmigkeit,* Orientalia Biblical et Christiana 9 (Wiesbaden: Harrassowitz Verlag, 1996), 71–89. In order to emphasize the parallelism between lowering and raising, I have chosen to translate ܡܟܟ literally instead of its usual rendering as "humility."

11. *LG* 593.17–19. Though Christ's lowliness is the example, human beings can never reach the same level as Christ: "But not even when we imitate the lowliness of our Lord is our lowliness a copy of his" (*LG* 664.14–16). The author also reminds his listeners that human beings are only required to imitate the Lord's lowliness, not his cursing, anger, or hate (*LG* 669.12–19). For a more detailed examination of the function and meaning of Christ in the Liber Graduum, see Juhl, *Askese im Liber Graduum.* According to Juhl, "Das Werk Christi, den ursprünglichen Menschen zu erneuern und die erneuerte Schöpfung in seiner eigenen Person sichtbar zu machen, erscheint durch die Aufforderung zur Imitatio Christi als vorbildliche Tat eines vollkommenen Menschen" (71). She especially notes the importance of imitating Christ's lowliness in the process of becoming perfect: "Der Wandel der Vollkommenen jedoch ist durch die Demut geprägt, die die Asketen sogar zur Feindesliebe befähigt" (163). This, she says, is one of the main differences between the author of the *Book of Steps* and Aphrahat, who "unterstreicht die einmalige Erlösungstat Christi, die in der Vernichtung der endgültigen Herrschaft des Todes besteht" (163).

12. *LG* 617.23–24.

13. *LG* 617.25–20.1. The author has Numbers 12:3 in mind here: "Now the man Moses was very meek, more than all men that were on the face of the earth" (Revised Standard Version [RSV]).

who was more lowly than Mary, Christ, who is the lowliest of all and who is the friend of lowliness, would have been given birth by her."[14] God especially loves lowliness because it is the most important of all the virtues.

Like "breaking one's mind," the activity of lowering one's self also leads to a transformation of the individual by removing inadequacies so that one may become closer to God. In one sense lowliness is achieved through ascetical acts such as suffering and keeping the commandments.[15] In another sense lowliness is what kills "the sin from the heart."[16] Lowliness is therefore the necessary prerequisite for interaction between the human and the divine. In memra 21 the author describes this positive effect of acquiring lowliness. Lowliness, he says, allows for the human mind to return to heaven and participate in the original human nature of Adam, which was lost in the fall.[17] Lowliness transports the ascetic to the spiritual Eden, or the heavenly Jerusalem, where he then openly dwells with God as Adam and Eve did in the original garden. This vision of God in heaven, however, should not be understood as an eschatological reality alone. As Alexander Golitzin has pointed out, union with God and participation in the heavenly life is available "in this world" (ܒܗܘ ܥܠܡܐ).[18] The author states in memra 15, "If he significantly lowers himself, the Lord will be revealed to him in this world and he will hear the voice of God."[19] Imitation of Christ's lowliness therefore transforms the ascetic into a person capable of dwelling with God and understanding the truth of scripture.[20]

We have just examined the author's use of two Syriac phrases, ܡܟܟ ܪܥܝܢܐ and

14. *LG* 625.1–4. The author has Luke 1:48 in mind here: "For he has regarded the low estate of his handmaiden. For behold, henceforth all generations will call me blessed" (RSV).

15. For an example of the importance of suffering in lowering oneself, see *LG* 296.15–18. For an example of the importance of following the commandments, see *LG* 432.10–14.

16. *LG* 341.14–15.

17. According to the author, the fall of Adam consisted primarily in his forsaking lowliness for pride at the suggestion of Satan; see, for example, the author's paraphrase of Satan's temptation, *LG* 609.9–12: "Cast off from yourself the ascetic life, renunciation, holiness, and lowliness (ܡܟܝܟܘܬܐ) and know both evil and good things and rise to honor (ܪܘܡ) and become like God."

18. Alexander Golitzin, "Recovering the 'Glory of Adam': 'Divine Light' Traditions in the Dead Sea Scrolls and the Christian Ascetical Literature of Fourth-Century Syro-Mesopotamia," in *The Dead Sea Scrolls as Background to Postbiblical Judaism and Early Christianity: Papers from an International Conference at St. Andrews in 2001,* edited by James R. Davila, 302 (Leiden: E. J. Brill, 2003).

19. *LG* 373.12–13.

20. The author concludes in memre 21 that one can only understand the truth of scripture while in a state of lowliness; see *LG* 624.2–4: "If there is no lowliness and kindness in a person, he is not known to the lowly ones and God does not dwell in him, nor does he comprehend the truth."

ܡܟܟ ܢܦܫܐ. Now we turn to a third technical term of prominent importance—namely, the act of "emptying" or "stripping" one's self (ܣܪܩ). In memra 1 the author shows that the act of emptying oneself is closely related to lowering oneself. With Philippians 2:7 in mind, the author says, "Let us abandon everything and enter into the lowliness of our Lord and into his self-emptying (ܒܣܘܪܩܢܗ)."[21] Elsewhere he connects this self-emptying of Christ with the act of atonement, saying that our Lord emptied himself into the form of a human being for the sake of creation so that all flesh "might pay attention to his death and servitude."[22] Emptying one's self, therefore, is more than just a way to achieve the lowliness necessary for the life of the Perfect; it is a way of sharing in the redeeming act of Christ who emptied himself through his crucifixion and death.

For this reason the author also upholds Stephen as an example of someone who "emptied himself and received the Paraclete."[23] Though the biblical account of Stephen's martyrdom refers to Stephen simply as "being full of the Holy Spirit," the self-emptying of Stephen is assumed by the author of the *Book of Steps* and is witness to the fundamental connection he sees between self-emptying and reception of the Paraclete.[24] As we shall see, emptying and being filled with the Paraclete are fundamentally related for the author of the *Book of Steps.*

When the author speaks of the process of self-emptying in the life of the human being in pursuit of perfection, he has both a physical and spiritual component in mind. Emptying one's self, for example, occurs through fasting. The author states, "When our Lord and the apostles emptied themselves, they emptied themselves completely and fasted fully with their bodies and their souls."[25] For the author of the *Book of Steps,* the intimate union between body and soul must not be taken for granted, which he says clearly in memra 1:

> If we wish to work and teach and be called great ones, we must wash and cleanse the inner self as the outer and the outer as the inner. Our bodies and souls become worthy together through fasting, prayer, and lowliness. . . . In

21. *LG* 16.8–9.

22. *LG* 548.9–10.

23. *LG* 77.24–26.

24. See Acts 7:55: "But he [Stephen], full of the Holy Spirit, gazed into heaven and saw the glory of God, and Jesus standing at the right hand of God" (RSV).

25. *LG* 268.3–5.

other words, if the soul is harmed, the body is harmed; and if the body is harmed, the soul is harmed. For there is no inner person without an outer person and there is no outer person without an inner person.[26]

Thus when the author speaks of fasting and its effects, he has in mind both bodily and spiritual fasting. While it is easy to understand how abstention from food and drink affects the self-emptying of the body, the concept of fasting with the soul is more obscure. The author ties the expression "fasting to the world" (ܨܐܡ ܠܗ ܠܥܠܡܐ), a phrase taken from the *Gospel of Thomas* 27, to the concept of fasting to the soul. In a short article devoted entirely to this phrase, Aelred Baker concludes that the expression was one that was used throughout Syria to signify the ascetic's withdrawal from the world through a life of celibacy.[27] The author of the *Book of Steps* describes "fasting to the world" as such: "If a person avoids evil things, gives alms, redeems the afflicted, and appeases the detestable, then he will rise (ܪܒܐ) to increasingly higher levels in his fast even when he eats and drinks well and when he dresses nicely and possesses wealth."[28] In other words, fasting to the world involves emptying oneself of the moral evils that come from living in the world.[29] In fact, it is this fasting that is the aim of all bodily fasting.

The result of breaking one's mind, lowering oneself, and emptying oneself through fasting is a state of being described as purity of heart (ܕܟܝܘܬܐ ܕܠܒܐ).[30] The importance of this term derives from Matthew 5:8, which the author refers to no less than seven times throughout the memre.[31] For the author of the *Book of Steps,* a pure heart is one where all sin and all affection for sin have been removed, and reaching this state is necessary because the heart is the lo-

26. *LG* 253.8–23.

27. Dom Aelred Baker, "Fasting to the World," *Journal of Biblical Literature* 84 (1965): 294; see also Antoine Guillamont, "ΝΗΣΤΕΥΕΙΝ ΤΟΝ ΚΟΣΜΟΝ (P.Oxy. 1, verso, l.5–6)," *Bulletin de l'Institut francais d'archeologie orientale* 61 (1962): 15–23.

28. *LG* 828.2–7.

29. Therefore the author can conclude that the whole reason the children of Adam are bound to the earth is that they have not emptied themselves of it through fasting; see *LG* 588.2–4.

30. The importance of this term has already been noted in the secondary literature; see, for example, Stewart, *"Working the Earth,"* 91: "Through imitation of Christ's lowliness and love . . . one strives for *kēnūtā* and then for *gmīrūtā*. The goal is new creation in Christ, when one is restored to Adam's purity of heart, freed from the 'course of desire,' filled with the Spirit of God." Stewart specifically refers to *LG* 581.5, where the author quotes Psalm 51 to describe purity of heart.

31. "Blessed are the pure in heart, for they shall see God" (RSV).

cus of the person that directly connects to God.[32] The author also discusses the role of the heart in the human encounter with the divine in memra 12, when he describes the three levels of the church: the heavenly church, the visible church, and the church of the heart.[33] He describes the Perfect as those who participate in the worship of the heavenly church through both the visible church and the spiritual worship that takes place on the "altar of the heart." Elsewhere, in memra 18, the author refers to the "eyes of the heart" as the faculty of the human being that can see God.[34]

In considering the important role that the state of the heart plays in the human relationship with God, we begin to see why the author of the *Book of Steps* develops the ascetical system described earlier. Breaking one's mind, lowering oneself, and emptying oneself are all meant to remove the impurities of the heart. As the author states, "The heart is not purified unless the hidden sin has vanished from it and [the heart] has put an end to evil thoughts which are hidden and buried in it through the power of sin dwelling in it."[35] It is only when impurities have been removed from the heart that God is able to enter into the heart and dwell in it.

So far we have seen how the author of the *Book of Steps* applies a technical vocabulary aimed at achieving a state described as "purity of heart." Purity of heart, however, is not itself the end of the ascetic life, but rather the necessary state for God to begin transforming the individual. Throughout the memre the author alludes to a constant pattern where one is lowered, broken, and emptied in order to be raised up and exalted by God. In such cases the author uses the *ettaphal* (a factitive verbal conjugation) form of ܪܘܡ (*rum*), which literally means to be raised up, but can also mean exalted.[36] For example, in memra 14 he says, "everyone is raised up (ܡܬܬܪܝܡ) according to his manner of life, his proportion, his broken mind (ܬܒܝܪ ܪܥܝܢܗ), and the lowliness of his soul (ܡܟܝܟ ܢܦܫܗ).[37] And in memra 17, "He [God] is teaching you, however, to be-

32. For example, see *LG* 252.24–53.8, where the author states that human lowliness and service are revealed to God through the heart, not the body.

33. For further discussion on this passages and echoes of it in the Pseudo-Macarian homilies and in Babai, see Robert Murray, *Symbols of Church and Kingdom: A Study in Early Syriac Tradition,* rev. ed. (London: T. and T. Clark; Piscataway, N.J.: Gorgias Press, 2004), 262–73.

34. *LG* 440.7.

35. *LG* 440.10–14.

36. Smith, *Compendious Syriac Dictionary,* 534–35.

37. *LG* 332.1–3.

come lowly and despicable like him, so that once you have lowered yourself like him, you will be raised up as he himself was raised up (ܐܬܬܪܝܡ)."[38]

If we have just examined the "negative aspect" of the ascetical system presented in the *Book of Steps,* the rest of the chapter will now examine the technical language of the "positive aspect" of the system—that is, "being raised up" into mystical relationship with God by means of the indwelling of the Paraclete. In other words, the ascetic breaks his mind so that God can raise him up with honor, he empties himself so that he can be filled by God, and he lowers himself so that he can be raised with Christ. These ascetical activities only make sense, therefore, when we understand that God uses acts of humility to enable the ascetic to share in the life of God through the redeeming work of Christ. Asceticism, in other words, is not only a program for a virtuous life, but rather is a way of experiencing God's redemption through mystical union with Christ.

Ascetical Terminology in the *Book of Steps:* The Positive Aspect

The author of the *Book of Steps* makes it clear that the ascetic empties himself of evil for the purpose of filling himself with the Spirit. Columba Stewart has already noted the importance of "filling" (ܡܠܐ) language in the *Book of Steps,* but the theme merits further examination here.[39] In memra 3 the author states that the one who empties himself "is made perfect by our Lord and filled (ܡܠܐ) with his Spirit, and whoever is filled with the Spirit of Christ does all sorts of good works."[40] As the author explains later on, however, the Spirit of Christ is the Paraclete. In memra 28, for instance, he connects the "inbreathing" of God during creation with the Spirit of Christ, who breathed onto the face of his disciples: "When that breath dwells in him, then he is a living soul in the same manner as on the day when the Lord breathed into him after He had created him. Likewise, our Lord breathed his Spirit onto the face of his disciples in order that they might be like Adam was before he sinned."[41] Having made this connection between the breath of God and the Spirit of Christ,

38. *LG* 420.4–6.

39. See Stewart, *"Working the Earth,"* 227–33.

40. *LG* 69.23–25. The reverse is also true—i.e., one who is not filled is not emptied; see *LG* 540.1–3: "If one is not filled with our Lord, his heart will not be emptied of sin and its fruits."

41. *LG* 788.8–13.

he then goes on to say that the "inbreathing" of the Spirit of God is the same as being filled with the Paraclete. He continues, "For if the vessel of his human soul is not filled with the Spirit of God, it does not receive that total breath by which it became a living soul in the beginning. And that gift which fills a person without any loss is called the Paraclete."[42] The result of this close association between the Spirit of God and the Paraclete means that the author needs to make a further distinction between the Spirit of God as the Paraclete and the Spirit of God acting in a lesser capacity.

The author makes this distinction by referring to the Spirit as given to the Upright in the form of a "limited Pledge" (ܪܗܒܘܢܐ) and to the Perfect in the form of the Paraclete.[43] This distinction is explained most fully in memra 28: "Although the Holy Spirit of God and the Paraclete are one, [scripture] speaks of the Paraclete and the Holy Spirit in order to distinguish the greater gifts from the lesser ones. Whoever receives the great gift is perfected, but those who have received the lesser gifts are not perfected since they are lacking; unless the great gift comes, they are not fulfilled."[44] The author's association of the Paraclete with the Spirit of Christ explains why he needs to make this distinction between the Holy Spirit of God and the Paraclete. Though both the Holy Spirit and the Paraclete are of God, one is only "made perfect" (ܡܬܓܡܪ) and "fulfilled" (ܡܫܬܡܠܐ) through the Paraclete—that is, the spirit of Christ.[45] The author's use of the *eshtaphal* (a factitive form) of ܡܠܐ (ܡܫܬܡܠܐ) is intriguing here, as it allows for a number of meanings with ascetical overtones. In addition to the cognate meanings with ܓܡܪ ("to become perfect or fulfilled"), ܡܫܬܡܠܐ also implies the sort of perfection that comes through martyrdom, baptism, chrismation, or confirmation.[46] It is possible, therefore, that the author chose this word to further refine his notion of ܡܬܓܡܪ. By adding the phrase ܡܫܬܡܠܐ, he ensures that his audience would associate the notion of perfection with sacramental actions in which the Spirit was already thought to be present. At any rate, the author is clear that the Paraclete—that is, the presence of God in the person of Christ—is both what gave life to Adam, as he was created in

42. *LG* 788.25–89.6.

43. For more on the difference between the Paraclete and the "limited pledge," see Stewart, *"Working the Earth,"* 199–200.

44. *LG* 789.23–92.5.

45. *LG* 789.15.

46. See Smith, *Compendious Syriac Dictionary,* 274.

his original, perfect state, and what now perfects human beings by re-creating them in Adam's original state.

The author uses similar language in memra 6 when he compares human beings to a king's treasure room. Just as a king daily fills (ܡܠܐ) a treasure house that has been made perfect (ܓܡܝܪ) with his precious objects, so also does the ascetic who has broken his mind, lowered himself, and emptied himself receive the treasure of the Paraclete and come to know the whole truth.[47] Once again, the Paraclete is identified with Christ in his role as creator. In this case the author describes Christ as the king who opens his gates and allows the perfect to dwell in his heavenly kingdom because he recognizes that "this person is now as perfect as on the day I fashioned him."[48] The language of dwelling with Christ is even stronger here than in memra 28. Upon arriving in the heavenly kingdom, which the author also refers to as the "spiritual Eden" and the "heavenly Jerusalem," the perfect are allowed to "enter and enjoy the riches of its mysteries (ܐܪ̈ܙܐ)."[49] These mysteries are then identified as Christ himself, who is the "glorious majesty": "When he has become Perfect and lowered himself (ܐܬܡܟܟ) more than others, he will ascend (ܣܠܩ) unto that glorious majesty, for there is his dwelling place. Such is that dwelling place with our Lord, which is for the lowly and meek and holy, who are the sons of the city of life."[50] Therefore, when the author talks about filling a treasure house with precious objects, he means that the mind of those who perform ascetical actions can be filled with the indwelling Christ, who exists as the "great glory."[51]

As we have just seen, in addition to filling language, the author of the *Book of Steps* also uses "ascending language" in connection with the activities of "breaking one's mind," "lowering oneself," and "emptying oneself." Two ascending words in particular stand out as technical terms for the author: ܣܠܩ and ܪܒܝ. One need only to look at the number of citations in the lexicon attached to Kmoskó's edition in order to appreciate the frequency with which these two words are used in the *Book of Steps.* Turning first to ܣܠܩ, the word

47. See *LG* 140–41.14.

48. *LG* 141.23–25.

49. *LG* 144.1–2.

50. *LG* 144.16–21.

51. In memra 28, the author connects the glory of the Lord with the humanity of Christ. After explaining that Moses was able to see the glory of the Lord (ܫܘܒܚܐ ܕܡܪܝܐ), he goes on to say that this same glory that Moses saw appeared to all the prophets and instructed them "like a human being" (ܐܝܟ ܒܪܢܫܐ). "Glory" and "our Lord" are in parallel in the text and equivalent in the mind of the author; see *LG* 801.7–23; see also Golitzin, "Recovering the Glory of Adam," 303, for more on this point.

for "ascend," we see that it occurs regularly in association with dwelling language (i.e., one ascends so that he can dwell with God in the heavenly places).[52] For example, the author says that it is on account of lowliness that a person is made "to ascend (ܡܣܩ) to the highest heavens, where God dwells and is visible."[53] The author also states that one "will not enter that great city and that place where our Lord is visible to him face to face, unless he comes to ascend (ܣܠܩ) these steps that are the major and promised commandments."[54]

In many of these passages where the author talks about ascending and dwelling with God, he has Christ specifically in mind. Thus in memra 15 the author states that when a person abandons the earth with his mind (ܫܒܩ ܠܐܪܥܐ ܒܪܥܝܢܗ), this mind becomes free to "ascend to heaven" (ܣܠܩ ܠܫܡܝܐ), which he refers to as "the peaceful place of his father's house."[55] This passage is Christological, since the author places it within the context of a discussion on John 14:21, where Christ says that he will come to whoever keeps the commandments.[56] For the author of the *Book of Steps,* "dwelling in the peaceful place of the father's house" is equivalent to the indwelling of Christ, and one ascends to this place by keeping the major commandments. In other places, such as memra 13, the author speaks of ascending in terms of reception of the Paraclete: "If he desires to become Perfect, he must empty himself, consecrate his life as holy, leave everything behind, become joined to our Lord in heaven, and become dead from the use of the world. He will then ascend (ܣܠܩ) to these great commandments and receive the Paraclete and know all truth as our Lord makes known to him."[57] The author, therefore, uses ܣܠܩ to describe the process of receiving the Paraclete and achieving mystical illumination from Christ.

While the author of the *Book of Steps* uses ܣܠܩ to express the mystical dimensions of ascending, he uses the phrase "raise to honor" (ܪܒܝ) to express the moral components of ascending. The verb is based on the Syriac ܪܒ, which means "great" or "big," and in a few places the author of the *Book of Steps* uses

52. For an analysis of the technical use of "dwelling" (ܥܡܪ) language in the *Book of Steps,* see Stewart, *"Working the Earth,"* 216–23.

53. *LG* 617.15–18.

54. *LG* 461.9–13.

55. *LG* 380.25–81.4.

56. "He who has my commandments and keeps them, he it is who loves me; and he who loves me will be loved by my Father, and I will love him and manifest myself to him" (RSV).

57. *LG* 316.2–7.

the *aphel* (factitive) form of the verb, which literally means to make big, to enlarge, or to widen. For example, in memra 7, the author says the following about David: "God saw the submission of his lowliness and the labor of his petition, and forgave him and raised him to honor (ܐܘܪܒ)."[58] A literal translation, however, is appealing because it brings out the poignancy of the paradox of lowering oneself in order to become bigger. Thus we might read, "God saw David's lowliness and enlarged him." Likewise, the Lord "enlarged" the apostles when they lowered themselves.[59]

Most of the time, however, the author uses ܪܒ in its root form. For instance, he consistently presents Old Testament figures as examples of people whose lowliness caused them to be raised to honor. Thus Moses and Abraham are both "raised in honor" on account of their moral superiority and lowliness.[60] He then urges his listeners to follow the model of these exemplars: "Let us lower ourselves before God and people, just as we see our Lord and all his preachers who lowered themselves and were raised to honor (ܪܒ) on account of their lowliness."[61] As we just saw with ܣܠܩ, one is raised to honor into the presence of Christ. Thus, in memra 15, the author states that "it would be better for each . . . to keep the commandments, so that he may rise to honor (ܪܒ) in the eyes of the great ones in the new world of our Lord Jesus Christ, the eternal King."[62] Along with ܣܠܩ, the word ܪܒ is used by the author to express a moral ascension, which is accompanied by Christ.

We have seen, then, that the author of the *Book of Steps* employs a technical vocabulary aimed at achieving a mystical relationship with Christ, the second person of the Trinity. Ascetical actions such as "breaking one's mind," "lowering oneself," and "emptying oneself" only make sense when their opposites are considered. One breaks his mind in order to rise to honor, one lowers himself in order to ascend, and one empties himself in order to be filled. In each case the second half of the equation, as it were, involves a mystical relationship with Christ (i.e., one rises to honor in Christ, ascends in order to dwell with Christ, and is filled with the Paraclete). Knowledge and virtue are not the end

58. *LG* 169.11–13.
59. *LG* 845.1–6.
60. For Moses, see *LG* 620.13, and for Abraham, see *LG* 928.12.
61. *LG* 256.6–10.
62. *LG* 384.26–85.2.

goals in themselves; rather, the end of ascetical activities is participation in the life of Christ. In addition, we have seen that this mystical relationship with Christ is available to human beings even now in this world.

Conclusion

The ascetical system just outlined reveals a sophisticated and coherent vision of the Christian life, which the author of the *Book of Steps* presents as necessary for those Christians who have chosen the way of life associated with the Perfect. Although it is my hope that a philological study of the technical words and phrases used in this ascetical system will be useful in its own right for future study of the *Book of Steps,* I also suggest that my exposition of the *Book of Steps* is useful for addressing two issues found within recent scholarship on the *Book of Steps.* The first issue is the tendency to view the asceticism of the *Book of Steps* as a unique phenomenon. While it is true that many aspects of the *Book of Steps'* ascetical system remain unique, the technical terms and phrases just discussed should be helpful in situating the *Book of Steps* within the larger trajectory of ascetical terminology being used in fourth-century Syriac, or even Greek, Christianity.[63]

Although more detailed study is required in the way of comparative studies between the *Book of Steps* and other texts, I will offer a very brief comparison between the *Book of Steps* and the writings of Aphrahat as an impetus for further contextual study. Aphrahat, writing during the fourth century, proposes an ascetical system similar to the *Book of Steps,* though with even more explicit Christological references. In *Demonstration* VI Aphrahat equates lowliness with heavenly dwelling: "He who loves lowliness will be an heir in the land of the living."[64] Later on in the same *Demonstration* he brings in the Christological component when he says that Christ lowered himself not only so that human beings could follow his example, but so that lowering himself into human nature, human beings could participate in his nature:

63. The author's preoccupation with the role of the mind in the life of the ascetic suggests parallels with Greek ascetical writers. The emphasis on humility as the starting point of the Christian life is commonly found within the writings of the desert fathers, as well as other Greek writers like Basil of Caesarea and the Cappadocians.

64. Aphrahat, *Demonstration* VI.1 (PS 252.3–4). All translations from Aphrahat are my own.

Our savior showed us all of this lowliness (ܡܟܝܟܘܬܐ) in Himself. Therefore, my beloved, let us also lower ourselves. When our Lord came outside of his nature, he walked in our nature. Let us remain in our nature so that in the day of justice we might partake in his nature. Our Lord took from us a pledge when he went and he left for us a pledge belonging to Him when he was raised up.[65]

As did the author of the *Book of Steps,* Aphrahat uses Isaiah 66:2 to prove that "Christ dwells in the peaceful and the lowly."[66] Though Aphrahat's use of ascending language is not as strong as in the *Book of Steps,* he clearly associates lowering one's self with ascent to mystical union with Christ.

Similarly, Aphrahat speaks of emptying one's self in order to be filled. Like the author of the *Book of Steps,* he uses the metaphor of filling a king's house with treasures. A king's house, he says, must first be emptied and prepared for habitation by "pure fasting."[67] At the same time he makes it clear that the house is not to be left in its emptied (ܡܣܪܩ) state, or else the king will not want to dwell in it.[68] Thus, in *Demonstration* 14, for example, he speaks of the sage being filled (ܡܠܐ) with a treasure of knowledge.[69] Once again, though differences exist, Aphrahat and the author of the *Book of Steps* seem to have some common understanding of technical terms in their ascetic vocabularies, as well as having similar metaphors and analogies.

A closer look at the ascetical system of the *Book of Steps* also addresses a second important issue—namely, the accusation that the author of the *Book of Steps* propose a model of redemption through example instead of one where redemption occurs through mystical union with Christ. According to Juhl, the author of the *Book of Steps* views the reception of the Paraclete as a reward for imitating the lowliness of Christ, whose life was primarily meant to be an example for others. She concludes, therefore, that the *Book of Steps'* emphasis on the imitation of Christ limits the need for the grace of God through Christ's redeeming work on the cross. In the *Book of Steps,* she says, "the acquisition of the Spirit is understood as a work of man and not as the grace of God."[70] In Juhl's reading the author of the *Book of Steps* sees Christ as exemplar rather than redeemer.

65. Aphrahat, *Demonstration* VI.10 (PS 277.19–25).

66. Aphrahat, *Demonstration* VI.17 (PS 304.16); cf. XVIII.5 (PS 829.15–18).

67. Aphrahat, *Demonstration* I.4 (PS 12.9).

68. Aphrahat, *Demontration* I.4 (PS 9.19–21).

69. Aphrahat, *Demonstration* XIV.35 (PS 664.20).

70. Juhl, *Askese im Liber Graduum,* 163: "Geistaneignung wird als Werk des Menschen und nicht als Gnade Gottes verstanden."

Although Juhl is correct to characterize the Christology and soteriology of the *Book of Steps* as one of imitation (i.e., Christ demonstrated the importance of "lowliness"), doing so to the exclusion of redemption through Christ would be misleading. For the author of the *Book of Steps,* Christ lowered himself so that human beings who do likewise cannot just imitate his example, but also mystically ascend into heaven and dwell with Christ himself. Though he does not explicitly mention the redeeming work of the incarnate Christ, he certainly alludes to it when he mentions Christ's self-emptying. Since human beings can participate in Christ's redemptive work through the reception of the Paraclete, who is the Spirit of Christ, salvation still comes through Christ. Ascetical activities, therefore, are not merely means to a reward, as Juhl proposes, but ways in which one can become united to the Godhead through Christ. This union is not accomplished by the work of the human being, but rather by the work of God, who transforms the ascetic by filling him with the Paraclete. We must remember that, for the author of the *Book of Steps,* salvation begins in heaven, as he states in memra 12: "Everything beautiful begins with the heavenly church and from there the light shines on us from all sides."[71]

71. *LG* 292.13–16.

BIBLIOGRAPHY

Abbeloos, Jean Baptiste, ed. "Acta Mar Kardaghi: Assyriae praefecti qui sub Sapore II martyr occubit." *Analecta Bollandiana* 9 (1890): 5–105. Translated by Joel Thomas Walker in *The Legend of Mar Qardagh,* 19–69.

AbouZayd, Shafiq. "Virginity in Aphrahat." In *V Symposium Syriacum, 1988: Katholieke Universiteit, Leuven, 29–31 août 1988,* edited by René Lavenant, 123–33. Orientalia Christiana Analecta 236. Rome: Pontificium Institutum Orientalium Studiorum, 1990.

———. *Ihidayutha: A Study of the Life of Singleness in the Syrian Orient, From Ignatius of Antioch to Chalcedon 451 AD.* Oxford: ARAM Society for Syro-Mesopotamian Studies, 1993.

———. "Violence and Killing in the *Liber Graduum.*" *ARAM* 12 (2000): 451–65.

Achelis, Hans. *Virgines subintroductae: Ein Beitrag zum VII. Kapital des 1. Korintherbriefs.* Leipzig: J. C. Hinrichs, 1902.

Adam, Alfred. *Texte zum Manichäismus.* Berlin: Verlag Walter De Gruyter, 1969.

Aland, Barbara, and Andreas Juckel, eds. *Das Neue Testament in Syrischer Überlieferung.* Vol. 2, *Die paulinischen Briefe.* Arbeiten zur Neutestamentlichen Textforschung 14. Berlin and New York: de Gruyter, 1991.

Algaze, Guillermo, Ray Breuninger, Chris S. Lightfoot, and Michael Rosenberg. "The Tigris-Euphrates Archaeological Reconnaissance Project: A Preliminary Report of the 1989–1990 Seasons." *Anatolica* 17 (1991): 175–240.

Alston, William P. *Beyond "Justification": Dimensions of Epistemic Evaluation.* Ithaca: Cornell University Press, 2005.

Althaus, Frank, and Mark Sutcliffe. *The Road to Byzantium: Luxury Arts of Antiquity.* London: Fontanka, 2006.

Ammianus Marcellinus, *Ammianus Marcellinus: History,* edited by John C. Rolfe. 3 vols. Loeb Classical Library. Cambridge, Mass.: Harvard University Press, 1935–39.

Anderson, Gary A. "Celibacy or Consummation in the Garden? Reflections on Early Jewish and Christian Interpretations of the Garden of Eden." *Harvard Theological Review* 82 (1989): 121–48.

———. "The Garden of Eden and Sexuality in Early Judaism." In *People of the Body: Jews *and Judaism from an Embodied Perspective,* edited by Howard Eilberg-Schwartz, 47–68. Albany: State University of New York Press, 1992.

———. *The Genesis of Perfection: Adam and Eve in Jewish and Christian Imagination.* Louisville: Westminster John Knox Press, 2001.

Aquino, Frederick D. "The Healing of Cognition in Deification: Towards a Patristic Virtue Epistemology." In *Immersed in the Life of God: The Healing Resources of the Christian Faith,* edited by Paul Gavrilyuk, Douglas M. Koskela, and Jason E. Vickers, 123–42. Grand Rapids, Mich.: Eerdmans, 2008.

Argárate, Pablo. "Das *Ktābā dmasqātā:* Forschung und Bedeutung des syrischen Liber Graduum." In *Bibel, Byzanz und Christlicher Orient: Festschrift für Stephen Gero zum 65. Geburtstag,* edited by E. Grypeou, A. Toepel, T. Sailors, and D. Bumazhnov. Orientalia Lovaniensia Analecta 187. Leuven: Peeters, 2010.

Asmussen, Jes P. "Christians in Iran." In *Cambridge History of Iran,* edited by Ehsan Yarshater, 3:924–48. Cambridge: Cambridge University Press, 1983.

Aune, David E. "Luke 20:34–36: A 'Gnosticized' Logion of Jesus?" In *Geschichte-Tradition-Reflexion: Festschrift für Martin Hengel zum 70. Geburtstag,* edited by Hubert Cancik, Hermann Lichtenberger, and Peter Schäfer, 3:187–202. Tübingen: Mohr Siebeck, 1996.

Aveta, Michela. "Ad instar angelorum: Per un'analisi storico-religiosa dell'antropologia del *Liber Graduum.*" *Christianesimo nella storia* 8 (1987): 481–500.

Axtell, Guy. "Recent Work in Virtue Epistemology." *American Philosophical Quarterly* 34 (1997): 1–27.

———. *Knowledge, Belief, and Character: Readings in Virtue Epistemology.* Lanham, Md.: Rowman and Littlefield, 2000.

———. "Blind Man's Bluff: The Basic Belief Apologetic as Anti-Skeptical Stratagem." *Philosophical Studies* 130 (2006): 131–52.

Baehr, Jason S. "Character in Epistemology." *Philosophical Studies* 128 (2006): 479–514.

———. "On the Reliability of Moral and Intellectual Virtues." *Metaphilosophy* 38 (2007): 456–70.

Baker, Aelred. "Fasting to the World." *Journal of Biblical Literature* 84 (1965): 291–94.

———. "The Gospel of Thomas and the Syriac Liber Graduum." *New Testament Studies* 12 (1965–66): 49–55.

———. "The Significance of the New Testament Text of the Syriac Liber Graduum." In *Studia Evangelica 5: Papers Presented to the Third International Congress on New Testament Studies, Held at Christ Church, Oxford, 1965; Part 2: The New Testament Message,* edited by F. L. Cross, 171–75. Berlin: Akademie-Verlag, 1968.

———. "Early Syriac Asceticism." *The Downside Review* 88 (1970): 393–409.

Ball, Warwick. "Seh Qubba, a Roman Frontier Post in Northern Iraq." In *The Eastern Frontier of the Roman Empire: Proceedings of a Colloquium Held at Ankara in September 1988,* edited by D. H. French and Chris S. Lightfoot, 1:7–18. BAR International Series 553. Oxford: British Institute of Archaeology at Ankara, 1989.

Ball, Warwick, Stuart Campbell, and St. John Simpson, eds. *Ancient Settlement in the Zam-*

mar Region: Excavations by the British Archaeological Expedition to Iraq in the Saddam Dam Salvage Project, 1985–86. BAR International Series 1096. Oxford: Archaeopress, 2003.

Bardy, Gustave, ed. *Eusèbe de Césaré: Les Martyrs en Palestine.* Sources Chrétiennes 55. Paris: Éditions du Cerf, 1958.

———, ed. *Eusèbe de Césaré: Histoire Ecclésiastique.* Sources Chrétiennes 31, 41, 55, 73. Paris: Éditions du Cerf, 1952–1971.

Barnes, Timothy D. *Constantine and Eusebius.* Cambridge, Mass.: Harvard University Press, 1981.

———. *The New Empire of Diocletian and Constantine.* Cambridge, Mass.: Harvard University Press, 1982.

———. "Constantine and the Christians of Persia." *The Journal of Roman Studies* 75 (1985): 126–36.

Barsoum, Ignatius A. *The Scattered Pearls: A History of Syriac Literature and Sciences.* Translated by Matti Moosa. 2nd ed. Piscataway, N.J.: Gorgias Press, 2003.

Barth, Karl. *Die kirchliche Dogmatik.* Zollikon-Zurich: Evangelischer Verlag, 1932–1970.

———. *Church Dogmatics.* Edited by G. W. Bromiley and T. F. Torrance. 14 vols. Edinburgh: T. and T. Clark, 1936–1969.

Bäss, Peter. "Der Liber Graduum—ein messalianisches Buch?" In *XVII. Deutscher Orientalistentag, vom 21. bis 27. Juli 1968 in Würzburg,* edited by Wolfgang Voigt, 2:368–84. Wiesbaden: Franz Steiner Verlag, 1969.

Baumstark, Anton. *Geschichte der syrischen Literatur: Mit Ausschluss der christlich-palästinensischen Texte.* Bonn: A. Marcus and E. Webers, 1922.

———. *Katalog 500: Orientalische Manuskripte: Arabische, syrische, griechische, armenische, persische Handschriften des 7.–18. Jahrhunderts.* Leipzig: Karl W. Hiersemann, 1922.

Beck, Edmund, ed. *Des heiligen Ephraem des Syrers Hymnen de Fide.* Corpus Scriptorum Christianorum Orientalium 154–55, Syr. 73–74. Louvain: Peeters, 1955.

———. *Des heiligen Ephraem des Syrers Hymnen contra haereses.* Corpus Scriptorum Christianorum Orientalium 169, 170. Louvain: L. Durbecq, 1957.

———. *Des heiligen Ephraem des Syrers Hymnen de Paradiso und Contra Julianum.* Corpus Scriptorum Christianorum Orientalium 175, 176. Louvain: Peeters, 1957.

———. *Des heiligen Ephraem des Syrers Hymnen de Nativitate (Epiphania).* Corpus Scriptorum Christianorum Orientalium 186, Syr. 82. Louvain: Secrétariat du Corpus SCO, 1959.

———. *Des heiligen Ephrem des Syrers Hymnen de Ecclesia.* Corpus Scriptorum Christianorum Orientalium 198, 117. Louvain: Peeters, 1960.

———. *Carmina Nisibena.* Corpus Scriptorum Christianorum Orientalium 240, 112. Louvain: Peeters, 1963.

———. *Des heiligen Ephraem des Syrers Hymnen de Virginitate.* Corpus Scriptorum Christianorum Orientalium 223, 224. Louvain: Peeters, 1962.

———. *Dorea und Charis—Die Taufe: Zwei Beiträge zur Theologie Ephräms des Syrers.* Corpus Scriptorum Christianorum Orientalium 457. Louvain: Peeters, 1984.

Becker, Adam H. "Anti-Judaism and Care for the Poor in Aphrahat's *Demonstration* 20." *Journal of Early Christian Studies* 10 (2002): 305–27.

———. *Fear of God and the Beginning of Wisdom: The School of Nisibis and Christian Scholastic Culture in Late Antique Mesopotamia.* Philadelphia: University of Pennsylvania Press, 2006.

Bedjan, Paul, ed. *Acta martyrum et sanctorum Syriace.* 7 vols. Paris and Leipzig: Harrassowitz Verlag, 1890–1897.

Beggiani, Seely J. *Introduction to Eastern Christian Spirituality: The Syriac Tradition.* London: Associated University Presses, 1991.

Behr, John. "The Rational Animal: A Rereading of Gregory of Nyssa's *De hominis opificio.*" *Journal of Early Christian Studies* 7, no. 2 (1999): 219–47.

Bell, Gertrude, and Marlia M. Mango. *Churches and Monasteries of the Tur 'Abdin.* London: Pindar Press, 1982.

Benjamins, Hendrik S. "Keeping Marriage out of Paradise: The Creation of Man and Woman in Patristic Literature." In *The Creation of Man and Woman: Interpretations of the Biblical Narrative in Jewish and Christian Traditions,* edited by Gerard P. Luttikhuizen, 94–106. Themes in Biblical Narrative, Jewish and Christian Traditions 3. Leiden: E. J. Brill, 2000.

Bettiolo, Paolo. "Confessare Dio in perfetta spogliazione: La via del discernimento dei comandamenti nel *Liber graduum.*" *Cristianesimo nella storia* 19 (1998): 631–51.

———. "Adamo in Eden e la liturgia celeste: Temi della meditazione cristiana nella Siria del IV secolo, tra Afraate e il Liber Graduum." *Rivista di Storia e Letteratura Religiosa* 37 (2001): 3–27.

Betz, Johannes. *Eucharistie in der Schrift und Patristik.* Handbuch der Dogmengeschichte IV. Freiburg: Herder, 1979.

Bevan, Anthony A., F. Crawford Burkitt, and Charles W. Mitchell, eds. *S. Ephraim's Prose Refutations of Mani, Marcion, and Bardaisan: Of Which the Greater Part Has Been Transcribed from the Palimpsest B.M. Add. 14623 and Is Now First Published.* London: Published for the Text and Translation Society by Williams and Norgate, 1912–21.

Bianchi, Ugo, ed. *La "doppia creazione" dell'uomo negli Alessandrini, nei Cappadoci e nella gnosi.* Nuovi Saggi 70. Rome: Ateneo and Bizzarri, 1978.

———. "The Religio-Historical Relevance of Luke 20:34–36." In *Studies in Gnosticism and Hellenistic Religions Presented to Gilles Quispel on the Occasion of His 65th Birthday,* edited by Roelof van den Broek and Maarten J. Vermaseren, 31–37. Leiden: E. J. Brill, 1981.

Bitton-Ashkelony, Brouria. *Encountering the Sacred: The Debate on Christian Pilgrimage in Late Antiquity.* Berkeley and Los Angeles: The University of California Press, 2005.

Blockley, Roger C. "The Roman-Persian Peace Treaties of A.D. 299 and 363." *Florilegium* 6 (1984): 28–49.

———. "Constantius II and Persia." In *Studies in Latin Literature and Roman History,* edited by Carl Deroux, 5:465–90. Brussels: Latomus, 1989.

———. *East Roman Foreign Policy: Formation and Conduct from Diocletian to Anastasius.* Leeds: Francis Cairns, 1992.

Blum, Georg G. "Zur religionspolitischen Situation der persischen Kirche im 3. und 4. Jahrhundert." *Zeitschrift für Kirchengeschichte* 91 (1980): 11–32.

Bonnet, Max, ed. *Acta Thomae: Graece partim cum novis codicibus contulit partim primus edidit, Latine recensuit.* Supplementum Codicis Apocryphi 1. Leipzig: H. Mendelssohn, 1883.

Bowersock, Glen W. *Julian the Apostate.* Cambridge, Mass.: Harvard University Press, 1978.

Bowman, John. "The Malef." *Abr-Nahrain* 20 (1981–1982): 1–19.

Boyarin, Daniel. *Carnal Israel: Reading Sex in Talmudic Culture.* Berkeley and Los Angeles: University of California Press, 1993.

Brakke, David. *Athanasius and the Politics of Asceticism.* Oxford: Clarendon Press, 1995. Reprinted as *Athanasius and Asceticism.* Baltimore: Johns Hopkins University Press, 1998.

Braun, Oscar, trans. *Ausgewälte Akten persischer Märtyres, mit einem Anhang: Ostsyrische Mönchsleben.* Kempten: Verlag der Jos Köselschen Buchandlungen, 1915.

Breccia, Gastone. "'Salus Orientis': Il nuovo sistema militare romano-orientale alla prova, 379–400." *Rivista di studi bizantini e Neollenici* 41 (2005): 3–72.

Brock, Sebastian P. "Review of G. Wiessner's 'Zur Märtyrerübelieferung.'" *Journal of Theological Studies* 19 (1968): 300–8.

———. "Early Syrian Asceticism." *Numen* 20 (1973): 1–19.

———. "A Martyr at the Sasanid Court under Vahram II: Candida." *Analecta Bollandiana* 96 (1978): 167–81.

———. "John the Solitary: On Prayer." *Journal of Theological Studies* 30 (1979): 84-101.

———. "Clothing Metaphors as a Means of Theological Expression in Syriac Tradition." In *Typus, Symbol, Allegorie bei den östlichen Vätern und ihren Parallelen im Mittelalter: Internationales Kolloquium, Eichstätt 1981,* edited by Margot Schmidt and Carl F. Greyer, 11–38. Eichstätter Beiträge 4. Regensburg: Friedrich Pustet, 1982.

———. "Christians in the Sasanian Empire: A Case of Divided Loyalties." In *Religion and National Identity: Papers Read at the Nineteenth Summer Meeting and the Twentieth Winter Meeting of the Ecclesiastical History Society,* edited by Stuart Mews, 1–19. Studies in Church History 18. Oxford: Published for the Ecclesiastical History Society by B. Blackwell, 1982. Reprinted in Sebastian P. Brock, *Syriac Perspectives on Late Antiquity,* 1984.

———. "Some Aspects of Greek Words in Syriac." In *Synkretismus im syrisch-persischen Kulturgebiet: Bericht über ein Symposion in Reinhausen bei Göttingen in der Zeit vom 4. Bis 8. Oktober 1971,* edited by A. Dietrich, 80–108. Göttingen: Vandenhoeck and Ruprecht, 1975. Reprinted in Brock, *Syriac Perspectives on Late Antiquity,* 1984.

———. *Syriac Perspectives on Late Antiquity.* London: Variorum Reprints, 1984.

———. *St. Ephrem the Syrian: Hymns on Paradise.* New York: St. Vladimir's Seminary Press, 1990.

———. *The Luminous Eye: The Spiritual World Vision of St. Ephrem the Syrian.* Kalamazoo: Cistercian Publications, 1992.

———. "Mingana Syr. 628: A Folio from a Revision of the Peshitta Song of Songs." *Journal of Semitic Studies* 40 (1995): 39–56.

———. "Le monachisme syriaque: histoire et spiritualité." In *Le Monachisme Syriaque: Aux premiers siècles de l'Église. IIe–Début VIIe siècle,* 21–31. Patrimoine Syriaque: Actes du colloque V. Antélias, Lebanon: *Éditions du Cerf,* 1998.

———. "Syriac into Greek at Mar Saba." In *The Sabaite Heritage in the Orthodox Church from the Fifth Century to the Present,* edited by Joseph Patrich, 203. Orientalia Lovaniencia Analecta 98. Leuven: Peeters, 2001.

———. "Traduzioni siriache degli scritti di Basilio." In *Basilio tra Oriente e Occidente: Convegno Internazionale "Basilio il Grande e il Monachesimo Orientale," Cappadocia, 5–7 ottobre 1999,* edited by E. Baudry. Monastero di Bose, Magnano, Italy: Edizioni Qiqajon, 2001.

———. "Without Mushē of Nisibis, Where Would We Be? Some Reflections on the Transmission of Syriac Literature." *Journal of Eastern Christian Studies* 56 (2004): 15–24.

———. "The Bridal Chamber of Light: A Distinctive Feature of the Syriac Liturgical Tradition." *The Harp* 18 (2005): 179–91.

———. "The Genealogy of the Virgin Mary in Sinai Syr. 16." *Scrinium* 2 (2006): 58–71.

———. *The Holy Spirit in Syrian Baptismal Tradition.* Piscataway, N.J.: Gorgias Press, 2008.

Brock, Sebastian P., and Susan Ashbrook Harvey. *Holy Women of the Syriac Orient.* Berkeley and Los Angeles: University of California Press, 1987.

Brooks, Ernest W., ed. *A Collection of Letters of Severus of Antioch from Numerous Syriac Manuscripts.* 2 vols. Patrologia Orientalis 12.2, 14.1. Paris: Firmin-Didot, 1915, 1920.

Brown, Peter R. "The Rise and Function of the Holy Man in Late Antiquity." *Journal of Roman Studies* 61 (1971): 80–101.

———. *Society and the Holy in Late Antiquity.* Berkeley and Los Angeles: University of California Press, 1982.

———. *The Body and Society: Men, Women, and Sexual Renunciation in Early Christianity.* New York: Columbia University Press, 1988.

———. *Authority and the Sacred: Aspects of the Christianisation of the Roman World.* Cambridge: Cambridge University Press, 1995.

———. "Christianisation and Religious Conflict." In *The Cambridge Ancient History.* Vol. 13, *The Late Empire, A.D. 337–425,* edited by Averil Cameron and Peter Garnsey, 632–64. Cambridge: Cambridge University Press, 1998.

Buber, Solomon, ed. *Midrash Tanhuma.* Warsaw: 1878.

Budge, Ernest A. W. ed., trans. *The Discourses of Philoxenus: Bishop of Mabbôgh, A.D. 485–519.* 2 vols. London: Asher, 1893–1894.

———. *The Histories of Rabban Hôrmîzd the Persian and Rabban Bar-'Idtâ.* 3 vols. London: Luzac, 1902.

———. *Miscellaneous Coptic Texts in the Dialect of Upper Egypt.* Coptic Texts 5. London: British Museum, 1915.

Bundy, David. "Marcion and the Marcionites in Early Syriac Apologetics." *Le Muséon* 101, nos. 1 and 2 (1988): 21–32.

———. "Vision for the City: Nisibis in Ephrem's *Hymns on Nicomedia.*" In *Religions of*

Late Antiquity in Practice, edited by Richard Valantasis, 189–206. Princeton: Princeton University Press, 2000.

Burgess, Richard W. "The Dates of the First Siege of Nisibis and the Death of James of Nisibis." *Byzantion* 69 (1999): 7–17.

———. "The Dates of the Martyrdom of Simeon bar Sabba'e and the 'Great Massacre.'" *Analecta Bollandiana* 117 (1999): 9–66.

Burgess, Richard W., and Witold Witakowski. *Studies in Eusebian and Post-Eusebian Chronography.* Stuttgart: F. Steiner, 1999.

Burkitt, F. Crawford, trans. *Euphemia and the Goth: With the Acts of Martyrdom of the Confessors of Edessa* [1913]. Amsterdam: APA–Philo Press, 1981.

Burris, Catherine, and Lucas Van Rompay. "Thecla in Syriac Christianity: Preliminary Observations." *Hugoye: Journal of Syriac Studies* 5 (2002): 225–36.

———. "Some Further Notes on Thecla in Syriac Christianity." *Hugoye: Journal of Syriac Studies* 6 (2003): 337–42.

Calzolari, Valentina. "Notes sur la traduction arménienne du texte syriaque des Actes de Thècle." In *Proceedings of the Fifth International Conference on Armenian Linguistics: McGill University, Montreal, Quebec, Canada, May 1–5, 1995,* edited by Dora Sakayan, 233–43. New York: Delmar, 1996.

Camelot, P. Thomas. "Les traités 'De virginitate' au IVe siècle." In *Mystique et continence: Travaux scientifiques du VIIe Congrès international d'Avon,* 273–92. Bruges: Desclée de Brouwer, 1952.

Cameron, Averil. *The Later Roman Empire, AD 284–430.* Cambridge, Mass.: Harvard University Press, 1993.

———. *The Byzantine and Early Islamic Near East.* Vol. 3, *States, Resources and Armies,* Studies in Late Antiquity and Early Islam 1. Princeton: Darwin Press, 1995.

Cameron, Averil, and Peter Garnsey. *The Cambridge Ancient History.* Vol. 13, *The Late Empire, A.D. 337–425.* Cambridge: Cambridge University Press, 1998.

Cameron, Averil, and Stuart G. Hall, trans. *Eusebius: Life of Constantine.* Clarendon Ancient History Series. Oxford: Oxford University Press, 1999.

Canepa, Matthew P. *The Two Eyes of the Earth: Art and Ritual of Kingship between Rome and Sasanian Iran.* Berkeley: University of California Press, 2010.

Caner, Daniel. *Wandering, Begging Monks: Spiritual Authority and the Promotion of Monasticism in Late Antiquity.* Berkeley and Los Angeles: University of California Press, 2002.

Canivet, Pierre, and Alice Leroy-Molinghen, ed. and trans. *Histoire des Moines de Syrie.* Sources Chrétiennes 234, 257. Paris: Éditions du Cerf, 1977, 1979. English translation: Richard M. Price, *A History of the Monks of Syria by Theodoret of Cyrrhus.* Kalamazoo, Mich.: Cistercian Publications, 1985.

Carrié, Jean-Michel, and Aline Rousselle. *L'Empire romain en mutation : Des Sévères à Constantin.* Nouvelle Histoire de l'Antiquité 10. Paris: Seuil, 1999.

Cecire, Robert C. *Encratism: Early Christian Ascetic Extremism.* PhD diss., The University of Kansas, 1985.

Chadwick, Henry. "Enkrateia." In *Reallexikon für Antike und Christentum,* edited by Theodor Klauser, 5:343–65. Stuttgart: Hiersemann, 1962.

Chahine, Charbel. *Abraham de Bēṯ-Neṭprā: Discours (Mēmrē): Introduction, texte critique et traduction.* PhD diss., Augustinianum: Roma, 2004.

Charlesworth, John H., ed. *The History of the Rechabites.* Vol. 1, *The Greek Recension.* Society of Biblical Literature. Texts and Translations 17. Chico: Scholars Press, 1982.

———. *The Old Testament Pseudepigrapha.* Vol. 2. New York: Doubleday, 1985.

Chaumont, Marie-Louise. *La christianisation de l'Empire iranien: Des origines aux grandes persécutions du IVe siècle.* Corpus Scriptorum Christianorum Orientalium 499. Louvain: Peeters, 1988.

Chialà, Sabrino. *Abramo di Kashkar e la sua comunità: La rinascita del monachesimo siro-orientale.* Comunità di Bose, Magnano, Italy: Edizioni Qiqajon, 2005.

Childers, Jeff W. "'Humility Begets Wisdom and Discernment:' Character and True Knowledge in Aphrahat." In *Studia Patristica,* edited by Frances Young, et al, 41:13–22. Leuven: Peeters, 2006.

———. "'We Must Seek the Truth': Theological Scholarship in the Early Syriac Tradition." *Restoration Quarterly* 49 (2007): 193–216.

Clabeaux, John J. "Abraham in Marcion's Gospel and Epistles: Marcion and the Jews." In *When Judaism and Christianity Began: Essays in Memory of Anthony J. Saldarini,* edited by A. J. Avery-Peck, D. J. Harrington, and Jacob Neusner, 69–92. Vol. 1, *Christianity in the Beginning.* Supplements to the Journal for the Study of Judaism 85. Leiden: E. J. Brill, 2004.

Clark, Elizabeth A. *Reading Renunciation: Asceticism and Scripture in Early Christianity.* Princeton: Princeton University Press, 1999.

Code, Lorraine. *Epistemic Responsibility.* Hanover, N.H.: University Press of New England for Brown University Press, 1987.

Cohen, Jeremy. *"Be Fertile and Increase, Fill the Earth and Master It": The Ancient and Medieval Career of a Biblical Text.* Ithaca: Cornell University Press, 1989.

Collins, John J. "In the Likeness of the Holy Ones: The Creation of Humankind in a Wisdom Text from Qumran." In *The Provo International Conference on the Dead Sea Scrolls: Technological Innovations, New Texts, and Reformulated Issues,* edited Donald W. Parry and Eugene Ulrich, 609–18. Studies on the Texts of the Desert of Judah 30. Leiden: E. J. Brill, 1999.

———. "The Angelic Life." In *Metamorphoses: Resurrection, Body, and Transformative Practices in Early Christianity,* edited by T. K. Seim and Jorunn Økland, 291–310. Ekstasis 1. Berlin: Walter de Gruyter, 2009.

Colson, Francis H., and George H. Whitaker, trans. *Philo Volume 1.* Loeb Classical Library 226. London: Heinemann, 1929.

———. "Before Constantine." In *The Cambridge Companion to the Age of Constantine,* edited by Noel E. Lenski, 35–58. Cambridge: Cambridge University Press, 2006.

Conybeare, Frederick C. *The Armenian Apology and Acts of Apollonius and Other Monuments of Early Christianity.* 2nd ed. New York: Macmillan, 1896.

Cook, Johann. "The Origin of the Tradition of the יצר הטוב and יצר הרע." *Journal for the Study of Judaism* 38, no. 1 (2007): 80–91.

Corbett, John H. "They Do Not Take Wives, or Build, or Work the Ground: Ascetic Life in the Early Syriac Church." *Journal of the Canadian Society for Syriac Studies* 3 (2003): 9–26.

Corcoran, Simon. *The Empire of the Tetrachs: Imperial Pronouncements and Government, AD 284–324*. Rev. ed. Oxford: Clarendon Press, 2000.

Coxe, A. Cleveland, ed. *Ante-Nicene Fathers*. Vol. 1, *The Apostolic Fathers: Justin Martyr, Irenaeus*. New York: Christian Literature Publishing, 1885.

Daniélou, Jean. "Terre et paradis chez les Pères de l'Église." *Eranos Jahrbuch* 22 (1953): 433–72.

———. *Etudes d'exégèse judéo-chrétienne: Les testimonia*. Paris: Beauchesne, 1966.

Davis, Stephen J. *The Cult of St. Thecla: A Tradition of Women's Piety in Late Antiquity*. Oxford: Oxford University Press, 2001.

Debié, Muriel. "Nisibe sauviée des eaux: les sources de Théodoret et la place des versions syriaques." In *Pèlerinages et lieux saints dans l'antiquité tardive et le moyen âge: mélanges offerts à Pierre Maraval*, edited by Beatrice Caseau, Jean-Claude Cheynet, and Vincent Déroche, 135–51. Paris: Association des amis du Centre d'histoire et civilisation de Byzance, 2006.

Decret, F. "Les conséquences sur le christianisme en Perse de l'affrontement des empires romain et sassanide." *Recherches Augustiniennes* 14 (1979): 91–152.

Dedering, Sven, and Raphael J. Bidawid, eds. *The Old Testament in Syriac according to the Peshitta Version*. Part 4, fasc. 3, *Apocalypse of Baruch; 4 Esdras*. Leiden: E. J. Brill, 1973.

De Halleux, André. *Philoxène de Mabbog: Sa vie, ses écrits, sa theologie*. Louvain: Imprimerie Orientaliste, 1963.

De Lagarde, Paul, ed. *Analecta Syriaca*. Lipsiae: B. G. Teubnerus, 1858.

———. *Titi Bostreni contra Manichaeos libri quattuor syriace*. Berlin: C. Schulze, 1859.

Dimant, Devorah. "Men as Angels: The Self-Image of the Qumran Community." In *Religion and Politics in the Ancient Near East*, edited by Adele Berlin, 93–103. Studies and Texts in Jewish History and Culture. Bethesda: University Press of Maryland, 1986.

Dixon, B. "Journeys in Kurdistan." *Geographical Journal* 35 (1910): 357–78.

Dodgeon, Michael H., and Samuel N. C. Lieu. *The Roman Eastern Frontier and the Persian Wars A.D. 226–363: A Documentary History*. London: Routledge, 1991.

Dolabani, Filoksinos Y. *Catalogue of Syriac Manuscripts in St. Mark's Monastery*. Syriac Patrimony 8. Aleppo: Syria Mardin, 1994.

Dörries, Hermann. *Die Theologie des Makarios/Symeon*. Abhandlungen der Akademie der Wissenschaft. Philologisch-historische Klasse. Series 3, nos. 103, 105. Göttingen: Vandenhoeck and Ruprecht, 1978.

Draguet, René. *Les cinq recensions de l'Ascéticon syriaque d'Abba Isaïe*. Corpus Scriptorum Christianorum Orientalium 289. Louvain: Secrétariat du Sorpus SCO, 1968.

Drijvers, Han J. W. *Bardaisan of Edessa*. Studia Semitica Neerlandica 6. Assen: Van Gorcum, 1966.

———. "Odes of Solomon and Psalms of Mani: Christians and Manichaeans in Third-Century Syria." In *Gnosticism and Hellenistic Religions Presented to Giles Quispel on the Occasion of his 65th Birthday,* edited by Roelof van den Broek and Maarten J. Vermaseren, 117–30. Leiden: E. J. Brill, 1981.

———. "Addai und Mani: Christentum und Manichäismus in dritten Jahrhundert in Syrien." In *Les contacts du monde syriaque avec les autres cultures: IIIe Symposium Syriacum 1980 (Goslar 7–11 Septembre 1980),* edited by René Lavenant. Orientalia Christiana Analecta 221. Rome: Pont. Institutum studiorum orientalium, 1983.

———. "Facts and Problems in Early Syriac-Speaking Christianity." In *East of Antioch: Studies in Early Syriac Christianity.* London: Variorum Reprints, 1984.

———. "Marcionism in Syria: Principles, Problem, Polemics." *The Second Century* 6, no. 3 (1987–88): 153–72.

Eadie, John. "The Transformation of the Eastern Frontier, 260–305." In *Shifting Frontiers in Late Antiquity,* edited by Ralph W. Mathisen and Sivan Hagith, 72–82. Aldershot: Variorum, 1996.

Edwell, Peter M. *Between Rome and Persia: The Middle Euphrates, Mesopotamia and Palmyra under Roman Control.* London: Routledge, 2008.

Elton, H. "Defining Romans and Barbarians." In *Shifting Frontiers in Late Antiquity,* edited by Ralph W. Mathisen and Sivan Hagith, 126–35. Aldershot: Variorum, 1996.

Fairweather, Abrol, and Linda Zagzebski, eds. *Virtue Epistemology: Essays on Epistemic Virtue and Responsibility.* New York: Oxford University Press, 2001.

Fedwick, Paul J. *Basilius Caesariensis: The Letters.* Bibliotheca Basiliana Universalis 1. Turnhout: Brepols, 1993.

Ferguson, J., trans. *Clement of Alexandria. Stromateis: Books One to Three.* The Fathers of the Church: A New Translation 85. Washington, D.C.: The Catholic University of America Press, 1991.

Feuerbach, Ludwig. *Das Wesen des Christentums.* In *Essence of Christianity,* translated by George Eliot. Leipzig: Otto Wigand, 1904.

Fiey, Jean-Maurice. "Les Marcionites dans les textes historiques de l'Église de Perse." *Le Muséon* 83, nos. 1 and 2 (1970): 183–88.

———. *Nisibe: Métropole syriaque orientale et ses suffragants des origines à nos jours.* Corpus Scriptorum Christianorum Orientalum 388. Louvain: Peeters, 1977.

———. *Saints syriaques.* Edited by Lawrence I. Conrad. Princeton: Darwin Press, 2004.

Fitschen, Klaus. *Messalianismus und Antimessalianismus: Ein Beispiel ostkirchlicher Ketzergeschichte.* Göttingen: Vandenhoeck and Ruprecht, 1998.

Fletcher-Louis, Crispin H. T. *All the Glory of Adam: Liturgical Anthropology in the Dead Sea Scrolls.* Studies on the Texts of the Desert of Judah 42. Leiden: E. J. Brill, 2002.

Fonrobert, Charlotte E. *Menstrual Purity: Rabbinic and Christian Reconstructions of Biblical Gender.* Contraversions: Jews and Other Differences. Stanford: Stanford University Press, 2000.

———. "The *Didascalia Apostolorum:* A Mishnah for the Disciples of Jesus." *Journal of Early Christian Studies* 9, no. 4 (2001): 483–509.

Foucault, Michel. "The Order of Discourse." In *The Archaeology of Knowledge,* translated by A. M. Sheridan Smith, 215–37. New York: Pantheon Books, 1972.

Fowden, Elizabeth Key. *The Barbarian Plain: Saint Sergius between Rome and Iran.* Berkeley and Los Angeles: University of California Press, 1999.

Frakes, R. M., ed. *Mosaicarum et Romanorum legum collatio.* In *Compiling the "Collatio Legum Mosaicorum et Romanarum" in Late Antiquity.* Oxford: Oxford University Press, 2011), §15.3, 191–92 (text); 233–34 (translation).

Frank, Karl S. *Angelikos Bios: Begriffsanalytische und Begriffsgeschichtliche Untersuchung zum "Engelgleichen Leben" im frühen Mönchtum.* Münster: Aschendorffsche Verlagsbuchhandlung, 1964.

Freeman, Philip, and D. L. Kennedy, eds. *The Defense of the Roman and Byzantine East: Proceedings of a Colloquium Held at the University of Sheffield in April 1986.* BAR International Series 297 (i–ii). Oxford: British Institute of Archaeology at Ankara, 1986.

French, D. H., and Chris S. Lightfoot, eds. *The Eastern Frontier of the Roman Empire: Proceedings of a Colloquium Held at Ankara in September 1988.* BAR International Series 553. Oxford: British Institute of Archaeology at Ankara, 1989.

Friedlander, Gerald, trans. *Pirke de Rabbi Eliezer: The Chapters of Rabbi Eliezer the Great according to the Text of the Manuscript belonging to Abraham Epstein of Vienna.* New York: Hermon Press, 1965.

Froehlich, Karlfried. *Biblical Interpretation in the Early Church.* Philadelphia: Fortress Press, 1984.

Fumerton, Richard. "Theories of Justification." In *The Oxford Handbook of Epistemology,* edited by Paul K. Moser, 205–33. Oxford: University Press, 2002.

Funk, Wolf-Peter, ed. *Kephalaia I: Zweite Hälfte (Lieferung 13–14).* Stuttgart: Kohlhammer, 1999.

———. *Kephalaia I: Zweite Hälfte (Lieferung 15–16).* Stuttgart: Kohlhammer, 2000.

Gaca, Kathy L. *The Making of Fornication: Eros, Ethics, and Political Reform in Greek Philosophy and Early Christianity.* Hellenistic Culture and Society 40. Berkeley and Los Angeles: University of California Press, 2003.

Gaddis, Michael. *There Is No Crime for Those Who Have Christ: Religious Violence in the Christian Roman Empire.* Berkeley and Los Angeles: University of California Press, 2005.

Gafni, Isaiah M. "The Political, Social and Economic History of Babylonian Jewry, 224–638 CE." In *The Cambridge History of Judaism: The Late Roman-Rabbinic Period,* edited by Steven T. Katz, 4:792–820. Cambridge: Cambridge University Press, 2006.

Gardner, Iain M. F., ed. *Kellis Literary Texts.* Vol. 1. Oxford: Oxbow Books, 1996.

Gardner, Iain M. F., and Samuel N. C. Lieu. "From Narmouthis (Medinet Madi) to Kellis (Ismant El-Kharab): Manichaean Documents from Roman Egypt." *Journal of Roman Studies* 86 (1996): 146–69.

Gasparro, Giulia Sfameni. "Asceticism and Anthropology: *Enkrateia* and 'Double Creation' in Early Christianity." In *Asceticism,* edited by Vincent L. Wimbush and Richard Valantasis, 127–46. Oxford: Oxford University Press, 1995.

Géhin, Paul. "Manuscrits sinaïtiques dispersés I: Les fragments syriaques et arabes de Paris." *Oriens Christianus* 90 (2006): 23–43.

Geiger, Abraham. *Judaism and Islam.* Translated by F. M. Young. Madras, India: Zohar Books, 1898.

Gignoux, P. "Church-State Relations in the Sasanian Period." *Bulletin of the Middle Eastern Culture Centre in Japan* 1 (1984): 72–80.

Gilhus, Ingvild S. *Animals, Gods and Humans: Changing Attitudes to Animals in Greek, Roman and Early Christian Ideas.* London: Routledge, 2006.

Goldman, Alvin I. *Epistemology and Cognition.* Cambridge, Mass.: Harvard University Press, 1986.

Golitzin, Alexander. "Recovering the 'Glory of Adam': 'Divine Light' Traditions in the Dead Sea Scrolls and the Christian Ascetical Literature of Fourth-Century Syro-Mesopotamia." In *The Dead Sea Scrolls as Background to Postbiblical Judaism and Early Christianity: Papers from an International Conference at St. Andrews in 2001,* edited by James R. Davila, 275–308. Leiden: E. J. Brill, 2003.

Goodblatt, David M. "The Poll Tax in Sasanian Babylonia: The Talmudic Evidence." *Journal of the Economic and Social History of the Orient* 22 (1979): 233–95.

Goshen-Gottstein, Moshe H. *Syriac Manuscripts in the Harvard College Library: A Catalogue.* Harvard Semitic Studies 23. Missoula, Mt.: Scholars Press, 1979.

Grand'Henry, Jacques. "La réponse de S. Basile a S. Grégoire: Édition critique de la lettre 2 en version arabe." *Le Muséon* 102 (1989): 321–59.

Greatrex, Geoffrey. *Rome and Persia at War: 502–532.* Leeds: Francis Cairns, 1998.

———. "The Background and Aftermath of the Partition of Armenia in A.D. 387." *Ancient History Bulletin* 14 (2000): 35–48.

———. Review of *The Cambridge Ancient History,* vol.14, ed. Averil Cameron, B. Ward-Perkins, and M. Whitby. *Phoenix* 57 (2003): 181–86.

———. "Roman Frontiers and Foreign Policy in the East." In *Aspects of the Roman East: Papers in Honour of Professor Fergus Millar FBA,* edited by Richard Alston and Samuel N. C. Lieu, 103–73. Turnhout: Brepols, 2007.

———. Review of *Ērān ud Anērān: Studien zu den Beziehungen zwischen dem Sasanidenreich und der Mittelmeerwelt,* by Josef Wiesehöfer and Philip Huyse. *Phoenix* 63 (2009): 208–11.

Greatrex, Geoffrey, and M. Greatrex. "The Hunnic Invasion of the East of 395 and the Fortress of Ziatha." *Byzantion* 69 (1999): 65–75.

Greatrex, Geoffrey, and Samuel N. C. Lieu. *The Roman Eastern Frontier and the Persian Wars (A.D. 363–630): A Narrative Sourcebook.* London: Routledge, 2002.

Grech, Prosper. "The Regula Fidei as a Hermeneutical Principle in Patristic exegesis." In *The Interpretation of the Bible: The International Symposium in Slovenia,* edited by Joze Krasovec, 589–601. Sheffield: Sheffield Academic Press, 1998.

Greco, John. "Virtues in Epistemology." In *The Oxford Handbook of Epistemology,* edited by Paul K. Moser, 287–335. Oxford: Oxford University Press, 2002.

Gribomont, Jean. "Monasticism and Asceticism: I. Eastern Christianity." In *Christian Spirituality: Origins to the 12th Century,* edited by Jean Leclercq, Bernard McGinn, and John Meyendorf, 1:89–112. World Spirituality 16. London: SCM, 1989.

Griffith, Sidney H. "'Singles' in God's Service: Thoughts on Ihidaye from the Works of Aphrahat and Ephraem the Syrian." *The Harp* 4 (1991): 145–59.

———. "Monks, 'Singles,' and the 'Sons of the Covenant': Reflections on Syriac Ascetic Terminology." In *Eulogema: Studies in Honor of Robert Taft, S. J.,* edited by E. Carr, 141–60. Studia Anselmiana 110. Rome: Pontificio Ateneo S. Anselmo, 1993.

———. "Asceticism in the Church of Syria: The Hermeneutics of Early Syrian Monasticism." In *Asceticism,* edited by Richard Valantasis and Vincent L. Wimbush, 220–46. New York: Oxford University Press, 1995.

Guillaumont, Antoine. *Les "Képhalaia gnostica" d'Évagre le Pontique et l'histoire de l'origénisme chez les Grecs et chez les Syriens.* Patristica Sorbonensia 5. Paris: Éditions du Seuil, 1962.

———. "ΝΗΣΤΕΥΕΙΝ ΤΟΝ ΚΟΣΜΟΝ (P.Oxy. 1, verso, l.5–6)." *Bulletin de l'Institut français d'archeologie orientale* 61 (1962): 15–23.

———. "Les 'arrhes de l'Esprit' dans le Livre des degrés." In *Mémorial Mgr Gabriel Khouri-Sarkis (1898–1968): Fondateur et directeur de l'Orient syrien, 1956–1967,* edited by François Graffin, 107–13. Louvain: Imprimerie Orientaliste, 1969.

———. "Situation et significance du 'Liber Graduum' dans la spiritualité syriaque." In *Symposium Syriacum 1972: Célébré dans les jours 26–31 octobre 1972 à l'Institut pontifical oriental de Rome: Rapports et communications,* edited by Ignacio Ortiz de Urbina, 311–25. Orientalia Christiana Analecta 197. Rome: Pontificium Institutum Orientalium, 1974.

———. "Liber Graduum." In *Dictionnaire de spiritualité ascétique et mystique: Doctrine et histoire,* 9:749–54. Paris: Beauchesne, 1976.

———. "Le dépaysement comme forme d'ascèse dans le monachism ancien." In *Aux origines du monachisme chrétien: Pour une phénoménologie du monachisme,* 89–116. Spiritualité Orientale 30. Bégrolles-en-Mauges, France: Abbaye de Bellefontaine, 1979.

Gunther, John J. "Syrian Christian Dualism." *Vigiliae Christianae* 25, no. 2 (1971): 81–93.

Hage, Wolfgang. "Die oströmische Staatskirche und die Christenheit des Perserreiches." *Zeitschrift für Kirchengeschichte* 84 (1973): 174–87.

Hartmann, U. "Mareades—ein sasanidischer Quisling?" In *Ērān ud Anērān: Studien zu den Beziehungen zwischen dem Sasanidenreich und der Mittelmeerwelt,* edited by Josef Wiesehöfer and Philip Huyse, 105–42. Oriens et Occidens 13. Stuttgart: Franz Steiner Verlag, 2006.

Harvey, Susan Ashbrook. "The Holy and the Poor: Models from Early Syriac Christianity." In *Through the Eye of a Needle: Judeo-Christian Roots of Social Welfare,* edited by Emily Albu Hanawalt and Carter Lindberg, 43–66. Kirksville, Mo.: Thomas Jefferson University Press, 1994.

———. "Creation and Asceticism: Syriac Christian Thought." In *Christian Thought: A Brief*

History, edited by Adrian Hastings, Alistair Mason, and Hugh S. Pyper, 33–37. Oxford: Oxford University Press, 2002.

Hasler, Victor Ernst. *Gesetz und Evangelium in der Alten Kirche bis Origenes: Eine auslegungsgeschichtliche Untersuchung.* Zürich: Gotthelf Verlag, 1953.

Hausherr, Irénée. "L'erreur fondamentale et la logique du messalianisme." *Orientalia Christiana Periodica* 1 (1935): 328–60.

———. "Quanam Aetate Prodierit 'Liber Graduum?'" *Orientalia Christiana Periodica* 1 (1935): 495–502.

Heither, Theresia, trans, ed. *Commentarii in Epistulam ad Romanos: Liber Septimus, Liber Octavus.* Fontes Christiani 2, 4. Freiburg: Herder, 1994.

Helderman, Jan. *Die Anapausis im Evangelium Veritatis.* Leiden: E. J. Brill, 1984.

Hewsen, Robert H., and Christopher C. Salvatico. *Armenia: A Historical Atlas.* Chicago: University of Chicago Press, 2001.

Hockel, Alfred. *Christus der Erstgeborene: Zur Geschichte der Exegese von Kol 1,15.* Düsseldorf: Patmos Verlag, 1965.

Hoffmann, Georg. *Auszüge aus syrischen Akten persischer Märtyrer.* 1994.. Leipzig: Brockhaus, 1880.

Hookway, Christopher. "How to Be a Virtue Epistemologist." In *Intellectual Virtue: Perspectives from Ethics and Epistemology,* edited by Michael R. DePaul and Linda T. Zagzebski, 183–202. Oxford: Clarendon Press, 2003.

Howard-Johnston, J. D. "The Great Powers in Late Antiquity: A Comparison." In *States, Resources and Armies: Papers of the Third Workshop on Late Antiquity and Early Islam,* edited by Averil Cameron, 3:157–226.

Hunt, Emily J. *Christianity in the Second Century: The Case of Tatian.* London: Routledge, 2003.

Hutter, M. "Manichaeism in Iran in the Fourth Century." In *Studia Manichaica: IV Internationaler Kongreß zum Manichäismus, Berlin, 14.–18. Juli 1997,* edited by R. Emmerick, W. Sundermann, and P. Zieme. Berlin: Akademie Verlag, 1997.

Jansma, Taeke, and Marinus D. Koester, eds. *The Old Testament in Syriac according to the Peshitta Version.* Part 1, fasc. 1, *Preface; Genesis–Exodus.* Leiden: E. J. Brill, 1977.

Jones, Arnold H., John R. Martindale, and J. Morris. *Prosopography of the Later Roman Empire. Vol. 1.* Cambridge: Cambridge University Press, 1971.

Jones, Frederick S. "Jewish Christianity of the *Pseudo-Clementines.*" In *A Companion to Second-Century Christian "Heretics,"* edited by P. Luomanen and A. Marjanen, 315–34. Supplements to Vigiliae Christianae 76. Leiden: E. J. Brill, 2005.

Juhl, Diana. *Die Askese im Liber Graduum und bei Afrahat: Eine vergleichende Studie zur frühsyrischen Frömmigkeit.* Orientalia Biblical et Christiana 9. Wiesbaden: Harrassowitz Verlag, 1996.

Jullien, Christelle, and Florence Jullien. "La chronique d'Arbèles: Propositions pour la fin d'une controverse. " *Oriens Christianus* 85 (2001): 41–83.

———. *Apôtres des confins: Processus missionaires chrétiens dans l'Empire Iranien.* Res Orientales 15. Bures-sur-Yvette: Groupe pour l'étude de la civilisation du Moyen-orient, 2002.

——— *Aux origines de l'église de Perse: les Actes de Mar Mari.* Corpus Scriptorum Christianorum Orientalium 604. Louvain: Peeters, 2003.

Kawerau, Paul, ed. *Die Chronik von Arbela* [*The Chronicle of Arbela*]. Corpus Scriptorum Christianorum Orientalium 467:45 (text); 468:51 (translation). Louvain: Peeters, 1985.

Kerschensteiner, Josef. *Der altsyrische Paulustext.* Corpus Scriptorum Christianorum Orientalium 315. Subsidia 37. Louvain: Secrétariat du Corpus Scriptorum Christianorum Orientalium, 1970.

Kessel, Grigory. "A Note on One Borrowing from Aphrahat: Ms. St. Petersburg Syr. 34." *Parole de l'Orient* 31 (2006): 295–307.

———. "The 'Letter' of Thomas the Monk: An Edition and Study of the Syriac Text and Its Author." *Journal of Eastern Christian Studies* 61 (2009): 43–100.

Khalek, Nancy. "Methods of Instructing Syriac-Speaking Christians to Care for the Poor: A Brief Comparison of the Eighth Memra of the Book of Steps and the Story of the Man of God of Edessa." *Hugoye: Journal of Syriac Studies* 8 (2005): 13–25.

Kieckhefer, Richard. *Magic in the Middle Ages.* Cambridge: Cambridge University Press, 2000.

Kister, Menahem. "'In Adam': 1 Cor 15:21–22; 12:27 in Their Jewish Setting." In *Flores Florentino: Dead Sea Scrolls and Other Early Jewish Studies in Honour of Florentino García Martínez,* edited by A. Hilhorst, É. Puech, and E. Tigchelaar, 687–90. Leiden: E. J. Brill, 2007.

———. "'First Adam' and 'Second Adam' in 1 Cor 15:45–49 in the Light of Midrashic Exegesis and Hebrew Usage." In *The New Testament and Rabbinic Literature,* edited by Reimund Bieringer, Florentino García Martínez, Didier Pollefeyt, and Peter J. Tomson, 351–62. Leiden: E. J. Brill, 2010.

Kitchen, Robert A. "The Gattung of the Liber Graduum: Implications for a Sociology of Asceticism." In *IV Symposium Syriacum 1984,* edited by Han J. W. Drijvers, et al, 173–82. Orientalia Christiana Analecta 229. Rome: Pontificium Institutum Studiorum Orientalium, 1987.

———. "The Development of the Status of Perfection in Early Syriac Ascetism with Special Reference to the Liber Graduum and Philoxenus of Mabbug." PhD diss., University of Oxford, 1997.

———. "Conflict on the Stairway to Heaven: The Anonymity of Perfection in the Syriac *Liber Graduum.*" In *Symposium Syriacum VII: Uppsala University, Department of Asian and African Languages, 11–14 August 1996,* edited by René Lavenant, 211–20. Rome: Pontificio Instituto Orientale, 1998.

———. "Becoming Perfect: The Maturing of Asceticism in the Liber Graduum." In *Journal of the Canadian Society for Syriac Studies* 2 (2002): 30–45.

———. "Syriac Additions to Anderson: The Garden of Eden in the Book of Steps and Philoxenus of Mabbug." *Hugoye: Journal of Syriac Studies* 6 (2003): 37–50.

———. "Making the Imperfect Perfect: The Adaptation of Hebrews 11 in the 9th Mēmrā of the Syriac Book of Steps." In *Reading and Interpretation of the Bible in Late Antiquity: Charles Kannengiesser Festschrift,* 227–51. Leiden: E. J. Brill, 2008.

Kitchen, Robert A., and Martien F. G. Parmentier, trans. *The Book of Steps: The Syriac Liber Graduum.* Kalamazoo, Mich.: Cistercian Publications, 2004.

Klijn, Albertus F. J., trans. "2 (Syriac Apocalypse of) Baruch." In *The Old Testament Pseudepigrapha,* edited by James H. Charlesworth, 1:615–52. New York: Doubleday, 1983, 1985.

———. *The Acts of Thomas: Introduction, Text, and Commentary.* 2nd ed. Supplements to Novum Testamentum. Leiden: E. J. Brill, 2003.

Kmoskó, Michael, ed. *Ammonii Eremitae Epistolae.* Patrologia Orientalis 10.6. Paris: Firmin-Didot, 1915.

———. *Liber Graduum.* Patrologia Syriaca 1.3. Paris: Firmin-Didot, 1926.

Kofsky, Aryeh. "The Renunciation of Will in the Monastic School of Gaza." *Liber Annuus* 56 (2006): 321–46.

Kofsky, Aryeh, and Serge Ruzer. "Justice, Free Will and Divine Mercy in Ephrem's Commentary on Genesis 2–3." *Le Muséon* 113 (2000): 315–32.

———. "Logos, Holy Spirit and Messiah: Aspects of Aphrahat's Theology Reconsidered." *Orientalia Christiana Periodica* 73 (2007): 347–78.

———. *Syriac Idiosyncrasies: Theology and Hermeneutic in Early Syriac Literature.* Leiden: E. J. Brill, 2010.

Koltun-Fromm, Naomi. "Yokes of the Holy-Ones: The Embodiment of a Christian Vocation." *Harvard Theological Review* 94, no. 2 (2001): 207–20.

Kowalski, Aleksander. "Adam i Ewa jako dzieci w egzegezie syryjskiej." *Roczniki Teologiczno-Kanoniczne* 30, no. 1 (1983): 117–22.

———. "Die Gebete im Liber Graduum." *Orientalia Christiana Periodica* 55 (1989): 273–81.

———. *Perfezione e giustizia di Adamo nel Liber Graduum.* Orientalia Christiana Analecta 232. Rome: Pontificium Institutum Orientale, 1989.

Kronholm, Tryggve. *Motifs from Genesis 1–11, in the Genuine Hymns of Ephrem the Syrian with Particular Reference to the Influence of Jewish Exegetical Tradition.* Upsala: Almqvist and Wiksell, 1978.

———. "The Trees of Paradise in the Hymns of Ephraem Syrus." *Annual of the Swedish Theological Institute Leiden* 1 (1978): 48–56.

Krueger, Derek. *Symeon the Holy Fool: Leontius's Life and the Late Antique City.* Berkeley and Los Angeles: University of California Press, 1996.

———. *Writing and Holiness: The Practice of Authorship in the Early Christian East.* Divinations: Rereading Late Ancient Religion. Philadelphia: University of Pennsylvania Press, 2004.

Kvanvig, Jonathan L. *The Intellectual Virtues and the Life of the Mind.* Savage, Md.: Rowman and Littlefield, 1992.

Labourt, Jérôme. *Le christianisme dans l'empire perse sous la dynastie sassanide (224–632).* 2nd ed. Bibliotheque de l'enseignement de l'histoire ecclesiastique. Paris: Librarie Victor Lecoffre, 1904.

Lambdin, Thomas O., trans. *Gospel of Thomas.* In *The Nag Hammadi Library in English,* edited by James M. Robinson and Richard Smith. 3rd ed. San Francisco: Harper and Row, 1988.

Lane, David J. "The Book of Grades, or Steps." *The Harp* 14 (2001): 81–88.

———. *Šubḥalmaran: The Book of Gifts.* Corpus Scriptorum Christianorum Orientalium 612, Scriptores Syri 236. Louvain: Peeters, 2004.

Lawlor, H. J., and J. E. L. Oulton, trans., ed. *Eusebius: Ecclesiatical History and Martyrs of Palestine.* London: S.P.C.K, 1927–28, 1:152.

Leadbetter, Bill. *Galerius and the Will of Diocletian.* London: Routledge, 2009.

Leclerc, Pierre, and Edgardo M. Morales, eds. *Jérôme: Trois vies de moines; Paul, Malchus, Hilarion.* Sources chrétiennes 508. Paris: Éditions du Cerf, 2007.

Lee, A. Douglas. *Information and Frontiers: Roman Foreign Relations in Late Antiquity.* Cambridge: Cambridge University Press, 1993.

———. *Pagans and Christians in Late Antiquity: A Sourcebook.* London: Routledge, 2000.

Leemhuis, Fred, Albertus F. J. Klijn, and Geert J. van Gelder, eds. *The Arabic Text of the Apocalypse of Baruch: Edited and Translated with a Parallel Translation of the Syriac Text.* Leiden: E. J. Brill, 1986.

Légasse, Simon. "Les autres voies de la mission." In *Histoire du Christianisme 1: Le Nouveau Peuple (des origines à 250),* edited by J.-M. Mayeur, et al. Paris: Desclée, 2000.

Leloir, Louis, ed. *Saint Éphrem: Commentaire de l'évangile concordant.* Scriptores armeniaci I. Corpus Scriptorum Christianorum Orientalium 137, 277. Louvain: Imprimerie Orientaliste L. Durbecq and Peeters, 1953–54.

Lemerle, Paul. *Les plus anciennes recueils des miracles de saint Démétrius et la penetration des Slaves dans les Balkans.* Paris: Éditions du Centre national de la recherche scientifique, 1979.

Lenski, Noel E., ed. *The Cambridge Companion to the Age of Constantine.* Cambridge: Cambridge University Press, 2006.

Levison, John R. *Portraits of Adam in Early Judaism: From Sirach to 2 Baruch. Journal for the Study of the Pseudepigrapha.* Supplement Series 1. Sheffield: JSOT Press, 1988.

Lieber, Andrea. "Jewish and Christian Heavenly Meal Traditions." In *Paradise Now: Essays on Early Jewish and Christian Mysticism,* edited by April D. DeConick, 313–39. SBL Symposium Series 11. Atlanta: Society of Biblical Literature, 2006.

Liebeschuetz, John H. W. G. "Epigraphic Evidence on the Christianisation of Syria." In *Akten des XI. Internationalen Limeskongresses,* 485–508. Budapest: Akadémiai Kiadó, 1981.

Lieu, Samuel N. C. *Manichaeism in the Later Roman Empire and Medieval China*, 2nd ed. Tübingen: J. C. B. Mohr, 1992.

———, ed. *The Emperor Julian: Panegyric and Polemic.* 2nd ed. Translated Texts for Historians. Liverpool: Liverpool University Press, 1989.

Lightfoot, Chris S. "Tilli: A Late Roman *Equites* Fort on the Tigris." In *The Defence of the Roman and Byzantine East: Proceedings of a Colloquium Held at the University of Sheffield in April 1986,* edited by Philip Freeman and D. L. Kennedy, 506–29. BAR International Series 297. Oxford: British Institute of Archaeology at Ankara, 1986.

———. "Facts and Fiction: The Third Siege of Nisibis (A.D. 350)." *Historia* 37 (1988): 105–25.

———." The Site of Roman Bezabde." In *Armies and Frontiers in Roman and Byzantine Anatolia: Proceedings of a Colloquium Held at University College, Swansea, in April 1981,* edited by Stephen Mitchell, 189–204. BAR International Series 156. Oxford: British Institute of Archaeology at Ankara, 1989.

———. "The Year's Work." *Anatolian Studies* 40 (1990): 19–24.

Louf, André. "Une ancienne exégèse de Phil 2:6 dans le Ketaba DeMasqata (Livre des Degrés)." In *Studiorum paulinorum congressus internationalis Catholicus 1961,* 2:523–33. Analecta Biblica 17–18. Rome: Pontificio Instituto Biblico, 1963.

Louth, Andrew. "Paradies: IV Theologiegeschichtlich." In *Theologische Realenzyklopädie,* edited by Gerhard Müller, 25:714–19. Berlin and New York: Walter de Gruyter, 1995.

Luther, Andreas. "Roms mesopotamische Provinzen nach der Gefangennahme Valerians (260)." In *Ērān ud Anērān: Studien zu den Beziehungen zwischen dem Sasanidenreich und der Mittelmeerwelt,* edited by Philip Huyse and Josef Wiesehöfer, 203–19. Stuttgart: Franz Steiner Verlag, 2006.

Maguire, Henry, ed. *Byzantine Magic.* Washington, D.C.: Dumbarton Oaks Research Library; Cambridge, Mass.: Harvard University Press, 1995.

Marcus, Ralph, trans. *Philo: Questions on Exodus.* Loeb Classical Library 401. Cambridge, Mass.: Harvard University Press, 1953.

Martikainen, Juoko. *Gerechtigkeit und güte Gottes: Studies zur Theologie von Ephrem und Philoxenos von Mabbug.* Göttinger Orientforschungen 1. Reihe: Syriaca 20. Wiesbaden: Harrossowitz Verlag, 1981.

———. "Das Böse in den Schriften des Syrers Ephrem, im Stufenbuch und in Corpus Macarianum." In *Makarios-Symposium über das Böse: Vorträge der Finnisch-Deutschen Theologentagung in Goslar 1980,* edited by Werner Strothmann, 36–46. Göttinger Orientforschungen 1. Reihe: Syriaca 24. Wiesbaden: Harrassowitz Verlag, 1983.

Marsh, Fred Shipley. *The Book Which Is Called the Book of the Holy Hierotheos: With Extracts from the Prolegomena and Commentary of Theodosios of Antioch, and from the "Book of Excerpts" and Other Works of Gregory Bar-Hebraeus.* London: Text and Translation Society, 1927.

May, Gerhard. *Markion: Gesammelte Aufsätze.* Edited by Katharina Greschat and Martin Meiser. Mainz: Von Zabern, 2005.

May, Gerhard, Katharina Greschat, and Martin Meiser, eds. *Marcion und seine kirchengeschichtliche Wirkung: Vorträge der Internationalen Fachkonferenz zu Marcion gehalten vom 15.–18. August 2001 in Mainz.* Berlin: Walter de Gruyter, 2002.

Mathisen, Ralph W., and Hagith Sivan, eds. *Shifting Frontiers in Late Antiquity.* Aldershot: Variorum, 1996.

Matthews, Edward G., and Joseph P. Amar, trans. *St. Ephrem the Syrian: Selected Prose Works.* The Fathers of the Church 91. Washington, D.C.: The Catholic University of America Press, 1994.

Matthews, John F. *The Roman Empire of Ammianus.* London: Duckworth, 1989.
McDonough, S. "Power by Negotiation: Institutional Reform in the Fifth-century Sasanian Empire." PhD diss., University of California, Los Angeles, 2005.
———. "A Second Constantine? The Sasanian King Yazdgard in Christian History and Historiography." *Journal of Late Antiquity* 1, no. 1 (2008): 127–41.
McKechnie, Paul, and John A. Crook. "Roman Law and the Laws of the Medes and Persians: Decius' and Valerian's Persecutions of Christianity." In *Thinking Like a Lawyer: Essays on Legal History and General History for John Crook on his Eightieth Birthday,* edited by Paul McKechnie, 253–69. Leiden: E. J. Brill, 2002.
McVey, Kathleen E., trans. *Ephrem the Syrian: Hymns on the Nativity, Hymns Against Julian, Hymns on Virginity and on the Symbols of the Lord.* The Classics of Western Spirituality. New York: Paulist Press, 1989.
Meinardus, Otto. "The Nestorians in Egypt." *Oriens Christianus* 51 (1967): 112–27.
Merkel, Helmut. *Die Widersprüche zwischen den Evangelien: Ihre polemische und apologetische Behandlung in der alten Kirche bis zu Augustin.* Tübingen: Mohr Siebeck, 1971.
———. *Die Pluralität der Evangelien als theologisches und exegetisches Problem in der alten Kirche.* Bern: Lang, 1978.
Miller, Patricia Cox. "Desert Asceticism and 'The Body from Nowhere.'" *Journal of Early Christian Studies* 2 (1994): 137–53.
Mitchell, Charles W., ed. *S. Ephraim's Prose Refutations of Mani, Marcion, and Bardaisan.* 2 vols. London: Williams and Norgate, 1912–21.
Mitchell, Margaret M. *The Heavenly Trumpet: John Chrysostom and the Art of Pauline Interpretation.* Louisville: Westiminster John Knox Press, 2002.
Montmarquet, James A. "Epistemic Virtue." *Mind* 96 (1987): 482–97.
———. *Epistemic Virtue and Doxastic Responsibility.* Boston: Rowman and Littlefield, 1993.
Morony, Michael G. "Population Transfers between Sasanian Iran and the Byzantine Empire." In *Convegno internazionale La Persia e Bisanzio: Roma, 14–18 ottobre 2002,* 161–80. Roma: Accademia nazionale dei Lincei, 2002.
Morrison, Craig E. "The Recasting of Elijah in Aphrahat's VI Demonstration." *The Harp* 20 (2006): 325–40.
Mosig-Walburg, Karin. "Zur Schlacht bei Singara." *Historia: Zeitschrift für Alte Geschichte* 48 (1999): 330–84.
———. "Zu Spekulationen über den sasanidischen 'Thronfolger Narse' und seine Rolle in den sasanidisch-römischen Auseinandersetzungen im zweiten Viertel des 4. Jahrhunderts n. Chr." *Iranica Antiqua* 35 (2000): 111–57.
———. "Zur Westpolitik Shâpûrs II." In *Iran, questions et connaissances.* Vol. 1, *La période ancienne actes du IVe Congrès européen des études iraniennes, Paris, 6–10 septembre 1999,* edited by Philip Huyse, 329–47. Paris: Association pour l'avancement des études iraniennes, 2002.
———. "Christenverfolgung und Römerkrieg—Zu Ursachen, Ausmaß und Zielrichtung der Christenverfolgung unter Shapur II." *Iranistik* 7 (2005): 5–84.

———. "Hanniballianus rex." *Millennium* 2 (2005): 229–54.
———. "Der Armenienkrieg des Maximinus Daia." *Historia: Zeitschrift für Alte Geschichte* 55 (2006): 247–55.
———. "Die Christenverfolgung Shâpûrs II: Vor dem Hintergrund des persisch-römischen Krieges." In *Inkulturation des Christentums im Sasanidenreich,* edited by Arafa Mustafa, Jürgen Tubach, and G. Sophia Vashalomidze, 171–86. Wiesbaden: Reichert, 2007.
———. *Römer und Perser: Vom 3. Jahrhundert bis zum Jahr 363 n. Chr.* Gutenberg: Computus, 2009.
Muehlberger, Ellen. "Ambivalence about the Angelic Life: The Promise and Perils of an Early Christian Discourse of Asceticism." *Journal of Early Christian Studies* 16, no. 4 (2008): 447–78.
Müller, C. D. G. "Stellung und Bedeutung des Katholikos-Patriarchen von Seleukia-Ktesiphon im Altertum." *Oriens Christianus* 53 (1969): 227–45.
Murray, Robert. "The Exhortation to Candidates for Ascetical Vows at Baptism in the Ancient Syrian Church." *New Testament Studies* 21 (1974–75): 58–79.
———. "The Features of the Earliest Christian Asceticism." In *Christian Spirituality: Essays in Honour of Gordon Rupp,* edited by Peter Brooks, 53–77. London: SCM, 1975.
———. "Some Themes and Problems of Early Syriac Angelology." In *V Symposium Syriacum, 1988: Katholieke Universiteit, Leuven, 29–31 août 1988,* edited by René Lavenant, 143–53. Orientalia Christiana Analecta 236. Rome: Pontificium Institutum Studiorum Orientalium, 1990.
———. *Symbols of Church and Kingdom: A Study in Early Syriac Tradition.* Rev. ed. London: T. and T. Clark; Piscataway, N.J.: Gorgias Press, 2004.
Muyldermans, Jules. *Evagriana syriaca: Textes inédits du British Museum et de la Vaticane.* Bibliothèque du Muséon 31. Louvain: Publications universitaires, 1952.
Naeh, Shlomo. "Freedom and Celibacy: A Talmudic Variation on Tales of Temptation and Fall in Genesis and Its Syrian Background." In *The Book of Genesis in Jewish and Oriental Christian Interpretation,* edited by Judith Frishman and Lucas van Rompay, 73–89. Traditio Exegetica Graeca 5. Louvain: Peeters, 1997.
Nagel, Peter. "Die 'Märtyrer des Glaubens' und die 'Märtyrer der Liebe' im syrischen Liber Graduum." In *Religion und Wahrheit: Religionsgeschichtliche Studien; Festschrift für Gernot Wiessner zum 65. Geburtstag,* edited by Gernot Wiessner and Bärbel Beinhauer-Köhler, 127–42. Wiesbaden: Harrassowitz Verlag, 1998.
———. "Das Gleichnis vom verlorenen Sohn (Lk 15, 11–32) im syrischen Liber Graduum." In *Dankesgabe für Heinrich Schützinger zum 75. Geburtstag,* 115–21. Hallesche Beiträge zur Orientwissenschaft 29. Halle: Institut für Orientalistik, 2000.
———. "Manichäisches im syrischen Liber Graduum?" In *Religionsbegegnung und Kulturaustausch in Asien. Studien zum Gedenken an Hans-Joachim Klimkeit,* edited by Wolfgang Gantke, Karl Hoheisel, and Wassilios Klein, 179–84. Studies in Oriental Religions 49. Wiesbaden: Harrassowitz Verlag, 2002.
Nau, François. "La version syriaque de la première lettre de Saint Antoine." *Revue de l'Orient Chrétien* 14 (1909): 282–97.

———. "L'histoire ecclésiastique de Bar Ḥadbešabba 'Arbaia et une controverse de Théodore de Mopsueste avec les macédoniens." *Revue de l'Orient Chrétien* 6 (1911): 234–38.

———. "Résumé de monographies syriaques." *Revue de l'Orient Chrétien* 20 (1915): 3–32.

Nedungatt, George. "The Covenanters of the Early Syriac-Speaking Church." *Orientalia Christiana Periodica* 39 (1973): 191–215, 419–44.

Neusner, Jacob, trans. *Aphrahat and Judaism: The Christian-Jewish Argument in Fourth-Century Iran.* Studia Post-Biblica 19. Leiden: E. J. Brill, 1971.

———. "Jews in Iran." In *The Cambridge History of Iran,* edited by Ehsan Yarshater, 3:909–23. Cambridge: Cambridge University Press, 1983.

Nikolsky, Ronit. *The Provenance of "The Journey of Zosimos."* PhD diss. The Hebrew University of Jerusalem, 2003 [in Hebrew].

Nöldeke, Theodor. *Geschichte der Perser und Araber zur Zeit der Sasaniden: Aus der Arabischen Chronik des Tabari.* Leiden: E. J. Brill, 1879.

Ortiz de Urbina, Ignacio. "Le Paradis eschatologique d'aprés Saint Ephrem." *Orientalia Christiana Periodica* 21 (1956): 467–72.

Outtier, Bernard. "Le sort des manuscrits du Katalog Hiersemann 500." *Analecta Bollandiana* 93 (1975): 377–80.

Pagels, Elaine H. "Adam and Eve, Christ and the Church: A Survey of Second Century Controversies Concerning Marriage." In *The New Testament and Gnosis: Essays in Honour of Robert McL. Wilson,* edited by A. H. B. Logan and A. J. M. Wedderburn, 146–75. Edinburgh: T. and T. Clark, 1983.

Palmer, Andrew. *Monk and Mason on the Tigris Frontier: The Early History of Tur 'Abdin.* Cambridge: Cambridge University Press, 1990.

Parisot, Jean, ed. *Aphraatis Sapientis Persae Demonstrationes.* Patrologia Syriaca 1.1. Paris: Firmin-Didot, 1894.

Parrott, Douglas M., ed. *Nag Hammadi Codices V, 2–5 and VI with Papyrus Berolinensis 8502, 1 and 4.* Nag Hammadi Studies 11. Leiden: E. J. Brill, 1979.

Parsons, Fiona J. "The Nature of the Gospel Quotations in the Syriac *Liber Graduum.*" PhD diss., University of Birmingham, U.K., 1969.

Payne, Richard E. "Christianity and Iranian Society in Late Antiquity, ca. 500–700." PhD diss., Princeton University, 2010.

Peeters, Paul. "Le martyrologe de Rabban Saliba." *Analecta Bollandiana* 27 (1908): 129–200.

Pentiuc, Eugen J. "'Renewed by Blood': Sheol's Quest in 2 Baruch 56.6." *Revue Biblique* 114, no. 4 (2007): 535–64.

Pierre, Marie-Joseph, trans. *Aphraate le sage persan: les exposés.* 2 vols. Sources Chrétiennes 349, 359. Paris: Les Éditions du Cerf, 1988–1989.

———. "Un synode contestataire à l'époque d'Aphraate le sage Persan." In *La controverse religieuse et ses formes,* edited by Alain Boulluec, 243–79. Paris: Les Éditions du Cerf, 1995.

Pingérra, Karl. *All-Erlösung und All-Einheit: Studien zum "Buch des heiligen Hierotheos" und seiner Rezeption in der syrisch-orthodoxen Theologie.* Wiesbaden: Reichert, 2002.

Poirier, Paul-Hubert. *L'hymne de la perle des Actes de Thomas: Introduction, texte-traduction, commentaire.* Louvain-la-Neuve: Centre d'histoire des religions, 1981.

Polotsky, Hans Jakob, and A. Böhlig. *Kephalaia I: Hälfte (Lieferung 1–10).* Stuttgart: Kohlhammer, 1940.

Polotsky, Hans Jakob, and Carl Schmidt. *Ein Mani-Fund in Ägypten: Originalschriften des Mani und seiner Schüler.* Berlin: Akademie der Wissenschaften, in Kommission bei W. de Gruyter, 1933.

Potter, David S. *Prophecy and History in the Crisis of the Roman Empire: A Historical Commentary on the Thirteenth Sibylline Oracle.* Oxford: Oxford University Press, 1991.

———. *The Roman Empire at Bay: A.D. 180–395.* London: Routledge, 2004.

Quispel, Gilles. "The Study of Encratism: A Historical Survey." In *La tradizione dell'enkrateia: motivazioni ontologiche e protologiche. Atti del Colloquio Internazionale, Milano 20–23 aprile 1982,* edited by Ugo Bianchi, 35–81. Roma: Ateneo, 1985.

Ramelli, Ilaria, trans. *Il Chronicon di Arbela: Presentacione, traducione e note essenziali.* Madrid: Universidad Complutense de Madrid, 2002.

Ratcliff, Robert A. "Steps Along the Way of Perfection: The *Liber Graduum* and Early Syrian Monasticism." PhD diss., Emory University, 1988.

Redgate, Anne E. *The Armenians.* Oxford: Blackwell, 1998.

Rees, Roger. *Diocletian and the Tetrarchy.* Edinburgh: Edinburgh University Press, 2004.

Reeves, John C. "Exploring the Afterlife of Jewish Pseudepigrapha in Medieval Near Eastern Religious Traditions: Some Initial Soundings." *Journal for the Study of Judaism* 30, no. 2 (1999): 148–77.

———. "Manichaean Citations from the *Prose Refutations* of Ephrem." In *Emerging from Darkness: Studies in the Recovery of Manichaean Sources,* edited by Jason BeDuhn and Paul A. Mirecki. Nag Hammadi and Manichaean Studies 43. Leiden: E. J. Brill, 1997.

Rehm, Bernhard, ed. *Die Pseudoklementinen. I: Homilien.* Die griechischen christlichen Schriftsteller der ersten drei Jahrhunderte 42. Berlin: Akademie Verlag, 1953.

Renoux, Charles, ed. and trans. *Ephrem de Nisibe: Memre sur Nicomédie.* Patrologia Orientalis 37.2, 3. Turnhout: Brepols, 1975.

Riad, Eva. *Studies in the Syriac Preface.* Studia Semitica Upsaliensia 11. Uppsala, Sweden: Uppsala University, 1988.

Riggs, Wayne D. "Understanding 'Virtue' and the Virtue of Understanding." In *Intellectual Virtue: Perspectives from Ethics and Epistemology,* edited by Michael DePaul and Linda Zagzebski, 203–26. Oxford: Clarendon Press, 2003.

Rignell, Lars Gösta, ed. *Briefe von Johannes dem Einsiedler.* Lund: Håkan Ohlssons Boktryckeri, 1941.

Rist, Josef. "Die Verfolgung der Christen in spätantiken Sasanidenreich: Ursachen, Verlauf und Folgen." *Oriens Christianus* 80 (1996): 17–42.

Ritter, Adolf Martin. *Charisma im Verständnis des Joannes Chrysostomos und seiner Zeit: Ein Beitrag zur Erforschung der griechisch-orientalischen Ekklesiologie in der Frühzeit der Reichskirche.* Göttingen: Vandenhoeck and Ruprecht, 1972.

Roberts, Robert C., and W. Jay Wood. "Humility and Epistemic Goods." In *Intellectual Virtue: Perspectives from Ethics and Epistemology,* edited by Michael DePaul and Linda Zagzebski, 257–80. Oxford: Oxford University Press, 2007.

———. *Intellectual Virtues: An Essay in Regulative Epistemology.* Oxford: Oxford University Press, 2007.

Robinson, James. "The Fate of the Manichaean Codices of Medinet Madi: 1929–1989." In *Studia Manichaica: II. Internationaler Kongress zum Manichäismus, 6.–10. August 1989, St. Augustin/Bonn,* edited by Hans-Joachim Klimkeit and Gernot Wiessner. Wiesbaden: Harrassowitz Verlag, 1989.

Robinson, Stephen E. "The Testament of Adam and the Angelic Liturgy." *Revue de Qumrân* 12 (1985): 105–10.

Rosen-Zvi, Ishay. *Demonic Desires: Yetzer Hara and the Problem of Evil in Late Antiquity.* Divinations: Rereading Late Ancient Religion. Philadelphia: University of Pennsylvania Press, 2011.

Rougé, Jean, ed. *Expositio Totius Mundi et Gentium.* Sources Chrétiennes 124. Paris: Éditions du Cerf, 1966.

Rousseau, Adelin, and Louis Doutreleau, eds. *Irénée de Lyon: Contre les hérésies. Livre I.* 2 vols. Sources Chrétiennes 253–64. Paris: Éditions du Cerf, 1979.

Roux, René. "The Doctrine of the Imitation of Christ in the *Liber Graduum:* Between Exegetical Theory and Soteriology." In *Studia Patristica: Biblica Et Apocrypha, Ascetica, Liturgica,* vol. 30, edited by Elizabeth A. Livingstone and E. Peters. Leuven: Peeters, 1997.

Rubin, Z. "The Reforms of Khusro Anūshirwān." In *States, Resources and Armies: Papers of the Third Workshop on Late Antiquity and Early Islam,* edited by Averil Cameron, 3:227–97. Byzantine and Early Islamic Near East. Studies in Late Antiquity and early Islam. Princeton: Darwin Press, 1995.

Russell, Norman. *The Doctrine of Deification in the Greek Patristic Tradition.* Oxford: Oxford University Press, 2005.

Russell, Paul S. "Nisibis as the Background to the Life of Ephrem the Syrian." *Hugoye: Journal of Syriac Studies* 8 (2005): 179–235.

Sachau, Eduard. *Verzeichniss der Syrischen Handschriften der Königlichen Bibliothek zu Berlin.* Vol. 2. Berlin: A. Asher, 1899.

Salvesen, Alison. "Infants or Fools in the Garden of Eden? An Ambiguity in Early Syriac Tradition." In *Hamlet on a Hill: Semitic and Greek Studies Presented to Professor T. Muraoka on the Occasion of His Sixty-Fifth Birthday,* edited by Martin F. J. Baasten and Wido T. van Peursen, 432–40. Orientalia Lovaniensia Analecta 118. Leuven: Peeters, 2003.

———. "Without Shame or Desire: The Pronouncements of Jesus on Children and the Kingdom, and Early Syriac Attitudes to Childhood." *Scottish Journal of Theology* 59, no. 3 (2006): 307–26.

Scher, Addai, ed. *Chronique de Séert.* Patrologia Orientalis 4. Turnhout: Brepols, 1908.

Schwen, Paul. *Afrahat: Seine Person und sein Verständnis des Christentums, Ein Beitrag zur Geschichte der Kirche im Osten.* Neue Studien zur Geschichte der Theologie und der Kirche 2. Aalen: Scientia-Verlag, 1973.

Séd, Nicholas. "Les Hymnes sur le Paradis de Saint Ephrem et les Tradition Juives." *Le Muséon* 81 (1968): 455–501.

Segal, J. B. *Edessa: The "Blessed City."* Oxford: Clarendon Press, 1970.

Sherwood, Polycarp. "Le fonds patriarcal de la bibliothèque manuscrite de Charfet." *L'Orient Syrien* 2 (1957): 93–107.

Simonetti, Manlio. *La crisi ariana nel IV secolo.* Rome: Institutum patristicum Augustinianum, 1975.

———. *Lettera e/o allegoria: Un contributo alla storia dell'esegesi patristica.* Rome: Institutum Patristicum Augustinianum, 1985.

Sinkewicz, Robert E. *Evagrius of Pontus: The Greek Ascetic Corpus.* Oxford: Oxford University Press, 2003.

Smith, Kyle. "The Persian Persecution: Martyrdom, Politics, and Religious Identity in Late Ancient Syriac Christianity." PhD diss., Duke University, 2011.

Smith, Jessie Payne, ed. *A Compendious Syriac Dictionary: Founded Upon the Thesaurus Syriacus of R. Payne Smith, DD.* Oxford: Oxford University Press, 1902; Eugene, Ore.: Wipf and Stock, 1999.

Smith, Robert Payne. *Thesaurus Syriacus.* 2 vols. Oxford: Clarendon, 1879–1901.

Smith, Thomas, Peter Peterson, and James Donaldson. "The Clementine Homilies." In *Ante-Nicene Christian Library: Translations of the Writings of the Fathers down to A.D. 325,* edited by A. Roberts and James Donaldson, 17:1–340. Edinburgh: T. and T. Clark, 1870.

Sommer, Michael. *Roms orientalische Steppengrenze: Palmyra, Edessa, Dura-Europos, Hatra; Eine Kulturgeschichte von Pompeius bis Diocletian.* Stuttgart: Franz Steiner, 2005.

Sōnī, Behnām. *Fihris al-maḫṭūṭāt al-baṭriarkīyya fī Dair aš-Šarfa: Lubnān/Le catalogue des manuscrits du Patrarcat au Couvent de Charfet—Liban.* Beirut: 1993.

Sosa, Ernest. "The Raft and the Pyramid: Coherence versus Foundations in the Theory of Knowledge." In *Studies in Epistemology,* edited by Peter French, Howard K. Wettstein, Robert Feleppa, and Theodore E. Uehling, Jr., 5:3–25. Midwest Studies in Philosophy 5. Minneapolis: University of Minnesota Press, 1980.

Stanton, Graham. "Jewish Christian Elements in the Pseudo-Clementine Writings." In *Jewish Believers in Jesus: The Early Centuries,* edited by O. Skarsaune and R. Hvalvik, 305–24. Peabody, Mass.: Hendrickson, 2007.

Stern, Sacha. "Near Eastern Lunar Calendars in the Syriac Martyr Acts." *Le Muséon* 117 (2004): 447–72.

Stewart, Columba. "*Working the Earth of the Heart": The Messalian Controversy in History, Texts, and Language to A.D. 431.* Oxford: Clarendon Press, 1991.

Stoneman, Richard. *Palmyra and Its Empire: Zenobia's Revolt against Rome.* Ann Arbor: University of Michigan Press, 1992.

Strothmann, Werner. *Johannes von Apamea.* Patristische Texte und Studien 11. Berlin: De Gruyter, 1972.

———. "Die orientalischen Handschriften der Sammlung Mettler (Katalog Hiersemann 500)." In *XIX. Deutscher Orientalistentag vom 28. September bis 4. Oktober 1975 in Freiburg im Breisgau. Vorträge, Sektion IV,* edited by Wolfgang Voigt. Zeitschrift der Deutschen Morgenländischen Gesellschaft. Supplement, vol. 3, part 1. Wiesbaden: Steiner, 1977.

———. *Die syrische Überlieferung der Schriften des Makarios.* 2 vols. Göttinger Orientforschungen I Reihe. Syriaca; Bd. 21. Wiesbaden: Harrassowitz, 1981.

Studer, B. *Schola Christiana: Die Theologie zwischen Nizäa (325) und Chalzedon (451).* Paderborn: Ferdinand Schöningh, 1998.

Tanghe, Antoine. "Memra de Philoxène de Mabboug sur l'inhabitation du Saint Esprit." *Le Muséon* (1960): 39–71.

Teule, Herman. "Les compilations monastiques syriaques." In *Symposium Syriacum VII: Uppsala University, Department of Asian and African Languages, 11–14 August 1996,* edited by René Lavenant, 249–62. Orientalia Christiana Analecta 256. Roma: Pontificio Istituto Orientale, 1998.

Theodore, Judah, and Chanock Albeck, ed. *Midrash Bereshit Rabbah.* Jerusalem: Wahrmann, 1965.

Tonneau, Raymond-Marie, ed. *Sancti Ephraem Syri in Genesim et in Exodum commentarii.* Corpus Scriptorum Christianorum Orientalium 152. Louvain: L. Durbecq, 1955.

Van de Gheyn, I., ed. "Passio Antiquior SS. Sergii et Bacchi." *Analecta Bollandiana* 14 (1895): 371–95.

Van der Horst, Pieter W. "A Note on the Evil Inclination and Sexual Desire in Talmudic Literature." In *Jews and Christians in Their Graeco-Roman Context: Selected Essays on Early Judaism, Samaritanism, Hellenism, and Christianity,* 59–65. Wissenschaftliche Untersuchungen zum Neuen Testament 196. Tübingen: Mohr Siebeck, 2006.

Van Eijk, Ton H. C. "Marriage and Virginity, Death and Immortality." In *Mélanges patristiques offerts au Cardinal Jean Daniélou,* edited by Jacques Fontaine and Charles Kannengiesser, 209–35. Paris: Beauchesne, 1972.

Van Rompay, Lucas. "Impetuous Martyrs? The Situation of the Persian Christians in the Last Years of Yazdgard I (419–420)." In *Martyrium in Multidisciplinary Perspective: Memorial Louis Reekmans,* edited by Mathijs Lamberigts, Louis Reekmans, and Peter van Deun, 363–75. Leuven: Peeters, 1995.

———. "An Ascetic Reading of the Book of Job: Fragments from a Syriac Commentary Attributed to John the Solitary; Ms. London, British Library, Add.18814, f. 91r–95r." *Le Muséon* 119, no. 1–2 (2006): 1–24.

Visotzky, Burton L. "Three Syriac Cruxes." *Journal of Jewish Studies* 42, no. 2 (1991): 167–75.

Vivian, Tim, and Apostolos N. Athanassakis. "Montanism, Heresy, or Proto-Monasticism? The Martyrdom of St. Theodotos of Ancyra and of the Seven Virgins with Him." *Studia Monastica* 44 (2002): 239–92.

Von Dobschütz, E., ed. *Die Akten der edessenischen Bekenner Gurjas, Samonas und Abibos.* Vol. 37, bk. 2 of *Text und Untersuchungen zur Geschichte der altchristlichen Literatur.* Leipzig: J. C. Hinrichs, 1911.

Vööbus, Arthur. *Celibacy: A Requirement for Admission to Baptism in the Early Syrian Church.* Papers of the Estonian Theological Society in Exile 1. Stockholm: Estonian Theological Society in Exile, 1951.

———. "*Liber Graduum:* Some Aspects of Its Significance for the History of Early Syrian Asceticism." In *Charisteria Iohanni Kopp octogenerio oblata,* 108–28. Papers of the Estonian Theological Society in Exile 7. Stockholm: Estonian Theological Society in Exile, 1954.

———. *Syriac and Arabic Documents Regarding Legislation Relative to Syrian Asceticism.* Papers of the Estonian Theological Society in Exile 11. Stockholm: Estonian Theological Society in Exile, 1960.

———. *The Didascalia Apostolorum in Syriac.* 4 vols. Corpus Scriptorum Christianorum Orientalium 401–2, 407–8, Syr. 175–76, 179–80. Louvain: Secrétariat du Corpus SCO, 1979.

———. *History of Asceticism in the Syrian Orient: A Contribution to the History of Culture in the Near East.* 3 vols. Corpus Scriptorum Christianorum Orientalium 184, 197, 500. Louvain: Secrétariat du Corpus SCO, 1958, 1960, 1988.

Walker, Joel Thomas. *The Legend of Mar Qardagh: Narrative and Christian Heroism in Late Antique Iraq.* Berkeley and Los Angeles: University of California Press, 2006.

Walter, Donald M. *The Old Testament in Syriac according to the Peshitta Version.* Part 2, fasc. 3, *The Book of Psalms.* Leiden: E. J. Brill, 1980.

Warmington, B. H. "Objectives and Strategy in the Persian War of Constantius II." In *Akten des XI. internationalen Limeskongresses,* edited by Jenó Fitz, 509–20. Budapest: Akadémiai Kiadó, 1977.

Webster, John B. *Holiness.* Grand Rapids: Eerdmans, 2003.

Westerhoff, Matthias. "Zur Paulus-Rezeption im Liber Graduum: der Apostel als Vorbild." In *Syriaca: Zu Geschichte, Theologie, Liturgie und Gegenwartslage der syrischen Kirchen,* edited by Martin Tamcke, 253–59. Münster: LIT Verlag, 2002.

———. *Das Paulusverständnis im Liber Graduum.* Berlin and New York: Walter de Gruyter, 2008.

———. "Das Bild vom Staat im *Liber Graduum.*" In *Christentum und Politik in der Alten Kirche,* edited by J. Van Oort and Otmar Hesse, 25–33. Leuven: Peeters, 2009.

Whittaker, Molly, ed. *Tatian: Oratio ad Graecos and Fragments.* Oxford: Clarendon Press, 1982.

Wickham, Lionel. "The *Liber Graduum* Revisited." In *VI Symposium Syriacum, 1992: University of Cambridge, Faculty of Divinity, 30 August–2 September 1992,* edited by René Lavenant, 177–87. Rome: Pontificio Instituto Orientale, 1992.

———. "Teachings About God and Christ in the Liber Graduum." In *Logos: Festschrift für Luise Abramowski zum 8. Juli 1993,* edited by Hanns Christof Brennecke, Ernst Ludwig Grasmück, and Christoph Markschies, 486–98. New York: Walter de Gruyter, 1993.

Wiesehöfer, Josef. "'Geteilte Loyalitäten': Religiöse Minderheiten des 3. und 4. Jahrhunderts n. Chr. im Spannungsfeld zwischen Rom und dem sasanidischen Iran." *Klio* 75 (1993): 362–82.

———. *Ancient Persia: From 550 BC to 650 AD.* London: I. B. Tauris, 1996.

Wiesehöfer, Josef, and Philip Huyse, eds. *Ērān ud Anērān: Studien zu den Beziehungen zwischen dem Sasanidenreich und der Mittelmeerwelt.* Oriens et Occidens 13. Stuttgart: Franz Steiner Verlag, 2006.

Wiessner, Gernot. *Zur Märtyrerüberlieferung aus der Christenverfolgung Schapurs II.* Göttingen: Vandenhoeck and Ruprecht, 1967.

———. *Untersuchungen zur syrischen Literaturegeschichte I. Zur Märtyrerüberlieferung aus der Christenverfolgung Schapurs II.* Göttingen: Vandenhoeck and Ruprecht, 1967.

Winkelmann, Friedhelm, ed. *Über das Leben des Kaisers Konstantins.* Rev. ed. Berlin: Akademie-Verlag, 1991.

Winter, Engelbert. "On the Regulation of the Eastern Frontier of the Roman Empire in 298." In *The Eastern Frontier of the Roman Empire: Proceedings of a Colloquium Held at Ankara in September 1988,* edited by D. H. French and Chris S. Lightfoot, 555–71. BAR International Series 553. Oxford: British Institute of Archaeology at Ankara, 1989.

Winter, Engelbert, and Beate Dignas. *Rome and Persia in Late Antiquity: Neighbours and Rivals.* Cambridge: Cambridge University Press, 2007.

Wirth, Gerhard. "Hannibalian: Anmerkungen zur Geschichte eines überflüssigen Königs." *Bonner Jahrbücher* 190 (1990): 201–31.

Wood, W. Jay. *Epistemology: Becoming Intellectually Virtuous.* Downers Grove, Ill.: Intervarsity Press, 1998.

Wray, Judith Hoch. *Rest as a Theological Metaphor in the Epistle to the Hebrews and the Gospel of Truth.* New York: Scholars Press, 1998.

Wright, William, trans., ed. *Apocryphal Acts of the Apostles, Edited from Syriac Manuscripts in the British Museum and Other Libraries.* 2 vols. London: Williams and Norgate, 1871.

———. *Catalogue of Syriac Manuscripts in the British Museum, Acquired since the Year 1838.* Vol. 2. London: British Museum, 1871.

Yarbrough, O. Larry. "Canons from the Council of Gangra." In *Ascetic Behavior in Greco-Roman Antiquity: A Sourcebook,* edited by Vincent L. Wimbush, 448–55. Studies in Antiquity and Christianity. Minneapolis: Fortress Press, 1990.

Yarshater, Ehsan, ed. *The Cambridge History of Iran.* Vol 3.1, *The Seleucid, Parthian and Sasanian Periods.* Cambridge: Cambridge University Press, 1983.

Zagzebski, Linda Trinkaus. *Virtues of the Mind: An Inquiry into the Nature of Virtue and the Ethical Foundations of Knowledge.* Cambridge: Cambridge University Press, 1996.

Zimonyi, István. "Kmoskó Mihály és a magyar ostörténet." In *Ostörténet és nemzettudat 1919–1931,* edited by É. Kincses Nagy, 89–93. Szeged: Magyar Őstörténeti Kutatócsoport, 1991.

Zotenberg, Hermann. *Catalogue des manuscrits syriaques et sabéens (mandaïtes) de la Bibliothèque Nationale.* Paris: Imprimerie nationale, 1874.

Zuckerman, C. "Les campagnes des tétrarques, 296–298: Notes de chronologie." *Antiquité tardive* 2 (1994): 65–70.

CONTRIBUTORS

Pablo Argárate is professor of patristics and ecumenical theology and the director of the Institut für Ökumenische Theologie, Ostkirchliche Orthodoxie und Patrologie at the Karl-Franzens-Universität Graz.

Kelli Bryant is a D.Phil. student in oriental studies at the University of Oxford. She holds an M.Phil. in Eastern Christian Studies from the University of Oxford and a Master of Divinity from Abilene Christian University.

Jeff W. Childers is Carmichael-Walling Chair of New Testament and Early Christianity at the Graduate School of Theology of Abilene Christian University.

Geoffrey Greatrex is a professor in the Department of Classics and Religious Studies at the University of Ottawa.

Tera Stidham Harmon is a Ph.D. candidate in church history at the Catholic University of America.

Kristian S. Heal is director of the Center for the Preservation of Ancient Religious Texts at Brigham Young University.

Grigory Kessel is a postdoctoral researcher in Syriac Christianity at the Theological Faculty of the Philipps University, Marburg.

Robert A. Kitchen is the minister of Knox-Metropolitan United Church, Regina, Saskatchewan. He is the author (with Martien F. G. Parmentier) of *The Book of Steps: The Syriac Liber Graduum* (Kalamazoo: Cistercian Publications, 2004).

Aryeh Kofsky is professor of comparative religion at the University of Haifa.

Thomas Kollamparampil is professor of theology and former president of the Pontifical Athenaeum, Dharmaran Vidya Kshetram in Bangalore, India.

Sergey Minov is a Ph.D. candidate at the Department of Comparative Religion of the Hebrew University of Jerusalem.

Martien F. G. Parmentier is emeritus professor of systematic theology at the University of Berne.

Timothy Pettipiece is a sessional lecturer at the University of Ottawa.

René Roux is professor of early church history, patrology, and eastern Christianity at the University of Erfurt.

Serge Ruzer is senior lecturer in the Department of Comparative Religion and senior research fellow at the Center for the Study of Christianity of the Hebrew University of Jerusalem.

Jason Scully is a lecturer at Seton Hall University.

Kyle Smith is assistant professor in the Department of Historical Studies at the University of Toronto, Mississauga, and the Department for the Study of Religion at the University of Toronto, Saint George.

Columba Stewart, OSB, is a Benedictine monk of Saint John's Abbey, Collegeville, Minnesota. He is executive director of the Hill Museum and Manuscript Library and professor of theology at Saint John's University.

Matthias Westerhoff is minister in the Evangelical Lutheran Church of Bavaria, presently serving at Hof. He is a Privatdozent at the Lehrstuhl für Ältere Kirchengeschichte, University of Erlangen-Nuremberg.

INDEX OF CITATIONS OF THE *BOOK OF STEPS*

SUBJECT INDEX

Breaking the Mind: New Studies in the Syriac "Book Of Steps" was designed and typeset in Garamond by Kachergis Book Design of Pittsboro, North Carolina. It was printed on 55-pound Natures Natural and bound by Sheridan Books of Ann Arbor, Michigan.